Lecture Notes in Computer Science

T0250710

Commenced Publication in 1973
Founding and Former Series Editors:
Gerhard Goos, Juris Hartmanis, and Jan van Leeuwen

Editorial Board

John Vicente   David Hutchison (Eds.)

Management of Multimedia Networks and Services

7th IFIP/IEEE International Conference, MMNS 2004
San Diego, CA, USA, October 3-6, 2004
Proceedings

 Springer

Volume Editors

John Vicente
Intel Corporation
Information Services and Technology Group Research
1900 Prairie City Road, Folsom, CA 95630, USA
E-mail: john.vicente@intel.com

David Hutchison
Lancaster University, Computing Department
Engineering Building, Lancaster, LA1 4YR, UK
E-mail: d.hutchison@lancaster.ac.uk

Library of Congress Control Number: 2004113133

CR Subject Classification (1998): C.2, H.5.1, H.3, H.5, K.3, H.4

ISSN 0302-9743
ISBN 3-540-23239-7 Springer Berlin Heidelberg New York

Springer is a part of Springer Science+Business Media

springeronline.com

© 2004 IFIP International Federation for Information Processing, Hofstrasse 3, A-2361 Laxenburg, Austria
Printed in Germany

Typesetting: Camera-ready by author, data conversion by Olgun Computergrafik
Printed on acid-free paper   SPIN: 11327004   06/3142   5 4 3 2 1 0

Preface

We are delighted to present the proceedings of the *7th IFIP/IEEE International Conference on Management of Multimedia Networks & Services (MMNS)*.

The MMNS 2004 conference was held in San Diego, California, USA on October 4–6, 2004. As in previous years, the conference brought together an international audience of researchers and scientists from industry and academia who are researching and developing state-of-the-art management systems, while creating a public venue for results dissemination and intellectual collaboration.

This year marked a challenging chapter in the advancement of management systems for the wider management research community, with the growing complexities of the Internet, the proliferation of alternative wireless networks and mobile services, intelligent and high-speed networks, scalable multimedia services, and the convergence of computing and communications for data and voice delivery. Contributions from the research community met this challenge with 84 paper submissions; 26 selected high-quality papers were subsequently selected to form the MMNS 2004 technical program. The diverse topics in this year's program included novel protocols in wireless systems, multimedia over wireless, mobility management, multimedia service control, proactive techniques for QoS management, MPLS traffic engineering and resiliency, distributed systems management, scalable multimedia systems, and adaptive methods for streaming multimedia.

The conference chairs would first like to thank all those authors who contributed to an outstanding MMNS 2004 technical program, second the Program Committee and Organizing Committee chairs for their support throughout the development of the program and conference, third the worldwide experts who assisted in a rigorous review process, and fourth the sponsors Intel Corporation, IFIP and IEEE, without whose support we would not have had such a professional conference. Last and certainly not least, we express grateful thanks to Marie Dudek who was instrumental in helping to ensure a top-quality MMNS 2004.

We truly feel that this year's proceedings mark another significant point in the development of MMNS as a primary venue for the advancement of network and service management, and also novel architectures and designs in technology and network services, to enable multimedia proliferation.

October 2004   David Hutchison and John Vicente

Program Committee

Nazim Agoulmine, University of Evry, France
Kevin Almeroth, University of California, Santa Barbara, USA
Greg Brewster, DePaul University, USA
Andrew Campbell, Columbia University, USA
Russ Clark, Georgia Institute of Technology, USA
Alexander Clemm, Cisco Systems, Inc., USA
Spyros Denazis, Hitachi Europe Ltd., France
Petre Dini, Cisco Systems, Inc. and Concordia University, USA
Dominique Gaiti, University of Technology of Troyes, France
Abdelhakim Hafid, Telcordia Technologies, Inc., USA
Masum Hasan, Cisco Systems, Inc., USA
Go Hasegawa, Osaka University, Japan
Ahmed Helmy, University of Southern California, USA
Doan Hoang, University of Technology, Sydney, Australia
Ahmed Karmouch, University of Ottawa, Canada
Lukas Kencl, Intel Corporation, UK
Dilip Krishnaswamy, Intel Corporation, USA
Alberto Leon-Garcia, University of Toronto, Canada
Raymond Liao, Siemens Technology-to-Business Center, USA
Songwu Lu, University of California, Los Angeles, USA
Hanan Lutfiyya, University of Western Ontario, Canada
Alan Marshall, Queen's University Belfast, UK
Jean-Philippe Martin-Flatin, CERN, Switzerland
Ahmed Mehaoua, University of Versailles, France
José Neuman de Souza, Universidade Federal do Ceará, Brazil
Dina Papagiannaki, Intel Research, Cambridge, UK
Gerard Parr, University of Ulster, UK
George Pavlou, University of Surrey, UK
Nicholas Race, Lancaster University, UK
Puneet Sharma, HP Labs, USA
Chien-Chung Shen, University of Delaware, USA
Rolf Stadler, KTH, Sweden
Ralf Steinmetz, Darmstadt University of Tech., Germany
Burkhard Stiller, UniBw Munich, Germany and ETH Zurich, Switzerland
John Strassner, Intelliden Corporation, USA
Michael Tchicholz, Fraunhofer Fokus, Germany
Chen-Khong Tham, National University of Singapore, Singapore
Bert-Jan van Beijnum, University of Twente, The Netherlands
Mihaela van der Schaar, University of California, Davis, USA
Theodore Willke, Columbia University and Intel Corporation, USA
Rita Wouhaybi, Columbia University, USA
Alaa Youssef, Alexandria University, Egypt
Murat Yuksel, Rensselaer Polytechnic Institute, USA

Organization Committee

Kevin Almeroth, UC Santa Barbara, USA
Ehab Al-Shaer, DePaul University, USA
Spyros Denazis, Hitachi Europe Ltd., France
Petre Dini, Cisco Systems, Inc. and Concordia University, USA
Marie Dudek, Intel Corporation, USA
Dominique Gaiti, University of Technology of Troyes, France
Go Hasegawa, Osaka University, Japan
David Hutchison, Lancaster University, UK
John Strassner, Intelliden Corporation, USA
John Vicente, Intel Corporation, USA

Reviewers

Ehab Al-Shaer, DePaul University, USA
Kevin Almeroth, University of California at Santa Barbara, USA
Chee Wei Ang, Institute for Incofomm Research, Singapore
Raouf Boutaba, University of Waterloo, Canada
Gregory Brewster, DePaul University, USA
Andrew Campbell, Columbia University, USA
Kartikeya Chandrayana, RPI, USA
Alexander Clemm, Cisco Systems, Inc., USA
Spyros Denazis, Hitachi Europe Ltd., UK
Justin Denney, Lancaster University, UK
Petre Dini, Cisco Systems, Inc. and Concordia University, USA
Ramy Farha, University of Toronto, Canada
Lars-Åke Fredlund, SICS,
Sweden Dominique Gaiti, University of Troyes, France
Alberto Gonzalez, KTH Royal Institute of Technology, Sweden
Hasan Guclu, Rensselaer Polytechnic Institute, USA
Abdelhakim Hafid, Telcordia Technologies, Inc., USA
Masum Hasan, Cisco Systems, Inc., USA
Go Hasegawa, Osaka University, Japan
Ahmed Helmy, University of Southern California, USA
Doan Hoang, University of Technology, Sydney, Australia
David Hutchison, Lancaster University, UK
Rajagopal Iyengar, Rensselaer Polytechnic Institute, USA
Ahmed Karmouch, University of Ottawa, Canada
Stamatis Karnouskos, Fraunhofer FOKUS, Germany
Lukas Kencl, Intel Corporation, UK
Dilip Krishnaswamy, Intel Corporation, USA
Alberto Leon-Garcia, University of Toronto, Canada
Raymond Liao, Siemens Technology-to-Business Center, USA
Koon-Seng Lim, KTH Royal Institute of Technology, Sweden

Yong Liu, National University of Singapore, Singapore
Michael Logothetis, University of Patras, Greece
Songwu Lu, University of California, Los Angeles, USA
Hanan Lutfiyya, University of Western Ontario, Canada
Alan Marshall, Queen's University Belfast, UK
Jean-Philippe Martin-Flatin, CERN, Switzerland
Ignacio Más Ivars, Royal Institute of Technology, KTH, Sweden
Ahmed Mehaoua, University of Versailles, France
Keith Mitchell, Lancaster University, UK
Agoulmine Nazim, University of Evry, France
José Neuman de Souza, Universidade Federal do Ceará, Brazil
Giovanni Pacifici, IBM T.J. Watson Research Center, USA
Konstantina Papagiannaki, Intel Corporation, UK
Gerard Parr, University of Ulster, UK
George Pavlou, University of Surrey, UK
Gokul Poduval, National University of Singapore, Singapore
Guy Pujolle, University of Paris, France
Nicholas Race, Lancaster University, UK
Vikram Ravindran, University of Toronto, Canada
Nancy Samaan, University of Ottawa, Canada
Puneet Sharma, Hewlett-Packard Labs, USA
Chien-Chung Shen, University of Delaware, USA
Harry Skianis, National Centre for Scientific Research 'Demokritos', Greece
Rolf Stadler, KTH, Sweden
Ralf Steinmetz, Darmstadt University of Technology, Germany
Burkhard Stiller, UniBw Munich, Germany and ETH Zurich, Switzerland
John Strassner, Intelliden Corporation, USA
Michael Tchicholz, Fraunhofer Fokus, Germany
Chen Khong Tham, National University of Singapore, Singapore
Omesh Tickoo, RPI, USA
Ali Tizghadam, University of Toronto, Canada
Andrei Tolstikov, National University of Singapore, Singapore
Bert-Jan van Beijnum, University of Twente, The Netherlands
Mihaela van der Schaar, University of California, Davis, USA
Hector Velayos, KTH, Royal Institute of Technology, Sweden
John Vicente, Intel Corporation, USA
Theodore Willke, Columbia University and Intel Corporation, USA
Rita Wouhaybi, Columbia University, USA
Daniel B. Yagan, National University of Singapore, Singapore
Lidia Yamamoto, Hitachi Europe Ltd., France
Alaa Youssef, Alexandria University, Egypt
Murat Yuksel, Rensselaer Polytechnic Institute, USA

Table of Contents

Mobility: Control and Management

Improving Interactive Video
in Wireless Networks Using Path Diversity[*]

Ahmed Abd El Al[1], Chitra Venkatramani[2], Tarek Saadawi[1], and Myung Lee[1]

[1] City College and Graduate Center of City University of New York,
New York, NY 10031
aabdelal@ieee.org, {saadawi,lee}@ccny.cuny.edu
[2] IBM T.J. Watson Research Center
Yorktown Heights, NY 10598
chitrav@us.ibm.com

Abstract. The increase in the bandwidth of wireless channels and the computing power of mobile devices increase the interest in video communications over wireless networks. However, the high error rate and the rapidly changing quality of the radio channels can be devastating for the transport of compressed video. In motion compensated coding, errors due to packet losses are propagated from reference frames to dependant frames causing lasting visual effects. In addition, the bounded playout delay for interactive video limits the effectiveness of retransmission-based error control. In this paper, we propose a mechanism that combines retransmission-based error control with path diversity in wireless networks, to provide different levels of protection to packets according to their importance to the reconstructed video quality. We evaluated the effectiveness of the mechanism under different network conditions. Simulation results show that the mechanism is able to maintain the video quality under different loss rates, with less overhead compared to error control techniques that depend on reference frame updates.

1 Introduction

The increase in the bandwidth of wireless channels and the computing power of mobile devices increase the interest in video communications over mobile wireless networks. However, in such networks there is no end-to-end guaranteed Quality of Service (QoS) and packets may be discarded due to bit errors. Wireless channels provide error rates that are typically around 10^{-2}, which range from single bit errors to burst errors or even intermittent loss of the connection. The high error rates are due to multi-path fading, which characterizes radio channels, while the loss of the connection can be due to the mobility in such networks. In addition, designing the wireless communication system to mitigate these effects can be complicated by the rapidly changing quality of the radio channel.

The effect of the high error rates in wireless channels can be devastating for the transport of compressed video. Video standards, such as MPEG and H.263, use mo-

---

[*] Prepared through collaborative participation in the Communications and Networks Consortium sponsored by the U.S. Army Research Laboratory under the Collaborative Technology Alliance Program, Cooperative Agreement DAAD19-01-2-0011.

J. Vicente and D. Hutchison (Eds.): MMNS 2004, LNCS 3271, pp. 1–12, 2004.
© IFIP International Federation for Information Processing 2004

tion-compensated prediction to exploit the redundancy between successive frames of a video sequence [1]. Although motion-compensated prediction can achieve high compression efficiency, it is not designed for transmission over lossy channels. In this coding scheme the video sequence consists of two types of video frames: *intra-frames* (I-frames) and *inter-frames* (P- or B-frames). I-frame is encoded by only removing spatial redundancy present in the frame. P-frame is encoded through motion estimation using preceding I- or P-frame as a reference frame. B-frame is encoded bi-directionally using the preceding and succeeding reference frames. This poses a severe problem, namely error propagation (or error spread), where errors due to packet loss in a reference frame propagate to all of the dependent frames leading to perceptible visual artifacts that can be long-lasting.

Different approaches have been proposed to tackle the error propagation problem. One approach is to reduce the time between intra-coded frames, in the extreme case to a single frame. Unfortunately, I-frames typically require several times more bits than P- or B-frames. While this is acceptable for high bit-rate applications, or even necessary for broadcasting, where many receivers need to resynchronize at random times, the use of the intra-coding mode should be restricted as much as possible in low bit rate point-to-point transmission, as typical for wireless networks. The widely varying error conditions in wireless channels limit the effectiveness of classic Forward Error Correction (FEC), since a worst-case design would lead to a prohibitive amount of redundancy. Closed-loop error control techniques like retransmission have been shown to be more effective than FEC and successfully applied to wireless video transmission. But for interactive video applications, the playout delay at the receiver is limited, which limits the number of admissible retransmissions [2].

In this paper, we propose a mechanism to provide error resilience to interactive video applications in wireless networks. The mechanism extends retransmission-based error control with redundant retransmissions on diverse paths between the sender and receiver. The mechanism factors in the importance of the packets as well as the end-to-end latency constraints to minimize the overhead and maximize the quality at the receiver. Our simulation results indicate that the proposed mechanism performs significantly better than reference frame update schemes in terms of perceived quality measured at the receiver as well as the transmission overhead.

This paper is organized as follows. Section 2 provides a review for related works. The proposed mechanism is presented in Section 3. Section 4 discusses the mechanism implementation. Section 5 presents experiments that we performed to examine the proposed mechanism and to compare it to reference frame update error control mechanism. Finally, conclusions are outlined in Section 6.

2   Related Work

Analysis for the effects of packet loss on the quality of MPEG-4 video is presented in reference [3], which also proposes a model to explain these effects. The model shows that errors in reference frames are more detrimental than those in dependant frames, due to propagation of errors, and therefore reference frames should be given a higher level of protection.

Forward error correction (FEC) has been proposed to provide error recovery for video packets by adding redundant information to the compressed video bit-stream so that the original video can be reconstructed in presence of packet loss. Reference [4], presents Priority Encoding Transmission (PET) where different segments of video data are protected with redundant information according to their priority, so that information with higher priority can have a higher chance of correct reception. Typical FEC schemes are stationary and must be implemented to guarantee a certain QoS requirement for the worst-case channel characteristics. Due to the fact that wireless channel is non-stationary, and the channel bit error rate varies over time, FEC techniques are associated with unnecessary overhead that reduces the throughput when the channel is relatively error free.

Unlike FEC, which adds redundancy regardless of correct receipt or loss, reference [5] proposes retransmission-based error control schemes, such as Automatic Repeat Request (ARQ), for real time data. Retransmission-based schemes resend only the packets that are lost, thus they are adaptive to varying loss characteristics, resulting in efficient use of network resources. However, retransmission schemes are limited by the receiver's playout delay, as well as the Round Trip Time *(RTT)*. Reference [6] presents Time-Lined TCP (TLTCP), which extends the TCP retransmission to support time-lines. Instead of treating all data as a byte stream TLTCP allows the application to associate data with deadlines.

An overview on different error concealment mechanisms proposed to minimize the visible distortion of the video due to packet loss is presented in [7]. Error concealment techniques depend on the smoothness property of the images as well as that the human eye can tolerate distortion in high frequency components than in low frequency components. Reference [2] shows that detectable artifacts can still exist after the error concealment, and that the degree of these artifacts depends on the amount of lost data, the type of the stream and the effectiveness of the concealment algorithm. High-quality concealment algorithms require substantial additional computation complexity, which is acceptable for decoding still images but not tolerable in decoding real-time video. In addition, the effectiveness of concealment depends on the amount and correct interpretation of received data, thus concealment becomes much harder with the bursty losses in wireless channels.

Error-resilient encoding, such as Multiple Description Coding (MDC) and Layered Coding (LC), are proposed to combat channel-induced impairments. MDC generates multiple equally important, and independent substreams, also called descriptions [8]. Each description can be independently decoded and is of equal importance in terms of quality, i.e. there is no decoding dependency between any two of the descriptions. When the decoder receives more descriptions, the quality can be gradually increased no matter which description is received. LC generates one base-layer bitstream and several enhancement-layer bitstreams [9]. The base-layer can be decoded to provide a basic video quality while the enhancement-layers are mainly used to refine the quality of the video that is reconstructed from the base-layer. If the base-layer is corrupted, the enhancement-layers become useless, even if they are received perfectly.

3 Prioritized Retransmission over Diverse Paths

The ability to successfully decode a compressed bitstream with inter-frame dependencies depends heavily on the receipt of reference frames, and to a lesser degree on dependent frames. Thus, we propose a mechanism to provide adaptive end-to-end unequal error protection for packets belonging to different frames, without sacrificing the timely-delivery requirement for interactive video. We achieve the unequal error protection through redundant retransmissions over diverse paths between the sender and receiver, based on the importance of the packets. There are several ways to set up multiple diverse paths in a wireless network. In single hop wireless network a mobile node would need to establish channels to multiple base stations. In a multi-hop wireless network, routing protocols can utilize the mesh structure of the network to provide multiple loop-free and maximally disjoint paths. Due to the statistical independence of the packet loss events over different paths, by re-transmitting the packets over separate paths, we are maximizing the probability that at least one packet is received error-free, in least number of retransmissions. With a network loss rate l, the error rate can be reduced to

$$\text{Error Rate} = l^{1+\sum_{i=1}^{L} M_i} \tag{1}$$

where L is the maximum number of retransmission trials, which is typically determined by the initial playout delay in the receiver as well as the round-trip delay. M_i is the number of retransmission copies during the ith retransmission, which depends on the importance of the retransmitted data to the reconstructed video quality. The maximum number of copies $\text{MAX}(M_i)$ is equal to the number of available paths between the sender and receiver.

The scheme is adaptive in the sense that the retransmission overhead will only be added when there is loss in the stream, and the degree of the overhead is proportional to the importance of the lost packets. To ensure in-time delivery of retransmitted packets, and to prevent retransmitting expired packets, the retransmission is controlled by the packet lifetime, as well as estimate(s) of the path delays.

The priority for each data unit in the stream is determined by the application. Thus in the context of motion compensated coding, the application can assign higher priority for I-frames data, than P- or B- frames data. Also P-frames might be assigned varying priority levels, since P-frames that are closer to the preceding I-frame are more valuable for preserving picture quality than later P-frames in the group of pictures (GOP). The prioritization scheme can also be applied on the macroblock basis in coding schemes which provides the encoder with the flexibility to select the coding mode, i.e. intra or inter coding, on the macroblock level [10].

4   Implementation

We implemented the mechanism as a sub-layer above Real Time Protocol (RTP) [11]. Fig. 1 shows the system architecture. We refer to this sub-layer as Multiple Path-RTP (MP-RTP).

MP-RTP is responsible for:

1. Maintaining the reliability level and the lifetime for each packet, as well as implementing delay constrained retransmission,
2. Monitoring the status of the available paths, and selecting the suitable path(s) for packet retransmission.

For each video frame, the sending application assigns a priority level, which is based on the frame's importance to the reconstructed video quality. I-frames are assigned higher reliability level than P- or B- frames. Also P-frames are assigned varying reliability levels based on their location in the GOP. In addition, the sending application calculates the lifetime for each video frame N, $T_L(N)$, as follows:

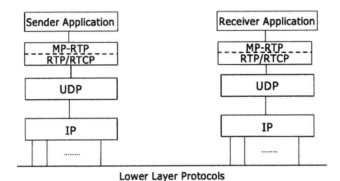

Fig. 1. System architecture.

$$T_L(N) = T_R(N) + D_S \qquad (2)$$

where $T_R(N)$ is an estimate for the rendering time of frame N at the receiver, and D_S is a slack term to compensate the inaccuracies in estimating the One-Way-Delay (OWD) from the sender to the receiver, as will be discussed later, as well as the receiver's processing delay. Assuming that there is no compression and/or expansion of total display time at the receiver, the rendering time for frame N, $T_R(N)$, is calculated as follows:

$$T_R(N) = T_0 + T_D + N/R \qquad (3)$$

where T_0 is the video session initiation time, T_D is the receiver's playout delay, which determines the rendering time for the first frame in the sequence. Playout delay can be obtained from the receiver during the session initiation. R is the frame rate. As the MP-RTP sub-layer receives a frame it fragments it, if required, into multiple packets, then RTP headers are added and the packets are sent to the receiver. In addition, a copy of each packet is kept in a retransmission buffer, along with its lifetime and priority. Typically, all the packets within one frame will have the same lifetime and priority. MP-RTP clears packets from the retransmission buffer, as it receives the Real Time Control Protocol-Receiver Reports (RTCP-RR), which are sent regularly from the receiver, indicating the highest sequence number received, as well as other information regarding the quality of the received stream [11]. Initially, packets are sent on a primary path with the receiver, selected by the sender during the session initiation.

The MP-RTP at the receiver is responsible for sending retransmission requests to the sender as soon as it detects a missing packet. The format of the retransmission request, shown in Fig. 2, is similar to RTCP-RR [11], except that it is extended to include the 32 bits sequence number of the missing packet. As the retransmission request is susceptible to losses, the MP-RTP retransmits these reports on different paths to the sender.

MP-RTP uses Heartbeat packets, shown in Fig. 3.a, to maintain an estimate for the *RTT* of the available paths. The *RTT* estimate is an exponential average of current and past *RTT* measurements. Each heartbeat packet includes a time stamp indicating the transmission time. The MP-RTP at the receiver responds to the heartbeat packet by

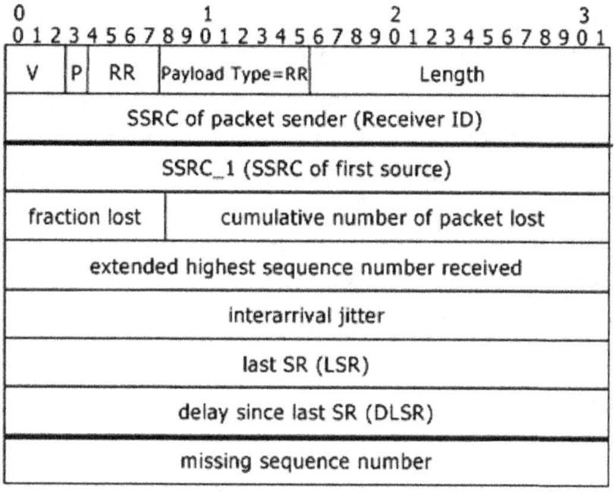

Fig. 2. Extended RTCP-RR to include the missing sequence number.

sending a Heartbeat-Acknowledgment packet, shown in Fig. 3.b, on the same path from which the heartbeat was received. The heartbeat-acknowledgement includes a copy of the timestamp in the corresponding heartbeat packet. The *RTT* estimates are used to obtain an approximation for the paths *OWD*, i.e., $OWD \approx RTT / 2$. The application can compensate the inaccuracies in the *OWD* approximation as it assigns the frames lifetime, as shown in equation 2. In addition, MP-RTP uses the *RTT* estimates to switch the primary path, which can break due to the mobility in the wireless network. To minimize the interruption for the interactive video session, as the primary path *RTT* increases beyond a certain threshold, MP-RTP sets the alternative path with the shortest *RTT* to be the primary path. The switching threshold can be based on the maximum delay allowed for the interactive video application. Currently, we are using a fixed value for the switching threshold. In future work, we are planning to investigate techniques to dynamically adapt the value of the switching threshold.

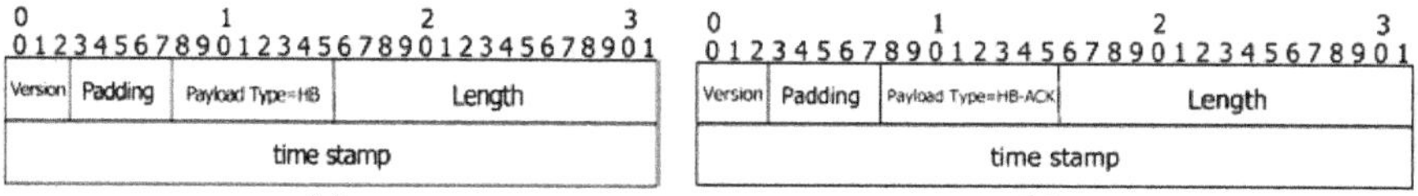

Fig. 3. (a) Heartbeat packet (b) Heartbeat acknowledgement packet.

As soon as the sender receives a retransmission request, it performs the following algorithm:

1. If the lost packet has a low priority, go to step 2, otherwise go to step 3
2. Check the round trip time estimate RTT_i for all the available paths, maintained using heartbeat packets. Select the retransmission path i with the minimum OWD_i, such that the following condition holds:

$$T_c + OWD_i < T_L(j) \tag{4}$$

where T_c is the current time at the sender and $T_L(j)$ is the lifetime for frame j, to which the retransmitted packet belongs.

3. For high priority packets, the sender selects all the available path(s) that satisfies condition 4, and retransmits the packet on these paths simultaneously.

By controlling the retransmission through the frames lifetime, as well as estimate(s) of the path(s) delay, MP-RTP prevents retransmission of expired packets while trying to meet the frames lifetime constraint. If no path(s) is suitable in step 2 or 3, the retransmission is discarded, as the packet will not be received before the rendering time for the frame to which it belongs. At the same time the upper layer application is notified about the dropped packet to allow the encoder to utilize schemes, such as error tracking, to limit the error propagation [2].

5 Performance Analysis

In order to examine the performance of the proposed mechanism, we implemented the mechanism in OPNET simulation and modeling tool [12]. We simulated a Multi Path Transport (MPT) system, with configurable number of single hop paths between the sender and receiver. For simplicity we assumed that the paths are identical in terms of available bandwidth, equal 2.0 Mbps. A two-state model Markov model, shown in Fig. 4, is used to simulate the bursty packet loss behavior in wireless channels [13].

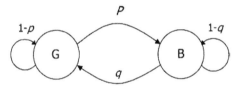

Fig. 4. A two-state Markov model to simulate burst packet losses.

The two state model, which is often referred to as Gilbert channel model, has been shown to be able to effectively capture the bursty packet loss behavior of the wireless channels. The two states of this model are denoted as *Good* (*G*) and *Bad* (*B*). In state *G*, packets are received correctly whereas, in state *B*, packets are assumed to be lost. This model can be described by the transition probabilities p from state G to B and q from state B to G. The average packet loss rate (*PLR*) is:

$$Average\ PLR = \frac{p}{p + q} \tag{5}$$

We vary the error characteristics for channel i by appropriately controlling the channel *Good* and *Bad* durations, according to an exponential distributions with averages p_i and q_i, respectively. Delay for channel i is modeled by an exponential distribution with the mean delay $D_i = 30$ msec. We set the path maximum transfer unit (MTU) of 400 bytes for all the paths. The heartbeat interval is set to 150 msec.

To generate the video sequence used in our simulation, we used open source XviD MPEG-4 compliant video codec [14]. Sixty seconds of a high motion video sequence (football match) are encoded at 15 frames per second (fps), which results in a sequence of 900 frames. The frame resolution is quarter common intermediate format (QCIF, 176 x 144 pixels), which is the most common format at low bit rates, and the coding rate is 200 Kbps. We repeated our experiments with limited motion video sequence (TV news) and we get similar results to that shown here. We limited the playout delay at the receiver to 100 msec., to represent an interactive video application. We set the switching threshold, discussed in Section 4, to 200 msec. We selected this value because given the channel delays and the playout delay at the receiver, having the *RTT* of the primary path higher than this threshold will result in all frames arriving later than their rendering time at the receiver and will be discarded.

The average Peak Signal to Noise Ratio (PSNR) is used as a distortion measure of objective quality. PSNR is an indicator of picture quality that is derived from the root mean squared error (RMSE). Without transmission losses, the average PSNR of the decoded frames for the video sequence used in our performance study is 27 dB.

After obtaining a transmission trace of a video sequence, we run the decoder on the trace to measure the image distortion due to packet losses, using the PSNR. In order to generate statistically meaningful quality measures, for each simulation scenario we repeated the experiment ten times with different seeds. The presented PSNR values are the average of the ten experiments.

In our performance study we set the application to choose I-frames and half of the P-frames starting from the I-frame in a GOP to be high priority frames, while other frames are set to low priority frames.

5.1 Effect of Packet Loss Rate on Video Quality

We tested MP-RTP using two diverse paths, namely path 0 and path 1, between the sender and the receiver. Path 0 was selected as the primary path during the video session initiation. The channel average packet loss rates for path 0 and path 1 were set to 0.2 and 0.1 respectively. We set the encoder so that the I-frame update period, i.e. interval between two consecutive I-frames, equal 3 seconds. Fig. 5 shows the PSNR for each frame in the video sequence. For comparison we repeated the experiment using the retransmission scheme with single path retransmissions, where missing packets are retransmitted on a single path selected randomly from the paths between the sender and receiver. As can be shown from the figure that the redundant retransmission scheme is able to maintain the video quality, at high packet loss rates. On the other hand, with the single path retransmission scheme, the video quality can be dropped for long durations due to loss of packets in reference frames, and under the high loss rate retransmitted packets can also be lost, leading to error propagation in the following dependent frames up to the next I-frame. Although the sender can keep retransmitting the packet, the receiver will discard these retransmissions, as they arrive after the frame rendering time.

Fig. 6, shows the average PSNR over the whole sequence versus different channel average packet loss rates for the primary path, i.e. path 0. The channel average packet loss rate for path 1 is set to 0.1. We repeated the same experiment with different I-frame update periods. For our mechanism we used an I-frame update period equal 3 seconds. As can be seen in Fig. 6, the single path retransmission scheme achieves a similar performance to MP-RTP only when the I-frame frequency is increased more than three times to one every 15 frames. As the I-frames have larger sizes than P- and B-frames, increasing the I-frame frequency for the same bit rate translates to reduced video quality since bits are now wasted to code I-frames. If the I-frame frequency is set to one in 45 frames for the single path case, it can be seen that the quality deteriorates rapidly.

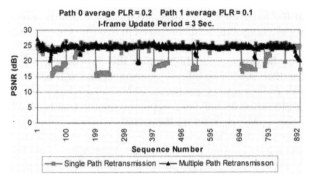

Fig. 5. PSNR versus frame number.

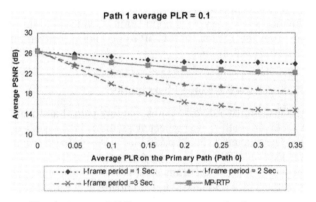

Fig. 6. Average PSNR versus average packet loss rate.

Again this is mostly due to losses in reference frames, as a result of the high packet loss rate and the bounded delay for interactive video. The errors are propagated from reference frames to the following frames up to the next I-frame. On the other hand, redundant retransmissions over diverse paths ensures that in the single retransmission allowed at least one copy of the packet will be received, preventing the error propagation.

5.2 Effect of Changing the Number of Paths

We tested the redundant retransmission mechanism with different number of paths between the sender and receiver. In all experiments the I-frame update period is equal 3 seconds.

We varied the channel average packet loss rate on the primary path, i.e. path 0, from 0.05 to 0.3. We represented the independent packet losses for the other paths, i.e. paths 1-3, by choosing different channel average packet loss rates 0.01, 0.1 and 0.2 respectively. As can be seen from Fig. 7, with a single path the quality deteriorates at high packet loss rates, due to error propagation. But, with MP-RTP, increasing the number of paths between the sender and the receiver, improves the quality due to the independent loss characteristics of the paths, which increases the probability that the retransmitted packets will be received before their deadline.

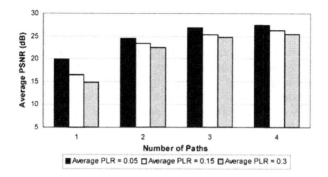

Fig. 7. Average PSNR versus number of paths.

5.3 Redundant Retransmission Overhead

In this experiment, we compared the overhead of MP-RTP, due to the redundant re-transmissions and heartbeats, to the overhead of error control mechanisms that depend on increasing the I-frame frequency to limit the error propagation.

We define the overhead ratio to be the total number of bytes sent in I-frame update scheme to the total number of bytes sent in MP-RTP, to attain a given video quality represented by the average PSNR. In order to calculate the maximum overhead for MP-RTP, we used 3 paths. We varied the channel average packet loss rate for the primary path, path 0, while the channel average packet loss rates for the other paths, path 1 and path 2, were set to 0.1 and 0.2 respectively.

Fig. 8 shows the overhead ratio for average PSNR equal 23 dB. As was shown before, the single path retransmission case required an I-frame frequency of almost 1 per second, while the MP-RTP required 1 per 3 seconds, for a video quality of around 23 dB. It can be seen from the figure that the overhead of our mechanism is less than that for the I-frames update scheme. The reason behind this is that the redundant retransmission mechanism implemented in MP-RTP is adaptive, in the sense that it only adds the retransmission overhead when there is loss in the video stream. In addition, the degree of the overhead is proportional to the importance of the lost packets. Although heartbeat packets are periodically sent, they have less contribution to the overhead, as they are small in size compared to the size of video frames.

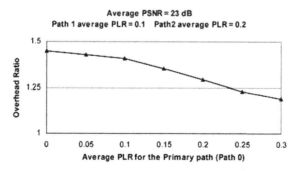

Fig. 8. Overhead ratio versus average packet loss rate on the primary path.

6 Conclusion

The nature of video encoded using motion compensation requires higher protection for reference frames than dependent frames, otherwise errors due to packet losses in reference frames propagate to dependent frames. Interactive video complicates the problem by bounding the time available for the error control. To tackle these problems, we propose a mechanism to provide unequal error protection to data within the video stream according to their importance to the reconstructed video quality. The unequal error protection is realized through extending the classic retransmission based error control, with redundant retransmissions on diverse paths, in order to increase the probability that at least one of the retransmitted packets arrive at the receiver in less number of retransmissions. The degree of redundant retransmission depends on the reliability level required for the data within the retransmitted packet. A delayed constrained retransmission, based on the packet lifetime and estimate of the delay from the sender to receiver, is used to prevent re-transmitting expired packets. We implemented the proposed mechanism as an extension to RTP, refereed to as Multi Path - RTP (MP-RTP). Performance results show that the mechanism is able to provide a good quality for interactive video under different packet loss rates. In addition, comparing the transmission overhead of the mechanism to the overhead of reference frame updates error control mechanism, it is shown that for a given video reconstruction quality MP-RTP has less overhead, which is an important feature required in wireless networks.

Disclaimer

The views and conclusions in this document are those of the authors and should not be interpreted as representing the official policies, either expressed or implied, of the Army Research laboratory or the U.S. Government.

References

1. International Organization for Standardization, Overview of the MPEG-4 Standard. (1999)
2. Girod, B., Farber, N.: Feedback-Based Error Control for Mobile Video Transmission. Proceedings of the IEEE, special issue on video for mobile multimedia, Vol. 97, No. 10, (1999) 1707-1723
3. Feamster, N., Balakrishnan, H.: Packet Loss Recovery for Streaming Video. International Packet Video Workshop (2002)
4. Albanese, A., Blomer, J., Edmonds, J., Luby, M., Sudan, M.: Priority Encoding Transmission. IEEE Transactions on Information Theory, Vol. 42, No. 6 (1996)
5. Dempsey, B.: Retransmission-Based Error Control for Continuous Media in Packet Switched Networks. Ph.D. thesis, University of Virginia (1994)
6. Mukherjee, B., Brecht, T.: Time-lined TCP for the TCP-friendly Delivery of Streaming Media. International Conference on Network Protocols (ICNP) (2000)
7. Wang, Y., Zhu, Q.: Error Control and Concealment for Video Communications: A Review. Proceedings of IEEE, Vol.86, No. 5 (1998)
8. Goyal, V.: Multiple Description Coding: Compression Meets the Network. IEEE Signal Processing Magazine, Vol. 18 (2001) 74-93

9. Lee, Y., Kim, J., Altunbasak, Y., Mersereau, R.: Layered Coded vs. Multiple Description Coded Video over Error Prone Networks. Signal Processing: Image Communication, Vol. 18 (2003) 337-356
10. ITU-T Recommendation, H.263, in Video Coding for Low Bitrate Communication (1997)
11. Schulzrinne H., Casner S., Frederick, R., Jacobson, V.: RTP: A Transport Protocol for Real-Time Applications. RFC 3550 (2003)
12. Opnet Simulation and Modeling Tool, www.opnet.com.
13. Gilbert, E.: Capacity of a burst-noise channel, Bell System Technical Journal, Vol. 39, No. 9 (1960) 1253-1265
14. XviD MPEG-4 video codec, www.xvid.org

A Bandwidth-Efficient Application Level Framing Protocol for H.264 Video Multicast over Wireless LANs

Abdelhamid Nafaa, Yassine Hadjadj Aoul, Daniel Negru, and Ahmed Mehaoua

University of Versailles, CNRS-PRiSM Lab.
45, av. des Etats Unis 78035, Versailles, France
Tel: +33 1 39 25 40 59, Fax: +33 1 39 25 40 57
{anaf,yana,dan,mea}@prism.uvsq.fr

Abstract. Optimizing wireless bandwidth utilization is one of the numerous challenges in wireless IP multimedia systems design. This paper describes and evaluates the performance of a novel Application Level Framing protocol for efficient transmission of H.264 video over error-prone wireless IP links. The proposed ALF protocol introduces an innovative loss spreading scheme for video streaming services which is based on (*i*) a bandwidth-efficient adaptive H.264 video fragmentation and (*ii*) an unequal-interleaved protection for improving FEC efficiency. Both video fragmentation and interleaving are coordinated in a frame-based granularity providing bounded end-to-end delays. Performance evaluation results show that the proposed protocol allows graceful video quality degradation over error-prone wireless links while minimizing the overall bandwidth consumption and the end-to-end latency.

1 Introduction

Wireless communication technology has gained widespread acceptance in recent years. The IEEE 802.11b 1 standard has led wireless local area networks (LANs) into greater use, providing up to 11 Mbps of shared bandwidth. With such high bandwidth, the demand for supporting time-sensitive traffic applications, such as video-on-demand and interactive multimedia, in wireless LANs has been increasing. Meanwhile, the recently adopted ITU-T H.264 standard 2 (known also as ISO/IEC International Standard 14496 Part 10) achieves efficient video encoding and bandwidth savings. H.264 experts have taken into account transmission over packet based networks in the video codec design from the very beginning. The overall performance of H.264 is as such that bit rate savings of 50% or more, compared to the current state of technology, are reported. Digital Satellite TV quality, for example, was reported to be achievable at 1.5 Mbit/s, compared to the current operation point of MPEG-2 video at around 3.5 Mbit/s. In this paper, we investigate H.264 video multicast communications over IEEE 802.11b wireless LAN. Though the proposed protocol is network independent and can support various media types as well.

In previous work 3, 4, we have addressed wireless video communication issue from an application point of view. Thus, we proposed a multimedia elementary streams classification and aggregation that provides wireless bandwidth savings and packet loss tolerance. However, the intrinsic wireless link characteristics involve unpredictable burst errors that are usually uncorrelated with the instantaneous available bandwidth. The resulting packet losses and bit errors can have devastating effects on multimedia quality. To overcome residual BER (Bit Error Rate), error control mechanisms of video streams is generally required. Error control mechanisms are

J. Vicente and D. Hutchison (Eds.): MMNS 2004, LNCS 3271, pp. 13–25, 2004.

popular on dealing with packet loss and delay over bandwidth limited fading wireless channels. Such mechanisms involve Forward Error Correction (FEC), Automatic Retransmission ReQuest (ARQ), and error resilience tools. FEC has been commonly suggested for real-time applications due to (*i*) its proven scalability for multicast communications and (*ii*) the strict delay requirements of media streams.

Typical communications over wireless networks involve high bit error rates that translate to correlated adjacent packets losses. In this case, the classical adaptive FEC approaches 5, 6, can be inefficient since they involve an excessive bandwidth usage. Actually, such approaches use FEC to protect consecutive original data packets, which reduce its effectiveness against burst packets losses. This often implies transmitting additional FEC packets to overcome the increasing BER. Hence, we propose a novel low-delay interleaved FEC protection scheme. The idea is to spread the burst loss before FEC recovering, so that the burst loss manifests itself as a number of disjoint packet losses in the FEC-recovered data stream. This process first consists of adaptively fragmenting the H.264 Frames in order to achieve a better link utilization. The second phase is based on the application of an unequal-interleaved media packet protection, which takes into account the H.264 video Frames relevance. Thus, our protocol minimizes burst errors consequences, as well as the video distortion at receivers' side, while minimizing the overall bandwidth consumption.

The remainder of this paper is as follows. Section 2 investigates reliable H.264 video multicasting over Wireless LAN. Then, the proposed protocol is presented in Section 3. Section 4 is devoted to the performance evaluation. Finally, Section 5 concludes the paper.

2 Related Works on H.264 Streaming over Wireless LAN

2.1 H.264 over Wireless IP Networks

A new feature of H.264 design 7 resides in the introduction of a conceptual separation between Video Coding Layer (VCL), which provides the core high-compression representation of the video picture content, and Network Adaptation Layer (NAL), which packages that representation for efficient delivery over a particular type of network.

The H.264 NAL design provides the ability to customize the format of the VCL data for delivery over a variety of particular networks. Therefore, a unique packet-based interface between the VCL and the NAL is defined. The packetization and appropriate signaling are part of the NAL specification, which is not necessarily part of the H.264 specification itself. For the transmission of video over WLANs with limited bandwidth and transmission power resources, the necessity for high compression efficiency is an obvious task. Besides, adaptation of the video data to the network fluctuation is an additional important task due to special properties of the wireless channel. These two design goals, compression efficiency and network friendliness, motivate the differentiation between the VCL for coding efficiency and the NAL to take care of network issues. In the H.264 framework, all information that was traditionally conveyed in sequences, group-of-picture, or picture headers is conveyed out of band. During the setup of the logical channel the capability exchange takes place. This procedure was already subject to many discussions within H.264, and it was agreed that a simple version/profile/level concept should be used; current work in the IETF 9 is underway to enable such features.

2.2   Reliable Multicast Communications over Wireless LAN

In order to reliably communicate over packet-erasure channels, it is necessary to exert some form of error control 8. Two classes of communication protocols are used in practice to reliably communicate data over packet networks: synchronous and asynchronous. Asynchronous communication protocols, such as ARQ operates by dividing the data into packets and appending a special error check sequence to each packet for error detection purposes. The receiver decides whether a transmission error occurred by calculating the check sequence. For each intact data packet received in the forward channel, the receiver sends back an acknowledgement. While this model works very well for data communication, it is not suitable for multimedia streams with hard latency constraints. The maximum delay of the ARQ mechanism is unbounded, and in the case of live streaming it is necessary to interpolate late-arriving or missing data rather than insert a delay in the stream playback. In synchronous protocols (i.e. FEC-based protocols), the data are transmitted with a bounded delay but generally not in a channel adaptive manner. The FEC codes are designed to protect data against channel losses by introducing parity packets. No feedback channel is required. If the number of lost packets is less than the decoding threshold for the FEC code, the original data can be recovered perfectly.

ARQ-based schemes are not appropriate for the multicast case for three reasons: (*i*) ACK explosion, that scales with the multicast group size; (*ii*) for significant loss rate, each user will require frequent packet retransmissions that are probably useless for the other multicast clients; and (*iii*) unbounded data transmission delays. Hence, using a FEC-based error control seems to be more appropriate for real time multicast communication.

The IEEE 802.11 standard 1 uses the same logical link layer as other 802-series networks (including the 802.3 wired Ethernet standard), and uses compatible 48-bit hardware Ethernet addresses to simplify routing between wired and wireless networks. As in the wired Ethernet, corrupted packets are dropped at the link layer (i.e. the packets with bit errors are unavailable to a multimedia application). The communication is complicated by the inability of radio transceivers to detect collisions as they transmit, and the potential for devices outside the network to interfere with network transmissions. Communication is also hampered by the hidden node problem. Therefore, the IEEE 802.11b standard uses a complex MAC protocol to cope with these wireless communication specificities. The basic medium access protocol is a DCF (Distributed Coordination Function) that allows medium sharing through the use of CSMA/CA (Carrier Sense Medium Access / Collision Avoidance). In addition, all directed traffic uses immediate positive acknowledgment (ACK frame) where retransmission is scheduled by the sender if no ACK is received. That is, within IEEE 802.11b unicast communications, all wireless data frames are acknowledged by the receiver. Furthermore, each retransmission introduces an additional latency due to triggering of the collision avoidance routine. The sender uses limited retransmission persistence, so the data can be dropped at the source after several retransmission attempts. In case of multicast or broadcast traffic, however, the data packets are not acknowledged, and hence no retransmission is performed on the MAC/Logical link layer; this mode of communication reduces transmissions delays while making communications less reliable.

2.3 Specific Related Works

Nowadays, most of the reliable multicast video distribution protocols propose the use of ARQ (see 10 and references therein). Besides, FEC for multicast streaming of different characteristic have been extensively studied in the literature 6, 12. In a multicast scenario, to tackle the problem of heterogeneity and to ensure graceful quality degradation, the use of multi resolution-based scalable bitstreams has been previously suggested in 10 and 13. These approaches are, however, dedicated to multilayer video coding throughout their design.

In wireless communications, packet loss can exhibit temporal dependency or burstiness. For instance, if packet n is lost, packet $n + 1$ is also likely to do so. This translates to burstiness in network losses, which may worsen the perceptual quality compared to random losses at the same average loss rate. As a consequence, the performance of FEC is affected, e.g., percentage of packets that cannot be recovered. Moreover, the final loss pattern after FEC recovering could be even burstier due to the dependency between losses, which affects audio/video quality and effectiveness of loss concealment. In order to reduce burst loss, redundant information has to be added into temporally distant packets, which introduces even higher delay. Hence, the repair capability of FEC is limited by the delay budget 14. Another sender-based loss recovery technique, interleaving, which does not increase the data rate of transmission, also faces the same dilemma. The efficiency of loss recovery depends on over how many packets the source packet is interleaved and spread. Again, the wider the spread, the higher the introduced delay.

In this paper, we introduce a novel technique that combines reliability and efficiency advantages of both interleaving and FEC coding. Our proposal is based on an adaptive H.264 streams fragmentation coordinated with an unequal-interleaved protection scheme. Thus, we improve the error resiliency while minimizing the overall bandwidth consumption and still meeting the delay constraints.

3 Unequal Interleaved FEC Protocol for Reliable Wireless Video Multicasting

3.1 Adaptive H.264 Video Fragmentation and Packetization

Basically, mobile devices are hand-held and constrained in processing power. In addition, the mobile environment is characterized by harsh transmission conditions in terms of fading and multi-user interference, which results in time- and location-varying channel conditions. Therefore, a mobile video codec design must minimize terminal complexity while still remaining efficient. Consequently, in our work we specially focus on H.264 Baseline Profile to reduce the receiver's decoder complexity. In this H.264 coder release the data partitioning features are not enabled.

Internally, the NAL uses NALU (NAL Units) 9. A NAL unit consists of a one-byte header and the payload byte string. A complete separation between the VCL and the NAL is difficult to obtain because some dependencies exist. The packetization process is an example: error resilience, in fact, is improved if the VCL is instructed to create slices of about the same size of the packets and the NAL told to put only one slice per packet. The error resilience characteristics of the transmission will take profit of it because all the data contained in a certain packet can be decoded independently from the others. Note that in H.264, the subdivision of a Frame into slices has not to be the same for each Frame of the sequence; thus the decoder can flexibly decide how to make the slices. However, they should not be too short because a decrease of the compression ratio would occur for two reasons, i.e. the slice headers would reduce the available bandwidth and the context-based entropy coding would become less efficient. Moreover, in wireless channels, the size of transmitted packets influences its error probability; longer packets are more likely to contain transmission errors 1516. In this paper the trade-off involved in the packet creation process will be investigated, studying the performances of the video transmission as a function of the packet size. Actually, we try to find, for each Frame to be transmitted, the optimal slice size that maximizes the bandwidth utilization taking into account the fluctuating wireless link conditions (it is assumed that a NALU corresponds to a Slice).

Let *FRAMEsize* be the Frame size, S the packet size in bytes, oh the header size in bytes and *Lr* the wireless channel loss rate. The link utilization, U, is then given by (1). U represents the original video data over the transmitted data (i.e. including the FEC redundancy).

$$U = \frac{FRAMEsize}{\left(\dfrac{FRAMEsize}{S - oh} + \left\lceil \dfrac{Lr \cdot FRAMEsize}{S - oh} \right\rceil \right) \cdot S} \tag{1}$$

Where, $NALUsize = S - oh$ and $oh + 1 \le S \le MTU$ In Fig. 1, U is plotted against S for *FRAMESize*=10000 and *oh*=40 at four different loss rates (i.e. $Lr = \{0, 0.05, 0.2$ and $0.3\}$).

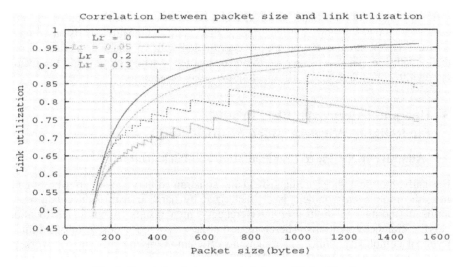

Fig. 1. Correlation between packet size and link utilization.

Fig. 1 depicts the wireless channel utilization for different packet loss rates. It is quite obvious that a small packet size provides better performance when the channel loss rate is too high. In the other hand, systematically choosing a small packet size does not necessarily give good channel utilization. Now, it is readily realized that the maximum of the utilization function is obtained by resolving the equation for S. Thus, *NALUSize* is determined for each Frame to be transmitted based on the measured loss rate. The fragmentation/encapsulation presented here, provides better wireless link utilization. Moreover, this scheme minimizes the dependency between adjacent RTP packets, which mitigate the dependency of H.264 decoder on any lost packet.

3.2   Unequal Interleaved FEC Protection Protocol

Fig. 2 illustrates a sample trace we obtained using an 802.11 AP (Access Point) and wireless receivers. Each point represents the packet loss rate measured at each receiver; we emphasize the channel behavior when multicasting video over wireless links. The AP sent multicast H.264 video packets and the receiving stations recorded the sequence number of the correctly received packets. It should be noted that this experience reveals an important number of adjacent packet losses as a consequence of the wireless burst errors. Furthermore, the packet loss rate is different at each receiver due to location-varying channel conditions.

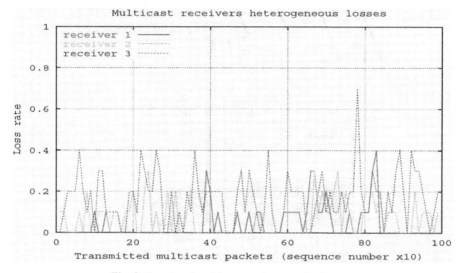

Fig. 2. Correlated multicast receivers packet losses.

Since the wireless link fluctuation occurs usually through unpredictable adjacent packets losses, we propose to use an interleaved FEC protection. As depicted in Fig. 3, the redundant FEC packets protect temporally scattered RTP packets in order to cope with wireless sporadic packet losses. This increases the FEC efficiency through improving the error resiliency at clients' side.

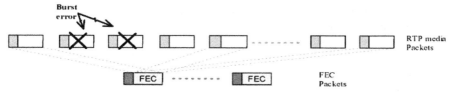

Fig. 3. Scattered video packets protection.

Within UI-FEC, the time is divided into transmission rounds. A transmission round ends when the sender transmits the last packet of a Frame. Each Frame is divided into several UBs (Unequal loss protection Block). An UB consists of $n = k + h$ packets (see Fig. 5). At this point, we define the interleaving factor (i) as the Sequence Number (SN) difference between each two successive protected RTP packets in the UB. The interleaving factor is fixed for the k protected RTP packets belonging to the same UB (see Eq.2). When $i = 1$, the interleaved protection is not applied and, hence, the FEC packets protect consecutive RTP packets. Fig. 4 summarizes the UI-FEC protocol working example for an interleaving $i = 3$. In this case, the adjacent video packets (in terms of transmission order) are protected in different FEC blocks. Here, the interleaving factor represents the interleaving stride[1].

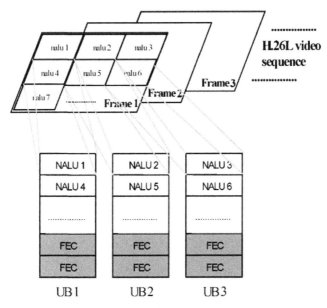

Fig. 4. UI-FEC Protocol.

Note that for a given Frame (F), the interleaving factor (i) represents the number of UBs constituting F. Moreover, i is fixed for all UBs belonging to the same Frame. For synchronization consideration the protected media data of a given UB must belong to the same Frame. In other words, each Frame is transmitted as an integer number of UBs. After applying FEC, the media packets are transmitted in their initial order (i.e. according to the sequence number order). Note that the delays introduced by the FEC interleaving do not have important consequences, since the interleaving is applied over a single Frame. The induced delays can be resolved through an initial buffering time. This novel interleaving schema over a single Frame is used to provide an adaptive and unequal FEC protection.

---

[1] By interleaving stride, we mean the separation (in terms of packet transmission order) between two consecutive data packets in the same FEC block. This is useful in spreading the burst loss, so that the burst loss manifests itself as a number of disjoint packet losses in the FEC-recovered data stream.

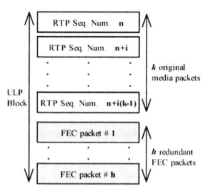

Fig. 5. UB structure details.

For FEC efficiency 6, it is suitable to keep the number of information packets (k) as high as possible with few redundant packets. Actually, a higher number of information packets leads to better granularity, which allows adjusting the redundancy rate more precisely according to wireless channel conditions. As an example, if a Frame to be transmitted has a size of 10 Kbytes, a packet payload size (*NALUSize*) of 1 Kbyte will result in 10 RTP packets. This makes the precision at which the error protection can be applied in units of 10%.

In our study, we take a minimum of 10 information packets for each UB (i.e. guarantying a minimum precision of 10%). This is insured using an appropriate $l \geq 10$ taking into account the mean Frame size (see formula (2)). For a fixed l, both interleaving factor (i) and the number (k) of media packet per UB are then easily stated; where the FRAMESize is obtained from the Frame header, while the *NALUSize* is fixed by our H.264 video packetization process (see section 3.1).

$$k = \left\lfloor \frac{FRAMESize}{i * NALUSize} \right\rfloor, where, i = \left\lfloor \frac{FRAMESize}{l * NALUSize} \right\rfloor \tag{2}$$

It is clear that the interleaving factor is tightly dependent on Frame size. Since the different Frames (pictures) of a coded H.264 video sequence have a different size, the interleaving factor (i) scales along with the Frame size. Consider that an intra-coded picture (picture-I) is larger than an inter-coded picture (picture-P or picture-B). Basically, the large inter-coded picture conveys a lot of motion vectors and error prediction information. Otherwise, the larger the inter-coded picture is, the more it codes a highly changeful scene with different texture, and the more it involves an important video distortion when lost. As a consequence, within our UI-FEC, the interleaving protection is applied differently based on Frame size and hence Frame relevance, which provides a better loss recovery for the most sensitive H.264 bitstream. Thus, the different Frames are interleaved unequally, protected, then transmitted based on their relevance and without using any previous video stream classification scheme.

The adaptive FEC scheme proposed in this paper is based on systematic RS(n, k) codes, where n, k and i are reassigned for each Frame to be transmitted based on the relevant priority of the Frame and the current loss rate of the communication channel. When using k source data in an UB, transmitting h FEC packets provides an erasure resiliency against a packet loss rate of h/n. Therefore, it is easy to calculate the amount of redundant packets (h) using the packet loss rate (p) and the number (k) of original media packets of current UB to be transmitted (see formula (3)).

$$h = \frac{p.k}{1-p} \qquad (3)$$

The amount of redundancy introduced is computed once per each Frame to be transmitted depending on (*i*) current transport-level packet loss rate (i.e. measured before FEC recovering) and (*ii*) video fragmentation parameters. This is achieved according to (1) and (3).

3.3 UI-FEC Signaling

In this section, we highlight the key components involved by UI-FEC deployments. Since the successive UBs will have different structure, we propose a simple signaling of required parameters for UB decoding (see Fig. 6). We transmit together within FEC stream (i.e. FEC header) the base RTP sequence number (*BSeq*) of the protected RTP packets, the UB size (n), the protected original data (k), and the interleaving factor (*i*). Thus, both interleaving and redundancy are adjusted to match the overall measured BER.

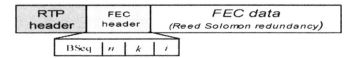

Fig. 6. FEC parameters signaling.

This signaling is sufficiently flexible to provide an adaptive error control based on the signaled FEC interleaving parameters. In addition, the original media stream is decoupled from the FEC stream and its associated parameters, which allows clients without FEC capabilities to decode the original media stream.

4 Performance Evaluation

UI-FEC is evaluated with Network Simulator v2 using different network configurations. We emphasize the robustness and efficiency of our proposal with the classical FEC protection (i.e. non interleaved FEC protection) for wireless multimedia communications.

4.1 Simulation Model

Video multicasting applications are considered for the simulation. With our proposed technique, the H.264 multicast server generates FEC packets that protect interleaved RTP media packets, while, with classical approach, FEC protection is applied to consecutive RTP media packets. It should be noted that both approaches are evaluated for the same network configurations and using the same amount of FEC protection as well. In our simulation, we use a QCIF Foreman H.264 coded sequence with a constant quantization parameter of 10 (sequence parameters are depicted in Table1); the video sequence was generated using the current release of the TML software, JM80. We choose a highly changeful video sequence in order to highlight the unequal-interleaved protection efficiency.

Table 1. Source Video Statistics.

Original video	Video configuration	Average bit-rate	Frame frequence
Foreman (13.33 seconds)	H.264 Baseline Profile	1783 Kb/s	30 Frame/s

We use the network simulation models depicted in Fig. 7 for evaluating and comparing our proposal with the classical approach. The MPEG-4 sender attached to the node "1" transmits a multicast MPEG-4 stream to the wireless receivers "5" and "7". We include constant-bit-rate (CBR) traffic over UDP to allow loading the network differently each time in order to get further information about UI-FEC behavior.

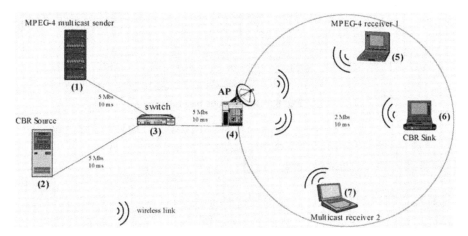

Fig. 7. Network model.

4.2   Results Analysis

Fig. 8 represents the final packet loss rates measured for each received H.264 Frame after recovering with FEC; it reveals relatively high bit error rates due to (1) wireless channel burst errors and (2) absence of MAC-level retransmissions in multicast communications. Consider that the measured high loss rates are often provoked by temporally consecutive packet losses affecting the same Frame. We observe that for the same network conditions, UI-FEC increases error resiliency at receivers' side through recovering more RTP packets.

Fig. 9 illustrates the bandwidth consumption measured during the simulation (i.e. for 400 Frames). UI-FEC is more bandwidth efficient than the classical FEC; the measured mean bandwidth saving is around 76 Kbps. This bandwidth saving is principally due to a better error resiliency, which implies a reduced FEC transmission. We observed that the unequal-interleaved FEC scheme provides better robustness in networks with a high BER and, consequently, a likely small MTU size. Moreover, UI-FEC behaves better when transporting high bit-rate video streams (i.e. video streams with a large mean Frame size).

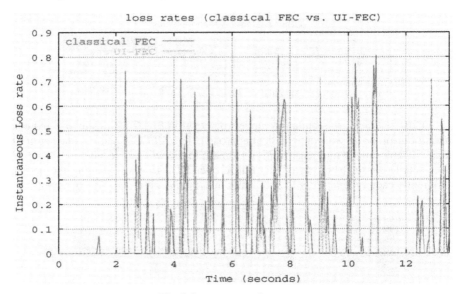

Fig. 8. Instantaneous loss rates.

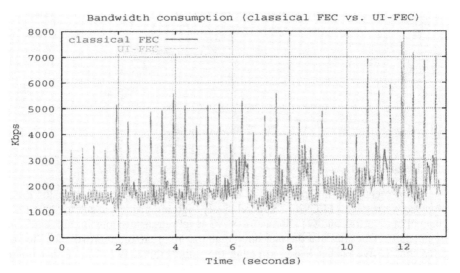

Fig. 9. Instantaneous bandwidth consumption.

We experienced 4 dropped Frames that can not be decoded when transmitting video protected by the classical adaptive FEC, whereas we were able to decode the whole video sequence (400 Frames) through using UI-FEC protocol. Fig. 10 depicts the objective quality measurements of reconstructed video streams when transmitted and protected using both FEC techniques. It is clear that UI-FEC protection achieves smoother video quality degradation than a classical FEC protection; the average PSNR gain over the whole communication is around 2.18 dB.

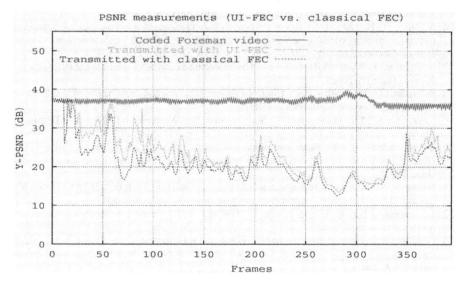

Fig. 10. Objective video quality measurements.

5 Conclusion

In this paper we designed, implemented and tested a new Application Framing Protocol named UI-FEC to cope with the problem of efficiently stream real-time compressed video over error-prone wireless links. A distinct feature of UI-FEC is the efficient wireless bandwidth management by means of an adaptive video stream fragmentation coupled with an unequal-interleaved FEC protection. UI-FEC performance was evaluated by simulation with an H.264 multicast distribution service. Results analysis show that UI-FEC offers considerable gains over conventional adaptive FEC in effectively protecting sensitive H.264 video frames, and consequently improving both bandwidth utilization and end-user perceived video quality.

References

1. Information technology, Wireless LAN medium access control (MAC) and physical layer (PHY) specifications, IEEE 802.11 standard, (August 1999).
2. "Draft ITU-T Recommendation and Final Draft International Standard of Joint Video Specification", *(ITU-T Rec. H.264 | ISO/IEC 14496-10 AVC)*, (May 2003).
3. A. Nafaa, T. Ahmed, Y. Hadjadj-Aoul, A. Mehaoua., RTP4mux: a novel MPEG-4 RTP payload for multicast video communications over wireless IP, *in Proc. of IEEE/PV'03,13[th] International Packet Video Workshop*, Nantes, France, (April 2003).

4. T. Ahmed, A. Nafaa, A. Mehaoua, An object-based MPEG-4 multimedia content classification model for IP QoS differentiation, *in Proc. of IEEE ISCC'03, IEEE International Symposium on Computer Communications 2003*, Turkey, (July 2003), 1091 - 10962

5. T. Ahmed, V. Lecuire, A. Mehaoua, MPEG-4 AVO streaming over IP using TCP-Friendly and unequal error protection, *in Proc. of IEEE ICME'03, IEEE Intentional Conference on Multimedia and Expo 2003*, Baltimore, USA, (July 2003), 317 – 320.

6. N. Nikaein, H. Labiod, C. Bonnet, MA-FEC: A QoS-based adaptive FEC for multicast communication in wireless networks, in *Proc. IEEE ICC'00, IEEE International Conference on Communications 2000*, New Orleans, USA, (Jun 2000), 954 – 958.

7. R. Schäfer, T. Wiegand, H. Schwarz, The emerging H.264/AVC standard, *EBU Technical Review*, (January 2003).

8. S. Lin and D.-J. Costello, Error Control Coding: Fundamentals and Applications, Prentice-Hall, Inc. Englewood Cliffs, N.J., (1983).

9. S. Wenger et M.M. Hannuksela, T. Stockhammer, M. Westerlund, D. Singer, RTP payload format for H.264 video, *IETF Draft, version 10,* expires (January 2005).

10. A. Mjumdar et al., Multicast and unicast real-time video streaming over wireless LANs, *IEEE Transaction on Circuits and Systems for Video Technology*, Issue: 6, 524 – 534, (June 2002).

11. Nafaa, A. Mehoua "A novel unequal interleaved protection for robust H.264 video multicasting" Technical report, http://prism.uvsq.fr/~anaf/tr02.pdf, (July 2003).

12. J. Nonnenmacher, E. Biersack, and D. Towsley, Parity-based loss recovery for reliable multicast transmission, *IEEE/ACM Transactions on Networking*, (August 1998), 349-361.

13. G. Liebl, M. Wagner, J. Pandel, and W. Weng, An RTP payload format for erasure-resilient transmission of progressive multimedia streams, *IETF Draft, draft-ietf-avt-uxp-05.txt*, expires (Sept. 2003).

14. J.-C. Bolot, End-to-end packet delay and loss behavior in the internet, *ACM SIGCOMM '93*, San Francisco, CA, USA, (September 1993).

15. M. Johanson, Adaptive Forward Error Correction for real-time Internet video, *in Proc. of IEEE/PV'03, 13th International Packet Video Workshop*, Nantes, France, (April 2003).

16. P. Lettieri and M. B. Srivastava, Adaptive frame length control for wireless link throughput, range, and energy efficiency, *in Proc. of IEEE INFOCOM'98, Conference on Computer Communications, San Francisco*, CA, (April 1998), 564 – 571.

Adaptive Video Streaming
in Presence of Wireless Errors

Guang Yang, Mario Gerla, and Medy Sanadidi

Computer Science Department, UCLA
Los Angeles, CA 90095, USA
{yangg,gerla,medy}@cs.ucla.edu

Abstract. Real-time video streaming with rate adaptation to network load/congestion represents an efficient solution to its coexistence with conventional TCP data services. Naturally, the streaming rate control must be efficient, smooth and TCP friendly. As multimedia clients become mobile, these properties must be preserved also over wireless links. In particular, they must be robust to random wireless losses. Existing schemes such as TCP Friendly Rate Control (TFRC) perform well in the wired Internet, but show serious performance degradation in the presence of random wireless losses. In this paper we introduce the Video Transport Protocol (VTP) with a new rate control mechanism based on the Achieved Rate (AR) estimation and Loss Discrimination Algorithm. We show that VTP can preserve efficiency without causing additional performance degradation to TCP, in both error-free and error-prone situations.

1 Introduction

Real-time video streaming is becoming increasingly important on the Internet. Unlike conventional applications, real-time streaming generally requires a minimum, continuous bandwidth guarantee as well as stringent bounds on delays and jitters. Earlier work largely relied on the unresponsive UDP traffic and imposed potential menace to network stability. Thus the more recent research is focused on adaptive schemes that respond to the network dynamics and avoid possible congestion collapses.

TCP, the dominant transport protocol on the Internet, has also been considered for streaming [11]. However, the instantaneous sending rate of TCP changes drastically such that buffering is needed at the receiver to accommodate rate fluctuations [14]. Buffering smoothes the playback rate but also brings up two concerns. First, it causes a startup delay. For Video-on-Demand (VoD) applications, startup delays of a few seconds or slightly longer are tolerable, but for real-time, interactive applications, e.g. video conferencing and online gaming, startup delays have to be tightly bounded [16]. The second concern is that more and more mobile/wireless devices are connected to the Internet. These devices are often small and inexpensive with limited computation and buffer capacities; storing a large amount of data is simply impractical.

J. Vicente and D. Hutchison (Eds.): MMNS 2004, LNCS 3271, pp. 26–38, 2004.
© IFIP International Federation for Information Processing 2004

To address the concerns, real-time streaming needs more intelligent *rate adaptation* or *rate control* mechanisms. Solutions are usually based on two types of feedback: *a)* cross-layer feedback from lower layers [9], or *b)* end-to-end feedback. On the Internet, cross-layer approaches require modifications on both end hosts and intermediate nodes, which is not practical, thus end-to-end rate control has been the preferred choice [3][7].

TCP Friendly Rate Control (TFRC) [7] is one of the most popular end-to-end streaming protocols and often used as the reference and benchmark. TFRC attempts to match the long-term throughput of legacy TCP (e.g. Reno) and is smooth, fair and TCP friendly in wired networks. However, with the increasing popularity of wireless Internet terminals and the demand for delivering multimedia to mobile users, it is necessary for streaming protocols to work efficiently also on wireless links, withstanding the high random wireless errors. Legacy TCP does not work well in this case; it tends to over-cut its window, leading to a severely degraded performance. Since TFRC attempts to faithfully match the throughput of TCP, it suffers the same low efficiency in the presence of moderate to high random errors [18].

Our goal is to develop a real-time streaming protocol that behaves well in the wired Internet, and moreover is robust to random errors and can be deployed with wireless links. We have proposed the Video Transport Protocol (VTP) [2], which measures the Achieved Rate (AR) and adapts its sending rate according to the network dynamics. However, we have recently found that the original VTP tends to be unfriendly to TCP in some scenarios. The main contribution of this paper is to refine the VTP rate control. The new mechanism should provide efficient and smooth rate control in both error-prone and error-free situations, while maintaining fairness and friendliness to coexisting flows.

The rest of the paper is organized as follows: Section 2 lists our design goals of the VTP rate control. The Achieved Rate (AR) estimation and Loss Discrimination Algorithm (LDA) are introduced in Section 3, followed by the VTP rate control mechanism in Section 4. We evaluate the performance of VTP in the Ns-2 simulator in Section 5. Related work is summarized in Section 6 and finally Section 7 concludes the paper.

2   Design Goals

In this section we discuss the main design goals of the VTP rate control mechanism, namely robustness to random errors and TCP friendliness.

2.1   Robustness to Random Errors

As the Internet evolves into a mixed wired-cum-wireless environment, more and more devices are interconnected via wireless technologies. Wireless links are usually error-prone due to interference, noise, fading, mobility, etc. [13]. However, popular error recovery techniques, such as Automatic Repeat reQuest (ARQ) and Forward Error Correction (FEC), may not completely solve this problem.

First of all, ARQ increases both the end-to-end delay and its variance, which is undesirable for real-time streaming. Applying ARQ in a single FIFO queue, as performed in the majority of commercial MAC layer implementations, also introduces the problem of head-of-of-line blocking, where retransmission of a packet forces subsequent packets in the same queue to wait. On the other side, FEC is more effective when errors are sporadic. In practice, errors are usually bursty due to the interference by external sources. In conclusion, after applying limited ARQ/FEC where appropriate, packet error rates of a few percent or higher are still expected in wireless networks [17]. This is the key working assumption that motivates the rest of the paper. The first design goal of VTP is to provide efficient streaming rate control in presence of random wireless errors.

2.2   TCP Friendliness

TCP is deployed virtually on every computer. Years of operation have proved that the well-designed congestion control in TCP contributes significantly to the stability of the Internet. New protocols must be *TCP friendly* to avoid potential congestion collapses.

Different definitions of "TCP friendliness" exist in the literature. A widely used one is based on *Jain's fairness index* [8], which belongs to the class of *max-min fairness*. Applying Jain's fairness index to TCP friendliness results in a statement like "a flow of the new protocol under evaluation must achieve a rate similar to the rate achieved by a TCP (usually Reno/NewReno) flow that observes the same round-trip time (RTT) and packet loss rate". VTP must comply with this definition in the region where TCP performs efficiently (i.e., with zero random errors) and can potentially use the entire bandwidth. In the case of frequent random errors, however, legacy TCP cannot achieve full bandwidth utilization. Thus the conventional definition of friendliness must be modified to allow a new, more efficient protocol to opportunistically exploit the unused bandwidth, even beyond the "fair share".

In this paper we introduce the notion of *opportunistic friendliness* to refer to the ability of a new flow to use the bandwidth that would be left unused by legacy flows. More precisely, a new protocol *NP* is said to be opportunistically friendly to legacy TCP if TCP flows obtain no less throughput when coexisting with *NP*, compared to the throughput that they would achieve if all flows were TCP (i.e., *NP* flows replaced by TCP). The second design goal of VTP is to have opportunistic friendliness to legacy TCP.

3   Achieved Rate and Loss Discrimination Algorithm

3.1   Achieved Rate

The Achieved Rate (AR), together with the Loss Discrimination Algorithm (LDA) that will be introduced shortly, are two important components in VTP. AR is the rate that the sender succeeds in pushing through the bottleneck. This is the rate that the receiver can measure, plus the fraction corresponding to packet losses at the exit of the bottleneck due to random errors.

For the time being, let us assume zero errors. The receiver samples and filters the receiving rate, using an Exponentially Weighted Moving Average (EWMA). AR has an intuitive interpretation. Assuming we start with an empty bottleneck, each sender can safely transmit for an unlimited time at AR and expect its packets to be delivered to the receiver with no buffer overflow. If the sender transmits at a rate higher than AR, there is a chance that the extra packets will get buffered at the bottleneck queue. The sender will typically transmit, over limited periods of time, at rates higher than AR to probe the bandwidth. However, following a packet loss, it will step back and restart at or below AR.

An AR sample S_k is obtained, by the receiver, as the number of received bytes during a time period of T, divided by of T. AR samples are reported back to the sender, which updates its smoothed AR value AR_k as

$$AR_k = \sigma \cdot AR_{k-1} + (1 - \sigma) \cdot \frac{1}{2}(S_k + S_{k-1})$$ (1)

where σ is a fraction close to 1.

The above scheme works well when no random errors are present. If packets can get lost at the exit of the bottleneck due to errors, they will not be received and counted by the receiver, although they do have succeeded in squeezing through the bottleneck. These packets should be included in the sender's AR value. This is done jointly with the LDA. Via the LDA, the VTP sender is able to estimate the fraction of packet losses that are error-induced, i.e., the error rate e. The AR sample reported by the receiver is then prorated by $1 + e$.

3.2   Loss Discrimination Algorithm

The Loss Discrimination Algorithm (LDA) allows VTP to distinguish error losses from congestion losses. Intuitively, it suffices to measure the RTT. If RTT is close to RTT_{min} measured on this connection, we know the bottleneck is not congested; the loss must be an error loss. On the contrary, if RTT is quite larger than RTT_{min}, the loss is likely to be due to congestion. We propose to use the Spike [4] scheme as the LDA in VTP. Spike, as illustrated in Figure 1, is an end-to-end algorithm based on RTT measurement. A flow enters the *spike* state if 1) it was not in the *spike* state, and 2) RTT exceeds a threshold B_{start}. Similarly, the flow exits the *spike* state if 1) it was in the *spike* state, and 2) RTT falls below another threshold B_{end}. B_{start} and B_{end} are defined as:

$$B_{start} = RTT_{min} + \alpha \cdot (RTT_{max} - RTT_{min})$$ (2)
$$B_{end} = RTT_{min} + \beta \cdot (RTT_{max} - RTT_{min})$$ (3)

where α and β are adjustable parameters. If a loss occurs when the flow is in the *spike* state, it is believed to be congestion-induced; otherwise it is error-induced.

We must point out that the above LDA works only if the error-prone link is also the bottleneck. If not, flows that share the bottleneck but do not traverse

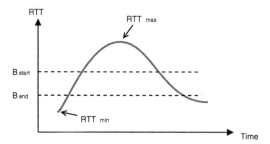

Fig. 1. Spike as a loss discrimination algorithm.

the "error" link will keep the bottleneck loaded and the value of RTT high. Other flows that also traverse the error link will suffer extra losses. However, the corresponding senders will not be able to classify these losses as error-induced due to the consistently high value of RTT. Those latter flows will reduce their rates and be "suppressed" by the flows that do not experience random errors. Fortunately, in virtually all wireless scenarios the wireless error-prone link is also the bottleneck, e.g. a satellite link or last-hop wireless segment. Thus all bottlenecked flows are subject to random errors. Our LDA scheme thus applies to most wireless situations.

4   VTP Rate Control

In this section we present the rate control mechanism in VTP. Similar to the Additive Increase in TCP congestion control, VTP linearly probes the bandwidth until congestion is detected. VTP does not perform Multiplicative Decrease though; instead it reduces the rate to AR, with extra adjustments required to mimic the TCP behavior.

4.1   TCP Behavior in Terms of Rate

While most streaming protocols operate on the concept of *rate*, TCP is window-based: a congestion window *cwnd* is used to control the number of outstanding packets. Due to this difference, streaming protocols must first understand the TCP behavior, in terms of its instantaneous sending rate rather than the window size, in order to achieve TCP friendliness.

We now consider TCP NewReno operating in congestion avoidance. We ignore slow start since it has less impact on the steady state performance. We also focus on the losses caused by congestion and assume no random errors. Consider the topology in Figure 2. C, B and P are the link capacity, queue buffer size and round-trip bandwidth-delay product (namely the pipe size), respectively. Assuming the buffer size is equal to the pipe size, we have $B = P$. *Cwnd* oscillates between P and $B + P = 2P$ as the left diagram in Figure 3 shows.

Although TCP increases *cwnd* at the speed of 1 packet/RTT, it does not necessarily increase the sending rate, since the extra packets may be buffered

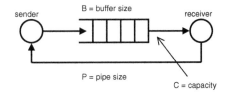

Fig. 2. A simple topology with buffer size equal to pipe size.

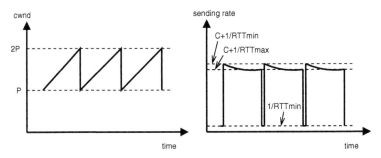

Fig. 3. Congestion window and instantaneous sending rate of TCP NewReno.

in the queue. With the assumption of $B = P$ in Figure 2, the sender detects a packet loss when the queue is full, i.e., $cwnd = 2P$. $Cwnd$ is then halved to P. Since there are $2P$ outstanding packets, the sender must temporarily stop sending and wait until P ACKs have been received, before it can resume the transmission. Having P outstanding packets means that the queue is drained while the pipe is full. Next, $cwnd$ will increase by 1 packet/RTT, allowing the sender to transmit an extra packet every RTT. Other than this, TCP is regularly transmitting at the rate of the bottleneck capacity C, limited by the arriving rate of ACKs (i.e., self-clocked).

The right diagram in Figure 3 illustrates the instantaneous *sending rate* of TCP as we discussed above. The sending rate of TCP in congestion avoidance, in the topology of Figure 2, is $C + 1/RTT$. Note that as RTT grows with more packets get buffered, the sending rate actually decreases slightly.

4.2   VTP Rate Control

As we explained earlier, TCP instantaneous sending rate drops drastically when $cwnd$ is cut by half, due to the fact that the sender must wait until half of the outstanding packets are drained from the queue/pipe. This rate reduction, as shown in Figure 3, can not be implemented as such in VTP. Yet VTP must respond to congestion by reducing, on average, its rate in the same way as TCP in order to be TCP friendly. The tradeoff is between the amount of rate reduction and the length of time this rate is maintained. Simply speaking, VTP may reduce the rate by less but keep it longer.

Figure 4 illustrates the VTP rate control mechanism and compares it to TCP. Note that Figure 4 reflects just one of the three cycles in Figure 3. Also, curves are approximated by line segments. In Figure 4, TCP chooses the "deep but short" strategy where its rate is cut to near zero for RTT_{min} and then restored to $C+1/RTT$ immediately. In contrast, VTP reduces its rate by a smaller portion but keeps it longer. The two shaded areas $A1$ and $A2$ in Figure 4 represent the amount of extra data that TCP and VTP would be able to transmit if the loss did not happen. To make VTP friendly to TCP, these areas should be equal.

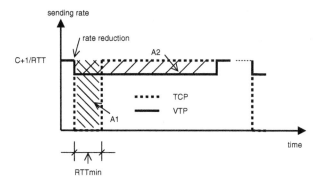

Fig. 4. Comparsion of rate control between TCP and VTP.

A parameter γ between 0 and 1 is selected as the tolerable rate reduction ratio. When congestion is detected, VTP reduces its rate to $\gamma \cdot AR$, where AR is equal to C in this case. Since $A1 = A2$, the interval over which the reduced rate is maintained is $\tau = A1/((1-\gamma) \cdot AR) = RTT/(2(1-\gamma)) = RTT_{max}/(2(1-\gamma))$. When τ has elapsed, VTP has given up the same amount of data transmission as TCP and should then enter congestion avoidance.

During congestion avoidance, VTP must match the TCP behavior. For convenience we introduce the concept of *equivalent window* in VTP and denote it as *ewnd*. *Ewnd* is defined as the number of packets transmitted by the sender during one RTT. The VTP sender computes its sending rate as follows:

1. The sender measures its current *ewnd* by counting the packets transmitted within the current RTT. Letting R be the current transmit rate, we have

$$ewnd = R \cdot RTT \qquad (4)$$

2. Following Additive Increase, the new window *ewnd′* is given as

$$ewnd' = R \cdot RTT + 1 \qquad (5)$$

3. Converting from window to rate, we have the new rate R' as

$$R' = (R \cdot RTT + 1)/(RTT + \Delta RTT) \qquad (6)$$

where ΔRTT is the RTT increase after a round.

4. Assuming RTT increases linearly at each round, then

$$R' = (R + 1/RTT)/(2 - RTT^{[-1]}/RTT) \qquad (7)$$

where $RTT^{[-1]}$ is the round-trip time during the previous round. Note that R' is lower than what would be derived from the conventional linear rate increase by 1 packet/RTT. All necessary quantities can be readily measured by the sender.

5   Performance Evaluation

In this section, we evaluate the performance of VTP in terms of efficiency, intra-protocol fairness and opportunistic friendliness, for both error-prone and error-free cases. We also examine the ability of VTP to adapt to bandwidth changes. The experiments are carried out with the Ns-2 simulator.

5.1   Simulation Setup

The topology in Figure 5, representing a mixed wired-cum-wireless scenario, is used throughout this paper. The Internet segment is abstracted as a set of error-free links, while the wireless segment, e.g. a wireless LAN, is abstracted as a shared error-prone link. The wireless link is the only bottleneck in the system which all traffic goes through. The round-trip propagation delay is 72 msec, a typical value for a cross-continent path. All queues are drop-tail; the bottleneck buffer size is 99 packets, equal to the pipe size. Simulation time is 300 seconds for all runs.

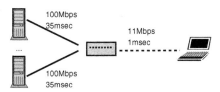

Fig. 5. Simulation setup.

5.2   Rate Adaptation and Robustness to Random Errors

First we test the rate adaptation of VTP to bandwidth changes under different error rates, where a solo VTP flow runs against varying rate CBR traffic. This test is indicative of the "agility" of the protocol and also of its efficiency in different loss rate conditions. For comparison we also replace VTP with TFRC and repeat all experiments.

Figure 6 shows the sending rates of VTP and TFRC as they adapt to the bandwidth changes caused by CBR traffic. Bandwidth available to VTP/TFRC,

computed as the bottleneck capacity minus the aggregate CBR rate, is included
in Figure 6 for reference. In the absence of random errors, both VTP and TFRC
manage to utilize the bandwidth efficiently, maintain a smooth rate, and react
to bandwidth changes quickly. When errors are present, e.g. 1% or 5% as shown,
VTP is able to maintain its efficiency in bandwidth utilization, while TFRC
suffers the inefficiency problem as we have discussed.

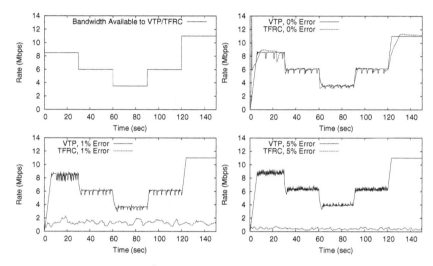

Fig. 6. Solo VTP/TFRC under different random error rates.

5.3   Inter-protocol Opportunistic Friendliness

We now evaluate the opportunistic friendliness between VTP and TCP under
different error rates. For each error rate we run a couple of experiments. In
the first experiment, one VTP flow and one TCP flow share the bottleneck.
VTP is then replaced by TCP and the experiment is repeated. According to the
definition, if the TCP throughput in the first experiment is comparable to that
in the second, VTP is said to be opportunistically friendly to TCP.

We show the experiment results in Figure 7. Graphs are grouped in pairs
by different error rates. In each pair, the left graph presents the instantaneous
sending rates of VTP and TCP when they coexist; the right graph presents
the rates when the VTP flow is replaced by TCP. More precisely, Table 1 lists
the long-term[1] throughput of a TCP flow when it coexists with either VTP or
another TCP flow. In all cases, impact of VTP on TCP throughput is minimal.
Moreover, VTP is able to utilize the residual bandwidth when errors are present,
a perfect reflection of opportunistic friendliness.

We need to point out that in the zero error case, TCP slow start tends to
overshoot the TCP window and result in multiple losses, where NewReno takes

---

[1] 500 seconds.

Table 1. TCP throughput: coexisting with VTP or itself under different error rates.

	TCP Throughput (Mbps): Coexisting with VTP	TCP Throughput (Mbps): Coexisting with Another TCP	TCP Performance Degradation
0% Error	5.09	5.14	1%
1% Error	1.22	1.21	0%
5% Error	0.38	0.38	0%

multiple RTTs to recover. During this period the TCP sending rate drops to near zero. Since VTP rate probing is less aggressive than slow start, TCP overshoots its window even higher when coexisting with VTP than with another TCP. Thus in Figure 7 the TCP recovery time is longer when coexisting with VTP. Once TCP is recovered, VTP is able to share the bandwidth in a friendly manner. We are still investigating this issue to make TCP recover faster.

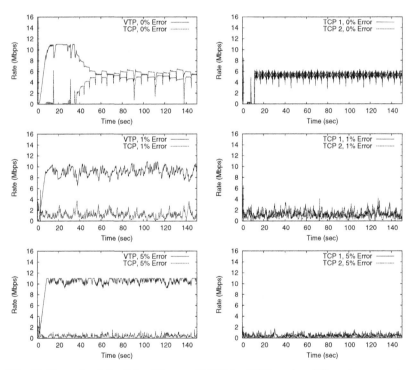

Fig. 7. Opportunistic Friendliness of VTP to TCP under different error rates.

5.4   Intra-protocol Fairness

By *fairness* we refer to the relationship between flows of the same protocol. To evaluate the fairness property of VTP, we run a set of experiments with two VTP flows sharing the bottleneck. Since both flows have identical network parameters, they should equally share the bottleneck bandwidth. Figure 8 presents the VTP sending rates in different error situations. In all tested cases, VTP flows are able to fairly share the bottleneck while achieving high link utilization in presence of random errors. This confirms that VTP has an excellent property of fairness to itself.

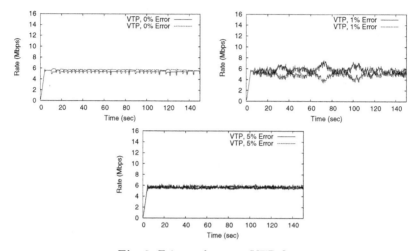

Fig. 8. Fairness between VTP flows.

6   Related Work

In this section we briefly summarize some of the related work. TCP Friendly Rate Control (TFRC) [7] is an equation-based protocol aiming to achieve the equivalent long-term throughput of TCP with less short-term fluctuation. TFRC per se is not robust to wireless losses, but extensions that can operate in mixed wired-cum-wireless environments have been recently reported. For example, [4] proposes to apply a LDA to the TFRC receiver and exclude error losses from the calculation of packet loss rate p used in the equation. [5] proposes another approach that creates multiple parallel TFRC connections when a single connection is inefficient. We plan to compare VTP to these TFRC extensions in the future work.

Rate Control Scheme (RCS) [17] uses low-priority dummy packets to probe the available bandwidth on the path. RCS is able to estimate an admissible rate similar to the AR and effectively distinguish between error and congestion losses. However, RCS requires all intermediate gateways to implement a multiple-priority mechanism. This feature is currently not available on the Internet.

Explicit Congestion Notification (ECN) [12] is a general method to handle error losses. It is often implemented in conjunction with Random Early Detection (RED) [6]. It stamps a packet with a designated bit to indicate buffer congestion. If the sender detects a loss but no ECN bit is reported, it assumes the loss to be random and does not trigger congestion recovery. The ECN scheme is generally used for TCP but can also be used for streaming. The main limitation again is the cost of the network layer implementation.

Binomial algorithms [3] aim to provide smoother rate control than AIMD for real-time streaming. Wireless losses are not specifically addressed. Streaming Control Transmission Protocol (SCTP) [15] and Datagram Congestion Control Protocol [10] are transport protocols that can be used for real-time streaming. Again they were designed mostly for wired networks and lack a rate control mechanism that handles wireless losses efficiently.

7   Conclusion and Future Work

In this paper we have proposed a new rate control mechanism for the adaptive real-time video streaming protocol VTP. This new protocol measures the end-to-end Achieved Rate (AR) and adjusts the sending rate accordingly when congestion is detected by the Loss Discrimination Algorithm (LDA). Rate decreases and increases are carefully designed so as to mimic the TCP behavior and maintain intra-protocol fairness and opportunistic friendliness to legacy TCP. We have shown via Ns-2 experiments that under all tested error rates (up to 5%), VTP is able to utilize the bandwidth efficiently, while at the same time keeping excellent properties of fairness and friendliness.

To our knowledge, VTP is one of the few truly end-to-end schemes that perform well in the wireless environment without requiring the support from lower layer feedback and AQM mechanisms. In the future we plan to compare VTP to the recently proposed TFRC extensions for the wireless scenario. We are currently in the process of developing a Linux-based implementation of VTP and will carry out testbed/Internet measurements in the near future.

References

1. Allman, M., Paxson, V., Stevens, W.: TCP Congestion Control. RFC 2581 (1999)
2. Balk, A., Maggiorini, D., Gerla, M., Sanadidi, M. Y.: Adaptive MPEG-4 Video Streaming with Bandwidth Estimation. QOS-IP 2003, Milano, Italy (2003)
3. Bansal, D., Balakrishnan, H.: Binomial Congestion Control Algorithms. IEEE Infocom 2001, Anchorage, AK (2001)
4. Cen, S., Cosman, P., Voelker, G.: End-to-end Differentiation of Congestion and Wireless Losses. IEEE/ACM Transactions on Networking, Vol. 11, Iss. 5 (2003)
5. Chen, M., Zakhor, A.: Rate Control for Streaming Video over Wireless. IEEE Infocom 2004, Hong Kong, China (2004)
6. Floyd, S., Jacobson, V.: Random Early Detection gateways for Congestion Avoidance. IEEE/ACM Transactions on Networking, V.1, N.4 (1993)
7. Floyd, S., Handley, M., Padhye, J., Widmer, J.: Equation-Based Congestion Control for Unicast Applications. SIGCOMM 2000, Stockholm, Sweden (2000)
8. Jain, R.: The Art of Computer Systems Performance Analysis. John Wiley and Sons (1991)

 9. Kazantzidis, M.: Adaptive Wireless Multimedia. Ph.D. Thesis, Computer Science Dept, UCLA (2002)
10. Kohler, E., Handley, M., Floyd, S.: Datagram Congestion Control Protocol (DCCP). Internert Draft (2004)
11. Mehra, P., Zakhor, A.: TCP-based Video Streaming Using Receiver-driven Bandwidth Sharing. Int'l Packet Video Workshop 2003, Nantes, France (2003)
12. Ramakrishnan, K., Floyd, S., Black, D.: The Addition of Explicit Congestion Notification (ECN) to IP. RFC 3168 (2001)
13. Rappaport, T.: Wireless Communications: Principles and Practice. Prentice Hall PTR, Upper Saddle River, NJ (1996)
14. Rejaie, R., Handley, M., Estrin, D.: Quality Adaptation for Congestion Controlled Video Playback over the Internet. ACM SIGCOMM 1999, Cambridge, MA (1999)
15. Stewart, R., Xie, Q., Morneault, K., Sharp, C., Schwarzbauer, H., Taylor, T., Rytina, I., Kalla, M., Zhang, L., Paxson, V.: Stream Control Transmission Protocol. RFC 2960 (2000)
16. Sun, M., Reibman, A. (ed.): Compressed Video over Networks. Marcel Dekker, Inc. (2001)
17. Tang, J., Morabito, G., Akyildiz, I., Johnson, M.: RCS: A Rate Control Scheme for Real-Time Traffic in Networks with High Bandwidth-Delay Products and High Bit Error Rates. IEEE Infocom 2001, Anchorage, AK (2001)
18. Yang, Y., Kim, M., Lam, S.: Transient Behaviors of TCP-friendly Congestion Control Protocols. IEEE Infocom 2001, Anchorage, AK (2001)

Content-Based Adaptation of Streamed Multimedia

Nikki Cranley[1], Liam Murphy[1], and Philip Perry[2]

[1] Department of Computer Science, University College Dublin,
Belfield, Dublin 4, Ireland
{Nicola.Cranley,Liam.Murphy}@UCD.ie
[2] School of Electronic Engineering, Dublin City University,
Glasnevin, Dublin 9, Ireland
PerryP@eeng.DCU.ie

Abstract. Most adaptive delivery mechanisms for streaming multimedia content do not explicitly consider user-perceived quality when making adaptations. We show that an Optimal Adaptation Trajectory (OAT) through the set of possible encodings exists, and that it indicates how to adapt encoding quality in response to changes in network conditions in order to maximize user-perceived quality. The OAT is related to the characteristics of the content, in terms of spatial and temporal complexity. We describe an objective method to automatically determine the OAT in response to the time-varying characteristics of the content. The OAT can be used with any transmission adaptation policy. We demonstrate content-based adaptation using the OAT in a practical system, and show how this form of adaptation can result in differing adaptation behaviour.

1   Introduction

Best-effort IP networks, particularly wireless networks, are unreliable and unpredictable. There can be many factors that affect the quality of a transmission, such as delay, jitter and loss. Adaptation techniques should attempt to reduce network congestion and packet loss by matching the rate of the video stream to the available network bandwidth. Without adaptation, any data transmitted exceeding the available bandwidth could be discarded, lost or corrupted in the network. This has a devastating effect on the playout quality of the received stream. A slightly degraded quality but uncorrupted video stream is less irritating to the user than a corrupted stream. In general, adaptation policies (whether sender-based [1], receiver-based [2],[3], or encoder-based are [4]) address the problem of how to adapt only in terms of adjusting the transmission rate or the window size and are thus bitrate centric. Other adaptation approaches include utility-based schemes [5],[6], which adapt video quality encoding configurations by using a utility function (UF). However, rapidly fluctuating quality should also be avoided as the human vision system (HVS) adapts to a specific quality after a few seconds and it becomes annoying if the viewer has to adjust to a varying quality over short time scales [7]. Controlled video quality adaptation is needed to reduce the negative effects of congestion on the stream whilst providing the highest possible level of service and perceived quality.

   In previous work we proposed that there is an optimal way in which multimedia transmissions should be adapted in response to network conditions to maximize the

J. Vicente and D. Hutchison (Eds.): MMNS 2004, LNCS 3271, pp. 39–49, 2004.
© IFIP International Federation for Information Processing 2004

user-perceived quality. Extensive subjective testing demonstrated the existence of an Optimum Adaptation Trajectory (OAT) in the space of possible encodings and that it is related to the content type [8]. However, due to the time-varying nature of content characteristics, there is a need to automatically and dynamically determine the OAT based on these contents characteristics in order to properly apply the OAT. This knowledge can then be used as part of a content-based adaptation strategy, which aims to maximize the user-perceived quality of the delivered multimedia content.

This paper is structured as follows. Section 2 describes the concept of an Optimum Adaptation Trajectory (OAT) that exists for each class of video content. Section 3 describes how content can be characterized by its spatial and temporal complexities. Section 4 presents an objective means of determining the OAT that is dynamic and can react to the time varying characteristics of content. Section 5 describes our content-based adaptive streaming system. The system is demonstrated using the existing Loss-Delay Adaptation (LDA) algorithm using a content-based dynamic OAT. Some preliminary simulation results from our system are presented to show system operation and behavior. Conclusions and directions for future work are presented in Section 6.

2   Optimum Adaptation Trajectories

In previous work, the concept of an Optimum Adaptation Trajectory (OAT) has been presented [8] and has been shown to complement the sender-based Loss-Delay Adaptation algorithm using a static OAT determined by subjective testing, or as the basis of a Perceptual Quality Adaptation (PQA) algorithm [9].

The OAT embodies the idea that there is an optimal way in which multimedia transmissions should be adapted (upgraded/downgraded) in response to network conditions to maximize the user-perceived quality. This is based on the hypothesis that within the set of different ways to achieve a target bit rate, there exists an encoding configuration that maximizes the user-perceived quality. If a particular multimedia file has n independent encoding configurations then, there exists an adaptation space with n dimensions. Adaptation space consists of all possible dimensions of adaptation for the content that can be implemented as part of an adaptive streaming server or adaptive encoder. When adapting the transmission from some point within that space to meet a new target bit rate, the adaptive server should select the encoding configuration that maximizes the user-perceived quality for that given bit rate. The example shown in Figure 1 indicates that, when degrading the quality from an encoding configuration of 25fps and a spatial resolution of 100%, there are a number of possibilities – such as reducing the frame rate only to 15fps, reducing the spatial resolution only to 70%, or reducing a combination of both the frame rate and resolution. The choice of which encoding configuration that should be adopted is determined as the encoding configuration that maximizes the user-perceived quality. When the transmission is adjusted across its full range, the locus of these selected encoding configurations should yield an OAT within that adaptation space.

There is much research into developing objective metrics for video quality assessment [10],[11],[12],[13]. The most commonly used objective metric of video quality

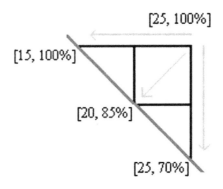

[Frame Rate, Resolution]

Fig. 1. Encoding Quality Options.

assessment is the Peak Signal to Noise Ratio (PSNR), which has been widely used in many applications and adaptation algorithms [14] to assess video quality. The advantage of PSNR is that it is very easy to compute using the Mean Square Error (MSE) of pixel values of luminance for frames from the degraded and reference clips. However, PSNR does not match well to the characteristics of the human vision system (HVS) [15]. However, the main problem with using PSNR values as a quality assessment method is that even though two images may be different, the visibility of this difference is not considered. The PSNR metric does not take into consideration any details of the HVS such as its ability to "mask" errors that are not significant to the human comprehension of the image. Several objective metrics, namely the Video Quality Metrics (VQM) and PSNR were investigated to determine whether they yielded an OAT. The ITU-T has recently accepted the VQM as a recommended objective video quality metric that correlates adequately to human perception in [16], [17], [18]. However, our findings were that these objective metrics produce an OAT which jumped through adaptation space with no sense of direction or continuity. In contrast, subjective methods were consistent across content types and produced a smooth graceful OAT through adaptation space.

The OAT is dependent on the characteristics of the content. There is a content space in which all types of video content exist in terms of spatial and temporal complexity (or detail and action). The OAT was discovered through extensive subjective testing for a number of different content types using the forced choice methodology. Subjective testing results showed that the OAT is logarithmic with the general form

$$Resolution = A*Ln(Frame\ rate) + B \qquad (1)$$

for some constants A and B. It was also found that the temporal and spatial complexity of the scene plays an important role in the curvature of the OAT. The usefulness of the OAT relies on the contents' spatial and temporal characteristics being known by the adaptive server. Since the spatial and temporal complexity of content will vary over time, we propose a method to automate the process of determining the OAT in response to these changing content characteristics.

3 Spatial and Temporal Complexity Metrics

User perception of video quality varies with the content type; for example, viewers perceive action clips differently from slow moving clips. Thus, there exists a different OAT for different types of content based on their spatial and temporal characteristics. The spatial and temporal complexity of content can be determined using the metrics Spatial Information (SI) and Temporal Information (TI).

The Spatial Information parameter, SI, is based on the Sobel filter, and is implemented by convolving two 3 x 3 kernels over the luminance plane in the video frame [19]. Let $Conv1_n(i, j)$ be the result of the first convolution for the pixel of the input nth frame at the ith row and jth column and let $Conv2_n(i, j)$ be the result of the second convolution for the same pixel. The output of the Sobel filtered pixel at the ith row and jth column in the nth frame, $y_n(i,j)$, is the square root of the sum of the squares of both convolutions. The SI value is the standard deviation (std_{space}) over all pixels in the nth frame and is computed as follows:

$$y_n(i, j) = \sqrt{[Conv1_n(i, j)]^2 + [Conv2_n(i, j)]^2} \qquad (2)$$

$$SI = std_{space}[y_n] \qquad (3)$$

This process is repeated for each frame in the video sequence and results in a time series of spatial information of the scene. The calculations are performed on a sub-image of the video frame to avoid unwanted edge and border effects. The size of the original image is QCIF (176x144 pixels) and so a centrally located sub-image of 100x100 was used.

The Temporal Information parameter, TI, is based upon the motion difference feature in successive frames. The motion difference, $M_n(i, j)$, is the difference between the pixel values in the ith row and jth column in nth frame $F_n(i, j)$, and the value for the same pixel in the previous frame, $F_{n-1}(i, j)$. The measure of Temporal Information, TI, is the standard deviation over all pixels in the sub-image space (std_{space}) and is computed as follows:

$$M_n(i, j) = F_n(i, j) - F_{n-1}(i, j) \qquad (4)$$

$$TI = std_{space}[M_n] \qquad (5)$$

Both the SI and TI values result in a time varying measure of the spatial and temporal complexity of a piece of content. This information can be used to create a time varying understanding of the characteristics and requirements of the content to generate the OAT. The calculation of the SI and TI complexity parameters is not computationally expensive for small image sizes such as QCIF.

4 Objective OAT

Upon analysis of the OATs discovered by subjective testing, it was observed that the OAT for different content types was not strongly dependent on the precise SI-TI values, but more influenced by the relationship between spatial and temporal complexity. For example, when the SI value was significantly greater than the TI value, the resulting OAT tended towards the spatial resolution, and vice versa. However, for a number of test sequences where the spatial and temporal complexities were approximately equal, the OATs were "neutral".

To represent the relative dominance of one characteristic over another, a weighting factor, W, is introduced which is determined using the SI and TI metrics. The factor W is the relative dominance of temporal complexity over the spatial complexity. Since the scales of spatial complexity and temporal complexity are different, both parameters were converted to their respective fractional values. The fractional SI value is thus the SI value divided by the maximum SI value; similarly, the fractional TI value is the TI value divided by the maximum TI value. The maximum SI and TI values can be found by applying the equations to the luminance plane of an image with alternating black and white pixels.

$$Fractional\_SI = SI\big/SI_{MAX} \tag{6}$$

$$Fractional\_TI = TI\big/TI_{MAX} \tag{7}$$

$$W = \text{Weighting factor} = \left(Fractional\_TI\big/Fractional\_SI\right) \tag{8}$$

From Figure 2, it can be seen that when SI=TI, the weighting factor, W, is equal to 1, therefore there is no dominant characteristic and the OAT is neutral. If SI>TI, then the weighting factor W<1 and the spatial complexity is dominant, and the resulting OAT should tends towards maintaining the spatial resolution during adaptation. Conversely, when SI<TI, the weighting factor W>1 and the resulting OAT should tend towards maintaining the frame rate during adaptation. The following empirical equation (Eqn. 9) was derived to relate the OATs discovered by subjective testing, the weighting factor, W, resolution and frame rate:

$$\text{Re}\,s = \left(\text{Re}\,s_{MAX}\big/Ln(F_{MAX})\right)\left(WLn(F) - (W-1)Ln(F_{MAX})\right) \tag{9}$$

where:

Res = Spatial resolution;
Res_{MAX} = Maximum spatial resolution = 100%;
F_{MAX} = Maximum frame rate = 25fps;
F = Frame rate.

From Figure 3 it can be seen that the OAT increases in curvature towards the frame rate with increasing values of W. For very low values of W only the spatial resolution should be degraded: this would be expected for film credits or panoramic still shots, where there is very low temporal information but high spatial resolution requirements. The objective OATs demonstrate that a piece of content containing a static still image (TI value of zero) should be adapted in the frame rate dimension only. However, it is not possible for a piece of content to have a zero SI value and a non-zero TI value.

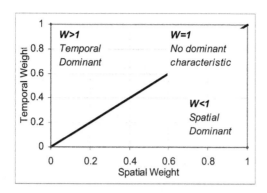

Fig. 2. Spatial-Temporal Space.

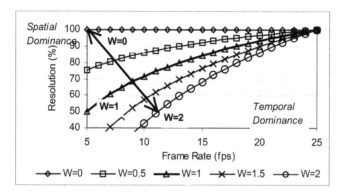

Fig. 3. Objective OAT variance with different weighting factors.

The objective OAT was validated by comparing the OAT discovered by subjective testing and that determined using the objective OAT. The SI and TI values for several different content types were measured to determine the weighting factor. From this, the objective OAT was calculated and then compared against the OAT discovered by subjective testing. The results in Figure 4 indicate a high degree of correlation between the objective OAT and the subjective OAT, which, in most cases was over 98%.

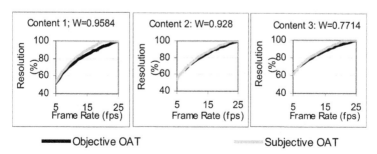

Fig. 4. Correlation of Subjective and Objective OATs.

5 Content-Based Adaptation

Dynamic content-based adaptation can be integrated into a client server system with either in a real-time system with real-time encoding and analysis (Figure 5) or else for streaming of pre-analyzed pre-encoded content (Figure 6). Our prototype system is of the latter architecture. Both client and server consist of the RTP/UDP/IP stack with RTCP/UDP/IP to relay feedback messages between the client and server. The content is pre-encoded and hinted with an MPEG-4 encoder. The content contains multiple tracks, each encoded with a different resolution. By switching tracks the server can dynamically and discretely adapt the resolution. The server can also apply a frame dropping policy to dynamically adapt the frame rate. By controlling these two operations the server is able to implement the two-dimensional adaptation trajectory given by the OAT.

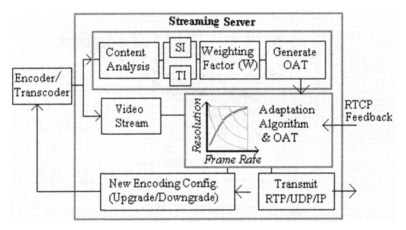

Fig. 5. Basic System Architecture for Live Content.

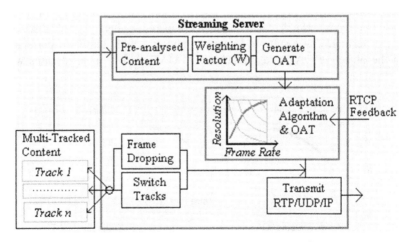

Fig. 6. Basic System Architecture for Pre-encoded Content.

To demonstrate how the objective OAT can be used to provide content-based adaptation to complement the LDA adaptation algorithm, a prototype client-server system was developed. The client returns standard RTCP-RR feedback containing information about loss, delay and bottleneck bandwidth values. When the server receives feedback from the client, the LDA algorithm indicates how the bit rate should be adjusted in response to fluctuations in the available end-to-end bit rate between client and server. The server finds the intersection of the OAT and the new target bit rate as determined by the adaptation algorithm. From this intersection point of the new target bit rate and the OAT, the server finds the corresponding encoding configuration on the OAT indicating the quality-encoding configuration that maximizes the user-perceived quality for the content. Having found this new encoding configuration, the server adjusts the frame rate and/or adapts the resolution by switching tracks. The OAT is constantly varied in response to the changing characteristics of the content.

Given that the weighting factor of the content typically changes in a subtle and gradual manner (with the exception of scene changes), the weighting factor was averaged over 20 second intervals. The time variance of the weighting factor can be seen in Figure 7(a). A challenging network condition has been selected to demonstrate the efficacy and use of content-based adaptation using the OATs with LDA. This would be typical of a wireless IP network where mobility can result in sudden and substantial changes in the available bit rate. In the simulations, RTCP feedback was fixed at every 5 seconds. The stability of our system and its ability to react to network conditions is entirely dependent on the frequency of feedback as the system can adapt on each feedback report. In the example below, Figure 7(b) shows how the server's

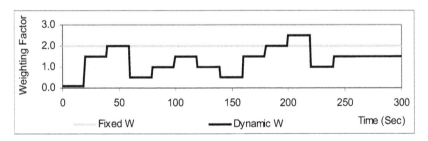

Fig. 7a. Weight factor variations with time.

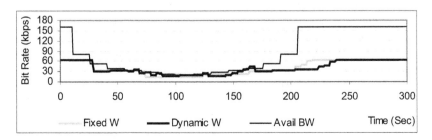

Fig. 7b. Bit rate variations with time.

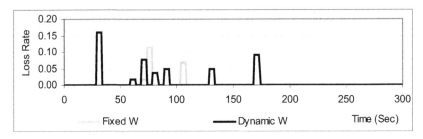

Fig. 7c. Loss rate variations with time.

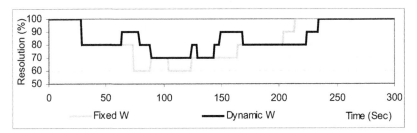

Fig. 7d. Resolution variations with time.

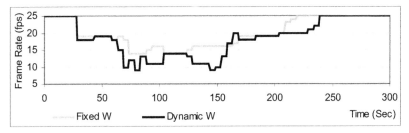

Fig. 7e. Frame rate variations with time.

transmission rate (using both a fixed weighting factor and a dynamic weighting factor) adapts in response to the available bandwidth ("Avail BW") at the client using the LDA algorithm whilst Figure 7(c) shows the loss rate. The intersection of the target transmission rate given by LDA and the intersection with the OAT gives the required resolution and frame rate. Figures 7(d) and Figure 7(e) show how the resolution and frame rates are adapted. Adaptation occurs in both dimensions of frame rate and resolution simultaneously as indicated by the OAT. These examples show the very different behaviors that can result from content-based adaptation. When the weighting factor is low, the resolution is increased faster during periods of no congestion and decreased at a slower rate when congestion occurs. By using an automatically generated OAT that is related to the characteristics of the content, it is expected that this would enhance the user perception and quality of the session since the quality is degraded and upgraded in a known and controlled manner that has the least negative impact on the perceptual quality of the content and is based on the characteristics of the content.

6   Conclusions and Future Work

We have built upon previous work in which the concept of an Optimum Adaptation Trajectory was proposed and shown to exist by subjective testing. The OAT proposed that there is an optimal way in which multimedia transmissions should be adapted (upgraded/downgraded) in response to network conditions to maximize the user-perceived quality. The OAT is related to the spatial and temporal characteristics of the content or more specifically the relative dominance of one characteristic over another. In this paper we have indicated how the characteristics of the content can be encapsulated by a weighting factor. This weighting factor plays an important role in the empirically derived equation used to generate the OAT. This equation was shown to correlate well to the OATs discovered by subjective testing. Finally, we showed how the dynamic content-based OAT can be used with the sender-based LDA algorithm.

Future work involves integrating content-based adaptation into an adaptation algorithm that uses the OAT directly as a means of adaptation. Further subjective testing is required to verify overall better user-perceived quality using content-based adaptation. It is possible to increase the feedback frequency and work is underway to implement and investigate the effects and efficacy of increased feedback frequency, as proposed by the 3GPP organization who suggest using a bandwidth modifier in the Session Description Protocol (SDP) to increase the RTCP feedback frequency [20] such that an RTCP feedback packet is sent at least once a second [21].

Acknowledgements

The support of the Research Innovation Fund and Informatics Research Initiative of Enterprise Ireland is gratefully acknowledged.

References

1. D. Sisalem, A. Wolisz LDA+: A TCP-friendly adaptation scheme for multimedia communication, IEEE International Conference on Multimedia and Expo (III) (2000).
2. D. Sisalem, A. Wolisz, MLDA: A TCP-friendly congestion control framework for heterogeneous multicast environments, Proc. Eighth International Workshop on Quality of Service (IWQoS 2000), Pittsburgh, PA, June (2000).
3. V. Jacobson S. McCanne, M. Vetterli. Receiver-driven layered multicast, Proc. of ACM SIGCOMM'96, Stanford, CA, August (1996).
4. D. Wu, Y. T. Hou, W. Zhu, H.-J. Lee, T. Chiang, Y.-Q. Zhang, H. J. Chao, On end-to-end architecture for transporting MPEG-4 video over the Internet, IEEE Trans. on Circuits and Systems for Video Technology, vol. 10, no. 6, Sept. (2000)
5. J.G. Kim, Y. Wang, S.F. Chang, Content-adaptive utility-based video adaptation, IEEE ICME 2003, Baltimore, July (2003)

6. Y. Wang, J.G. Kim, S.F. Chang, Content-based utility function prediction for real-time MPEG-4 transcoding, ICIP 2003, Barcelona, Spain, September 14-17, (2003).
7. G. Ghinea, J.P. Thomas, R. Fish, Multimedia, Network Protocols and Users - Bridging the Gap, ACM Multimedia '99, pp. 473-476, Orlando, Florida, (1999)
8. N.Cranley, L. Murphy, P. Perry, User-Perceived Quality Aware Adaptive Delivery of MPEG-4 Content, Proc. NOSSDAV'03, Monterey, California, June (2003)
9. N.Cranley, L. Murphy, P. Perry, Perceptual Quality Adaptation (PQA) algorithm for 3GP and multi-tracked MPEG-4 content over wireless networks, Proc. 15th IEEE Intl. Symp. on Personal, Indoor and Mobile Radio Communications, Barcelona, Spain, Sept. (2004)
10. M.J. Nadenau, S. Winkler, et al., Human Vision Models for perceptually Optimized Image Processing - A Review, Proceedings of the IEEE 2000, (2000)
11. S. Winkler, Vision Models and Quality Metrics for Image Processing Applications, Ph.D. Thesis, Ecole Polytechnique Federale de Lausanne (EPFL), (2000)
12. Z. Yu, H.R. Wu, Human visual system based objective digital video quality metrics, in Proc. Intl. Conf. on Signal Processing of IFIP World Computer Conference 2, August (2000)
13. M. Masry, S.S Hemami, Models for the perceived quality of low bit rate video, Proc. of IEEE International Conference on Image Processing, Rochester, NY, September (2002)
14. J.G. Kim, Y. Wang, S.F. Chang, Content-adaptive utility-based video adaptation, IEEE ICME 2003, Baltimore, July (2003)
15. C. Van den Branden Lambrecht, O. Verscheure, Perceptual Quality Measure using a Spatio-Temporal Model of the Human Visual System, Proceedings of SPIE 96, San Jose, CA, (1996)
16. Institute for Telecommunication Sciences, Technical Report, 2002, ITU-T and Related U.S. Standards Development, http://its.bldrdoc.gov/tpr/2002/itu_related_standards.pdf, (2002)
17. ITU-T Recommendation J.149, Method for specifying accuracy and cross-calibration of Video Quality Metrics (VQM), (2004)
18. ITU-T Recommendation J.148, Requirements for an objective perceptual multimedia quality model, (2003)
19. ITU-T P.910 Recommendation, Subjective video quality assessment methods for multimedia applications, (1996)
20. 3GPP TSG-SA WG4, Tdoc S4-030019, RTCP Packet Frequency for very low bit rate sessions, (2004)
21. S. Casner, SDP Bandwidth Modifier for RTCP Bandwidth, <draft-ietf-avt-rtcp-bw-05.txt>, (2002)

Performance Assessment
of the Quality-Oriented Adaptation Scheme

Gabriel-Miro Muntean[1], Philip Perry[1], and Liam Murphy[2]

[1] School of Electronic Engineering, Dublin City University,
Glasnevin, Dublin 9, Ireland
{munteang,perryp}@eeng.dcu.ie
http://www.eeng.dcu.ie/~munteang
[2] Computer Science Department, University College Dublin,
Belfield, Dublin 4, Ireland
liam.murphy@ucd.ie

Abstract. This paper focuses on the experimental performance assessment of the Quality-Oriented Adaptation Scheme (QOAS) when used for streaming high quality multimedia-based services via local broadband IP networks. Results of objective tests using a QOAS simulation model show very efficient adaptation in terms of end-user perceived quality, loss rate, and bandwidth utilization, compared to existing adaptive streaming schemes such as LDA+ and TFRCP. Subjective tests confirm these results by showing high end-user perceived quality of the QOAS under various network conditions.

1 Introduction

Bursty losses, or excessive and extremely variable delays, caused by increased traffic have a devastating effect on multimedia delivery over IP networks by severely affecting the end-users' perceived quality. Regardless of the infrastructure architecture used for delivering rich content multimedia-based services [1], the service providers and network operators aim at increasing its utilization and thus their revenues. On the other hand the customers always want the best quality for the services at the lowest price possible.

The Quality-Oriented Adaptation Scheme (QOAS) - an end-to-end application-level adaptive control solution proposed in [2], [3] and described in [4], [5], [6] - balances these opposing requirements and works best in increased traffic conditions. The adaptation is based on a client-located grading scheme that maps some network-related parameters' values and variations to application-level scores that describe the quality of delivery. In order to maximize the quality of service in existing conditions, estimates of end-user perceived quality are actively considered during this grading process. The computed quality scores are used by a server-side feedback-controlled QOAS mechanism to take adaptive decisions.

Results of extensive testing that assess QOAS in local broadband IP-networks [7] are presented and discussed in this paper. They illustrate QOAS performance and its potential benefits for delivering multimedia-based services to the customers. These tests involve both simulations and subjective perceptual testing and their results are

J. Vicente and D. Hutchison (Eds.): MMNS 2004, LNCS 3271, pp. 50–62, 2004.

presented in section 4. Section 2 discusses some related work whereas section 3 gives details about QOAS. At the end of the paper, performance analysis, conclusions and possible future work directions are presented.

2 Related Work

Extensive research has focused on proposing different adaptive schemes based on rate control and various directions have been taken. They were mainly classified in the literature [8], [9], [10] according to the place where the adaptive decision is taken.

Source-based adaptive control techniques require the sender to respond to variations in the delivery conditions. Among them there are solutions based on *probing tests* that try to estimate the available bandwidth while maintaining the loss rate below a certain threshold [11], [12].

Other solutions follow a *throughput model* that determines the transmission rate in certain conditions. The TCP-Friendly Rate Control Protocol (TFRCP)-based adaptive scheme [13] relies only on the TCP model proposed in [14], whereas the Loss-Delay Adjustment Algorithm (LDA) [15] also uses another model for rate adaptation.

A third direction that *relies on heuristic knowledge, experimental testing* and *models* encompasses many of the proposed schemes. Among the most significant are the Loss-Delay-based Adaptation Algorithm (LDA+) [16] that extends LDA; the Rate Adaptation Protocol (RAP) [17] which uses a similar approach to TCP's AIMD adaptation; Layered Quality Adaptation (LQA) [18] that bases its rate control on a layered approach; and the scheme described in [19] that bases its adaptation on information about the network state acquired by a TCP-like mechanism.

Receiver-based schemes provide mechanisms that allow for the receivers to select the service quality and/or rate, such as Receiver-driven Layered Multicast (RLM) [20] and Receiver-driven Layered Congestion Control (RLC) [21]. Among the **hybrid adaptive mechanisms** that involve both the sender and the receiver in the adaptation process, the TCP Emulation At Receivers (TEAR) scheme was described in detail in [22]. **Transcoder-based solutions** focus on matching the available bandwidth of heterogeneous receivers through transcoding or filtering, and significant solutions were presented in [23], [24].

Commercial adaptive streaming solutions like Real Networks' SureStream [25] and Microsoft's Multimedia Multi-bitrate (MBR) solution [26] are proprietary and detailed technical information has never been revealed. However the available information states that they were specially designed to allow for adaptations at very low bit-rates, unlike QOAS which addresses high quality high bit-rate video streaming.

3 Quality-Oriented Adaptation Scheme (QOAS)

Although the adaptive schemes presented in the "Related Work" section have shown good adaptation results in certain scenarios, their adjustment policies are not directly related to the quality of the streaming process as perceived by the customers. Unlike them, QOAS bases its adaptation process on estimates of the end-user perceived quality made at the receiver. This perceived quality is estimated in-service using the no-reference moving picture quality metric-Q proposed in [27] that describes the joint impact of MPEG rate and data loss on video quality. More details about Q and its usage are presented in [4].

QOAS is distributed and consists of server-side and client-side components. It makes use of a client-located Quality of Delivery Grading Scheme (QoDGS) and of a Server Arbitration Scheme (SAS) that co-operate in order to implement the feedback-controlled adaptation mechanism. The QOAS principle is schematically illustrated in Figure 1 for pre-recorded multimedia streaming used for Video-on-Demand (VoD) services, and is briefly described next.

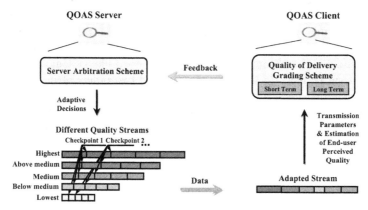

Fig. 1. QOAS principle, illustrated for pre-recorded multimedia streaming.

3.1 Principle of Quality-Oriented Adaptive Scheme

Multimedia data is received at the client where the QoDGS continuously monitors both some network-related parameters such as loss rate, delay and jitter and the estimated end-user perceived quality. According to their values and variations, QoDGS grades the quality of delivery (QoD) in terms of application-level quality scores (QoD_{Scores}) that are sent to the server as feedback. These scores are analyzed by the SAS that may suggest taking adaptive decisions in order to maximize the end-user perceived quality in existing delivery conditions. These decisions affect an internal state defined for the QOAS server component that was associated with the streamed multimedia clip's quality as shown in Figure 1. The figure presents the five-state quality model used during testing with the following states: excellent, good, average, poor and bad. Between adjacent states the adaptation step is 0.5 Mbps in the experiments described in this paper. Any QOAS server state modification affects the multimedia data transmission rate. For example, when increased traffic in the network affects the client-reported quality of delivery, SAS switches to a lower quality state. This results in a reduction in the quantity of data sent, thus helping to improve the situation. This is performed because research has shown [28] that viewers prefer a controlled reduction in multimedia quality to the effect of random losses on the streamed multimedia data. In improved delivery conditions, the QOAS server component gradually increases the quality of the transmitted stream and therefore the transmission rate. In the absence of loss this causes an increase in end-user perceived quality.

3.2 Quality of Delivery Grading Scheme (QoDGS)

QoDGS maps some transmission related parameters values and variations and estimates of end-user perceived quality into application-level scores that describe the quality of delivery. It monitors some parameters such as delay, jitter and loss rate, computes estimates of end-user perceived quality using Q and analyses their short-term and long-term variations. Short-term monitoring is important for learning quickly about transient effects, such as sudden traffic changes, and for quickly reacting to them. The long-term variations are monitored in order to track slow changes in the overall delivery environment, such as new users in the system. These short-term and long-term periods are set to be an order and two orders of magnitude (respectively) greater than the feedback-reporting interval in the experiments described here.

In the first of QoDGS's three stages, instantaneous values of the monitored parameters are saved in different length sliding windows and their short-term and long-term variations are assessed. At the same time, session-specific lower and higher limits are maintained for each parameter, allowing for corresponding partial scores to be computed in comparison with them. In the second stage, the relative importance of all the monitored parameters in this delivery infrastructure is considered (by weighting their contributions) and the partial scores are used to compute short-term (QoD_{ST}) and long-term (QoD_{LT}) quality of delivery grades. This second stage also takes into account estimates for short-term and long-term end-user perceived quality. In the third stage, QoD_{ST} and QoD_{LT} are weighted to account for their relative importance and the overall client score (QoD_{Score}) is computed.

Extensive tests were performed in order to make sure that the design of QODGS ensures that best results will be obtained in terms of adaptiveness, responsiveness to traffic variations, stability, link utilization, and end-user perceived quality in local broadband IP-networks. A detailed presentation of QoDGS is given in [4].

3.3 Server Arbitration Scheme (SAS)

SAS takes adaptive decisions based on the values of a number of recent feedback reports, in order to minimise the effect of noise in the QoD_{Scores}. This arbitration process is *asymmetric*, requiring fewer feedback reports to trigger a decrease in quality than for a quality increase. This ensures a fast reaction during bad delivery conditions, helping to eliminate their cause and allowing the network conditions to improve before any quality upgrade. These adaptive decisions are taken to maintain system stability by minimising the number of quality variations. The late arrival of a number of feedback messages is considered as an indication of network congestion, and triggers quality degradations. This permits the streaming scheme to work even if feedback is not available. More details about SAS are presented in [4].

4   Testing Results

In order to test QOAS performance when delivering multimedia clips in local multi-service broadband IP-networks to home residences and business premises, QOAS was implemented by both a simulation model, built using Network Simulator 2 (NS-2) [29], and a prototype system, built using Microsoft Visual C++ 6.0. The simulation model was used for objective testing whereas the prototype system was used for subjective assessment of the end-users' perceived quality.

4.1   Objective Testing of QOAS

The objective testing employs NS-2 simulations in order to assess the QOAS performance. The simulation setup requires a network topology, simulation models, multimedia clips, simulation scenarios and performance assessment principles. These issues and the simulation results are presented next.

Network Topology. The NS-2 simulations use a "Dumbbell" topology that assumes a single shared bottleneck link with characteristics as in Figure 2. The 100 ms latency was chosen such the adaptation of the feedback-based schemes in highly loaded delivery conditions is tested. The sources of traffic, including QOAS server application instances and a source of multimedia-like background traffic are located on one side of the bottleneck link, and the receivers are on the other side. The links are provisioned such as the only significant delays and packet drops are caused by congestion that occurs on the bottleneck.

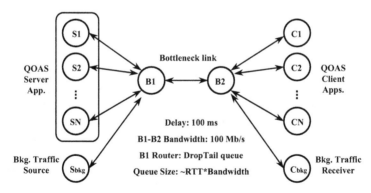

Fig. 2. "Dumbell" topology for NS-2 simulation tests.

Simulation Models. For testing QOAS a simulation model that implements the mechanism described in section III was built, using a five-quality state model for the server. The SAS upgrade period was 6 s and the downgrade one was 1 s. The QoDGS short-term and long-term periods were set to 1 s and 10 s, respectively.

When comparing QOAS to other adaptive schemes, NS-2 models for TFRCP [13] and LDA+ [16] were used and maximum rate of 4 Mb/s was imposed for consistency.

TFRCP uses estimates of round-trip delay and loss rates to determine the adaptive policy. When loss occurs, the rate of transmission is limited to the one computed by the TCP model [14]. In case of no loss, the current rate is doubled. This TFRCP model uses 5 s for rate update intervals, as suggested in [13] for latencies greater than 0.1s, as in this setup.

LDA+ is an AIMD algorithm based on estimates of network condition and bandwidth share used. In zero loss periods, the sender increases its rate with minimum from an estimated bandwidth share rate increase, a bottleneck bandwidth share rate limit, and a corresponding TCP rate update. In nonzero loss periods, the server reduces its rate by a value that depends on the current rate and the rate determined by the TCP model [14]. The LDA+ implementation used an RTCP feedback interval of 5 s as suggested in [16].

Multimedia Clips. Five video sequences were selected from movies with various types and different degrees of motion content: *diehard1* – high, *jurassic3* and *dontsayaword* – average, *familyman* – low, whereas *roadtoeldorado* is a typical cartoon sequence. The clips were MPEG-2 encoded at five rates between 2 Mb/s and 4 Mb/s using the same frame rate (25 frames/sec) and the same IBBP frame pattern (9 frames/GOP). Traces were collected, associated with QOAS server states and used during simulations. Statistics related to the ratio between the peak and mean rates for each version of the multimedia sequences used during simulations are presented in Table 1. Peak/mean rate ratios are close related to both the motion complexity and type of multimedia sequences and are the cause for the burstiness of transmissions.

Simulation Scenarios and Results. Simulations involved streaming each multimedia clip indicated in Table 1 for 500s, but 50s long transitory periods at the beginning and the end were not considered when analysing the results. Since in local multi-service broadband IP networks multimedia is expected to account for the majority of traffic, the complex multimedia-like background traffic presented in Figure 3 is used. This traffic simulates possible user interactions such as consecutive *play* commands that increase the traffic in a staircase-up manner, different frequency *pause-play* interactions applied on different rate clips and consecutive *stop's*. In order to create highly loaded network conditions, CBR-UDP background traffic with a rate of 95.5 Mb/s is generated using NS-2. This traffic represents the well-multiplexed aggregation of a high number of data flows of different types commonly expected in IP networks.

Table 1. Peak/mean rate ratio for all quality versions of the clips used during simulations.

Quality Version (average rate) Clip Name	2.0 Mb/s version	2.5 Mb/s version	3.0 Mb/s version	3.5 Mb/s version	4.0 Mb/s version
diehard1	7.48	7.43	6.31	5.65	4.06
roadtoeldorado	6.91	6.51	6.23	6.12	6.05
dontsayaword	5.56	4.51	4.36	4.08	3.56
jurassic3	4.83	4.38	4.04	3.71	3.41
familyman	3.99	3.67	3.42	3.09	2.93

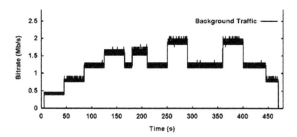

Fig. 3. Multimedia-like background traffic on top of 95.5 Mb/s CBR traffic.

Table 2. Performance comparison when streaming *diehard1* with QOAS, TFRCP and LDA+.

Streaming Scheme	Avg. Tx. Rate (Mb/s)	Avg. Loss (%)	Avg. Quality (1-5)	Avg. Utilis. (%)
QOAS	3.21	0.013	4.42	99.91
TFRCP	3.16	1.057	3.79	99.88
LDA+	2.95	1.465	3.77	99.67

Table 2 presents comparative performance statistics gathered when streaming *diehard1* using QOAS, TFRCP and LDA+, respectively in these traffic conditions. The performance was assessed in terms of average bit-rate, end-user perceived quality, loss rate and infrastructure utilization. End-user quality is computed using the no-reference metric Q [28] and is expressed on the ITU-T five-point scale [30].

Since QOAS maintains very low loss rate (0.01%) by successfully adapting even to most difficult background traffic variations, the consequent average end-user perceived quality is between "good" and "excellent" quality level (4.42). Higher loss rates than 1% are experienced when using both TFRCP and LDA+, determining decreases of the end-user perceived quality much below the "good" perceptual level.

Tests were performed using multimedia clips with different motion content and the results were similar. For exemplification Figure 4 presents a comparison between end-user perceived quality variations when streaming a single multimedia sequence with very complex motion content - *diehard1* using QOAS, TFRCP and LDA+. QOAS successfully adapts to the staircase-up increase in the background traffic that exceeds the available bandwidth, reducing the quantity of data transmitted and avoiding losses that significantly degrade end-user perceived quality in the TFRCP and LDA+ cases.

When the background traffic varies in a periodic manner with steps comparable to the adaptation step of 0.5 Mb/s (see Table 1), QOAS obtains better results in terms of perceived quality in comparison to both other solutions due to its conservative policy of slowly increasing the transmission rate to a level determined according to long-term information it maintains. Both LDA+ and TFRCP use a more aggressive manner of recovery after network problems and increase their transmission rate faster. This policy achieves in generally high throughput, but when the background traffic varies sharply like in this situation, it leads to packet loss.

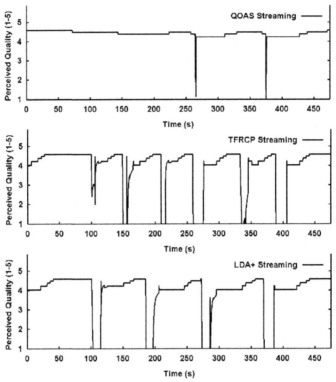

Fig. 4. Comparison between end-user perceived quality when streaming *diehard1* with QOAS, TFRCP and LDA+.

The effect of a steep increase in the background traffic when the system is already heavily loaded is tested at 250s and 360s. QOAS performs significantly better that both TFRCP and LDA+-based adaptations, reacting much faster to the sharp change in traffic. This minimizes the losses and therefore reduces the period when the perceived quality is degraded from 20s in TFRCP case and 17s in LDA+ case to only 1.2s.

At the end, the effect of stopping the multimedia cross traffic was tested. All the adaptive schemes increased their rates to compensate for the decrease in background traffic, but TFRCP and LDA+ did this faster than QOAS. However, the difference in the perceived quality between the consequent results was less than 2%.

After obtaining similar results when the other multimedia clips were used for streaming, it can be concluded that the QOAS-based solution showed superior performance to both TFRCP and LDA+. QOAS reacts quickly to changes in network traffic, reducing the quantity of the transmitted data, both preventing and minimizing losses, if they occur. Therefore the consequent end-user perceived quality was much higher than in the other cases when it even reached the "very annoying" level for long periods. QOAS's more conservative upgrade approach pays off if unexpected delivery problems occur. In terms of average utilization, all the solutions have highly performed, although QOAS slightly out-performs the other schemes.

4.2 Subjective Testing of QOAS

Subjective tests were performed in order to verify the objective end-user quality results obtained during simulations. They have involved the prototype system and 60 s long multimedia sequences taken from movies with different motion content (see Table 1). Increased traffic conditions were emulated using the NistNet network emulator [31] determining QOAS-based adaptations and consequent variations in the viewers' perceived quality.

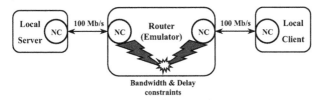

Fig. 5. Testbed setup for subjective testing.

The testbed presented in Figure 5 was set up, testing conditions suggested in [30] were ensured and the Single Stimulus Method with explicit reference was selected as testing methodology for two perceptual tests. These aimed at testing the subjects' perceived quality when using QOAS for streaming in very difficult delivery conditions, as shown by the simulations. The effects of consecutive *play* commands in the delivery system that are emulated by background traffic that varies in a staircase-up manner are tested in *Test1*. The effects of periodic variation of traffic with steps of 0.7 Mb/s, higher than the adaptation step of 0.5 Mb/s, are assessed in *Test2*. Figure 6 and Figure 7 show both the background traffic variations and the consequent QOAS rate adaptations during these tests, when the *diehard1* clip was selected for streaming. Similar results were obtained when the other clips were used.

In each of the two tests 42 subjects, aged between 18 and 48, graded the quality of each streamed clip on the 1-5 ITU-T R. P.910 scale [30]. Among the subjects, 19 and 16 in the first and the second tests respectively wore glasses or contact lenses and none had other visual impairments that may affect their perception of multimedia quality. From the subjects, 23 and 21 respectively were familiar with multimedia streaming, 1 and 2 respectively have considered themselves experts.

The results presented in Table 3 show how QOAS streaming was very appreciated by the test subjects, scoring on average above 4, the "good" quality level on the ITU-T scale, for all the movies and close to the "good" level for the cartoons sequence.

Table 3. Subjective Test Results: mean end-user perceived quality scores for *Test1* and *Test2*.

Sequence	Motion Content / Type	Test 1	Test 2
diehard1	High / Movie	4.00	4.22
dontsayaword	Average / Movie	4.18	3.98
familyman	Low / Movie	4.21	4.24
roadtoeldorado	Average / Cartoons	3.74	3.85

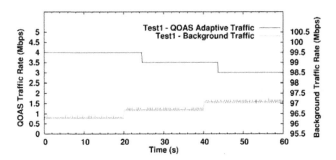

Fig. 6. Test 1: QOAS bit-rate adaptation with background traffic variation when streaming *diehard1*.

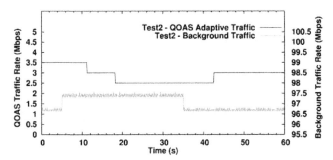

Fig. 7. Test 2: QOAS bit-rate adaptation with background traffic variation when streaming *diehard1*.

The results of *Test1* suggest that the higher the motion complexity of a sequence the lower the subjective appreciation in loaded delivery conditions is, fact supported by an ANOVA test which indicated that the results are significantly different ($p <$ 0.05). However, during *Test2* when the delivery conditions have triggered loss, the viewers' perceived quality was affected independent from the motion content as shown in Table 3. This finding was supported by an ANOVA test that found the results significantly different ($p < 0.05$).

Although the results of the second set of subjective test seem higher than those of the first set of tests, by performing t-tests on *Test1* and *Test2* results for each multimedia sequence involved in testing, the null hypothesis that there is no statistical difference between the results of *Test1* and *Test2* respectively cannot be rejected. This finding is stated with a very high level of confidence of 99% (significance level $\alpha =$ 0.01).

At the same time there is a significant statistical difference between the subjective scores obtained for the clips that contain movie scenes and the cartoons clip. This result was confirmed by paired t-tests that were performed for each movie sequence and the cartoons sequence with a significance level of $\alpha = 0.01$. A potential cause might be the different MPEG-2 encoding output for the cartoons sequences as shown in Table 1. Unlike for the movie content, for cartoons content the peak/mean ratio computed in relation to the size of the encoded frames does not significantly increase with the decrease in the average encoding bit-rate. Also the content with many colors and edges might be more affected in terms of the end-user subjective quality corrupted during streaming.

In conclusion, although slightly lower than the simulation test results obtained in the same conditions (for example when streaming the *diehard1* sequence the mean scores were 4.42 and 4.22 respectively) the subjective test results verify them and confirm the very good performance of QOAS.

5   Performance Analysis

The significant advantages of a QOAS-based solution come with a cost in terms of extra processing requirements and some bandwidth used for feedback.

The fact that this processing is distributed among the QOAS clients whose QoDGSs monitor and grade the quality of streaming at the receivers, significantly reduces the load of the QOAS server machine that runs only the SAS. The QOAS server has only to acquire the client transmitted QoD_{Scores}, to process them (this can be performed incrementally) and to take adaptive decisions (this does not involve excessive CPU load).

Regarding the feedback, it is significant to mention that each feedback report consists only of a QoD_{Score}. If RTCP packets are used, for standard values for the headers' sizes (20 Bytes – IP header, 8 Bytes – UDP header, 8 Bytes – RTCP receiver report packet header) and for a 4-Byte payload, the feedback packet size becomes 40 Bytes long. For a very low inter-feedback transmission time of 0.1 sec the bandwidth used by feedback for a single client becomes $BW_{feedback}$ = 400 Bytes/s. Since QOAS was designed for local broadband multi-service IP-networks, this represents an insignificant bandwidth usage. For example over 300 customers that are served simultaneously via a gigabit Ethernet infrastructure consume only 0.1 % of the available bandwidth for feedback.

6   Conclusions and Further Work

The Quality-Oriented Adaptation Scheme (QOAS) is an end-to-end application-level solution for streaming multimedia that considers the end-user perceived quality as an active factor in the adaptation process. The scheme is tested in conditions expected for delivering multimedia-based services to residential homes or businesses premises via a local broadband multi-service IP network.

Simulation-based objective tests have shown very good performance of QOAS, assessed in terms of remote user perceived quality, average loss rate and network infrastructure utilization when streaming multimedia in loaded network conditions and in the presence of highly variable multimedia-like background traffic. The perceived quality was between the "good" and "excellent" ITU-T quality levels, the loss rate was around 0.01 % and the utilization greater than 99.9 %, results that out-perform those obtained when other adaptive schemes such as TFRCP and LDA+ were tested in the same conditions. Subjective tests performed in difficult emulated traffic conditions verify these results.

These results highly recommend QOAS as a very efficient solution for delivering good quality multimedia-based services in local broadband IP-network to customers, even in increased and highly variable traffic conditions.

Further work will test in detail the performance of QOAS if deployed in local broadband multi-service IP networks against different types of individual traffic flows such as long-lived or short-lived TCP. These tests will study not only the effect this traffic has on multimedia streams transmitted using QOAS, but also the effect QOAS streaming has on the other traffic. In this context QOAS's degree of TCP friendliness is of significant importance. Also experiments that involve streaming of more than one type of multimedia clips at the same time are envisaged. Next QOAS will be extended for multicast transmissions, taking into account some multicast specific characteristics such as multiple feedback and arbitration of heterogeneous client reports in order to make more efficient live multimedia streaming.

Acknowledgements

The support of the Research Innovation Fund and Informatics Research Initiative of Enterprise Ireland is gratefully acknowledged.

References

1. Barnett, S. A., Anido, G. J.: A Cost Comparison of Distributed and Centralized Approaches to Video-on-Demand, IEEE Journal Sel. Areas in Comm., vol. 14, no. 6, (1996), 1173-1183
2. Muntean, G.-M., Murphy, L.: An Adaptive Mechanism For Pre-recorded Multimedia Streaming Based On Traffic Conditions, W3C WWW Conf., Honolulu, HI, USA, (2002)
3. Muntean, G.-M., Murphy, L.: Adaptive Pre-recorded Multimedia Streaming, IEEE GLOBECOM, Taipei, Taiwan, (2002)
4. Muntean, G.-M., Perry, P., Murphy, L.: A New Adaptive Multimedia Streaming System for All-IP Multi-Service Networks, IEEE Trans. on Broadcasting, vol. 50, no. 1, (2004), 1-10
5. Muntean, G.-M., Perry, P., Murphy, L.: Performance Comparison of Local Area Video Streaming Systems, IEEE Communication Letters, vol. 8, no. 5, (2004), 326-328
6. Muntean, G.-M., Perry, P., Murphy, L.: A Quality-Orientated Adaptation Scheme for Video-on-Demand, IEE Electronic Letters, vol. 39, no. 23, (2003), 1689-1690
7. Dravida, S., Gupta, D., Nanda, S., Rege, K., Strombosky, J., Tandon, M.: Broadband Access over Cable for Next-Generation Services: A Distributed Switch Architecture, IEEE Comm. Magazine, vol. 40, no. 8, (2002), 116–124
8. Wang, X, Schulzrinne, H.: Comparison of Adaptive Internet Multimedia Applications, IEICE Trans. on Comm., vol. E82-B/6, (1999), 806 – 818
9. Wu, D., Hou, Y. T., Zhu, W., Zhang, Y.-Q., Peha, J. M.: Streaming Video over the Internet: Approaches and Directions, IEEE Trans. on Circuits and Systems for Video Technology, vol. 11, no. 3, (2001), 282–300
10. Wu, D., Hou, Y. T., Zhang, Y.-Q.: Transporting Real-time Video over the Internet: Challenges and Approaches, Proc. IEEE, vol. 88, no. 12, (2000)

11. Kanakia, H., Mishra, P., Reibman, A.: An Adaptive Congestion Control Scheme for Real-time Packet Video Transport, Proc. ACM SIGCOMM, San Francisco, USA, (1993), 20-31
12. Bolot, J.-C., Turletti, T.: A Rate Control Mechanism for Packet Video in the Internet, Proc. IEEE INFOCOM, Toronto, Canada, (1994), 1216-1223
13. Padhye, J., Kurose, J., Towsley, D., Koodli, R.: A Model Based TCP Friendly Rate Control Protocol, Proc. ACM NOSSDAV, New Jersey, (1999)
14. Padhye, J., Firoiu, V., Towsley, D., Kurose, J.: Modeling TCP Throughput: A Simple Model and its Empirical Validation, Proc. ACM SIGCOMM, Vancouver, Canada, (1998)
15. Sisalem, D., Schulzrinne, H.: The Loss-Delay Adjustment Algorithm: A TCP-friendly Adaptation Scheme, Proc. ACM NOSSDAV, UK, (1998)
16. Sisalem, D., Wolisz, A.: LDA+ TCP-Friendly Adaptation: A Measurement and Comparison Study, Proc. ACM NOSSDAV, USA, (2000)
17. Rejaie, R., Handley, M., Estrin, D.: RAP: An End-to-end Rate-based Congestion Control Mechanism for Realtime Streams in the Internet, Proc. IEEE INFOCOM, New York, NY, USA, (1999), 1337-1345
18. Rejaie, R., Handley, M., Estrin, D.: Layered Quality Adaptation for Internet Video Streaming, IEEE J. Sel. Areas of Comm., vol. 18, no. 12, (2000), 2530-2543
19. Jacobs, S., Eleftheriadis, A.: Streaming Video Using Dynamic Rate Shaping and TCP Congestion Control, Journal of Visual Comm. and Image Repres., vol. 9, no. 3, (1998), 221-222
20. McCanne, S., Jacobson, V., Vetterli, M.: Receiver-Driven Layered Multicast, Proc. ACM SIGCOMM, Stanford, USA, (1996), 117-130
21. Vicisano, L., Crowcroft, J., Rizzo, L.: TCP-like Congestion Control for Layered Multicast Data Transfer, Proc. IEEE INFOCOM, vol. 3, (1998), 996-1003
22. Rhee, I., Ozdemir, V., Yi, Y.: TEAR: TCP Emulation at Receivers - Flow Control for Multimedia Streaming, Technical Report, CS Department, NCSU, (2000)
23. Yeadon, N., García, F., Hutchison, D., Shepherd, D.: Filters: QoS Support Mechanisms for Multipeer Communications, IEEE J. Sel. Areas in Comm., vol. 14, no. 7, (1996), 1245-1262
24. Wang, L., Luthra, A., Eifrig, B.: Rate Control for MPEG Transcoders, IEEE Trans. on Circuits and Systems for Video Technology, vol. 11, no. 2, (2001)
25. RealNetworks, SureStream, [Online]. Available: http://www.realnetworks.com
26. Microsoft, Windows Media, MBR, [Online]. Available: http://www.microsoft.com
27. Ghinea, G., Thomas, J. P., QoS Impact on User Perception and Understanding of Multimedia Video Clips, Proc. ACM Multimedia, Bristol, UK, (1998)
28. Verscheure, O., Frossard, P., Hamdi, M.: User-Oriented QoS Analysis in MPEG-2 Video Delivery, Journal of Real-Time Imaging, vol. 5, no. 5, (1999), 305-314
29. Network Simulator-2, [Online]. Available: http://www.isi.edu/nsnam/ns/
30. ITU-T Recommendation P.910: Subjective Video Quality Assessment Methods for Multimedia Applications, (1999)
31. NIST Net, [Online]. Available: http://snad.ncsl.nist.gov/itg/nistnet

An Adaptive Batched Patch Caching Scheme for Multimedia Streaming*

Shaohua Qin[1], Weihong He[2], Zimu Li[3], and Jianping Hu[1]

[1] School of Computer Science, Beijing University of Aeronautics & Astronautics,
Beijing 100083,China
{shqin,jianpinghu}@buaa.edu.cn
[2] Hengyang Branch of Hunan University, Hengyang 421101, China
hwh@hnbmc.edu.cn
[3] Network Research Center of Tsinghua University, Beijing 100084,China
zmli@cernet.edu.cn

Abstract. Large-scale steaming media applications usually consume a significant amount of server and network resources due to the high bandwidth requirements and the long-lived nature of the streaming media objects. In this paper, we address the problem of efficiently streaming media object to the clients over a distributed infrastructure consisting of video server and proxy caches. We build on the earlier work and propose an adaptive batched patch caching scheme, which tightly combine the transmission scheduling with proxy caching. This scheme adaptively caches the next segment data at proxy from the ongoing entire stream, which depends on the current batching interval that has non-zero requests. We demonstrate the benefits of our scheme compare to the classical streaming strategies. Our evaluations show that this scheme can reduce significantly the consumption of aggregate bandwidth on backbone link within much wider range of request arrival rate.

Keywords: Streaming media, Batched patch, Proxy cache, Multicast, Server scheduling.

1 Introduction

The emergence of the Internet as a pervasive communication medium, and a mature digital video technology have led to a rise of various networked streaming media applications such as video-on-demand, distance learning, video game and video conferencing. As access providers are rolling out faster last-mile connections, the bottleneck is shifting upstream to the provider's backbone, peering links and best-effort Internet. Due to the large size, long-lived nature of the streaming objects, they need to consume much more network bandwidth and server system resource in distribution and delivery. At the same time, the I/O capacity of the video server and network bandwidth are impossible to be unrestrained enhancement because of hardware costs limitation. So, in the process of distributing streaming media over the Internet, how to reduce the backbone bandwidth consumption and efficiently utilize the video server system resource have become the research hotspot in the area of streaming media applications in recent years.

Existing research has focused on developing transmission schemes that use multicast or broadcast connections in innovative ways to reduce server and network loads,

---

* This work is supported by the NNSF of China under grant 60103005.

J. Vicente and D. Hutchison (Eds.): MMNS 2004, LNCS 3271, pp. 63–73, 2004.

for serving a popular video to multiple asynchronous clients. Batching [1], Patch [2], [4], HMSM[11] and Optimized Batch Patching [3] are reactive in that the server transmits video data only on demand, in response to arriving client requests. These schemes have an underlying requirement that the multicast or broadcast connectivity between the server and the clients is available. However, IP multicast deployment in the Internet has been slow and even today remains severely limited in scope and reach. Therefore, transmission schemes that can support efficient delivery in such predominantly unicast settings need to be developed..

Another attractive solution for reducing server loads, backbone network traffic and access latencies is the use of proxy caches. This technique has proven to be quite effective for delivering traditional Web objects. However, streaming media object can be very large, and traditional techniques for caching entire objects are not appropriate for such media. Caching strategies that have been proposed in recent years [7],[12],[13],[14] cache a portion of streaming media object at the proxy. These prefix and segmentation-based caching methods have a number of advantages including reducing startup latency and jitter on the server-proxy path, while saving bandwidth usage along that path. However, they do not take the issue of the transmission scheduling into consideration. Recent work [10] combines prefix caching with proxy-assisted reactive transmission schemes for reducing the transmission cost of multiple heterogeneous videos. Another work [5],[6],[8],[9] combines multicast-based server scheduling with proxy caching to minimize the aggregate bandwidth usage. In particular, the Batched Patch Caching (BPC) proposed in [5] which caches the patch data at caching proxy in order to make more clients to share it, and as thus achieve better performance. However, when the request arrival rate is very high, these schemes mentioned above are still consume quite a few system resources.

In this paper, we build on early work and propose an adaptive batched patch caching scheme knows as ABPC which combines dynamic caching at the proxy with scalable transmission scheme at the origin server. In this scheme, the server-proxy network connections only provide unicast service, and on the proxy-client path offers multicast capability. By adaptive pre-caching the patch data for the upcoming request in the next batching interval, it achieves lower bandwidth consumption than the BPC scheme over a wider range of request arrival rate.

The rest of this paper is organized as follows. In section 2, some previous works in the multicast and streaming media caching areas are reviewed. In section 3, we present and formulate our scheme in detail. Section 4 shows results that compare the performance of new scheme and BPC. Finally we present our conclusions and ongoing work in section 5.

2   Previous Work

Streaming media objects over multicast consumes less network bandwidth and imposes less of a load on the server than does streaming media objects over multiple unicast channels. Batching is a simple scheduling strategy based on multicast. It delays the earlier arrival request to wait for much more clients, and serves them over a single channel. Patching is certainly one of the most efficient techniques. The server streams the entire video sequentially to the very first client. A later client receives its future playback data by listening to an existing ongoing multicast of the same video, and the server only transmits afresh only the missing portion (patch data).

The concept of optimized batch patching (OBP) in literature [3] has recently been proposed, which aimed at minimizing the average backbone rate. Basically, client requests are batched together on an interval basis before requesting either a patch or a regular multicast from the server. There is an optimal patching window after which it is more bandwidth efficient to start a new entire stream rather than send patches. This scheme outperforms other multicast-based techniques such as optimal patching [4] in terms of average backbone rate over a large range of request rates [3].

The Batched Patch Caching (BPC) was built on the Optimized Batch Patching idea. Upon reception of a patch, the proxy stores it in the buffer for a period of the patching window size, so that it is available for the last requests of the same patching window and consequently reduces the bandwidth usage of the extra channel. By caching the patch data in the proxy, this scheme demands the average backbone rate smaller than that of OBP scheme. But, it needs to retransmit all of the patch data.

We differ from all the above works in that we develop a new mechanism to prefetch the patch data from the ongoing entire stream along the unicast connection of the server and the proxy. At the same time, the pre-fetching data is cached dynamically at the proxy. They can serve the requests of the same patching window. Moreover, by varying the size of the patching window according to popularity of the streaming media object, the minimum consumption of the backbone bandwidth can achieve, and limited storage space of proxy can utilize efficiently.

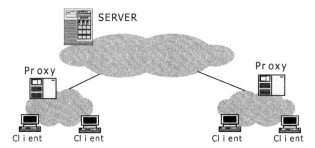

Fig. 1. Illustration of proxy cache for streaming media.

3   Adaptive Batched Patch Caching Scheme

In this section, we consider a delivering architecture of streaming media object, which composed of an origin server, a set of proxies, and a finite set of media objects. Each proxy is responsible for a group of clients as shown in Fig.1. We assume reliable transmissions over the server-proxy path, and the access network (proxy-client) is lossless and multicast enabled. We further assume that the clients are always request play back from the beginning of the media object. Moreover we impose the proxy to play the role of a client for server. That is, all the streaming media object data streamed out of the server are requested by the proxy and are thereby forwarded through it. A proxy streams the prefix directly to its clients if a prefix of the media object is present locally, and contacts the server for the remainder (suffix) of the stream. Otherwise, the proxy sends the server a request to start a full stream (unicast) and multicasts it to a set of clients. In order to shield the client-perceived startup latency, the proxy immediately sends client the first segment data by unicast channel once a request arrives in each batching interval. This unicast stream will terminate at the boundary of the batching interval. At this time, the client will join the full stream and the patch data stream that started by the proxy via multicast channel.

We next introduce the notations used in this paper, as presented in Table 1. We consider a server with a repository of M Constant-Bit-Rate (CBR) media objects. Let media object $m \in M$ is characterized by its playback rate r_m, duration L_m, and average access rate λ_m.

Table 1. Parameters used in this paper.

Para.	Definition
M	Number of the media objects
L_m	Length of media object m (sec.)
r_m	Playback rate of media object m(bps)
S	The cache size of proxy
Ω	Normalized transmission rate
λ_m	Average request arrival rate for object m
W_m	Patching window size for object m
μ_m	Total patch data for object m
b_m	The batching interval

3.1 Scheme Description

The basic idea of the adaptive batched patch caching is that whenever a full stream is started, the proxies that receive the data from this stream allocate a buffer size of b_m units to cache the upcoming data. And at the end of each batch in the same patching window, these proxies check to see whether or not there are requests. If there are requests, these proxies separately add b_m units to the buffer and cache the ongoing stream continuously. Otherwise they stop caching. Since we do not cache the data segments at the end of each batch of zero requests, the proxy will need to start an extra channel to afresh them if there are requests in the subsequent batching intervals.

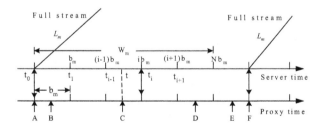

Fig. 2. Timing Diagram for adaptive batched patch caching.

Our scenario is illustrated in Fig.2, The proxy divides uniformly the time axis into intervals $[t_{i-1}, t_i]$ of duration b_m, Assume a request arrives at the proxy at time $t \in [t_{i-1}, t_i]$, and the most recent full stream was started at time t_0. If t_i is such that $t_i < t_0 + W_m$, the proxy need to transmit patch data of duration $t_i - t_0 = ib_m$ to the client at time t_i, also the proxy joins the full stream at time t_i, and multicasts it to the clients. However, if $t_i > t_0 + W_m$, a new full stream will be started at time t_i. Since the first segment data $[0, b_m]$ of the streaming media object has been stored at the proxy at time t_1 after the full stream is started, whether the subsequent segment data need to be cached depends on the current batching intervals that have no-zero requests before time t_i. This is better explained with the following example.

Suppose there are eight batching intervals in the patching window, that is $W_m=8b_m$. The full stream was started at time t_0. Also at time t_0 the proxy began to buffer the first segment data from this steam. Suppose $[t_0, t_1]$ had requests, then at time t_1 the proxy adds b_m units to the buffer and caches the ongoing stream continuously. This makes the proxy can serve the requests arrive at time intervals $[t_0, t_1]$ and $[t_1, t_2]$, and does not request server for any patch bytes. Suppose the next two intervals do not have any requests, and the proxy does not cache the corresponding data segment $[2b_m, 3b_m]$, $[3b_m, 4b_m]$ continuously. If the fourth interval $[t_3, t_4]$ has requests, at time t_4, the buffer of the proxy has only contained two segment data $[0, b_m]$ and $[b_m, 2b_m]$. The requests arrive in the fourth interval requires the patches to be $4b_m$-long, and so the proxy expands the buffer from having $2b_m$ units to having $5b_m$ units, and then fetches the missing patch data $[2b_m, 3b_m]$ and $[3b_m, 4b_m]$ from the server by the extra channel while storing the segment data $[4b_m, 5b_m]$ from the ongoing full stream. The processing method for subsequence intervals is similar to that for the preview intervals. At last, whether the eighth interval $[t_7, t_8]$, has requests or not, the proxy will not store the next segment data from the full stream at time t_8.

Our scheme has a remarkable characteristic. That is, the more probability of the request arrival each batching interval has (That means the request arrival rate is very high), the little patch data need to be transmitted afresh become. When each batched interval of patching window has no-zero requests, the pre-fetching mechanism can assure that the demanded patching data just obtaining from full stream can satisfy all the request arrived in the same patching window. On the other hand, if only the last batching interval has requests, the proxy will need to fetch the patch data up to $(N-1)b_m$ via the extra channel.

3.2 Scheme Analyses and Problem Formulation

For simplicity of exposition, we ignore network propagation latency. In order to derive analytic expressions in evaluating the performance of our scheme, we first make an abstract of our scheme as follows:

- Assume the access rate of media object m are modeled by Poisson process with parameter λ_m such that $p = e^{-\lambda_m b_m}$ is the probability to have an empty batch (zero request) of duration b_m.
- The proxy stores the patch data in the buffer at least for a period of $W_m=Nb_m$, so that it is available for the all requests arrived in the same patching window.
- Suppose x_i denotes the requests that arrive in the ith batching interval $[t_{i-1}, t_i]$. Let $x_1, x_2, ..., x_N$ be a sequence of independent random variables with common probability distribution.

- Whether the proxy need to fetch the patch data by extra channel at time t_i depends on the values of x_1, x_2, …,x_{i-1} and x_i. In particular if $x_1 = x_2 = \ldots = x_i = 0$ or $x_1 = x_2 = \ldots = x_i \neq 0$, the proxy does not request server for any patch bytes.
- Assume the proxy request server for the patches size is ψ in the patching window. It is obviously ψ will likely take one among the values $0, 1b_m, 2b_m, \ldots, (N-1)b_m$, we might as well let p_i denotes the probability of $\psi = ib_m$, that is $p(\psi = ib_m) = p_i$, $i = 0, 1, 2, \ldots, N-1$.

With the above assumption, we can achieve the mean value of η, namely

$$E\psi = b_m \sum_{i=0}^{N-1} i \cdot p_i = b_m \sum_{i=1}^{N-1} i \cdot p_i \qquad (1)$$

Now we need to determine p_i. Obviously,

$$
\begin{aligned}
p_0 &= p(\psi = 0) \\
&= p(x_1 = \cdots = x_N \neq 0) + p(x_1 = \cdots = x_{N-1} \neq 0, x_N = 0) \\
&\quad + p(x_1 = \cdots = x_{N-2} \neq 0, x_{N-1} = x_N = 0) + \cdots \\
&\quad + p(x_1 \neq 0, x_2 = \cdots = x_N = 0) + p(x_1 = \cdots = x_N = 0) \\
&= (1-p)^N + (1-p)^{N-1} p^1 + (1-p)^{N-2} p^2 + \cdots \\
&\quad + (1-p)^2 p^{N-2} + (1-p) p^{N-1} \\
&= C_{N-0}^0 (1-p)^N + C_{N-1}^0 (1-p)^{N-1} p^1 + C_{N-2}^0 (1-p)^{N-2} p^2 \\
&\quad + \cdots + C_1^0 (1-p)^1 p^{N-1} + C_0^0 p^N \\
&= \sum_{j=0}^{N} C_{N-j}^0 (1-p)^{N-j} p^j
\end{aligned}
$$

$$
\begin{aligned}
p_1 &= p(\psi = 1b_m) \\
&= C_{N-1}^1 (1-p)^{N-1} p + C_{N-2}^1 (1-p)^{N-2} p^2 + \cdots \\
&\quad + C_2^1 (1-p)^2 p^{N-2} + C_1^1 (1-p) p^{N-1} \\
&= \sum_{j=1}^{N-1} C_{N-j}^1 (1-p)^{N-1-j+1} p^{1+j-1}
\end{aligned}
$$

$$
\begin{aligned}
p_2 &= p(\psi = 2b_m) \\
&= C_{N-1}^2 (1-p)^{N-2} p^2 + C_{N-2}^2 (1-p)^{N-3} p^3 + \cdots \\
&\quad + C_3^2 (1-p_k^m)^2 p^{N-2} + C_2^2 (1-p) p^{N-1} \\
&= \sum_{j=1}^{N-2} C_{N-j}^2 (1-p)^{N-2-j+1} p^{2+j-1}
\end{aligned}
$$

$$
\begin{aligned}
p_3 &= p(\psi = 3b_m) \\
&= C_{N-1}^3 (1-p)^{N-3} p^3 + C_{N-2}^3 (1-p)^{N-4} p^4 + \cdots \\
&\quad + C_4^3 (1-p)^2 p^{N-2} + C_3^3 (1-p) p^{N-1} \\
&= \sum_{j=1}^{N-3} C_{N-j}^3 (1-p)^{N-3-j+1} p^{3+j-1}
\end{aligned}
$$

Thus the expression of p_i can be written as:

$$p_i = \sum_{j=1}^{N-i} C_{N-j}^i (1-p)^{N-(i+j)+1} p^{i+j-1} , \quad i = 0,1,2,\cdots,N-1. \tag{2}$$

Substituting equation (2) into equation (1), by computing all the different possibilities of batching interval along the patching window, we get the average number of patched data segments, μ_m at proxy. It is given by

$$\mu_m = E\psi = b_m \sum_{i=1}^{N-1}\sum_{j=1}^{N-i} i \cdot C_{N-j}^i (1-p)^{N-(i+j)+1} p^{i+j-1} \tag{3}$$

The aggregate transmission rate on the backbone link, R_m, includes the transmission of patches (μ_m) and the full stream of duration L_m from the server. Its normalized transmission rate Ω is thus obtained from:

$$\Omega = \frac{R_m}{r_m} = \frac{L_m + \mu_m}{I_m} \tag{4}$$

Where I_m represents the interval duration between two adjacent full streams:

$$I_m = (N+1)b_m + 1/\lambda_m \tag{5}$$

The average buffer capacity S needed for caching at proxy is then given by

$$S = (\mu_m + \mu_m')r_m \tag{6}$$

Where μ' denotes the segment data received from the full stream. According to the buffer allocating mechanism in our scheme, μ' is given by

$$\mu_m' = b_m + (N-1)(1-p)b_m \tag{7}$$

We now compute the proxy network bandwidth. Recall that the proxy deliver the first segment data to clients via unicast channel, and forwards the full stream and the other patching data via multicast channel. Thus its normalized bandwidth B_{proxy} is given by:

$$B_{porxy} = \frac{\lambda_m(N+1)b_m^2 r_m + (1-p)\dfrac{N(N+1)b_m}{2}r_m}{I_m} + \Omega \tag{8}$$

4   Numerical Results and Comparisons

In this section, we evaluate the performance of our proposed scheme ABPC and contrast it against BPC in three aspects using numerical result. Suppose the duration of the streaming media object is 120 minutes, and its average play back rate is 1.5 Mbps (MPEG-1).

First, we examine the transmission quantities of patching data that needed to get by the extra channel with respect to the request arrival rate and the patching window size. As shown in Fig.3, adopting the ABPC scheme, the average number of transmitted patches decreases rapidly as the request arrival rate increases, and that close to zero.

This indicates that ABPC scheme only needs to fetch few patch data through the extra channel while the request arrival rate reaches relative high. But the BPC scheme needs to fetch all the patch data through the extra channel, and that close to the patching window size. In other words, whatever the request arrival rate and the patching window change, under the same conditions, the ABPC scheme can save much more bandwidth of extra channel than the BPC scheme.

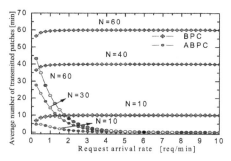

Fig. 3. Average number of transmitted patches through extra channel versus the request arrival rate, $b_m=1$[min].

Secondly, we compare the normalized backbone rate demanded in the case of transmitting one media object for both schemes ABPC and BPC by showing in Fig. 4(a) ~ (d). From these diagrams we see that the normalized backbone rate required in the ABPC scheme is always smaller than that in the BPC scheme at different values of the patching window as well as request arrival rate. Also, as the patching window size increases, the normalized backbone rate decreases.

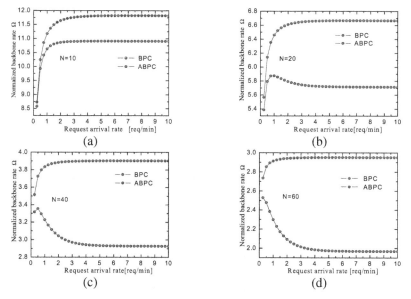

Fig. 4. Normalized backbone rate versus request arrival rate at different values of patching window, $b_m=1$[min].

Thirdly, we show in Fig.5 (a) ~ (d) the buffer requirement at proxy to deal with one media object for both schemes ABPC and BPC with respect to the patching window size and the request arrival rate. As the patching window size increases, the buffer requirement also increases. Moreover, under the same conditions, both of these schemes consume almost the same buffers at proxy, especially in the high request arrival rate. This evidence indicates that ABPC scheme archives the lower bandwidth saving than the BPC scheme, while it does not consume much more buffer size.

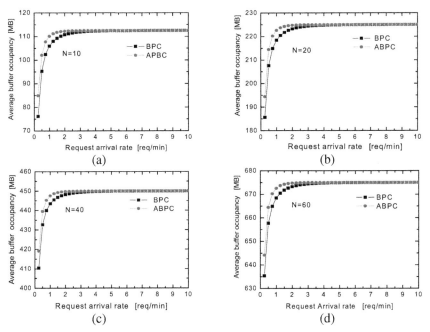

Fig. 5. Average buffer occupancy at proxy versus request arrival rate at different values of patching window, $b_m=1[\min]$.

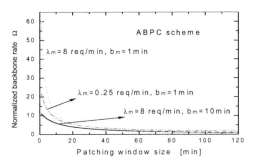

Fig. 6. Normalized backbone rate versus patching windows size.

Finally, Fig.6 shows the evolution of the normalized backbone rate Ω versus the duration of the patching windows under different request arrival rate and the batching interval by adopting ABPC scheme. We clearly find that the normalized backbone rate may no longer exhibit a minimum value for the patching window duration within T_m. Moreover, the longer the duration of patching window, the higher buffer size required at the proxy. Accordingly, in practice the initial value of the patching window can be determined using the expression in literature [3], afterwards, we let the patching window size to adaptively expand or shorten in terms of request arrival rate. Intuitively, if all batches during the duration of the stream have no-zero requests, this media object is really very popular and we ought to expand the patching window in order to much cache this entire object at proxy and not have to request from the server. With such a dynamical control of patching window, it instructs the proxy to implement an optimal cache for each media object, thereby achieving the better trade-off between backbone bandwidth and storage requirements.

5   Conclusions and Ongoing Work

In this paper, we proposed an adaptive batched patch caching scheme that joints server scheduling and proxy caching aimed at reducing the bandwidth streamed from the server. We formulate the on-demanded numbers of normalized backbone transmission rate for considering a particular streaming media object. Compared with the traditional batched patch-caching scheme, the proposed scheme achieves much more savings of backbone bandwidth by adaptive pre-caching the patch data from full stream. In addition, the adaptability of the proposed scheme keeps on very well within wide range of request arrival rate. The numerical results show that the adaptive batched patch caching is a highly efficient method that alleviates bottlenecks for the delivery of streaming media objects.

For simplicity of exposition, we ignore network propagation latency throughout the paper. Note that our scheme can be easily adapted to the scenario when the network propagation latency along server-proxy path is not ignorable. In order to hide the transmission delay for a streaming media object from the server, the proxy cache has to be allocated to accommodate a prefix for each media object.

We are currently investigating the trade-offs between bandwidth reduction and buffer occupancy at proxy. We are also exploring the scenarios based on ABPC where the proxies can cooperate.

References

1. A. Dan, D. Sitaram, P. Shahabuddin: Scheduling policies for an on-demand video server with batching. In Proc. ACM Multimedia, San Francisco, California, (1994) 15–23
2. K. A. Hua,Y. Cai, S. Sheu: Patching: A multicast technique for true video-on-demand services", in Proc. ACM Multimedia, Britstol UK, (1998)191–200
3. P. P. White, J. Crowcroft: Optimized batch patching with classes of service, ACM Communications Review, Vol. 30, No.4, (2000)
4. Y.Cai, K. Hua, K.Vu: Optimizing Patching Performance. In proc. of ACM/SPIE Multimedia Computing and Networking, (1999) 203–215
5. O.Verscheure,C.Verkatramani, P. Froassard, L. Amini: Joint server scheduling and proxy caching for video delivery. Computer Communications, Vol.25, No. 4, (2002) 413–423
6. C. Venkatramani, O. Verscheure, P. Frossard, K. W. Lee: Optimal proxy management for multimedia streaming in content distribution networks. In proc. of ACM NOSSDAV 2002, Miami Beach, FL, USA, May (2002)147–154

7. S. Sen, J. Rexford, D. Towsley: Proxy prefix caching for multimedia steams. In proc. of IEEE INFOCOM'99, New York, USA, (1999)1310–1319
8. Pascal Frossard, Oliver Verscheure: Batched patch caching for streaming media. IEEE Communications Letters, Vol.6, No.4, (2002), 159–161
9. S.-H. Gary Chan, Fouad Tobagi: Distributed servers architecture for networked video services. IEEE/ACM Trans. on Networking, Vol.9, No.2, (2001) 125–136
10. B. Wang, S. Sen, M. Adler, D. Towsley: Optimal proxy cache allocation for efficient streaming media distribution. IEEE Trans. on Multimedia, Vol.6, No.2, (2004) 366–374
11. D. Eager, M. Vernon, J. Zahorjan: Minimizing Bandwidth Requirements for On-Demand Data Delivery. IEEE Trans. on Knowledge and Data Engineering, Vol. 13, No. 5, (2001) 742–757
12. K. Wu, P. S. Yu, J. Wolf: Segment-based proxy caching of multimedia streams. In Proc. of WWW, Hong Kong, may (2001) 36–44
13. S. Chen, B. Shen, S. Wee, X. Zhang: Adaptive and lazy segmentation based proxy caching for steaming media delivery. In proc. of ACM NOSSDAV'03, Monterey, CA, (2003) 22–31
14. S. Chen, B. Shen, S. Wee, X. Zhang: Investigating performance insights of segment-based proxy caching of streaming media strategies. In proc. of MMCN'2004, San, CA, (2004) 148–165

Dynamic Cell-Based MAC Protocol
for Target Detection Applications
in Energy-Constrained Wireless Networks

Sonia Waharte and Raouf Boutaba

University of Waterloo, School of Computer Science
200, University Av. West, Waterloo, Canada N2L 3G1
{swaharte,rboutaba}@bbcr.uwaterloo.ca

Abstract. Today's advances in sensor technology make it feasible to embed sensing, communication and computation capabilities in small untethered nodes. However, node lifetime is still severely restricted by the limitations of power supply. By improving power consumption efficiency of sensor node operations, a sensor node's lifetime can be significantly extended. A well designed MAC protocol can achieve this goal by minimizing the amount of data transmitted through the network. In scenarios where data retrieval operations are infrequent and localized (e.g. target detection applications), pre-configuring an entire sensor network is detrimental to power conservation. Therefore, restricting data gathering operations to nodes with valuable information can significantly reduce energy consumption. In this paper, we propose and evaluate a new MAC protocol, and demonstrate the advantages of our scheme for specific types of applications.

1   Introduction

Recent technological advances have enabled the development of tiny devices embedding communication, sensing and computation capabilities. These devices are self-organized after deployment and coordinate themselves to perform some common tasks, such as sensing the environment, retrieving accurate data, and gathering data for further processing. Sensor networks are envisioned to find applications in diverse fields such as environment monitoring, battlefield surveillance, target tracking, traffic analysis, etc. They are intended to be deployed in any environment, outdoor or indoor, and cover large-scale areas, often making it infeasible to replace the nodes' limited power supply. As some applications (environment monitoring, fire detection, etc.) require sensor nodes to have a lifetime in the range of several months or years, one solution to extend the lifetime of the sensor nodes is to reduce the number of messages sent through the network during data gathering operations and during the network self-organization process. In the recent literature, the most commonly proposed solution relies on the concept of cluster formation [1], [2], [3], [4]. Some nodes in the sensor network are elected to act as cluster heads and collect data from the other nodes located

J. Vicente and D. Hutchison (Eds.): MMNS 2004, LNCS 3271, pp. 74–87, 2004.
© IFIP International Federation for Information Processing 2004

in their close vicinity. This configuration is particularly adapted to applications that require constant data retrieval from all the nodes in the network. However, cluster formation is not advantageous for applications needing only infrequent sensing operations on localized events.

Consider an application such as target tracking. Only the sensor nodes in proximity to the tracked target should participate in the data gathering process. Thus, the overall network lifetime can be significantly improved if we consider the formation of cells (groups of nodes located in the same vicinity), created in reaction to the detection of a specific stimulus, instead of a proactive network organization. Such approach is also more adapted to the tracking of moving targets.

We propose a Dynamic Cell-based MAC Protocol (DCP) whose principle is the following: using a multi-frequency mechanism, a self-elected cell head coordinates the data transmission of a set of neighboring nodes in order to minimize data collision. This paper describes the features of DCP and its performance in comparison to a traditional Time Division Multiple Access scheme. In this paper, we focus only on local node organization and we are therefore not concerned with the routing aspect of data transmission.

The paper is organized as follows. After a discussion of related works in Section 2, we present the design and implementation of DCP in Section 3. In Section 4, we show the results of the conducted simulations and demonstrate the advantages of DCP for the targeted application scenarios.

2   Related Works

An important research effort in wireless sensor networks has been conducted to reduce energy consumption of sensor nodes operations in order to increase the network's lifetime. Several mechanisms have been proposed to achieve this goal by turning on/off the sensor nodes or by implementing data gathering processes aiming at decreasing the overall traffic load. In this paper, we focus on the latter mechanism.

Several data gathering mechanisms have been designed for wireless sensor networks. They essentially adopt the same clusters formation approach excepted PEGASIS [5], which proposes to construct a chain among the nodes in the sensor network, with the election of a random leader node responsible for the transmission of the gathered data to the destination station.

Among the clustering approaches, a cyclic scheme has been proposed by LEACH (Low-Energy Adaptive Clustering Hierarchy) [6]. At the beginning of each round, each node decides to elect itself as a cluster head with a probability directly related to its energy level. To avoid collision, a transmission schedule is then established between the cluster head and the nodes in its cluster. Instead of a proactive configuration of the network, our proposal tries to avoid the synchronization problem through a reactive cell formation.

Chevallay, Van Dyck and Hall [1] took a different approach by limiting the number of nodes per cluster (they suggested 8). The cluster heads then form the backbone of the network. The clusters can be merged according to a predefined criterion called *attractiveness* (geographical proximity of the cluster heads). This protocol assumes the existence of node and group identifiers. DCP eliminates the problem of node identifiers using the multi-frequency approach described in the next section.

Krishnan and Starobinski proposed in [3] a node organization based on a growth budget defined by an initiator node (the growth budget corresponds to the number of children a node is allowed to have). Two algorithms for clusters formation are proposed: in the first one, *Algorithm Rapid*, the initiator node sends a message to its neighbors, which, according to the allocated budget, forward this message to their neighbors except the parent node. The process stops when the budget is exhausted. If a node is a leaf node, the allocated budget is wasted. In the second algorithm, *Algorithm Persistent*, a system of reallocation of unutilized budgets was introduced as an improvement of the first algorithm. In our approach, the node acting as initiator node does not have to be aware of the number of existing neighbor nodes.

Zhang and Arora proposed an algorithm for self-organization and self-healing of wireless sensor networks based on a cellular structure [7]. The destination station is defined as the center of the first cell. The algorithm begins by determining the heads of the neighboring cells. The cell heads thus selected run the same algorithm and the process goes on until the discovery of the whole network. Nodes are supposed to be able to detect the locations of other nodes, facilitating the process of self-healing in case of failure of the cell heads. After selection of the cell heads, the remaining nodes decide to join the cell with which the communication is the least energy-consuming (the cell head is the nearest geographically). This scheme and DCP explore the same idea of cell formation but in different ways. Whereas [7] assumes a fixed cellular topology, we propose a dynamic cell creation with the self-election of the cell head at the location where the targeted event takes place.

Some schemes based on the dynamic formation of cells have been recently proposed. However, they often rely on the assumption of the presence of nodes with enhanced capabilities, which are able to assume the role of cluster head [8]. In this paper, we intend to alleviate such constraints by considering the election of what we call *cell coordinators* at close vicinity to the event being monitored without any assumption on their capabilities. In addition, only the nodes with relevant information transmit data to the cell coordinator.

3   Dynamic Cell-Based MAC Protocol (DCP)

DCP is best suited for applications with sporadic data retrievals, such as safety applications (threat detection), surveillance systems or alarm generation. We believe that due to the infrequency of data retrieval operations, triggered by specific localized phenomena, only a limited number of nodes should be involved in the data gathering process. Such localized event does not justify the cost of pre-configuring an entire sensor network. For these applications, dynamic network organization is more suitable than traditional clustering approaches.

The idea underlying DCP is as follows: after detecting a specific event, a node informs its neighbors of its intention to report the results of its sensing operations to the remote destination station. Through this action, it automatically elects itself as the cell coordinator and becomes responsible for organizing data transfers from its neighbors, via a registration process. We devise a transmission schedule among registered nodes based on a time slot scheme. One major advantage of our model is that only the neighbor nodes willing to transmit information to the cell coordinator have to go through the registration process. As the cell coordinator is elected only for one data gathering process, the process of cell formation is repeated every time a node has information to report to the remote destination station.

We assume that the nodes in proximity of each other have correlated and often identical data to send to the destination station. Indeed, the perception of the same event occurring in a localized area will not differ significantly from one sensor node to another. Thus, if a sensor node dies (energy depletion, failure, etc), its loss will not affect the accuracy of the data sent by the surrounding nodes to the destination station.

DCP presents two apparent advantages. First, it is non-cyclic and therefore requires no synchronization. Second, we do not have any loss of bandwidth due to unused time slot because the node organization is dynamic, reactive, and involves only nodes with relevant information to send.

3.1   DCP Design

At any time, upon detection of an external event requiring an immediate report to the destination station, a node can initiate the cell creation process. We adopt a multi-frequency approach with simultaneous registrations to reduce the overhead entailed by node identification. Nodes are identified by the frequency they choose to register on. Moreover, for the implementation of our protocol, we assume that a control frequency f is set before the deployment of the sensor network. The control frequency is used to avoid multiple cell formations at the same time, in the same location. Prior to electing itself as a cell coordinator, a node has to listen to the control channel for a predetermined period of time. If the channel is idle, it then deduces that it can proceed with the cell formation process. A group of frequencies $f_1, \ldots, f_N$ is also set for the registration process.

The data gathering process can be divided into three phases (Figure 1):

1. The self-elected cell coordinator informs its neighbors that it has data to report to the destination station. This information is conveyed to its neighbors via a TR_INFO packet sent on the control frequency (Figure 1 (a)).

2. The nodes located in the cell (range of emission of the cell coordinator) register themselves by replying with a TR_RESP message, if they have information to send. Each node chooses a random frequency among the group specified in the TR_INFO message (Figure 1 (b)). To address the problem of multiple nodes colliding on the same frequency, each node begins its transmission after a random backoff time. During this period, the nodes listen

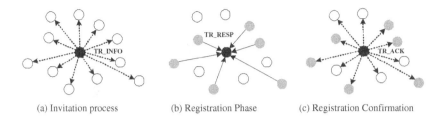

(a) Invitation process	(b) Registration Phase	(c) Registration Confirmation

Fig. 1. Data gathering mechanism

to the chosen channel. If the channel is busy, a node immediately chooses another channel and resumes its waiting period. If the new chosen channel is also busy, the node then considers that the information it wants to transmit is redundant (as a number of other nodes in close vicinity will transmit the same information), and switches to sleep mode.

During the transmission of TR_RESP signals, the cell coordinator scans the range of frequencies to determine which frequency is in use (if a frequency is used, that means that a node wants to register).

3. The cell coordinator builds a list of the frequencies used and sends it back to the nodes in a TR_ACK packet (Figure 1 (c)).

Finally, the registered nodes wait until their allocated time slot to wake up and transmit their data.

3.2   Dimensioning of the Number of Frequencies

In wireless environments, where the number of frequencies available is highly restricted, loss of bandwidth due to data collision is a critical problem that can be partially alleviated by the implementation of collision avoidance mechanisms such as the CSMA/CA MAC protocol. In multi-frequency approaches, further constraints are introduced in that the same frequency should not be allocated to neighboring cells (inter-cell collision) or to neighboring nodes in the same cell (intra-cell collision). Moreover, as the number of frequencies per group and the number of frequency groups directly impact the throughput available for data transmission, a tradeoff has to be made between these two factors.

Inter-cell Collisions. If several nodes elect themselves as cell coordinators in the same geographical area, formation of overlapping cells may occur. Hence, if the same frequency is selected by several neighboring cells, the chance of data collision will increase dramatically. In order to avoid this situation, different frequency groups have to be defined, so that each cell will choose a group different from its neighbors, such as no inter-cell collision occurs. To achieve this objective, we need to determine the exact number of frequency groups needed, which is mainly dependent on the cell distribution in the sensor field. By considering the worst case, illustrated in Figure 2, we can derive an upper bound for the

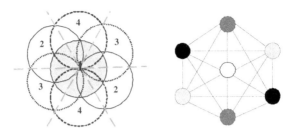

Fig. 2. Overlapping cells - This is similar to the Graph-Coloring problem, where two adjacent cells (graphically represented with a disk) must not transmit on the same frequency band

maximum possible number of adjacent cells and then choose an average number of frequency groups. Actually, by using 4 different frequency bands, it is possible to avoid inter-cell interference.

Some inter-cell collisions may appear during the cell formation (collisions on TR_INFO packets). The use of random backoff time before the transmission of a TR_INFO packet reduces the probability of collision but cannot totally prevent it from happening. One feasible solution is to implement a process of negative acknowledgments. While listening to the control channel, if a node (any node in the cell but the cell coordinator which can not detect a collision while transmitting) detects a collision, it sends on the control channel a busy tone warning the cell coordinators that a collision occurred on the TR_INFO packets. As some nodes may not be aware of the collision, the cell coordinators have to send another busy tone on the control channel to inform every node in the cell that a collision occurred and that a new cell formation process has to be started again.

Intra-cell Collisions. The probability of *intra-cell collision* is defined as the probability of two or more nodes deciding to choose the same frequency for the registration process (we suppose that the choice of a frequency is random).

In the following, we assume that the network density is such that the number of frequencies available will always be greater than the number of nodes willing to register in a specific cell. Let us consider a group of k sensor nodes located geographically in the same cell, $F = \{f_i, i = 1..N\}$ the set of frequencies available for the registration process and $C = \{c_i, i = 1..k\}$ the frequencies selected by the nodes.

The probability of collision can be defined as:

$$P(\text{collision}) = 1 - P(D_{k,N}) \tag{1}$$

where $D_{k,N}$ is the event where k nodes choose k different frequencies among N, such that:

$$D_{k,N} = \bigcap_{i=1}^{k} F_{i,N}$$

where $F_{i,N}$ is the event that node i chooses a frequency different from node j, for all $j < i$, among a group of N frequencies available.

We can then deduce the probability of collision:

$$P(\text{collision}) = 1 - P(F_{k,N}|D_{k-1,N})P(D_{k-1,N})$$

$$P(\text{collision}) = 1 - P(D_{1,N}) \prod_{i=2}^{k} P(F_{i,N}|D_{i-1,N})$$

This probability, dependent on the number of frequencies available N and on the number of nodes willing to register k, can be expressed as:

$$P(\text{collision}) = 1 - \frac{N!}{(N-k)!N^k} \qquad (2)$$

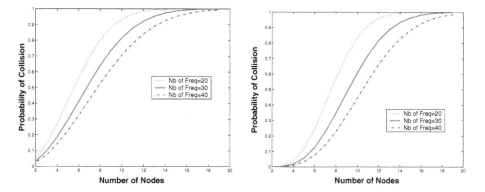

Fig. 3. (a) Probability of collision (b) Probability of collision with the "second chance" mechanism

In Figure 3 (a), by varying the number of frequencies per frequency group, we illustrate the probability of intra-cell collisions based on the number of nodes. We observe that as the number of nodes in a neighborhood increases, regardless of the number of frequencies available for use, the probability of collision tends to unity. To have a probability of collision below 50% with a number of frequencies equal to 30 requires that the number of nodes in a neighborhood be below 6. To relax this constraint, we introduce a "second chance" mechanism. In this scheme, every node (that has information to report) attempts to register itself twice. During the first attempt, if the randomly chosen frequency appears to be busy, the node will randomly choose another frequency and repeat the registration process.

Using the same method as for the previous calculation of the probability of collision, we define the probability of collision when using the "second chance" mechanism as:

$$P(\text{collision}) = P(C_2|C_1)P(C_1)$$

where C_2 is the event where at least one over k nodes experiences a collision during the second round of the registration process and C_1 is the event where at least one over k nodes experiences a collision during the first round of the registration process. Then, an approximation can be derived as:

$$P(\text{collision}) = P(C_2)P(C_1)$$

$$P(\text{collision}) = (1 - P(D_{1,N-1}))\prod_{i=2}^{k}(P(F_{i,N-1}|D_{i-1,N-1})))$$

$$(1 - P(D_{1,N}))\prod_{i=2}^{k}P(F_{i,N}|D_{i-1,N}))$$

This probability of collision, shown in Figure 3 (b), can be expressed as:

$$P(\text{collision}) = (1 - \frac{(N-1)!}{(N-k)!(N-1)^{k-1}})(1 - \frac{N!}{(N-k)!N^k}) \qquad (3)$$

Tradeoff. Let *Scan_Time* denote the time to scan the range of frequencies, *Detect_Time* denote the time to detect energy on a channel, *Hop_Time* denote the time to switch from one frequency to another and N the number of frequencies so that:

$$\text{Scan\_Time} = \text{Detect\_Time} * N + \text{Hop\_Time} * (N - 1)$$

The number of frequencies per group has a direct impact on the scan time, and hence, on the overall registration delay. An under-proportioned number of frequencies would lead to a high level of collisions and a limited number of registered nodes. At the opposite end, an over-proportioned number of frequencies would allow more registration possibilities but a longer registration process.

If we consider 30 frequencies per group and 21 frequency groups (5 times the minimum required plus 1 group for the control channel), the bandwidth available[1] per frequency group becomes:

$$\frac{\text{ISM band}}{\text{Number of Frequency Groups}} = \frac{26}{21} = 1.238\text{MHz}$$

As there is no synchronization between the cells, the probability that two cells would decide to transmit at the same time is negligible. In order for two cells to transmit simultaneously, they must first contend for the control channel and then choose the same frequency group. This scenario happens with a probability of the order of 10^{-6} for an initial contention window of 31.

The local synchronization during data transmission is maintained thanks to the geographical proximity of all the nodes in a cell. Actually, every node in a cell is at most 20m away from the cell coordinator. Upon reception of the TR_ACK

---

[1] We consider the 902-928 MHz Industrial, Scientific and Medical (ISM) band.

packet, the nodes go to sleep and wake up during their allocated time slots. For each time slot, the maximum overlapping period lasts 66ns (propagation time for a distance of 20m at 300000 km/s). Knowing that the precision of a GPS system is around 200ns [9], we can consider that the cell coordinator acts as a beacon and synchronizes all the nodes in the cell by sending first the TR_INFO packet and next the TR_ACK packet.

4   Performance Evaluation

4.1   Energy Consumption Evaluation

We present our analysis and evaluate our framework according to the radio propagation model described in [2]. The energy E_{Tx} to transmit a packet and E_{Rx} to receive a packet can be stated as:

$$E_{Tx} = lE_{elec} + l\epsilon d^2$$

$$E_{Rx} = lE_{elec}$$

where $E_{elec} = 50nJ/bit$, l is the packet size, $\epsilon = 100pJ/bit/m^2$ and d is the transmission distance.

By applying these formulas to our protocol, we obtain:

$$E_{coordinator} = E_{Tx,TR\_INFO} + E_{Tx,TR\_ACK} + NE_{Rx,Scan} \qquad (4)$$
$$E_{non-coordinator} = E_{Rx,TR\_INFO} + E_{Rx,TR\_ACK} + E_{Tx,TR\_RESP}$$

$$E_{non-coordinator} = E_{Rx,TR\_INFO} + E_{Rx,TR\_ACK} + E_{Tx,TR\_RESP}$$

Let us suppose that we have k nodes in the cell and N frequencies available for the registration process, the total energy consumption can thus be expressed as:

$$E_{total} = E_{Tx,TR\_INFO} + E_{Tx,TR\_ACK} + NE_{Rx,Scan} + (k-1)(E_{Rx,TR\_INFO}$$
$$+ E_{Rx,TR\_ACK} + E_{Tx,TR\_RESP})$$

$$E_{total} = (kl_{TR\_INFO} + kl_{TR\_ACK} + (k-1)l_{TR\_RESP} + Nl_{Scan})E_{elec}$$
$$+ (l_{TR\_INFO} + l_{TR\_ACK} + (k-1)l_{TR\_RESP})\epsilon d^2$$

In this analysis, we use a 100x100 meters network, and vary the number of nodes per cell. For simplicity, we consider that the transmission distance can not exceed 20 meters. The area covered by one cell is thus in the order of $1200m^2$. Thus a minimum of 8 simultaneous cells (called clusters) can be formed. We compare three types of network organizations: a single cell, three cells and 8 cells, with varying network density (we suppose a uniform node distribution).

Intuitively, the result obtained is not surprising. The energy saving obtained from a single cell formation (DCP 1 cell) is advantageous when the data retrieval

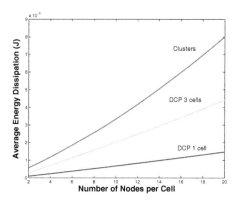

Fig. 4. Energy dissipation evaluation

is infrequent. When considering three cell formations, we can see that the energy consumption increases. But the gain of dynamic cells formations compared to a global network organization is largely dependent on the size of the network (this analysis only considers a very small number of clusters). This model is best adapted for scenarios where the data retrieval is localized and infrequent. As previously mentioned, some real world applications like target tracking exhibit these characteristics. A cell of $1200m^2$ is large enough for such applications. Moreover, the advantage of our model is more apparent in large scale networks.

4.2 Simulation Parameters

We evaluate the performance of our model by simulations using OMNET++ [10], an object-oriented discrete event simulator. We compare our design to a cell formation based on a TDMA scheme without acknowledgment process. The initial schedule is established by contention according to the IEEE 802.11 specifications. For simplicity, we kept the same designation for the name of the packets, even if the packets exchanged in both models are different. In the TDMA approach, TR_INFO packets are composed of a header and a 2-byte cell coordinator identifier. TR_RESP packets also include a header, the cell coordinator identifier and the sender node identifier. TR_ACK packets are composed of a header, the cell coordinator identifier and the list of IDs of the registered nodes.

We set our simulation parameters as follows:

- The time to detect energy on a frequency is set to $Detect\_Time$=15 μs [11].
- The hop time to change from one frequency to another is set to Hop_Time= 224 μs [11].
- We consider only the case of one cell formation.
- DCP is based on a combination of FDMA, TDMA and Direct Sequence Spread Spectrum (to reduce narrowband interference and noise effects) with a nominal data rate fixed at 112kbps.

- For the cell formation process based on TDMA, we consider a Direct Sequence Spread Spectrum over 21 frequency bands of 1.2MHz each[2]. The nominal data rate is fixed at 112kbps.
- Time intervals are set to 15 μs.
- Packet headers are set to 25 bytes.

In DCP, at the beginning of each registration process, the nodes randomly choose a frequency and transmit a busy tone on this frequency after a random backoff time. In the simulations, we set the contention window to 44. Thus, we have 45 time slots (1 time slot=15 μs) for the backoff period, which corresponds to 3 times the average number of neighbor nodes in case of a node density of 0.01 nodes/m^2.

We evaluate our protocol according to two criteria. First, we study the registration delay in order to demonstrate the effectiveness of our scheme for time-sensitive applications such as target detection. Second, we estimate the number of registered nodes, a critical indicator for the accuracy of the sensing operations. In fact, it is necessary to ensure that the number of nodes successfully registered is above a certain threshold (the determination of this threshold is application-dependent).

4.3   Simulation Results

By increasing the number of nodes in a cell, we show that DCP still performs better than the TDMA scheme in terms of delay, while maintaining a high level of node registration rate. We define the *Registration Delay* as the global setup time of the registration process (from sending the TR_INFO packet to the reception of the last TR_ACK packet) and *Number of Nodes* as the total number of nodes in the cell, including the cell coordinator. Hence the maximum number of registered nodes at most equals to the total number of nodes minus 1.

Figure 5(a) depicts the average registration delay as defined previously and the corresponding number of nodes in the cell. The top curve represents the registration delay for the TDMA-based cell formation (referred as Cluster). The simulation is performed over multiple iterations, where the number of nodes in the cell is incremented per iteration. For each iteration, the simulation is repeated 100 times. The registration delay increases almost linearly with the number of nodes. This increase in registration delay corresponds to the time needed to transmit the TR_RESP packet to the cell coordinator. The bottom curve depicts the registration delay for DCP. We only observe a slight increase in the delay corresponding to the increase in the size of the TR_ACK packets (the TR_ACK packets include the ID/frequencies of the registered nodes). DCP performs better than a classic TDMA-based cell formation when the number of nodes in the cell increases above 3 nodes. This result can be explained by

---

[2] The number of orthogonal codes being limited, the occurrence of inter-cells interference can be reduced by the addition of a frequency band division technique, whose description is beyond the scope of this paper.

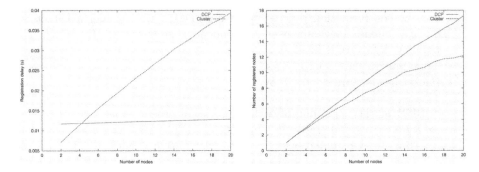

Fig. 5. (a) Average Delay (b) Average number of registered nodes

the implementation of the scanning process in DCP, which involves a minimum registration delay that is rapidly amortized when the number of neighbors is above 2.

Figure 5(b) depicts the average number of registered nodes, as well as the total number of nodes in the cell. The top curve represents the average number of registered nodes for the DCP model. Similar to the above case, we run the simulations 100 times and compute the average. The bottom curve represents the average number of registered nodes for a cluster formation without acknowledgment process. The "second chance" mechanism implemented in our protocol allows the nodes two attempts to register and accounts for the performance gain over the cluster formation.

In order to analyze the efficiency of our protocol, we implemented a cluster of 15 nodes, and ran the simulation for 200 iterations. We only consider the registration process without data transmission. The results of the simulations are summarized in Table 1 and in Table 2.

The analysis of the standard deviation for the registration delay and for the number of registered nodes gives insights on the stability of both protocols. DCP appears to be much more stable than the TDMA scheme, and performs significantly better in terms of number of registered nodes and registration delay. This is due to the fact that the fluctuations of the TDMA scheme are directly corre-

Table 1. Analysis of the TDMA scheme behaviour over a large number of simulation runs for 15 nodes per cell

	Number of Registered Nodes	Registration Delay (ms)
Mean	10.285	31.751185
Maximum	14	35.986
Minimum	5	26.086
Standard Deviation	2.21547209	2.466758021
95% Confidence Interval	0.307042937	0.341868729
99% Confidence Interval	0.403523385	0.449292298

Table 2. Analysis of DCP behaviour over a large number of simulation runs for 15 nodes per cell

	Number of Registered Nodes	Registration Delay (ms)
Mean	13.395	12.579045
Maximum	14	12.622
Minimum	10	12.338
Standard Deviation	0.756197177	0.05369
95% Confidence Interval	0.104801592	0.007440913
99% Confidence Interval	0.137732832	0.009779031

lated to the number of collisions that occurred during the registration process. For DCP, the slight fluctuations are due to the number of unregistered nodes (decreasing the size of the TR_ACK packet). Concerning the number of registered nodes, our model guarantees a better performance compared to a classic cluster formation. The minimum number of registered nodes for a cell of 15 nodes (including the cell coordinator) is 10 for DCP, whereas for the cluster formation this number drops to 5. The 95% and 99% confidence intervals illustrate the improvement of DCP over the TDMA scheme.

Overall, DCP performs better than the TDMA scheme both in terms of registered nodes and in terms of delay, particularly when the number of nodes in the network increases. More precisely, our protocol initially outperforms the cluster formation approach based on a TDMA scheme. This performance gain wanes over time, because the performance of cluster formation is amortized over several rounds. The advantage of our model is the dynamic and rapid cell formation.

5   Conclusion

Given that some applications need only infrequent sensing operations, we proposed a MAC protocol based on the creation of cells in the vicinity of the targeted event. The proposed Dynamic Cell-based MAC Protocol adopts a reactive approach, with a data gathering process that is triggered by the detection of a specific stimulus requiring an immediate report to the destination station. The advantages of our protocol are to reduce bandwidth loss due to unused time slots in TDMA schemes and to provide a faster cell formation while avoiding data collisions. At the same time, our multi-frequency approach does not require node identification. Moreover, no global synchronization is necessary because the cell coordinator is used as a beacon node to organize the data transmission process.

The preliminary analysis of energy consumption gives an estimate of the amount of energy dissipation during the cell formation process and supports the theory that if the data retrieval is localized and infrequent, a complete network organization is expensive. The results of the conducted simulations show that DCP performs better than traditional TDMA approaches in terms of delays and collisions reduction. The sending of tones on a frequency range during the registration process reduces the overall delay and decreases packet header size by avoiding the exchange of node identification.

References

1. Chevallay, C., Dyck, R.V., Hall, T.: Self-organization protocols for wireless sensor networks. In: Conference on Information Sciences and Systems. (2002)
2. Heinzelman, W., Chandrakasan, A., Balakrishnan, H.: An application-specific protocol architecture for wireless microsensor networks. In: IEEE Transactions on Wireless Communications. Volume 1. (2002) 660–670
3. Krishnan, R., Starobinski, D.: Message-efficient self-organization of wireless sensor networks. In: IEEE Wireless Communications and Networking Conference. (2003)
4. Mirkovic, J., Venkataramani, G., Lu, S., Zhang, L.: A self-organizing approach to data forwarding in large-scale sensor networks. In: IEEE International Conference on Communications. ICC 2001. Volume 5. (2001) 1357 –1361
5. Lindsey, S., Sivalingam, K.: Data gathering algorithms in sensor networks using energy metrics. IEEE Transactions on Parallel and Distributed Systems **13** (2002) 924–935
6. Catterall, E., Laerhoven, K.V., Strohbach, M.: Self-organization in ad hoc sensor networks: an empirical study. (2002) http://www.comp.lancs.ac.uk/ strohbach/.
7. Zhang, H., Arora, A.: GS3: scalable self-configuration and self-healing in wireless networks. In: Proceedings of the twenty-first annual symposium on Principles of distributed computing. (2002)
8. Chen, W.P., Hou, J., Sha, L.: Dynamic clustering for acoustic target tracking in wireless sensor networks. In: 11th IEEE International Conference on Network Protocols. (2003) 284 – 294
9. Elson, J., Estrin, D.: Time synchronization for wireless sensor networks. In: Proceedings of the 15th International Parallel and Distributed Processing Symposium., IEEE (2001) 1965–1970
10. OMNET++ simulator: ("http://whale.hit.bme.hu/omnetpp/")
11. IEEE Std 802.11 Information Technology- telecommunications And Information exchange Between Systems-Local And Metropolitan Area Networks-specific Requirements-part 11: Wireless Lan Medium Access Control (MAC) And Physical Layer (PHY) Specifications: (1997)

Reliable Collaborative Decision Making
in Mobile Ad Hoc Networks

Theodore L. Willke[1,2] and Nicholas F. Maxemchuk[1]

[1] Columbia University, Dept. of Electrical Engineering
1312 S.W. Mudd, 500 West 120th Street, New York, NY 10027
tlw24@columbia.edu, nick@ee.columbia.edu
[2] Intel Corporation, Enterprise Platforms Group
2800 Center Drive, M/S DP3-307, DuPont, WA 98327
theodore.l.willke@intel.com

Abstract. Mobile units, such as vehicles in a traffic flow or robots in a factory, may use sensors to interact with their environment and a radio to communicate with other autonomous units in the local area. Collaborative decision making can be carried out through information sharing amongst these units and result in cooperative problem solving. Examples of solutions include coordinated vehicle control for collision avoidance and executing complementary path plans for robots on a factory floor. We propose an application-level protocol that enables units to contribute their local knowledge and actions to a shared global view of the problem space. The protocol uses a time-driven token ring architecture to permit any unit to reliably broadcast a message to the entire group. The protocol ensures that all units commit the same set of received messages in the same order by a deadline, and it upholds these guarantees in the presence of channel failures, hidden units, and a changing set of collaborators. Units in the network are made aware of when others fail to maintain the global view. Failing units may be required to operate autonomously, pending information recovery.

1 Introduction

The growing ubiquity of both mobile computing and wireless networking will motivate new applications for this technology, including cooperative problem solving. Mobile units, such as vehicles in a traffic flow, tanks on a battleground, or robots in a factory, may be equipped with sensors to interact with their local environment, a radio to share information with other autonomous units in the immediate area, and a computer to execute a program. These resources enable the units to collaborate in the collection and dissemination of environmental information that can be used to make decisions that ultimately result in a single coherent solution to a problem. Examples of solutions include coordinated vehicle control for collision avoidance and computing non-intersecting trajectories for robots on a factory floor.

Units are enabled to act coherently and achieve common goals if they use a communication protocol that permits their local knowledge and actions to contribute to a shared global view of the problem space. Units may either carry out local, decentralized decisions or be directed by one or more units making centralized decisions. In the former case, the global view supports local decision making so that globally-optimal behavior results. In the latter case, the global view permits any unit to take the role of decision maker if communication with a centralized resource is lost. Both approaches

J. Vicente and D. Hutchison (Eds.): MMNS 2004, LNCS 3271, pp. 88–101, 2004.
© IFIP International Federation for Information Processing 2004

must contend with an environment where communication channel limitations and unit failures can result in a continuously changing set of collaborating units.

We propose an application-level protocol, the Mobile Reliable Broadcast Protocol (M-RBP), that is particularly well-suited to collaborative decision making in this environment. The protocol permits any unit to reliably send a message to every other unit in the group and is time-driven to ensure that all units commit the same set of received messages in the same message order by a maximum delay following initial message acknowledgement; this enables the global view to be kept up-to-date in a timely fashion. Units also learn when they have lost the global view and may be required to operate autonomously using a different, more conservative set of assumptions until sufficient information is recovered. Other units in the group are made aware of these failures and can react appropriately.

The remainder of this paper is organized as follows. The scope of the network considered is described in Section 2. Section 3 introduces the architecture of M-RBP and its operation. Section 4 presents a comparison of M-RBP with other existing reliable broadcast and multicast protocols for this application. Section 5 briefly discusses protocol scalability and performance tradeoffs, and Section 6 concludes the paper.

2   Scope of the Networking Problem

Figure 1 is an example of the scope of networking that we will address for collaborative decision making. A number of mobile units (e.g., *a* through *f*) are collaborating in a localized geophysical region, or LAN. Some units may be within direct communication range of all other units, while others may separated (i.e., hidden) from each other by greater than one hop distance and need to rely on neighboring units to relay information (e.g., *a* to *c*, *e*, or *f*). The relaying of information may also be required when an obstruction prevents direct communication between units (e.g., *d* and *e*).

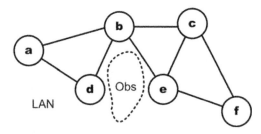

Fig. 1. Scope of the collaborative decision making network.

Our protocol provides delivery guarantees for broadcast transmissions from any of the units to the rest of the group. Some of the guarantees, such as maximum delay, scale with the network hop diameter and number of units. Although this protocol will function properly on larger multi-hop networks, it is best suited to implementations in which most units can directly communicate with one another. Providing a global view for the group remains difficult, even for small-diameter networks, due to a changing set of collaborators and the unreliability of wireless network connectivity.

3 M-RBP Architecture

M-RBP is an application-layer protocol that accepts data from user applications and transmits it using the IP broadcast address. We assume a networking stack consisting of UDP/IP services and an IEEE 802.11 MAC and PHY design [1] with the distributed coordination function. This medium provides physical signaling, a broadcast addressing scheme, and carrier sensing with collision avoidance. It does not provide a request-to-send, clear-to-send handshake or a data transfer acknowledgement.

Mobile units that share the global view participate in a token ring protocol. Previous work on token ring protocols for reliable broadcast and multicast focused on wired network implementations [2], [3], [4]. Figure 2 is an illustration adapted from the Reliable Broadcast Protocol [4] of a token ring comprised of receivers in a broadcast group. In our application, n mobile units can serve as both message sources and receivers. Sources transmit messages at will into the medium, with an identification of the source unit, s, and a source-specific sequence number, M_s. M_s is incremented for each unique broadcast message so that duplicate transmissions may be identified.

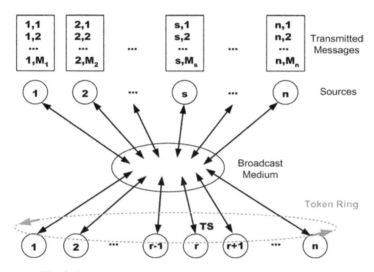

Fig. 2. Receivers in the broadcast group belong to a token ring.

A token is passed amongst the units in the receiver group on a timed schedule. The receiver with the token is referred to as the token site, and it is responsible for acknowledging any source messages received from the source unit, s, while in possession of the token, as well as some additional messages described in Section 3.5. The token site acknowledges messages using a single bulk acknowledgement (ACK) that references the messages and assigns them a relative sequence order. Sources retransmit messages until they receive an acknowledgement from a token site. Units that do not receive the token site's ACK shortly after its scheduled transmission time are permitted to broadcast a retransmission request. Units that receive the ACK broadcast a negative acknowledgement (NACK) for any messages that they are missing. The NACK is repeated until a peer services the retransmission request or other criteria described in Section 3.3 is met. Broadcast retransmissions include the original message identifier (s, M_s) and the retransmitter's source identifier; this prevents retransmissions from being mistaken for transmissions from the message source.

On a timed schedule, the group collectively determines what ACKs to use for global message ordering and what messages should be committed. By a specific deadline, all surviving units learn what messages are committed by their peers.

In the following sections, we describe aspects of the protocol in more detail.

3.1 Implicit Time-Based Token Passing

The token site is responsible for acknowledging messages and initiating global sequencing. In several token ring protocols [2], [3], [4], an explicit handshake is used to: 1) acknowledge source messages, 2) confirm acceptance of the token from the previous token site, and 3) request transfer of the token to the next token site, as shown in Figure 3. This approach prevents continuous circulation of the token in the presence of frequent unit and communication failures because, in these cases, the required handshake may not transpire.

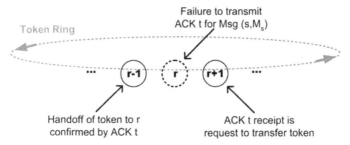

Fig. 3. Explicit ACK handshake used by many token ring protocols. If the token site, r, fails then the token ceases to circulate until the ring completes a lengthy repair process [2].

M-RBP, by contrast, uses a token that is passed based on time, without further qualification. Each receiver holds the token for a duration of Δ_T seconds in a time slot specified by a token passing list (TPL) and is expected to transmit a single ACK at the end of its assigned token passing interval. In addition to its role in message acknowledgement, the ACK is used to indicate continued participation of the acknowledging unit and enables each receiver, through an algorithm described in Section 3.2, to keep identical, and perform the same maintenance on, local copies of the TPL. Because no explicit handshake is required to pass the token, the communication with the token site may fail without disrupting token circulation. Relative synchronization of units is required, but is not addressed in this work.

3.2 Maintaining the Token Ring Using a Distributed Time-Driven Algorithm

A unit can infer that a token site has failed if its scheduled ACK broadcast is not recovered by a deadline. Individual units, however, may disagree on the failure, depending on how successful their own recovery efforts are. Units could use a gossip protocol [5], [6] to spread the ACK or the token site could require positive acknowledgement of its ACK by every other unit in the group, but these approaches would only provide highly probable agreement by a deadline. We have devised a distributed time-driven token ring repair process that ensures agreement by a deadline.

A conceptual timeline for the ring repair process is shown in Figure 4. Since all units have a copy of the TPL and can identify when a specific unit is scheduled to transmit its ACK as the token site, they all know when to expect the ACK and can begin attempting recovery (described below) shortly thereafter. Each unit that does not recover the ACK by a deadline assumes the token site has failed. After making a determination, each unit in the group broadcasts a "yes" or "no" vote to drop the unit in question. All units attempt to recover as many of these votes from peers as possible and, at a prescheduled deadline, they each attempt to determine a group consensus using an agreement function. The consensus will either be to take no action or to remove the unit from the TPL. If the unit is removed, its TPL entry is deleted and the entries below are shifted up to fill the void.

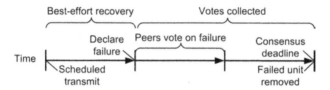

Fig. 4. Timeline for the time-driven distributed token ring repair process.

In M-RBP, the votes are transmitted in ACK messages to minimize control overhead. The relationship between scheduled ACKs and the votes they carry is shown in Figure 5. A token site is assigned a time slot of Δ_T seconds based on its offset in the TPL. The offset numbers are shown on the x-axis, with token round x having m_x slots. As shown on the y-axis, each token site transmits an ACK with a sequence number j at the end of its time slot. The set of scheduled ACK transmissions is delineated by the *solid line* on the chart. The units attempt to recover each ACK using a time-driven process involving k iterations, each of length Δ_k. The parameters for the process are chosen so as to guarantee a high probability of ACK recovery by the final iteration. The recovery period for each ACK is shown by the *gray band* in the chart, the end of which is delineated by a *dashed line*. Each unit that did not receive an ACK by the end of its recovery phase indicates this by including a drop field in its next ACK transmission that references the source and sequence number of the missing ACK (a vote against unit removal is implied by the absence of this field). In the example shown in Figure 5, the votes applying to the ACK transmitted by unit a, at the position labeled 1, are transmitted by peers in subsequent ACKs with sequence numbers j_3 through j_4.

Because each peer transmits its ACK, including votes, only once per token ring cycle, each ACK carries votes pertaining to all ACKs that reached the end of the recovery phase in the last token ring cycle. For example, the ACK transmitted by unit b at the position labeled 2 includes votes relevant to ACKs with sequence numbers j_1 through j_2.

When all of the ACKs associated with a particular vote (e.g., the range labeled 1 and associated with the ACK transmitted by unit a) have themselves completed their recovery phase, the group decides on whether to take action and remove the respec-

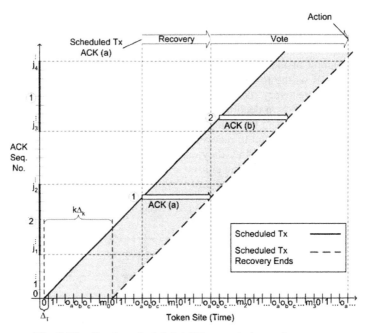

Fig. 5. Timeline for scheduled ACK transmission and recovery.

tive unit from the TPL. If all units take the same action at this point in time, their TPLs will be adjusted in the same manner and time slot reassignment can take place to fill in the vacant slot. However, attaining unanimous agreement is complicated by the fact that each unit may recover a different subset of the ACKs associated with a particular vote.

The units ensure unanimous agreement on TPL changes through the use of a majority agreement function that returns one of three possible values. If a unit recovers a sufficient number of ACKs to determine that the group consensus is "yes" or "no" on an action, the function returns a value of Y or N, respectively. If a unit fails to recover enough ACKs to determine the group consensus, the function returns a value of U for "unknown". In this case, the unit must forfeit its time slot in the token ring until it has rejoined the token ring with a new time slot assignment (see Section 3.4).

To make a decision based on a majority, each unit must determine that either greater than 50% of the expected vote transmissions, V, are "yes" votes or at least 50% of the transmissions are "no" votes. The total number of votes received by each unit is less than or equal to the number transmitted because some of the units may not transmit a vote (e.g., due to failure) and some votes may not reach a particular unit by the time the consensus deadline is reached. Given that unit i recovers Y_i "yes" votes and N_i "no" votes, the tri-valued function F is expressed as:

$$F(Y_i, N_i, V) = \begin{cases} Y & \text{if } Y_i > \left\lceil \dfrac{V}{2} \right\rceil \\ N & \text{if } N_i \geq \left\lceil \dfrac{V}{2} \right\rceil \\ U & o.w. \end{cases} \qquad (1)$$

We have chosen to use threshold values that require either a majority of "yes" votes or a majority of "no votes to be recovered to determine group consensus with certainty. Our choice minimizes the maximum number of "yes" or "no" votes that a unit must recover in order to avoid an "unknown" determination. Other threshold choices may better maximize a unit's probability of survival, especially if the selection is based on estimated probabilities of receiving a "yes" vote or a "no" vote. In any case, the thresholds chosen must guarantee a mutually-exclusive "yes" or "no" determination by F, no matter how many votes an individual unit successfully recovers. This can be accomplished by ensuring that the following holds for the choice "yes" and "no" thresholds, T_Y and T_N:

$$T_y + T_N \geq V + 1 \, , \tag{2}$$

In summary, by using F to determine the voting consensus and by acting in accordance with the consensus at the prescribed deadline, all units remaining in the token ring maintain identical copies of the TPL.

3.3   Reliable and Consistent Messaging with a Delay Guarantee

The distributed protocol used to maintain each unit's TPL can also be used to provide reliable and consistent message delivery between all sources and receivers. For real-time collaborative decision making, we desire to provide: 1) global sequencing of messages; 2) consistent commitment of messages across the group of receivers; and 3) notification of message commitment between each unit and its peers. Because the protocol provides units with a concept of time and units take action on a schedule, we can offer reliable and consistent message delivery with a delay guarantee.

A typical approach to defining the probability of reliable message delivery, $P_r(t)$, is to state that it monotonically increases to a value sufficient to meet application requirements at some time τ following a number of retransmission attempts, as shown in Figure 6. We desire a definition of reliability that is more suited to a continuously changing receiver set and that offers a specific reliability guarantee at a deadline. To this end, we pursue a guarantee that a receiver remaining in contact with its peers and participating in the token ring protocol for $> \tau_1$ seconds after a message is initially acknowledged will commit that message if the group reaches a consensus to do so. Furthermore, if the receiver remains in the group for $> \tau_2$ seconds, where $\tau_2 > \tau_1$, its peers can verify that it has committed the message.

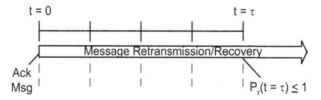

Fig. 6. Typical reliability guarantee.

The timeline for providing the new reliability guarantee is shown in Figure 7. The timeline starts at time t with acknowledgement of message (s, M_s) by scheduled

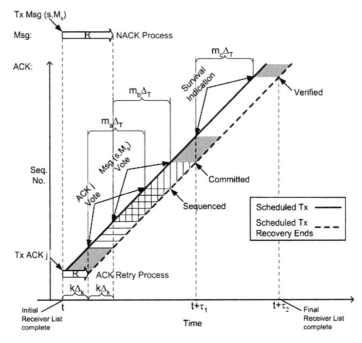

Fig. 7. Time-driven process for global message ordering, commitment, and delivery confirmation.

ACK j. The process proceeds in three phases, with each phase involving information recovery followed by a group consensus vote on the success of the recovery. Since the token ring length may increase or decrease by one unit each Δ_T, the number of expected votes associated with each phase is labeled uniquely as m_a, m_b, and m_c. A unit that cannot determine the voting consensus for any vote must relinquish its place on the TPL.

The first phase of the process involves recovery of the scheduled ACK j that acknowledges the source message of interest, in this case message (s, M_s). Since the ACK is also used to infer the token site's continued operation, the first vote both determines whether the associated token site is considered operational and whether the ACK will be used for message sequencing.

Some messages referenced by dropped ACKs may never be referenced again by future ACKs. These may be discarded $> \tau_1$ seconds after their reception without concern that they need be committed.

The second phase involves message recovery. Units that successfully recover the ACK attempt to recover the associated message(s) until one of the following events occur: 1) the message is recovered; 2) the group reaches a consensus to not use the ACK; or 3) the deadline for message recovery is reached. The deadline for message recovery follows the deadline for ACK recovery by $k \cdot \Delta_k$ seconds. At the deadline for message recovery, each unit that recovered ACK j, but not message (s, M_s), conveys this in its next scheduled ACK transmission by voting to drop (s, M_s). In general, the ACK may indicate that one or more messages be dropped in a variable-length field. If the voting unit did not recover ACK j, it votes generically to drop all messages referenced by the ACK. Message reception is implied for all messages referenced in ACK j that are not listed in the drop field of the ACK used in the vote. If a majority verifies message reception, the message is committed. If the majority votes to drop the message, it is discarded.

In the third phase, ACK recovery is used to determine the set of receivers that survived to commit the message. A unit determines that a peer has survived to receive the message if the peer transmits its scheduled ACK in the token round starting at $t+\tau_1$. If the unit either directly receives the peer's ACK or if any other peer indicates that it received the peer's ACK via a vote, then the peer in question survived to commit the message. A unit can verify the set of peers that received the message by applying this test to each peer in the TPL after time $t + \tau_1$. This verification is complete no later than time $t + \tau_2$. τ_1 and τ_2 are a deterministic function of the number of units in the group during several token ring cycles as well as a few protocol time constants.

This three-step process ensures that every unit that continues to collaborate in decision making has committed a message within, at most, three recovery periods and one token ring cycle of when it was initially acknowledged and that every unit knows what peers have committed the message within, at most, four recovery periods and two token ring cycles.

3.4 Join Requests

Units that intend to join the ring for the first time, or that were dropped and want to rejoin, must transmit a source message with a Join Request field. The token site that acknowledges this message will respond with an ACK that includes a copy of the TPL and protocol parameters. The unit is neither admitted to the token ring, nor does it begin sharing the global view, until its source message is committed by the group. The new unit is assigned the TPL entry corresponding to the first token passing interval that begins after the time of message commitment.

The unit must be ready to participate in the ring repair process as soon as it is added to the TPL. Therefore, it must begin to recover ACKs and monitor vote outcomes as soon as its message is acknowledged. Since all transmissions, scheduled or not, include source identifiers, the unit can maintain an updated list of one-hop neighbors. It may transmit unicast ACK Retry messages to these neighbors in a round-robin fashion each Δ_k seconds. The addressed neighbor may service the request by retransmitting it or, if the requested ACK was dropped by the group, respond with a unicast ACK that includes a drop field for the requested ACK. Changes to the TPL are inferred through the ACK history.

Units that are rejoining the group after being recently dropped and that desire to maintain a continuous global view must, in addition, request missing source messages via unicast NACK messages. The addressed neighbor may service the request with a message retransmission or respond with a unicast ACK that includes a drop field for the requested message(s).

3.5 Dealing with Hidden Units

The presence of hidden units challenges the delivery of messages to receivers hidden from a source and the acknowledgement of messages when the token site is hidden from a source. To solve these problems, ACK and source message retransmission requests are serviced by nearest-neighbor peers using a time-based recruitment process.

During the recovery window for a particular ACK, the units on the TPL are progressively recruited to service retransmission requests for the ACK and to request its retransmission themselves. The recruitment starts with the unit on the TPL that was originally scheduled to transmit the ACK and continues until the entire TPL is recruited. The number of units recruited per iteration may adhere to any number of profiles. For example, one strategy may be to exponentially recruit units until the entire TPL is recruited, so that a total of 2^j units are recruited $j \cdot \Delta_k$ seconds following the scheduled time of the ACK transmission. Another strategy would be to recruit one unit in the first iteration and all remaining units in the second iteration. In any case, the process halts when some k, where $k > j$, number of recovery iterations of length Δ_k have occurred. This mechanism grants all units an opportunity to service and request ACK retransmissions while lowering initial contention for the broadcast medium. Carrier sensing and collision avoidance is the MAC layer's responsibility and is outside the scope of this research.

Source message retransmissions, driven by NACKs, use the same mechanism, with the only difference being when the recovery window starts, and completes (see Figure 7). The recruitment process for message retransmissions begins when the ACK recovery process completes, and continues for a period of $k \cdot \Delta_k$ seconds. The process is executed independently for each source message, and starts with the unit that originally acknowledged the message.

An example of message recovery between units hidden from one another is shown in Figure 8. All four of the units shown participate in the token ring, and unit 3 is the token site when unit 4 transmits message $(4, M_1)$. The message is received by units 2 and 3. Unit 3 acknowledges message $(4, M_1)$ with ACK Y. A specified delay after the scheduled transmission of ACK Y, unit 1 realizes that it missed the transmission and repeatedly transmits a retry for ACK Y. This retry is eventually received by unit 2, which services the retry by transmitting the ACK. Unit 1 then repeatedly transmits a NACK for $(4, M_1)$. This NACK is eventually received by unit 2, which services the NACK by retransmitting the source message.

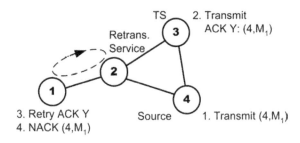

Fig. 8. ACK and source message recovery for hidden units.

Another problem that arises with hidden units is that a source transmitting a message may be hidden from the token site. To deal with this, the source retransmits the message at regular intervals of Δ_T seconds until it receives an ACK that references the message. The ACK may be either a scheduled ACK transmitted by a token site or an unscheduled ACK transmitted by any unit within one hop. Units other than the token site may be recruited to respond to the transmission if it is repeated one or more times. The neighbors are recruited in growing numbers (e.g., exponentially) according to their relative offset in the TPL from the unit that was token site during the original message transmission. Unscheduled ACKs (i.e., those not transmitted by the token site) do not have an ACK sequence number and are not used for message ordering; they simply inform the source that the message will be acknowledged later when the responding unit becomes the token site.

3.6 Global Message Ordering

As described previously, each ACK includes a sequence number j, indicating that it was transmitted at scheduled time $t_j = j{\cdot}\Delta_T$. ACK j assigns each message received, identified by the label (s, M_s), the relative sequence number k. Messages that were either acknowledged by a unit during the previous token round using an unscheduled acknowledgement, or received during its token passing interval, are assigned relative sequence numbers $k = 1, 2, ...$ in the order received. The 2-tuple (j, k) is used to assign message (s, M_s) a global order.

The received messages associated with ACK j are not assigned a global sequence number until all messages associated with ACK i, for $\forall i < j$, are sequenced. Duplicate references to message (s, M_s) may arise because sources can retransmit messages and because messages may reach units after a variable amount of propagation delay. To resolve this, all units commit messages according to the ACK with the lowest sequence number that references the message, and discard duplicate references. Then, the remaining messages associated with ACK j are ordered by increasing, not necessarily contiguous, relative sequence number k. This procedure results in the same message sequencing in all units that received the same acknowledgements.

4 Attributes of M-RBP

Token ring protocols have been studied for application to mobile ad hoc networks (MANETs) [7], [8]. The work described in [7] is limited to the study of several algorithms that permit a token to circulate amongst all members of a graph. WTRP [8] was developed for communication between unmanned vehicles. To provide bandwidth guarantees, each source is only permitted to transmit source messages in a time slot assigned by its position in the token ring. WTRP does not support mechanisms for reliable message delivery.

Numerous reliable broadcast and multicast protocols have been proposed for MANETs that do not use token rings [5], [6], [9], [10], [11], [12], and cannot provide global message ordering for many-to-many communication in multi-hop networks. These protocols are compared with M-RBP in Table 1, where attributes important for the support of collaborative decision making in a MANET are listed. None of these protocols were specifically developed for this application, and they all lack support for either message delivery confirmation with the source, or peer retransmission service. Furthermore, the gossip-based protocols, which do provide peer retransmission service, provide relatively weak reliability guarantees due to their probabilistic nature.

Because M-RBP was specifically developed to support collaborative decision making, it possesses all of the desirable characteristics.

Table 1. A comparison of M-RBP with other reliable broadcast and multicast protocols. Support of attributes that enable collaborative decision making in a MANET is indicated.

Protocol Class	Scheme	Support Many-to-Many[1]	Peer Service[2]	ACK-Based Delivery[3]	Confirm Delivery w/ Source	Global Ordering[4]
MAC	BMW w/ ODMRP [9]	✓	✓	✓		
Source Service	RALM [10]	✓		✓	On retry	
	RMA [11]	✓		✓	✓	
Hierarchical Service	FAT [12]	In omni mode	✓	✓		
Gossip Service	AG [5]	✓	✓			
	RDG [6]	✓	✓			
Time-Driven Token	M-RBP	✓	✓	✓	✓	✓

[1] Assuming a single instance of the protocol on each unit.
[2] Information may be recovered from any peer, even if source fails.
[3] Retry until positive acknowledgement.
[4] For many-to-many broadcast or multicast.

5 Comments on M-RBP Performance

Units that fail to recover ACKs and messages used in the global view are temporarily removed from the token ring. Therefore, the more effectively units recover information, the more likely they are to remain participating members of the group. As previously discussed, hidden units recover information using time-based retransmission protocols. Using a larger iteration interval, Δ_k, in these protocols provides units with more time to retransmit information and deal with congestion. However, the delay guarantees, τ_1 and τ_2, relax as Δ_k increases. This trade-off between delay guarantees and probability of unit failure will be analyzed in future work using the QualNet simulator [13].

The number of iterations, k, required of the time-based recovery processes has not yet been discussed. Independent of the profile used to qualify units to retry, or service retransmissions (e.g., one unit in the first iteration and all remaining units in the second iteration, exponential unit recruitment, etc.), the worst-case number of iterations occurs when: 1) all units, other than the token site, did not receive the original transmission, 2) the last unit permitted to retry is the only 1-hop neighbor of the token site, and 3) the network diameter is maximal, given the number of units (i.e., m - 1).

A worst-case network topology is illustrated in Figure 9. In this example, unit 1 is required to recover information from unit m by the end of the recovery period.

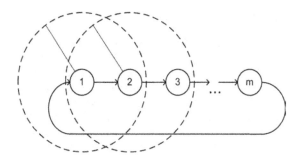

Fig. 9. Worst-case network topology (token ring shown) for a recovery process.

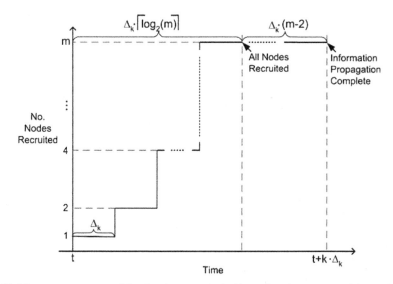

Fig. 10. Worst-case recovery delay for the scenario in Figure 9, using exponential recruitment.

The worst-case recovery process delay for the network depicted in Figure 9 using an exponential unit recruitment example is depicted in Figure 10. For this example and m units, the maximum number of iterations, k, required is:

$$k = \lceil \log_2 m \rceil + m - 2 . \tag{3}$$

In contrast, for a recruitment policy of a single unit in the first iteration and all units in the second, the relationship between iterations required and unit count is simply $k = m$. However, with this policy, medium contention may increase.

As an example of ACK recovery using the described network and exponential unit recruitment process, if $m = 9$ and unit 9 is the token site, it takes 11 iterations of the recovery process for unit 1 to recover unit 9's ACK. Thus, recovery is complete $11 \cdot \Delta_k$ after the scheduled transmission of the ACK, if the network remains connected.

6 Concluding Remarks

In this paper, we have discussed the problem of collaborative decision making in a mobile ad hoc networking environment. We have introduced an application-level protocol, the Mobile Reliable Broadcast Protocol, that provides the services necessary for collaborating mobile units to construct and share a real-time global view of the problem space, despite the potential for communication failures, a continuously-changing set of collaborators, and units that are hidden from one another. To the best of our knowledge, this support is not offered by any other existing protocol.

M-RBP uses a time-based token ring protocol to provide specific reliability and delay guarantees for source message commitment, something that is difficult, if not impossible, to accomplish with an event-driven protocol. It was shown that the delay guarantees provided can be tuned to alter the scalability of the protocol. It was also shown how novel time-based decision processes incorporated into M-RBP enable collaborating units to globally commit and order messages.

References

1. IEEE Standard for Wireless LAN Medium Access Control (MAC) and Physical Layer (PHY) Specifications, P802.11, (1999)
2. Chang, J.-M., Maxemchuk, N.F., Reliable Broadcast Protocols, ACM Trans. Comp. Sys., vol. 2, no. 3, (1984) 251-73
3. Maxemchuk, N.F., Shur, D., An Internet Multicast System for the Stock Market, ACM Trans. Comp. Sys., vol. 19, no. 3, (2001) 384-412
4. Maxemchuk, N.F., Reliable Multicast with Delay Guarantees, IEEE Comm. Mag., vol. 40, no. 9, (2002) 96-102
5. Chandra, R., Ramasubramanian, V., Birman, K., Anonymous Gossip: Improving Multicast Reliability in Mobile Ad-Hoc Networks, Proc. IEEE ICDCS, (2001) 275-283
6. Luo, J., Eugster, P. Th., Hubaux, J.-P. , Route Driven Gossip: Probabilistic Reliable Multicast in Ad Hoc Networks, IEEE Proc. INFOCOM, (2003) 2229-2239
7. Malpani, N., Chen, Y., Vaidya, N.H., Welch, J.L., Distributed Token Circulation on Mobile Ad Hoc Networks, to appear in IEEE Trans. Mobile Computing, (2004)
8. Lee, D., Attias, R., Sengupta, R., Tripakas, S., A Wireless Token Ring Protocol for Ad-Hoc Networks, Proc. IEEE Aerospace Conf., (2002)
9. Tang, K., Gerla, M., MAC Reliable Broadcast in Ad Hoc Networks, IEEE MILCOM, (2001) 1008-1012
10. Tang, K., Obraczka, K., Lee, S.-J., Gerla, M., Reliable Adaptive Lightweight Multicast Protocol, Proc. IEEE Intl. Conf. on Comm., vol. 2, (2003) 1054-1058
11. Gopalsamy, T., Singhal, M., Panda, D., Sadayappan, P., A Reliable Multicast Algorithm for Mobile Ad Hoc Networks, Proc. ICDCS, (2002) 563-570
12. Liao, W., Jiang, M.-Y., Family ACK Tree (FAT): Supporting Reliable Multicast in Mobile Ad Hoc Networks, IEEE Trans. Veh. Tech., vol. 52, no. 6, (2003) 1675-1685
13. QualNet User's Manual, version 3.6, Scalable Network Technologies, Inc., (2003)

Minimum-Cost Multicast Routing
for Multi-layered Multimedia Distribution

Hsu-Chen Cheng and Frank Yeong-Sung Lin

Department of Information Management, National Taiwan University
50, Lane 144, Keelung Rd., Sec.4, Taipei, Taiwan, R.O.C.
{d7725002,yslin}@im.ntu.edu.tw

Abstract. In this paper, we attempt to solve the problem of min-cost multicast routing for multi-layered multimedia distribution. More specifically, for (i) a given network topology (ii) the destinations of a multicast group and (iii) the bandwidth requirement of each destination, we attempt to find a feasible routing solution to minimize the cost of a multicast tree for multi-layered multimedia distribution. This problem has been proved to be NP-hard. We propose two adjustment procedures, namely: the tie breaking procedure and the drop-and-add procedure to enhance the solution quality of the modified T-M heuristic. We also formally model this problem as an optimization problem and apply the Lagrangean relaxation method and the subgradient method to solve the problem. Computational experiments are performed on regular networks, random networks, and scale-free networks. According to the experiment results, the Lagrangean based heuristic can achieve up to 23.23% improvement compared to the M-T-M heuristic.

1 Introduction

Multimedia application environments are characterized by large bandwidth variations due to the heterogeneous access technologies of networks (e.g. analog modem, cable modem, xDSL, and wireless access etc.) and different receivers' quality requirements. In video multicasting, the heterogeneity of the networks and destinations makes it difficult to achieve bandwidth efficiency and service flexibility. There are many challenging issues that need to be addressed in designing architectures and mechanisms for multicast data transmission [1].

Unicast and multicast delivery of video are important building blocks of Internet multimedia applications. Unicast means that the video stream goes independently to each user through point-to-point connection from the source to each destination, and all destinations get their own stream. Multicast means that many destinations share the same stream through point-to-multipoint connection from the source to every destination, thus reducing the bandwidth requirements and network traffic. The efficiency of multicast is achieved at the cost of losing the service flexibility of unicast, because in unicast each destination can individually negotiate the service contract with the source.

Taking advantage of recent advances in video encoding and transmission technologies, either by a progress coder [2] or video gateway [3] [4], different destina-

J. Vicente and D. Hutchison (Eds.): MMNS 2004, LNCS 3271, pp. 102–114, 2004.
© IFIP International Federation for Information Processing 2004

tions can request a different bandwidth requirement from the source, after which the source only needs to transmit signals that are sufficient for the highest bandwidth destination into a single multicast tree. This concept is called single-application multiple-stream (SAMS). A multi-layered encoder encodes video data into more than one video stream, including one *base layer* stream and several *enhancement layer* streams. The base layer contains the most important portions of the video stream for achieving the minimum quality level. The enhancement layers contain the other portions of video stream for refining the quality of the base layer stream. This mechanism is similar to destination-initiated reservations and packet filtering used in the RSVP protocol [5].

The minimum cost multicast tree problem, which is the Steiner tree problem, is known to be NP-complete. Reference [6] and [7] surveyed the heuristics of Steiner tree algorithms. For the conventional Steiner tree problem, the link costs in the network are fixed. However, for the minimum cost multi-layered video multicast tree, the link costs are dependent on the set of receivers sharing the link. It is a variant of the Steiner tree problem. The heterogeneity of the networks and destinations makes it difficult to design an efficient and flexible mechanism for servicing all multicast group users.

Reference [8] discusses the issue of multi-layered video distribution on multicast networks and proposes a heuristic to solve this problem, namely: the modified T-M heuristic (M-T-M Heuristic). Its goal is to construct a minimum cost tree from the source to every destination. However, the reference provides only experimental evidence for its performance. Reference [9] extends this concept to present heuristics with provable performance guarantees for the Steiner tree problem and proof that this problem is NP-hard, even in the special case of broadcasting. From the results, the cost of the multicast tree generated by M-T-M heuristics was no more than 4.214 times the cost of an optimal multicast tree. However, no simulation results are reported to justify the approaches in [9]. The solution approaches described above are heuristic-based and could be further optimized. Consequently, for multimedia distribution on multicast networks, we intend to find the multicast trees that have a minimal total incurred cost for multi-layered video distribution.

In this paper, we extend the idea of [8] for minimizing the cost of a multi-layered multimedia multicast tree and propose two more precise procedures (tie-breaking procedure and drop-and-add procedure) to improve the solution quality of M-T-M heuristic. Further, we formally model this problem as an optimization problem. In the structure of mathematics, they undoubtedly have the properties of linear programming problems. We apply the Lagrangean relaxation method and the subgradient method to solve the problems [10][11]. Properly integrating the M-T-M heuristics and the results of Lagrangean dual problems may be useful to improve the solution quality. In addition, the Lagrangean relaxation method not only gets a good feasible solution, but also provides the lower bound of the problem solution which helps to verify the solution quality. We name this method Lagrangean Based M-T-M Heuristics.

The rest of this paper is organized as follows. In Section 2, we describe the detail of the M-T-M heuristic and present the evidence that the M-T-M heuristic does not perform well under some often seen scenarios. We propose two procedures to improve the solution quality. In Section 3, we formally define the problem being studied, as well as a mathematical formulation of min-cost optimization is proposed. Section 4 applies Lagrangean relaxation as a solution approach to the problem. Section 5, illustrates the computational experiments. Finally, in Section 6 we present our conclusions and the direction of future research.

2 Heuristics of Multi-layered Multimedia Multicasting

Reference [12] proposes an approximate algorithm named T-M heuristic to deal with the Steiner tree problem, which is a min-cost multicast tree problem. The T-M heuristic uses the idea of minimum depth tree algorithm (MDT) to construct the tree. To begin with, the source node is added to the tree permanently. At each iteration of MDT, a node is temporarily added to the tree until the added node is a receiver of the multicast group. Once the iterated tree reaches one of the receivers of the multicast group, it removes all unnecessary temporary links and nodes added earlier and marks the remaining nodes permanently connected to the tree. The depth of the permanently connected nodes is then set to zero and the iterations continue until all receivers are permanently added to the tree. In [8], the author gives examples of the performance of the T-M heuristic and shows that in some cases the T-M heuristic does not achieve the optimum tree.

Reference [8] modified the T-M heuristic to deal with the min-cost multicast tree problem in multi-layered video distribution. For multi-layered video distribution, which is different from the conventional Steiner tree problem, each receiver can request a different quality of video. This means that each link's flow of the multicast tree is different and is dependent on the maximum rate of the receiver sharing the link. The author proposes a modified version of the T-M heuristic (M-T-M heuristic) to approximate the minimum cost multicast tree problem for multi-layered video distribution.

The M-T-M heuristic separates the receivers into subsets according to the receiving rate. First, the M-T-M heuristic constructs the multicast tree for the subset with the highest rate by using the T-M heuristic. Using this initial tree, the T-M heuristic is then applied to the subsets according to the order of receiving rate from high to low. For further details of the M-T-M heuristic, please refer to reference [8].

2.1 Some Scenarios of the Modified T-M Heuristic

In most networks, the performance of the Modified T-M heuristic is better than the T-M heuristic in multi-layered video multicasting. But, in some scenarios, we have found that the M-T-M does not perform well.

Consider the network in Figure 1 with node 1 as the source and nodes 3 and 4 as the destinations requiring rates 2 and 1, respectively. Assume the base costs of all links are the same, which is 1. First, the M-T-M heuristic separates the receivers into two subsets, one for rate 1 and the other for rate 2. It then runs a MDT algorithm such as Dijkstra algorithm to construct the tree with the highest rate subset. At Step 4, the

T-M heuristic reaches the destination with the highest rate and removes all unnecessary intermediate links. After setting the depth of the permanently connected nodes to zero, it continues the search process for the other destinations. At Step 5, the M-T-M heuristic tree is found and the sum of the link costs is 5. But the sum of the link costs for the optimum tree shown is 4.

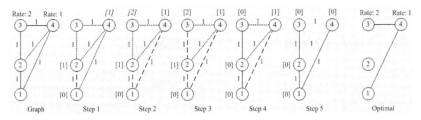

Fig. 1. Example of the M-T-M heuristic for multi-layered distribution with constant link cost.

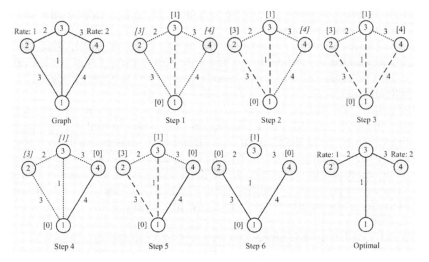

Fig. 2. Example of the M-T-M heuristic for multi-layered distribution with arbitrary link cost.

Consider the other network in Figure 2 with node 1 as the source and nodes 2 and 4 as the destinations requiring rates 1 and 2, respectively. The link costs are indicated by the side of the links. At Step 6, the M-T-M heuristic tree is found and the sum of the link costs is 11. But, the sum of the link costs for the optimum tree shown is 10.

2.2 Enhanced Modified T-M Heuristic

With reference to the above scenarios, we propose two adjustment procedures to improve the solution performance. The first one is the *tie breaking procedure*, which is used to handle the node selection when searching the nearest node within the M-T-M heuristic. The second is the *drop and add procedure*, which is used to adjust the multicast tree resulting from the M-T-M heuristic in order to reach a lower cost.

Tie Breaking Procedure. For the MDT algorithm, ties for the nearest distinct node may be broken arbitrarily, but the algorithm must still yield an optimal solution. Such ties are a signal that there may be (but need not be) multiple optimal solutions. All such optimal solutions can be identified by pursuing all ways of breaking ties to their conclusion. However, when executing the MDT algorithm within the M-T-M heuristic, we found that the tie breaking solution will influence the cost of the multicast tree. For example in Figure 2, the depth of nodes 2 and 4 is the same and is minimal at Step 1. The tie may therefore be broken by randomly selecting one of them to be the next node to update the depth of all the vertices. In general, we choose the node with the minimal node number within the node set of the same minimal depth for implementation simplicity. Although we choose node 1 as the next node to relax, node 2 is the optimal solution.

We propose a tie breaking procedure to deal with this situation. When there is a tie, the node with the largest requirement should be selected as the next node to join the tree. The performance evaluation will be shown in section 5.

Drop and Add Procedure. The drop and add procedure we propose is an adjustment procedure to adjust the initial multicast tree constructed by M-T-M heuristic. Nevertheless, redundantly checking actions may cause a serious decline in performance, even if the total cost is reduced. Therefore, we consider the most useful occurrence to reduce the total cost and control the used resources in an acceptable range. The details of procedures are:

1. Compute the number of hops from the source to the destinations.
2. Sort the nodes in descending order according to {incoming traffic/its own traffic demand}.
3. In accordance with the order, drop the node and re-add it to the tree. Consider the following possible adding measures and set the best one to be the final tree. Either adds the dropping node to the source node, or to other nodes having the same hop count, or to the nodes having a hop count larger or smaller by one.

3   Problem Formulation

3.1   Problem Description

The network is modeled as a graph where the switches are depicted as nodes and the links are depicted as arcs. A user group is an application requesting transmission in this network, which has one source and one or more destinations. Given the network topology, the capacity of the links and bandwidth requirement of every destination of a user group, we want to jointly determine the following decision variables: (1) the routing assignment (a tree for multicasting or a path for unicasting) of each user group; and (2) the maximum allowable traffic rate of each multicast user group through each link.

By formulating the problem as a mathematical programming problem, we intend to solve the issue optimally by obtaining a network that will enable us to achieve our goal, i.e. one that ensures the network operator will spend the minimum cost on con-

Table 1. Description of Notations.

Given Parameters	
Notation	**Description**
a_l	Transmission cost associated with link l
α_{gd}	Traffic requirement of destination d of multicast group g
G	The set of all multicast groups
V	The set of nodes in the network
L	The set of links in the network
D_g	The set of destinations of multicast group g
h_g	The minimum number of hops to the farthest destination node in multicast group g
I_v	The incoming links to node v
r_g	The multicast root of multicast group g
I_{r_g}	The incoming links to node r_g
P_{gd}	The set of paths destination d of multicast group g may use
δ_{pl}	The indicator function which is 1 if link l is on path p and 0 otherwise
Decision Variables	
Notation	**Descriptions**
x_{gpd}	1 if path p is selected for group g destined for destination d and 0 otherwise
y_{gl}	1 if link l is on the subtree adopted by multicast group g and 0 Otherwise
m_{gl}	The maximum traffic requirement of the destinations in multicast group g that are connected to the source through link l

structing the multicast tree. The notations used to model the problem are listed in Table 1.

3.2 Mathematical Formulation

According to the problem description in pervious section, the min-cost problem is formulated as a combinatorial optimization problem in which the objective function is to minimize the link cost of the multicast tree. Of course a number of constraints must be satisfied.

Objective function (IP):

$$Z_{IP} = \min \sum_{g \in G} \sum_{l \in L} a_l \, m_{gl} \tag{1}$$

subject to:

$$\sum_{p \in P_{gd}} x_{gpd} \alpha_{gd} \delta_{pl} \leq m_{gl} \qquad \forall g \in G, d \in D_g, l \in L \tag{2}$$

$$m_{gl} \in [0, \max_{d \in D_g} \alpha_{gd}] \qquad \forall l \in L, g \in G \tag{3}$$

$$y_{gl} = 0 \text{ or } 1 \qquad\qquad \forall l \in L, g \in G \qquad\qquad (4)$$

$$\sum_{l \in L} y_{gl} \geq \max\{h_g, |D_g|\} \qquad\qquad \forall g \in G \qquad\qquad (5)$$

$$\sum_{d \in D_g} \sum_{p \in P_{gd}} x_{gpd} \delta_{pl} \leq |D_g| y_{gl} \qquad\qquad \forall g \in G, l \in L \qquad\qquad (6)$$

$$\sum_{l \in I_v} y_{gl} \leq 1 \qquad\qquad \forall g \in G, v \in V - \{r_g\} \qquad\qquad (7)$$

$$\sum_{l \in I_{r_g}} y_{gl} = 0 \qquad\qquad \forall g \in G \qquad\qquad (8)$$

$$\sum_{p \in P_{gd}} x_{gpd} = 1 \qquad\qquad \forall d \in D_g, g \in G \qquad\qquad (9)$$

$$x_{gpd} = 0 \text{ or } 1 \qquad\qquad \forall d \in D_g, g \in G, p \in P_{gd} \qquad\qquad (10)$$

The objective function of (1) is to minimize the total transmission cost of servicing the maximum bandwidth requirement destination through a specific link for all multicast groups G, where G is the set of user groups requesting connection. The maximum bandwidth requirement on a link in the specific group m_{gl} can be viewed so that the source would be required to transmit in a way that matches the most constrained destination.

Constraint (2) is referred to as the capacity constraint, where the variable m_{gl} can be interpreted as the "estimate" of the aggregate flow. Since the objective function is strictly an increasing function with m_{gl} and (1) is a minimization problem, each m_{gl} will equal the aggregate flow in an optimal solution. Constraint (3) is a redundant constraint which provides upper and lower bounds on the maximum traffic requirement for multicast group g on link l. Constraints (4) and (5) require that the number of links on the multicast tree adopted by the multicast group g be at least the maximum of h_g and the cardinality of D_g. The h_g and the cardinality of D_g are the legitimate lower bounds of the number of links on the multicast tree adopted by the multicast group g. Constraint (6) is referred to as the tree constraint, which requires that the union of the selected paths for the destinations of user group g forms a tree. Constraints (7) and (8) are both redundant constraints. Constraint (7) requires that the number of selected incoming links y_{gl} to node is 1 or 0, while constraint (8) requires that there are no selected incoming links y_{gl} to the node that is the root of multicast group g. As a result, the links we select can form a tree. Finally, constraints (9) and (10) require that only one path is selected for each multicast source-destination pair.

4   Solution Approach

4.1   Lagrangean Relaxation

Lagrangean methods were used in both the scheduling and the general integer programming problems at first. However, it has become one of the best tools for optimization problems such as integer programming, linear programming combinatorial optimization, and non-linear programming [10][11].

The Lagrangean relaxation method permits us to remove constraints and place them in the objective function with associated Lagrangean multipliers instead. The optimal value of the relaxed problem is always a lower bound (for minimization problems) on the objective function value of the problem. By adjusting the multiplier of Lagrangean relaxation, we can obtain the upper and lower bounds of this problem. The Lagrangean multiplier problem can be solved in a variety of ways. The subgradient optimization technique is possibly the most popular technique for solving the Lagrangean multiplier problem [10] [13].

By using the Lagrangean Relaxation method, we can transform the primal problem (IP) into the following Lagrangean Relaxation problem (LR) where Constraints (2) and (6) are relaxed. For a vector of non-negative Lagrangean multipliers, a Lagrangean Relaxation problem of (1) is given by

Optimization Problem (LR):

$$
\begin{aligned}
Z_D(\beta,\theta) = \min \quad & \sum_{g \in G} \sum_{l \in L} a_l m_{gl} + \sum_{g \in G} \sum_{d \in D_g} \sum_{l \in L} \sum_{p \in P_{gd}} \beta_{gdl} x_{gpd} \alpha_{gd} \delta_{pl} - \sum_{g \in G} \sum_{d \in D_g} \sum_{l \in L} \beta_{gdl} m_{gl} \\
& + \sum_{g \in G} \sum_{l \in L} \sum_{d \in D_g} \sum_{p \in P_{gd}} \theta_{gl} x_{gpd} \delta_{pl} - \sum_{g \in G} \sum_{l \in L} \theta_{gl} \left| D_g \right| y_{gl}
\end{aligned}
\tag{11}
$$

subject to: (3) (4) (5) (7) (8) (9) (10).

Where β_{gdl}, θ_{gl} are Lagrangean multipliers and β_{gdl}, $\theta_{gl} \geq 0$. To solve (11), we can decompose (11) into the following three independent and easily solvable optimization subproblems.

Subproblem 1: (related to decision variable x_{gpd})

$$
Z_{Sub1}(\beta,\theta) = \min \sum_{g \in G} \sum_{d \in D_g} \sum_{p \in P_{gd}} [\sum_{l \in L} \delta_{pl} (\beta_{gdl} \alpha_{gd} + \theta_{gl})] x_{gpd}
\tag{12}
$$

subject to: (9) (10).

Subproblem 1 can be further decomposed into $|G||D_g|$ independent shortest path problems with nonnegative arc weights. Each shortest path problem can be easily solved by Dijkstra's algorithm.

Subproblem 2: (related to decision variable y_{gl})

$$
Z_{Sub2}(\theta) = \min \sum_{g \in G} \sum_{l \in L} (-\theta_{gl} \left| D_g \right|) y_{gl}
\tag{13}
$$

subject to: (4) (5) (7) (8).

The algorithm to solve Subproblem 2 is:

Step 1   Step 1   Compute $\max\{h_g, |D_g|\}$ for multicast group g.
Step 2   Step 2   Compute the number of negative coefficients $(-\theta_{gl} |D_g|)$ for all links in the multicast group g.
Step 3   Step 3   If the number of negative coefficients is greater than $\max\{h_g, |D_g|\}$ for multicast group g, then assign the corresponding negative coefficient of y_{gl} to 1 and 0 otherwise.

Step 4   Step 4   If the number of negative coefficients is no greater than $\max\{h_g,$ $|D_g|\}$ for multicast group g, assign the corresponding negative coefficient of y_{gl} to 1. Then, assign $[\max\{h_g, |D_g|\}-$ the number of positive coefficients of $y_{gl}]$ numbers of the smallest positive coefficient of y_{gl} to 1 and 0 otherwise.

Subproblem 3: (related to decision variable m_{gl})

$$Z_{Sub3}(\beta) = \min \sum_{g \in G} \sum_{l \in L} (a_l - \sum_{d \in D_g} \beta_{gdl}) m_{gl} \tag{14}$$

subject to: (3).

We decompose Subproblem 3 into $|L|$ independent problems. For each link $l \in L$:

$$Z_{Sub3.1}(\beta) = \min \sum_{g \in G} (a_l - \sum_{d \in D_g} \beta_{gdl}) m_{gl} \tag{15}$$

subject to: (3).

The algorithm to solve (15) is:

Step 1   Compute $a_l - \sum_{d \in D_g} \beta_{dgl}$ for link l of multicast group g.

Step 2   If $a_l - \sum_{d \in D_g} \beta_{dgl}$ is negative, assign the corresponding m_{gl} to the maximum traffic requirement in the multicast group, otherwise assign the corresponding m_{gl} to 0.

According to the weak Lagrangean duality theorem [13], for any β_{gdl}, $\theta_{gl} \geq 0$, $Z_D(\beta_{gdl}, \theta_{gl})$ is a lower bound on Z_{IP}. The following dual problem (D) is then constructed to calculate the tightest lower bound.

Dual Problem (D):

$$Z_D = \max Z_D(\beta_{gdl}, \theta_{gl}) \tag{16}$$

subject to:

$$\beta_{gdl}, \theta_{gl} \geq 0$$

There are several methods for solving the dual problem (16). The most popular is the subgradient method, which is employed here [14]. Let a vector s be a subgradient of $Z_D(\beta_{gdl}, \theta_{gl})$. Then, in iteration k of the subgradient optimization procedure, the multiplier vector is updated by $\omega^{k+1} = \omega^k + t^k s^k$. The step size t^k is determined by $t^k = \delta(Z_{IP}^h - Z_D(\omega^k))/\|s^k\|^2$. Z_{IP}^h is the primal objective function value for a heuristic solution (an upper bound on Z_{IP}). δ is a constant and $0 < \delta \leq 2$.

4.2 Getting Primal Feasible Solutions

After optimally solving the Lagrangean dual problem, we get a set of decision variables. However, this solution would not be a feasible one for the primal problem since some of constraints are not satisfied. Thus, minor modification of decision variables, or the hints of multipliers must be taken, to obtain the primal feasible solution of problem (IP). Generally speaking, the better primal feasible solution is an upper bound (UB) of the problem (IP), while the Lagrangean dual problem solution guarantees the lower bound (LB) of problem (IP). Iteratively, by solving the Lagrangean dual problem and getting the primal feasible solution, we get the LB and UB, respectively. So, the gap between UB and LB, computed by (UB-LB)/LB*100%, illustrates the optimality of problem solution. The smaller gap computed, the better the optimality.

To calculate the primal feasible solution of the minimum cost tree, the solutions to the Lagrangean Relaxation problems are considered. The set of x_{gpd} obtained by solving (12) may not be a valid solution to problem (IP) because the capacity constraint is relaxed. However, the capacity constraint may be a valid solution for some links. Also, the set of y_{gl} obtained by solving (13) may not be a valid solution because of the link capacity constraint and the union of y_{gl} may not be a tree.

Here we propose a comprehensive, two-part method to obtain a primal feasible solution. It utilized a Lagrangean based modified T-M heuristic, followed by adjustment procedures. While solving the Lagrangean relaxation dual problem, we may get some multipliers related to each OD pair and links. According to the information, we can make our routing more efficient. We describe the Lagrangean based modified T-M heuristic below.

Lagrangean Based Modified T-M Heuristic

Step 1   Use $a_l - \sum_{d \in D_g} \beta_{dgl}$ as link l's arc weight and run the M-T-M heuristic.

Step 2   After getting a feasible solution, we apply the drop-and-add procedure described earlier to adjust the result.

Initially, we set all of the multipliers to 0, so we will get the same routing decision as the M-T-M heuristics followed by the drop-and-add procedure at the first iteration.

5   Computational Experiments

In this section, computational experiments on the Lagrangean relaxation based heuristic and other primal heuristics are reported. The heuristics are tested on three kinds of networks- regular networks, random networks, and scale-free networks. Regular networks are characterized by low clustering and high network diameter, and random networks are characterized by low clustering and low diameter. The scale-free networks, which are power-law networks, are characterized by high clustering and low diameter. Reference [15] shows that the topology of the Internet is characterized by power laws distribution. The power laws describe concisely skewed distributions of graph properties such as the node degree.

Two regular networks shown in Figure 3 are tested in our experiment. The first one is a grid network that contains 100 nodes and 180 links, and the second is a cellular network containing 61 nodes and 156 links. Random networks tested in this paper are generated randomly, each having 500 nodes. The candidate links between all node pairs are given a probability following the uniform distribution. In the experiments, we link the node pair with a probability smaller than 2%. If the generated network is not a connected network, we generate a new network.

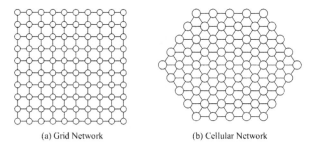

(a) Grid Network   (b) Cellular Network

Fig. 3. Regular Networks.

Reference [16] shows that the scale-free networks can arise from a simple dynamic model that combines incremental growth with a preference for new nodes to connect to existing ones that are already well connected. In our experiments, we applied this preferential attachment method to generate the scale-free networks. The corresponding preferential variable (m_0, m) is (2, 2). The number of nodes in the testing networks is 500.

For each testing network, several distinct cases, which have different pre-determined parameters such as the number of nodes, are considered. The traffic demands for each destination are drawn from a random variable uniformly distributed in pre-specified categories {1, 2, 5, 10, 15, 20}. The link costs are randomly generated between 1 and 5. The cost of the multicast tree is decided by multiplying the link cost and the maximum bandwidth requirement on a link. We conducted 2,000 experiments for each kind of network. For each experiment, the result was determined by the group destinations and link costs generated randomly. Table 2 summaries the selected results of the computational experiments.

In general, the results of LR are all better than the M-T-M heuristic (MTM), the M-T-M heuristic with tie breaking procedure (TB), and the M-T-M heuristic followed by drop-and-add procedure (DA). This is because we get the same solution as the M-T-M heuristic at the first iteration of LR. For each testing network, the maximum improvement ratio between the M-T-M heuristic and the Lagrangean based modified T-M heuristic is 16.18 %, 23.23%, 10.41 %, and 11.02%, respectively. To claim optimality, we also depict the percentile of gap in Table 2. The results show that 60% of the regular and scale free networks have a gap of less than 10%, but the result of random networks show a larger gap. However, we also found that the M-T-M heuristic perform well in many cases, such as the case D of grid network and case D of random network.

According to the experiments results, we found that the tie breaking procedure we proposed is not uniformly better than random selection. For example, the case H of cellular network, the performance of M-T-M (1517) is better than TB (1572). Consequently, we suggest that in practice we can try both tie breaking methods (randomly select or the method we proposed), and select the better result. The experiments results also show that the drop and add procedure does reduce the cost of the multicast tree.

Table 2. Selected Results of Computational Experiments.

CASE	Dest. #	M-T-M	TB	DA	UB	LB	GAP	Imp.
Grid Network						Max Imp. Ratio: 16.18 %		
A	5	332	330	332	290	286.3714	1.27%	14.48%
B	5	506	506	506	506	503.6198	0.47%	0.00%
C	10	158	153	148	136	123.1262	10.46%	16.18%
D	10	547	547	547	547	541.8165	0.96%	0.00%
E	20	522	507	502	458	397.8351	15.12%	13.97%
F	20	1390	1405	1388	1318	1206.235	9.27%	5.46%
G	50	2164	2229	2154	1940	1668.448	16.28%	11.55%
H	50	759	700	759	693	588.3226	17.79%	9.52%
Cellular Network						Max Imp. Ratio: 23.23 %		
A	5	182	167	172	167	160.4703	4.07%	8.98%
B	5	119	119	119	109	105.9671	2.86%	9.17%
C	10	194	185	190	180	156.9178	14.71%	7.78%
D	10	174	174	170	150	138.0774	8.63%	16.00%
E	20	382	349	382	310	266.1146	16.49%	23.23%
F	20	815	800	811	756	689.6926	9.61%	7.80%
G	50	602	595	602	567	479.9626	18.13%	6.17%
H	50	1517	1572	1503	1357	1187.332	14.29%	11.79%
Random Networks						Max Imp. Ratio: 10.41 %		
A	5	107	107	107	107	94.70651	12.98%	0.00%
B	5	88	88	88	86	74.63349	15.23%	2.27%
C	10	170	170	170	170	134.6919	26.21%	0.00%
D	10	123	125	123	123	97.90988	25.63%	0.00%
E	20	317	317	317	284	221.2635	28.35%	10.41%
F	20	226	216	226	216	168.0432	28.54%	4.42%
G	50	850	860	850	806	558.5077	44.31%	5.18%
H	50	702	715	702	690	446.9637	54.37%	1.71%
Scale-Free Networks						Max Imp. Ratio: 11.02 %		
A	5	82	82	82	82	78.35047	4.66%	0.00%
B	5	79	75	75	75	73.70663	1.75%	5.33%
C	10	210	210	210	208	196.3969	5.91%	0.96%
D	10	528	528	528	506	505.4039	0.12%	4.35%
E	20	886	896	886	854	770.9776	10.77%	3.75%
F	20	1068	1050	1022	962	920.2371	4.54%	11.02%
G	50	1869	1871	1869	1754	1502.061	16.77%	6.56%
H	50	1911	1946	1911	1891	1598.817	18.27%	1.06%

TB: The result of the modified T-M heuristic with the tie breaking procedure
DA: The result of the modified T-M heuristic followed by the drop-and-add procedure
UB and LB: Upper and lower bounds of the Lagrangean based modified T-M heuristic
GAP: The error gap of the Lagrangean relaxation
Imp.: The improvement ratio of the Lagrangean based modified T-M heuristic

6   Conclusions

In this paper, we attempt to solve the problem of min-cost multicast routing for multi-layered multimedia distribution. Our achievement of this paper can be expressed in terms of mathematical formulation and experiment performance. In terms of formulation, we propose a precise mathematical expression to model this problem well. In terms of performance, the proposed Lagrangean relaxation and subgradient based algorithms outperform the primal heuristics (M-T-M heuristic). According to the experiment results, the Lagrangean based heuristic can achieve up to 23.23% improvement compared to the M-T-M heuristic. We also propose two adjustment procedures to enhance the solution quality of the M-T-M heuristic.

Our model can also be easily extended to deal with the constrained multicast routing problem for multi-layered multimedia distribution by adding capacity and delay constraints. Moreover, the min-cost model proposed in this paper can be modified as a max-revenue model, with that objective of maximizing total system revenues by totally, or partially, admitting destinations into the system. These issues will be addressed in future works.

References

1. Wu, D., Hou, Y.T., Zhu, W., Zhang, T.Q., Peha, J.: Streaming Video over the Internet: Approaches and Directions. IEEE Transactions on Circuits and Systems for Video Technology, Vol. 11, No. 3 (2001) 282-300
2. Karlsson, G., Vetterli, M.: Packet Video and Its Integration into the Network Architecture. IEEE Journal on Selected Areas in Communications, Vol. 7 (1989) 739–751
3. Amir, E., McCanne, S., Zhang, H.: An Application Level Video Gateway. Proceedings of ACM Multimedia (1995) 255-265
4. Turletti, T., Bolot, J.C.: Issues with Multicast Video Distribution in Heterogeneous Packet Networks. Proceedings of the 6th International Workshop on Packet Video (1994)
5. Zhang, L., Deering, S., Estrin, D., Shenker, S., Zappala, D.: RSVP: A New Resource Reservation Protocol. IEEE Network, Vol. 7 (1993) 8–18
6. Winter, P.: Steiner Problem in Networks: A Survey. Networks (1987) 129-167
7. Hwang, F.K.: Steiner Tree Problems. Networks (1992) 55-89
8. Maxemchuk, N.F.: Video Distribution on Multicast Networks. IEEE Journal on Selected Areas in Communications, Vol. 15, No. 3 (1997) 357-372
9. Charikar, M., Naor, J., Schieber, B.: Resource Optimization in QoS Multicast Routing of Real-time Multimedia. IEEE/ACM Transactions on Networking, Vol. 12, No. 2 (2004) 340-348
10. Fisher, M.L.: The Lagrangian Relaxation Method for Solving Integer Programming Problems. Management Science, Vol. 27 (1981) 1-18
11. Ahuja, R.K., Magnanti, T.L., Orlin, J.B.: Network Flows: Theory, Algorithms, and Applications. Prentice Hall (1993)
12. Takahashi, H., Matsuyama, A.: An Approximate Solution for the Steiner Problem in Graphs. Math Japonica, Vol. 6 (1980) 573-577
13. Geoffrion, A.M.: Lagrangean Relaxation and Its Uses in Integer Programming. Math. Programming Study, Vol. 2 (1974) 82-114
14. Held, M., Karp, R.M.: The Traveling Salesman Problem and Minimum Spanning Trees: Part I. Operations Research, Vol. 18 (1970) 1138-62
15. Faloutsos, C., Faloutsos, P., Faloutsos, M.: On Power-law Relationships of the Internet Topology. Proceedings of the ACM SIGCOMM (1999)
16. Barabasi, A.-L., Albert, R.: Emergence of Scaling in Random Networks. Science, Vol. 286 (1999) 509–512

Efficient Management
of Multimedia Attachments*

Itai Dabran[1], Philippe Klein[2], and Danny Raz[1]

[1] Computer Science Department, Technion, Haifa 3200, Israel
[2] Telrad Mediagate Ltd, P.O. Box. 488, Rosh Haayin 48091, Israel

Abstract. In a modern heterogeneous environment, where users use a variety of devices such as smart phones, PDAs, and laptops, and a variety of network connections such as Wireless LAN, and GPRS to connect to the email system, handling of email and attachment messages and ensuring readability becomes an important management challenge. In some cases it is necessary to transcode the multimedia attachment to a format supported by the recipient device, and appropriate for the connection used, in order to allow the recipients to view the multimedia attachment. This transcoding could be done at the sender mail server, the receiver mail server, or at a proxy point in the middle. In addition the message may be addressed to several recipients in the receiver server, each may have different preferences and characterizations. This paper proposes an efficient scheme for handling email messages with multimedia attachments. We describe an architectural and algorithmic framework that allows service maximization to the end users (depending on their devices and connectivity) with minimum cost to the organizations in terms of storage, transcoding, and communication. We also provide a simulation study indicating that the proposed scheme is feasible and results in very efficient solutions.

1 Introduction

The increased importance of email in commercial applications, and the increased popularity of using rich media attachment files, makes efficient handling of email and attachment messages an important challenge. In addition to being the source for an endless increase in the demand for more storage resources, handling attachment files requires that the recipient of the message will have the ability to open the attachment file format. This problem becomes much more challenging when considering the modern heterogeneous environment, where users use a variety of devices such as smart phones, PDAs, laptops, and high-end desktops to connect to the email system. Each of these devices has a different capability in terms of color and screen resolution, memory, and available CPU. Moreover, the characterizations of the lines connecting the user to the mail server also vary in a significant way. A client that uses a PDA device and a GPRS network to

---

* This work is part of the STRIMM consortium operates under MAGNET program of the Chief Scientist of the Israeli Ministry of Trade and Industry (www.strimm.org).

J. Vicente and D. Hutchison (Eds.): MMNS 2004, LNCS 3271, pp. 115–126, 2004.

connect to his email server, may have a limited bandwidth and a considerable loss on the link, while the same user may have better connectivity when the PDA is connected via, say, wireless LAN (WLAN). Handling multimedia attachments efficiently in such a heterogeneous environment presents significant management challenges. This paper deals with an efficient scheme for handling email messages with multimedia attachments in today's heterogeneous environments. Clients are usually connecting to their email server using the popular IMAP [1] or PoP3 [2] protocols. These protocols use the Multipurpose Internet Mail Extensions (MIME) [3] that support various attachment encoding methods. Email messages between mail servers across the Internet are mostly carried by the Simple Mail Transfer Protocol (SMTP) [4]. The objective of the SMTP is to transfer mail reliably and efficiently between mail servers, it is independent of a particular transmission subsystem and is capable of relaying mail over several transport services in a Wide Area Network (WAN). It runs between e-mail servers where the sender establishes a two-way transmission channel to a receiver that may be either the ultimate or an intermediate destination.

Consider a typical scenario in which a user wants to send an email message with a multimedia attachment to another user, or more generally to a set of users. These users may be connected to the same mail server, or they may be using different mail servers. Each of the recipients has its own preferences in term of the end device he uses (PDA or smart phone), and its connectivity characteristics (wireless, wire line). Thus, in order for the recipients to view the attachment, it may be necessary to transcode the attached file into a different media format (or in some case several different formats). This transcoding could be done at the sender mail server, the receiver mail server, or at a proxy point in the middle. Each of the receiving mail servers, can then decide how to store the attached file and in which format. This decision has a critical impact both on the storage capability of the server, and on the ability to stream the media to the client when the end user opens his mail message and wants to view the attached multimedia content.

In this paper we concentrate on the connection between two SMTP servers, that is, we focus on the case where an email message containing a multimedia attachment is sent from one mail server to another mail server. The message may be addressed to several recipients in the receiver server, each may have different preferences and characterizations as described above. Our goal is to describe an architectural and algorithmic framework that allows an efficient handling of the multimedia attachments, in a way that allows service maximization to the end users (depending on their devices and connectivity) with minimum cost to the organizations in terms of storage, transcoding, and communication.

The first step toward achieving this goal is to allow mail servers to exchange information regarding users' preference and storage limitations. This information can then be used by the sender mail server in order to decide how to handle the multimedia attachment.

The cost of sending a message with a multimedia attachment is combined of three components. The transcoding cost reflects the computation resources used to perform file format transcoding. The communication cost reflects the use of network resources in order to send the information. Note that since different multimedia formats have different sizes, this cost may vary when the transcoding location changes from the sender mail server to the receiver mail server. The third component of the cost is the storage cost. In this paper we assume that the receiving mail server decides what multimedia formats are wanted, and this decision takes into account both the preference of the recipients, as well as storage constraints. Thus, the storage cost is not part of the algorithmic scheme but rather a part of the input.

There are few possible options to transfer the message: the format transcoding may be done at the sender server, or the multimedia attachment may be sent as is to the receiver server to be transcoded there. In addition, more than one format can be sent. In this paper we develop an algorithmic scheme that uses the information retrieved via the Capability Exchange phase in order to optimize the cost of the multimedia attachment sending process.

2   Related Work

The problem of efficient transcoding was addressed recently by several research papers ([5], [6], [7], and [8]). In [5] software and algorithmic optimizations for a real time MPEG-2 to MPEG-4 video transcoder is presented. This optimization results in a reduction of over 86% in the MPEG-4 transcoding time. The variation of the transcoding cost is also mentioned in [6] and [7]. In these papers the authors suggest to allow a caching proxy to perform the transcoding process. Variants of a video object can be delivered by transcoding the cached content to the appropriate format, instead of accessing it at the content origin. By this, heterogeneous clients with various network conditions, receive videos that are suited for their capabilities, as content adaptation can easily be done at the network edges. Another work [9] presents a complexity-quality analysis of various transcoding architectures for reduced spatial resolution, whereas to enable broadcast-quality video streams to be decoded and displayed on mobile devices, transcoding from MPEG-2 MP@ML to MPEG-4 Simple Profile is needed. This conversion implies a reduction in bit-rate from approximately 6Mbps to 384kbps and lower, as well as a reduction in spatial resolution from 720x480 interlace to 352x240 progressive.

The demand for multimedia information is increasing beyond the capabilities of a single storage device and may lead to the necessity of a new storage architecture [10], transcoding proxies [6] or server replications [11]. There are storage prototypes designed to address the real-time demands of digital video and audio. [10] presents a scalable storage architecture based on the replication of high performance storage instances, employing load balancing techniques of static file replication (whereas each server instance holds a copy of all other server instances' files and has a pre-allocated number of clients) and network striping (whereas the multimedia file is distributed over a number of cooperating server instances in a highly capable network) to minimize the load on individual servers and interconnecting networks.

However all of the work mentioned above deals with real-time streaming and do not consider our problem of off-line transcoding cost of multimedia attachments.

3   Architecture

The SMTP protocol was defined in 1982 [4] and was initially designed to deliver short text messages coded in American ASCII characters. During the last 30 years several extensions such as DSN (Delivery Status Notifications) [12], and DRN (Delivery Report Notifications) [13] were added. When email messages contained only American ASCII characters the readability of the messages was 100% i.e. every successfully delivered message could be correctly read by the recipient. However, once users started sending messages coded in other character sets, and using attachment files, the readability of the message could not be assured any more. DSN and DRN give an indication of successful delivery of the message and a notification that the message was opened by the recipient, but there is no guaranty that the message could also be successfully read. In fact, the current heterogeneous environment, where mail clients can be located at different devices supported by various operating systems, creates a situation where in many cases the attached file format is not supported and cannot be opened by the mail recipient. The increasing use of rich-media attachments exacerbates this message readability problem. Therefore, there is a need to upgrade the protocol and model used, so that not only delivery but also readability is ensured. A first step in this direction is to allow the sender mail server to query the recipient mail server regarding the recipient capability or restriction before sending the message. In this way recipients can report for example, maximal attachment size accepted and different media format supported. The sender mail server can then either adjust the outgoing message according to the new information or notify the actual sender and ask for an appropriate format. This will be done using minimal storage and communication resources, as the large (unreadable) attachment is not sent.

In the current architecture, mail is sent using the SMTP protocol from the client to the outgoing mail server. The mail may contain an attachment file and the encoding is done using the Multipurpose Internet Mail Extensions (MIME) [3] format. The outgoing mail server then sends the message to the receiver mail server. This is done by establishing a two-way transmission channel between the sender and a receiver that may be either the ultimate or an intermediate destination. In most cases the current practice is to establish such a channel to the ultimate destination, i.e. the recipient mail server. The message is then accepted by the mail server, and the recipient client can access it via the popular IMAP [1] or PoP3 [2] protocols.

In our architecture we add an initial phase that allows the sender mail server to retrieve information regarding the capabilities of the recipient in terms of size and supported format. This phase is termed Capability Discovery, and can be implemented within the SMTP protocol framework using a well defined text or XML messages.

When an email message is sent to a distribution list, the Capability Discovery information exchange becomes more challenging, because some of the information needed such as storage limits or supported format may be different for different members of the list and since individual information regarding members of the list cannot be exposed. When using multimedia attachments, and when transcoding at the mail servers is feasible, the information retrieved in the Capability Discovery phase can be used in order to decide the best format of this attachment. If the recipient list contains more than one receiver at the target mail server, then more than one format can be sent. Thus, in order to establish an efficient system, one needs to decide what are the best formats, and where to do the transcoding (at the sender or receiver server). We address this question in Section 4. However, in order to deploy the Capability Discovery phase, one needs to agree on a set of agreed parameters. In particular we need to define a set of profiles and formats that can be used. An example for such profiles for MPEG-4 can be found in Figure 1.

Profile / Level	L0	L1	L2	L3	L4
N-Bit			2 Mbps		
Advanced Coding Efficiency		384 Kbps	2 Mbps	15 Mbps	38.4 Mbps
Main		234 Kbps	2 Mbps	15 Mbps	38.4 Mbps
Core scalable		768 Kbps	1.5 Mbps	4 Mbps	
Advanced Core		384 Kbps	2 Mbps		
Core		384 Kbps	2 Mbps		
Simple scalable		128 Kbps	256 Kbps		
Advanced Real Time Simple		64 Kbps	128 Kbps	384 Kbps	2 Mbps
Simple	64Kbps	64 Kbps	128 Kbps	384 Kbps	

Fig. 1. Example of MPEG-4 Different Profile and levels

4   The Multimedia Attachments Problem

In this section we study the algorithmic aspects of our problem. We consider an outgoing mail server that has an email message with a multimedia attachment in a given format, and a list of receivers at another mail server. As explained in Section 3, we assume that capability discovery is possible and the outgoing mail server can exchange relevant information with the receiving mail server. We also assume, as described above, that transcoding is possible in both mail servers. In the general case the attachment file is needed in several formats at the receiver, thus one needs to decide what transcoding is needed and where to perform the transcoding (i.e., at which mail server – sender or receiver). Once such a decision is made, the format of the multimedia attachment that is sent over the network is also decided. Note that in some cases, when the message is sent to a list of users with different preferences, more than one copy of the message, each with a different attachment format, may be sent from the sender mail server to the receiver mail server.

Our goal is to make the most efficient decision that is the one that requires minimum resources. Note that there are two different resource types we consider here. One is the CPU and time needed for the transcoding. The second resource we consider is the communication cost which depends on the amount of information (bits) we send over the network. A third resource type, which may be critical in this context, is the storage ability at the receiving server. However, in our framework this aspect is covered in the Capability Discovery protocol, and is part of the receiving server decision to determine what formats are needed. Note that comparing CPU utilization at the servers and communication over the network is hard and thus we need to define a cost for each of the operations, and try to find the minimal solution, i.e., the one with the minimal cost.

The first input to the algorithm is thus, the format of the multimedia attachment at the sender, and the requested format(s) at the receiver. As explained in the previous section, there could be many requested formats, and thus we assume a small number of relevant agreed formats, for examples the formats described in the tables of the previous section.

The second part of the input is the ability of the different servers to perform transcoding, and the relative cost of such a transcoding between two given formats in each server. The transcoding capability and the transcoding time depends on the hardware capabilities and the software in use, and the difference may be significant as described for example in [5, 7, 9]. We present this information for each server by a transcoding graph. In this graph every node represents a multimedia file format, and a link (directed edge) between format A and format B represents the ability of the server to perform transcoding between these formats. Each such link is associated with a cost; this cost represents the resources needed for that transcoding in terms of time and CPU. An example for such a graph is presented in the top part of Figure 2a. This figure shows two graphs that represent the source format in the vertexes upper level and the destination formats as "target vertexes" in the lower level. Note that for our problem we get two graphs, one for the sending server and one for the receiving server.

The third part of the input information represents the communication cost. For each relevant multimedia format we need to define the cost associated with sending an attachment in this format between the two mail servers. This is represented in our model by a link connecting the node representing the format in one server (sender), with the node representing the same format in the second server (receiver). The cost of the link is the communication cost of the specific format. Since different formats have different sizes, the communication cost between the same sender and receiver varies according to the different formats. The required output is a list of transcoding needed to be performed in each of the servers, and a list of the different formats that are needed to be sent from the sender to the receiver server. We want, of course, to choose the output that induces minimal cost (i.e., minimal resource utilization). We formulate the Multimedia Attachment Problem in the following way:

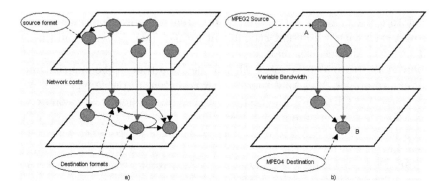

Fig. 2. Transcoding graph example

Definition 1. *Given a set of formats V, two weighted graphs $G_S = (V, E_S)$, $G_R = (V, E_R)$, where $E_S(v_1, v_2)$ $(E_R(v_1, v_2))$ represents the cost at the sender (receiver) for transcoding format v_1 to format v_2, a sender format v_S, a set of required receiving formats $v_{r_1}, \ldots, v_{r_l}$, and communication cost $C(v_i)$ representing the cost to send format v_i, find the minimal tree, rooted at v_S in G_s, and connecting all v_{r_i} in G_R.*

The problem as defined above is an instance of the minimal Steiner tree problem [14], and is NP-Complete. Thus, an algorithm that finds an optimal solution with a polynomial time complexity is unlikely to exist. One can thus take one of the following two approaches. The first approach is to use heuristics methods or proven approximation algorithms. These algorithms will find in polynomial time a solution to the Multimedia Attachment Problem, however, the solution may be sub-optimal in terms of cost. That is, if we have an R-approximation algorithm, it can find a solution with cost up to R times larger than the optimal solution.

The second approach is to try to find the optimal solution to the problem in hand. In this case we will be able to complete the task only if the input graph is small. The exact meaning of 'small' here depends on the structure of the graph, and the actual values of the costs. We discuss several running examples in the next section. Since most practical cases are small, we chose at this point to try to find the optimal solution using the A-Star algorithm [15]. This is a general search algorithm which uses a heuristic function in order to create a "minimal weighted path tree". However, a good choice of the heuristic function can guarantee that the best (i.e. the lightest) tree will be found eventually. Thus, the appropriate way to use this algorithm in this case is to run it for a limited amount of time, and if the optimal solution was not found during this time, to run an approximation algorithm and get a sub-optimal solution. In all examples we present in the next section the optimal solution was found by the A-star algorithm.

A good way to describe the algorithm is the following. At each step we have a list of 'open trees', and a list of 'closed trees'. All trees contain the root node (i.e. the sender format). The trees are ordered by their overall weight – the sum of the links weights. At each step we chose the first (i.e. lighter) tree in the open list. If it covers all the target nodes (i.e. all needed formats at the receiver), then we finish and output this tree. Otherwise, we move the tree to the 'closed trees' and add all the trees that can be created by adding one node to this tree, to the 'open trees' list. One can prove that this usage of the A-star algorithm guarantees finding the best solution. However, as explained above, in some cases the number of possible trees may be exponential, and the running time of the pure A-star algorithm may be infeasible. We implemented the above algorithm, where XML is used to describe and present the input graphs. The definition of an XML based notation helps to specify the dependencies and costs of all the components in our network in a similar way to the use of XML in [16].

5   Simulation Study

In order to demonstrate the benefit of our purposed architecture and algorithmic solution we present several realistic scenarios to study the various possible solutions for the multimedia attachment problem. We start with a very simple example. In this example the sender wants to send an email attachment that contains a 150Mbit MPEG-2 video clip (duration of 30 seconds, 5Mbps with a resolution of 720X480 (Format1)). The destination is a single user in the receiver server, which needs the attachment in 10 frames per second MPEG-4 format with a resolution of 352X240 (Format2). The size of the attachment needed by the destination is about 12Mbit[1].

We evaluated the costs in terms of seconds for the process of transmission and transcoding to the needed format. We tested the transcoding process with and without our algorithm, over various bit rates. In our simulation we used 31.18 seconds as the transcoding time at the server, and 3.53 seconds as the transcoding time at the receiver. Such a transcoding was performed in [5] using a Pentium 4 Dell workstation with 1.8 GHz processor, 512MB memory and running Windows 2000, with and without MMX optimization software. The transmission time of the MPEG-2 format file and the MPEG-4 format file is derived from the file size that is approximately 150Mb for the MPEG-2 format and approximately 12Mbit for the MPEG-4 format. In Figure 3(a) we show the cost in terms of time for sending and transcoding the Format1 file from node A to Format2 file at node B, when each of the options is used, while in Figure 3(b) we show our solution for the needed format when transcoding is done in the most efficient way. We see that each of the transmission routes is not optimal, while our solution chooses to switch between them in order to find the optimal solution.

Suppose that the cost of the communication line is a function of more factors than the bandwidth. Maintaining a satellite communication link or using cellular communication may cost much more. In our second simulation we checked the problem described in figure 2b, but with a variable cost of the communication link. Figure 4 depicts two areas. The first area (marked by x) presents the range

---

[1] These values are only similar to the values depicted in the tables of the previous section. This is done since we are using real measurements reported in [5].

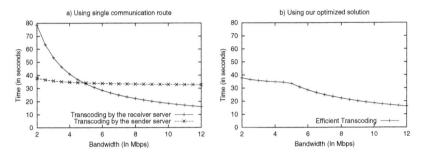

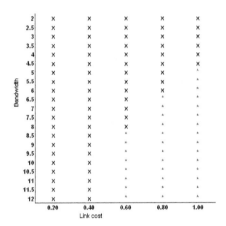

Fig. 3. The cost of multimedia transmission

Fig. 4. A Communication Link with a variable cost

where a decision to transmit the multimedia file and afterwards to transcode it
is taken and the second one (marked by *) presents the range where a decision
to transcode the multimedia file and afterwards to transmit it is taken. Both
areas present the most optimal way to handle the multimedia attachment. Next
we consider a somewhat more complex example. In this case the same sender
is sending again the same format (Format1) but this time there are two users
in the receiver server, whereas one of them needs the multimedia attachment in
Format1, and the other in Format2. The sender server and the receiver server are
connected in a 10Mbps communication link. Figure 5 presents this example. In
this case there are two options: a) The sender server transcodes the multimedia
attachment and sends a copy in Format1 and another copy in Format2 to the
destination server, and b) The sender server sends an attachment in Format1
to the receiver server and the receiver server saves one copy in Format1, and
a transcoded copy in Format2. Figure 6a depicts both options as a function of
the transcoding time of the receiver server. We see that when the first option
is executed and the source transcoding time is constant, the time it takes to
transmit the multimedia attachment remains constant. When the second option

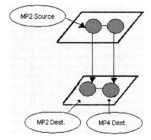

Fig. 5. When two formats are needed at the receiver server

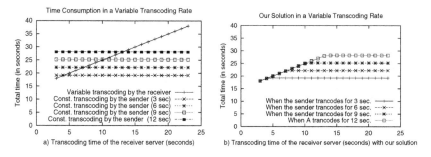

Fig. 6. A variable transcoding time of the receiver server with and without our solution

is done, the time it takes to transmit the multimedia attachment is a linear function that depends on the receiving server transcoding time. Figure 6b depicts our solution which optimizes each of the options presented in Figure 6a. We see that as the transcoding process in the sender server increases, our proposed solution requires that the transcoding process will be at the destination server.

Figure 7a presents a much more complicated problem, where the source has an AVI format and needs to transmit it to a destination server, where 3 formats are needed: MPEG-2, MPEG-4 and AVI. The solution produced by our simulator shows that the most optimal way is as shown by the wide arrows on Figure 7b. Note that this is indeed the optimal solution which indicates that our algorithmic solution can handle rather complex input.

6   Conclusions

In this paper we addressed the problem of efficient management of email messages containing multimedia attachments. We identified the need for capacity exchange between the mail servers, and presented an efficient algorithmic solution. This framework allows a mail server to decide how to handle multimedia attachment files, if and where to perform transcoding, and to what format. However, the results presented here are only a first step and very many interesting

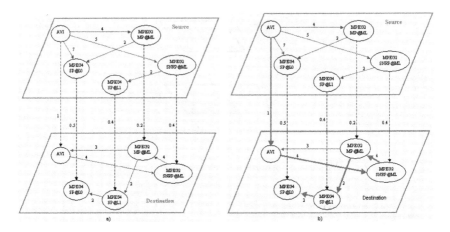

Fig. 7. A complex example

problems are left open. A basic problem is the generalization of the algorithm to multiple receiving servers. A more complex problem is related to proxy servers. In many cases it will be more efficient to store the multimedia attachments at separate servers that might be collocated with the mail servers, or located elsewhere in the network. In such a case, the multimedia attachment can be replaced by a link to the data in the appropriate media storage and streaming server, as done in Corsoft Aileron (url: http://www.corsoft.com). In this case the problem of finding the appropriate multimedia format and the optimal location for the attachment files becomes much more interesting and complicated. Finding good algorithms for the more general problem is a very challenging topic for future research. One has also to take into account economic considerations such as who pays for the mail (sender or receiver) and what is the business model of the transcoding services.

Acknowledgments

The simulation tool was developed in the LCCN Lab by Assaf Karpel, Oren Kaminer and Guy Gurfinkel, CS Department, Technion, Haifa, ISRAEL.

References

1. Crispin, M.: Internet Message Access Protocol – Version 4 rev1. IETF RFC 2060 (1996)
2. Myers, J., Rose, M.: Post Office Protocol – Version 3. IETF RFC 1939 (also STD0053) (1996)
3. Borenstein, N., Freed, N.: MIME(Multipurpose Internet Mail Extensions): Mechanisms for Specifying and Describing the Format of Internet Message Bodies. RFC-1341 (1992)

4. Postel, J.: Simple Mail Transfer Protocol. IETF RFC 2821 (also STD0010) (2001)
5. Hari Kalva, Anthony Vetro and Huifang Sun: Performance Optimization of an MPEG-2 to MPEG-4 Video Transcoder . SPIE Conference on VLSI Circuits and Systems, Vol. 5117, pp. 341-350 (2003)
6. Bo Shen, Sung-Ju Lee: Transcoding-Enabled Caching Proxy System for Video Delivery in Heterogeneous Network Environments. In: Proceedings of IASTED IMSA 2002, Kauai, HI. (2002)
7. Bo Shen, Sung-Ju Lee, and Sujoy Basu: Performance Evaluation of Transcoding-enabled Streaming Media Caching System. Proceedings of the 4th International Conference on Mobile Data Management pp. 363-368 (1997)
8. Youssef Iraqi and Raouf Boutaba: Supporting MPEG video VBR traffic in wireless networks. (Computer Communications 24 (2001) 1188-1201)
9. Anthony Vetro, Toshihiko Hata, Naoki Kuwahara, Hari Kalva, and Shun-ichi Sekiguchi: Complexity-Quality Analysis of Transcoding Architectures for Reduced Spatial Resolution. IEEE Transactions on Consumer Electronics, ISSN: 0098-3063, Vol. 48, Issue 3, pp. 515-521 (2002)
10. D. Pegler, D. Hutchison, P. Lougher, A. Scott, and D. Shepherd: Scalability issues for a networked multimedia storage architecture. (Multimedia Tools and Applications) http://www.comp.lancs.ac.uk/computing/users/phillip/scams.html.
11. Raouf Boutaba and Abdelhakim Hafid: A generic platform for scalable access to multimedia-on-demand systems. IEEE JOURNAL ON SELECTED AREAS IN COMMUNICATIONS, VOL. 17, NO. 9 (1999)
12. Moore, K.: SMTP service extension for delivery status notifications. IETF RFC 1891 (1996)
13. Vaudreuil, G.: The multipart report content type for the reporting of mail system administrative messages. IETF RFC 1892 (1996)
14. Hwang, F.K., Richards, D.S., Winter, P.: The Steiner Tree Problem. Volume 53 of ADM. North-Holland, Amsterdam, Netherlands (1992)
15. Rabin, S.: AI Game Programming Wisdom. Charles River Media, Hingham, Massachusetts (2002)
16. Ensel, C., Keller, A.: Managing Application Service Dependencies with XML and the Re source Description Framework. In: Proceedings of the 7th International IFIP/IEEE Symposium on Integrated Management (IM 2001), IFIP/IEEE, IEEE Publishing (2001)

A New Class of Scheduling Policies for Providing Time of Service Guarantees in Video-on-Demand Servers

Nabil J. Sarhan[1] and Chita R. Das[2]

[1] Department of Electrical & Computer Engineering
Wayne State University, Detroit, MI 48202
nabil@ece.eng.wayne.edu
[2] Department of Computer Science & Engineering
The Pennsylvania State University, University Park, PA 16802
das@cse.psu.edu

Abstract. Recent advances in storage and communication technologies have spurred a strong interest in *Video-on-Demand* (VOD) services. Providing the customers of VOD servers with time of service guarantees offers two major advantages. First, it makes VOD services more attractive by improving customer-perceived quality of service (QoS). Second, it improves throughput through the enhanced resource sharing attained by motivating the customers to wait. In this paper, we propose a new class of scheduling policies, called *Next Schedule Time First* (NSTF), which provides customers with schedule times and performs scheduling based on these schedule times. NSTF guarantees that customers will be serviced no later than scheduled and ensures that the schedule times are very accurate estimates of the actual times of service. We present alternative implementations of NSTF and show through simulation that NSTF works as expected and delivers outstanding performance benefits.

1   Introduction

Multimedia information has become an integral and an essential part of the World Wide Web (WWW). Multimedia data differ significantly from textual and numeric data in two main ways. First, they require high storage capacity and high transfer rates. Second, they consist of media quanta, which convey meaningful information only when presented continuously in time. Multimedia networking applications can be classified into three main classes: *Video-on-Demand* (VOD), *Live Streaming*, and *Interactive Real-time* (such as Internet telephony and video conferencing).

The application of interest in this paper is VOD. By contrast with broadcast-based systems such as cable TV, VOD servers enable customers to watch the videos they want at the times of their choosing and allow them to apply VCR-like operations. Besides its use for entertainment, VOD has been of great importance in education and distant learning in particular.

The number of customers that can be serviced concurrently by a VOD server is highly constrained by the stringent requirements of the real-time playback and the high transfer rates. Thus, a wide spectrum of techniques has been developed to enhance the performance of VOD servers, including *resource sharing* and *scheduling* [5], [10], [20],

J. Vicente and D. Hutchison (Eds.): MMNS 2004, LNCS 3271, pp. 127–139, 2004.

[1], [11], [12], [16], *admission control* [21], *disk striping* [19], [3], *data replication* [8], [4], *disk head scheduling* [14], and *data block allocation and rearrangement* [8], [15].

The performance of VOD servers can be significantly improved by servicing multiple requests from a common set of resources. The main classes of resource sharing strategies for VOD servers include *batching* [5], [7], [20], [1], [16], *patching* [11], [18], *piggy-backing* [10], *broadcasting* [12], [13], and *interval caching* [6], [17]. Batching off-loads the storage subsystem and uses efficiently server bandwidth and network resources by accumulating the requests to the same videos and servicing them together by utilizing the multicast facility. Patching expands the multicast tree dynamically to include new requests, thereby reducing the request waiting time and improving resource sharing, but it requires additional bandwidth and buffer space at the client. Piggy-backing offers similar advantages to patching, but it adjusts the playback rate so that the request catches up with a preceding stream, resulting in a lower-quality presentation of the initial part of the requested video and leading to significant implementation difficulties. Broadcasting techniques divide each video into multiple segments and broadcast each segment periodically on dedicated server channels. The improved resource sharing and the fixed waiting times for the playbacks of popular videos come at the expense of requiring relatively very high bandwidth and buffer space at the client. Interval caching caches intervals between successive streams in the main memory of the server. This technique shortens the request waiting time and increases server throughput without increasing the bandwidth or the space requirement at the client, but it increases the overall cost of the server.

The exploited degrees of resource sharing depend greatly on how VOD servers schedule the waiting requests. Through intelligent scheduling, a server can support more concurrent customers, can reduce their waiting times for service, and/or can meet some other objectives. Batching systems rely entirely on scheduling to boost up their performance. VOD systems that employ other resource sharing techniques also benefit from intelligent scheduling. (Note that only the most popular videos are broadcasted when a broadcasting technique is used.) This paper focuses on VOD servers that employ batching as the primary resource sharing technique without forcing any minimum waiting times and assumes that the multicast facility is deployed. Multicast is already employed or can be easily employed in most enterprise and local area networks (LANs), and it has incrementally been deployed over the Internet. In fact, a ubiquitous wide-scale deployment of native (non-tunneled) multicast across the Internet is becoming a reality [9].

Scheduling policies for VOD servers include *First Come First Serve* (FCFS) [5], *Maximum Queue Length* (MQL) [5], and *Maximum Factored Queue Length* (MFQL) [1]. To facilitate scheduling, a VOD server maintains a waiting queue for every video and services all the requests in a selected queue together using only one stream. FCFS selects the queue with the oldest request, whereas MQL selects the longest queue, and MFQL selects the queue with the largest *factored length*. The factored length of a queue is equal to its length divided by the square root of the access frequency of its corresponding video.

Providing time of service guarantees through scheduling can enhance customer-perceived QoS and can influence customers to wait, thereby increasing server throughput. Unlike most other policies, FCFS is believed to provide time of service guarantees [20]. In contrast, we show that FCFS may violate these guarantees because it considers only the waiting times in scheduling decisions, and not all customers continue to wait for services. We also show that FCFS is incapable of producing accurate time of service guarantees. Specifically, the average deviation of the actual times of service from the time of service guarantees ranges from 20 seconds to more than 4.5 minutes! Customers, however, would appreciate receiving accurate guarantees so that they can plan accordingly.

We propose a new class of scheduling policies, called *Next Schedule Time First* (NSTF), which eliminates the shortcomings of FCFS and also provides outstanding performance benefits. NSTF provides customers with schedule times, and it guarantees that they will be serviced no later than and accurately at their schedule times. The basic idea of the NSTF is to assign schedule times to incoming requests and to perform scheduling based on these schedule times rather than the arrival times. In the absence of VCR-like operations, a VOD server knows exactly when resources will become available for servicing new requests because each running stream requires a fixed playback time. Hence, when a new request calls for the playback of a video with no waiting requests, NSTF assigns the request a new schedule time that is equal to the closest unassigned completion time of a running stream. If the new request, however, is for a video that has already at least one waiting request, then NSTF assigns it the same schedule time assigned to the other waiting request(s) because all requests for a video can be serviced together using only one stream. Applying VCR-like operations, which are typically supported by using contingency channels [7], leads to early completions and thus servicing some requests earlier than scheduled.

When all customers waiting for the playback of a video defect (i.e., cancel their requests), their schedule time become available and can be used by other customers. This leads to two variants of NSTF: *NSTFn* and *NSTFo*. NSTFn assigns freed schedule times to incoming requests, whereas NSTFo assigns them to existing requests with waiting time guarantees beyond a certain threshold, and thus likely to defect. We also present three variants of NSTFo: *NSTFo-FCFS*, *NSTFo-MQL*, and *NSTFo-MFQL*, which differ in the selection criterion of existing requests that will be assigned better schedule times. These variants select requests on a FCFS, a MQL, or a MFQL basis, respectively. NSTFo-MQL and NSTFo-MFQL combine the advantages of FCFS and MQL/MFQL.

We show the effectiveness of the proposed policies through extensive simulation. We consider five performance metrics: the overall customer reneging (defection or turn-away) percentage, the average request waiting time, the number of violations of time of service guarantees, the average deviation from the time of service guarantees, and unfairness. The reneging percentage is the most important metric because it translates to the number of customers serviced concurrently and to server throughput. Unfairness measures the bias against unpopular videos. All other performance metrics signify QoS. We also study the impacts of customer waiting tolerance and server capacity (or server load) on the results.

The results demonstrate that NSTF achieves outstanding performance benefits, especially in terms of server throughput and accuracy of time of service guarantees. The main results can be summarized as follows. (1) The proposed NSTF policies meet their time of service guarantees and provide accurate schedule times. In particular, the average deviations of the actual times of service from the schedule times produced by NSTFn and NSTFo are within 6 seconds and 0.2 second, respectively. (2) NSTFo-MQL is the clear winner among the four variants of NSTF because of its superiority in both throughput and waiting times. (3) NSTFo-MQL achieves higher throughput and, in certain situations, shorter request waiting times than FCFS that may provide limited time of service guarantees. (4) NSTFo-MQL generally outperforms MQL and MFQL (both of which cannot provide time of service guarantees) in terms of throughput, especially for high server capacities, but MQL and MFQL achieve shorter waiting times. (5) NSTFo-MQL is fairer than MQL and MFQL for high server capacities because schedule times are assigned on a FCFS basis.

The rest of the paper is organized as follows. In Section 2, we discuss the main scheduling objectives and policies and explain why FCFS may violate its time of service guarantees. We then present NSTF and its variants in Section 3. In Section 4, we discuss the simulation platform, the workload characteristics, and the main simulation results. Finally, we draw conclusions in the last section.

2   Scheduling Objectives and Policies

Let us now discuss the major scheduling objectives and policies and then explain why FCFS may violate its time of service guarantees.

2.1   Objectives

Scheduling for VOD differs from that for processors and other parts of general-purpose computer systems. In particular, a VOD server maintains a waiting queue for every video, routes incoming requests to their corresponding queues, and applies a scheduling policy to select an appropriate queue for service whenever it has an available *channel*. A channel is a set of resources (network bandwidth, I/O bandwidth, etc.) needed to deliver a multimedia stream. All requests in the selected queue can be serviced together using only one channel. The number of channels is referred to as *server capacity*.

All scheduling policies are guided by one or more of the following primary objectives.

1. Minimize the overall customer reneging probability.
2. Minimize the average request waiting time.
3. Provide time of service guarantees.
4. Minimize unfairness.
5. Eliminate starvation.
6. Minimize the implementation complexity.

The reneging probability is the probability that a new customer leaves the server without being serviced because of a waiting time exceeding the user's tolerance. It is the most important metric because it translates to the number of customers that can be serviced concurrently and to server throughput. The second, third, and fifth objectives are indicators of customer-perceived quality of service (QoS). By providing time of service guarantees, a VOD server can also encourage customers to wait, thereby increasing server throughput. It is also usually desirable that VOD servers treat equally the requests for all videos. Unfairness measures the bias of a policy against cold (i.e., unpopular) videos and can be obtained by the following equation: $unfairness = \sqrt{\sum_{i=1}^{N_v}(r_i - \bar{r})^2/(N_v - 1)}$, where r_i is the reneging probability for the waiting queue i, $\bar{r}$ is the mean reneging probability across all waiting queues, and N_v is the number of waiting queues (and number of videos as well). Finally, minimizing the implementation complexity is a secondary issue in VOD servers because the CPU and memory are not performance bottlenecks.

2.2 Existing Policies

The following is a description of the common scheduling policies for VOD servers.

- *First Come First Serve* (FCFS) [5] - This policy selects the queue with the oldest request.

- *FCFS-n* [5] - With this policy, the server broadcasts periodically the n most common videos on dedicated channels and schedules the requests for the other videos on a FCFS basis. When no request is waiting for the playback of any one of the n most common videos, the server uses the corresponding dedicated channel for the playback of one of the other videos.

- *Maximum Queue Length* (MQL) [5] - This policy selects the longest queue.

- *Maximum Factored Queue Length* (MFQL) [1] - This policy attempts to minimize the mean request waiting time by selecting the queue with the *largest factored length*. The factored length of a queue is defined as its length divided by the square root of the relative access frequency of its corresponding video. MFQL reduces waiting times optimally only if the server is fully loaded and customers always wait until they receive service (i.e. no defections).

- *Group-Guaranteed Server Capacity* (GGSC) [20] - This policy preassigns server channel capacity to groups of requests in order to optimize the mean request waiting time. It groups objects that have nearly equal expected batch sizes and schedules requests in each group on a FCFS basis on the collective channels assigned to each group.

FCFS is the fairest and the easiest to implement. MQL and MFQL reduce the average request waiting time but tend to be biased against cold videos, which have relatively few waiting requests. Unlike MQL, MFQL requires periodic computations of access frequencies. FCFS can prevent starvation, whereas MQL and MFQL cannot. GGSC does not perform as well as FCFS in high-end servers [20], so we will not consider it further in this paper. Similarly, we will not analyze FCFS-n because [20] shows that it performs either as well as or worse in certain situations than FCFS. A detailed investigation of scheduling policies can be found in [16].

2.3 Time of Service Guarantees Through FCFS

In this subsection, we show that FCFS may violate its time of service guarantees because it only considers waiting times in scheduling decisions. We have also observed violations of time of service guarantees during simulations that use the same model of waiting tolerance used in [20]. Let us discuss first how a server may provide time of service guarantees and let us assume, just for now, the absence of VCR-like operations (pause, resume, fast forward, and fast rewind). In the absence of these operations, a VOD server knows exactly when each running stream will complete. A channel becomes available whenever a running stream completes, so the server can assign completion times of running streams as time of service guarantees to incoming requests. Obviously, the server should assign the closest completion times first. Thus, when a request comes and joins an empty waiting queue, the server grants that request a new time of service guarantee. If the incoming request, however, joins a queue that has at least one request, then the new request can be given the same time of service guarantee as the other request(s) waiting in the queue because of batch scheduling. Let us now discuss the impact of VCR-like operations. Applying a pause, a fast forward, or a fast rewind can be considered as an early completion if the corresponding client is the only recipient of the stream because VOD servers typically support interactive operations by using contingency channels [7]. Early completions lead to servicing some requests earlier than their time of service guarantees.

The following example explains why with FCFS, the server may violate time of service guarantees. Let us assume that $t1 < t2 < t3 < t4 < t5 < t6$ and that $i \neq j$. Let us also assume that at the current state of the server, $t5$ is the next stream completion time that has not yet been assigned, and $t6$ is the completion time that immediately follows. At time $t1$, a new request, $R1$, arrives and joins the empty waiting queue i. Thus, the server gives $R1$ the time of service guarantee $t5$. At time $t2$, a new request, $R2$, arrives and joins the empty waiting queue j. Hence, the server gives $R2$ the time of service guarantee $t6$. At time $t3$, a new request, $R3$, arrives and joins the waiting queue i, which already has the request $R1$. So, the server assigns $R3$ the time of service guarantee $t5$. Assume that at time $t4$, $R1$ defects (probably because it was given a far time of service guarantee). Thus, using FCFS, the server will service $R2$ before $R3$, although $R3$ was given a better time of service guarantee. (Note that FCFS by definition continues to select the queue with the oldest request and thus ignores the potential impact of request defections on the time of service guarantees.) Assuming that the time of service guarantee $t4$ is precise (i.e., equal to the actual time of service for the request(s) granted this guarantee), the server will violate the time of service guarantee of $R3$!

3   Next Schedule Time First (NSTF)

We propose a new class of scheduling policies, called *Next Schedule Time First* (NSTF), which eliminates the shortcomings of FCFS. In particular, NSTF assigns schedule times to incoming requests, and it guarantees that they will be serviced no later than scheduled. In addition, it ensures that these schedule times are very close to the actual times of service. NSTF, therefore, improves both QoS and server throughput. Improving throughput is attained by influencing the waiting tolerance of customers. In the absence of any time of service guarantees, customers are more likely to defect because of the uncertainty of when they will start to receive services. Another desirable feature of NSTF is the ability to prevent starvation (as FCFS).

NSTF selects for service the queue with the closest schedule time. The schedule times are assigned as follows. When a new request for a video with no waiting requests arrives, NSTF assigns that request a new schedule time. This schedule time is equal to the closest unassigned completion time of a running stream. By contrast, when a new request joins a waiting queue that has at least one request, NSTF assigns the new request the same schedule time assigned to the other request(s) because all requests in a queue can be serviced together. Note that a schedule time estimates the time when the server starts to deliver a stream and not the time when the presentation actually starts. Thus, it does not include the network latency or the buffering time at the client for smoothing out the delay jitter.

As discussed in the previous section, VCR-like operations can lead only to servicing requests earlier than scheduled and thus will not result in any violations of time of service guarantees.

NSTF can be implemented in different ways. When all waiting requests for a video are canceled, their schedule time becomes available and can be used by other requests. This leads to two variants of NSTF: *NSTFn* and *NSTFo*. NSTFn assigns the freed schedule times to incoming requests, whereas NSTFo assigns them to existing requests with waiting time guarantees beyond a certain threshold, and thus likely to defect without being assigned better schedule times. Hence, requests that are assigned schedule times that require them to wait beyond a certain threshold should be notified that they may be serviced earlier. This notification may influence them to wait. All other requests, however, should be given hard time of service guarantees. NSTFn is simpler than NSTFo, but it is more biased against old requests.

Let us now discuss how NSTFo works. NSTFo assigns each freed schedule time to an appropriate waiting queue that meets the following three conditions. (1) It is nonempty. (2) Its assigned schedule time is worse than the freed schedule time. (3) Based on its assigned schedule time, the expected waiting time for each request in it is beyond a certain threshold. This threshold is set to 5 minutes in this paper because of the studied waiting tolerance models (Subsection 4.2). If no candidate is found, NSTFo grants the freed schedule time to a new request. In contrast, if more than one queue meet these conditions, it selects the most appropriate one. We thus present three variants of NSTFo: *NSTFo-FCFS*, *NSTFo-MQL*, and *NSTFo-MFQL*. These variants differ in the selection criterion of existing requests that will be assigned better schedule times. NSTFo-FCFS selects the queue with the longest waiting time, whereas *NSTFo-MQL* selects the longest queue, and *NSTFo-MFQL* selects the queue with the largest factored length. NSTFo-MQL and NSTFo-MFQL combine the benefits of FCFS and MQL/MFQL by assigning schedule times on a FCFS basis and re-assigning freed schedule times on a MQL/MFQL basis.

The next section demonstrates that NSTF not only provides hard time of service guarantees but also yields outstanding performance gains.

4   Performance Evaluation

We analyze the effectiveness of the proposed policies through simulation. In the analysis, we refer to FCFS that may provide time of service guarantees (which may be violated as shown earlier) as *FCFSg*, and to FCFS that provides no guarantees simply as *FCFS*. We start our discussion with the simulation environment and workload characteristic, and then we present the main results.

4.1   Simulation Platform

We have developed a simulator for a VOD server that supports various scheduling policies. The simulated server starts with a state close to the steady state of the common case to accelerate the simulation. In that state, the server delivers its full capacity of running streams, whose remaining times for completion are uniformly distributed between zero and the normal video length. We have validated many of these results against those generated by simulating an initially unloaded server. The simulation stops after a steady state analysis with 95% confidence interval is guaranteed.

4.2   Workload Characteristics

Like most prior studies, we assume that the arrival of the requests to a VOD server follows a Poisson Process with an average arrival rate λ. Hence, the inter-arrival time is exponentially distributed with a mean $T = 1/\lambda$. We also assume as in previous work that the accesses to videos are highly localized and follow a Zipf-like distribution [2]. With this distribution, the probability of choosing the nth most popular video is $C/n^{1-\theta}$ with a parameter θ and a normalized constant C. The parameter θ controls the skewness of video access. Note that the skewness reaches its peak when $\theta = 0$, and that the access becomes uniformly distributed when $\theta = 1$. In accordance with prior studies, we assume that $\theta = 0.271$.

We characterize the waiting tolerance of customers by two models. In *Model A*, customers who receive time of service guarantees will wait for service if their waiting times will be less than or equal to five minutes; the waiting times of all other customers follow an exponential distribution with a mean of 5 minutes. *Model B* is used in [20] and is the same as Model A except that a truncated normal distribution with a mean of 5 minutes and a standard deviation of 1.67 minutes is used in place of the exponential distribution. Truncation excludes the waiting times that are negative or greater than 12 minutes. In both these models, we assume that the customers who are expected (according to their time of service guarantees) to wait longer than 12 minutes will defect immediately. Although they differ significantly, both normal and exponential distributions were used in previous studies.

We study a VOD server with 120 videos, each of which is 120-minute long. We examine the server at different loads by fixing the request arrival rate at 40 requests per minute and varying the number of channels (server capacity) generally from 500 to 1750. VCR-like operations can be supported using contingency channels [7]. Thus, the relative performance of various scheduling policies in terms of reneging probability, waiting times, and unfairness does not depend on these operations as long as the fraction of server channels used for these operations is kept the same (which is typically the case). Therefore, we will not consider VCR-like operations in this simulation study in favor of keeping the analysis focused. The results in terms of reneging probability, waiting times, and unfairness can be generalized by assuming that the number of server channels excludes the contingency channels. The accuracy of schedule times, however, is likely to change because VCR-like operations lead to early completions and thus to servicing requests earlier than scheduled. The change increases with the frequency of these operations.

4.3   Result Presentation and Analysis

Let us now compare the performance of various NSTF policies with each other, with FCFSg, and with policies that do not provide time of service guarantees: FCFS, MQL, and MFQL. We consider five performance metrics: the number of violations of time of service guarantees, the average deviation from these guarantees, the overall customer reneging percent, the average request waiting time, and unfairness.

Table 1 compares FCFSg, NSTFn, and the three variants of NSTFo in terms of the number of violations of time of service guarantees and the average deviation of these guarantees from the actual times of service. (The schedule times given by NSTF act as time of service guarantees.) The results are shown for the two models of customer waiting tolerance. The numbers of violations are collected per 1000 requests, and the arrows show the variations as the server capacity increases from 500 to 1500. For example, with FCFSg under Model A, an average of 11.6 out of 1000 time of service guarantees are violated when the server capacity is 500, compared with 0.03 violations when the capacity is 1500. The number of violations decreases with the server capacity as expected. The results demonstrate that FCFSg may violate its time of service guarantees, but these violations happen very occasionally (especially for high server capacities) because FCFSg tends to overestimate significantly these guarantees. In fact, overestimating these guarantees is the most critical problem of FCFSg. With FCFSg, the actual times of service differ from the time of service guarantees by 20 seconds to more than 4.5 minutes on the average! The inaccuracy of time service guarantees leads to uncertainty of when customers will start to receive services. Customers would greatly appreciate receiving accurate schedule times so that they could plan accordingly. Moreover, customers are more likely to defect if their waiting times are overestimated. In contrast with FCFSg, NSTF produces accurate schedule times and services requests no later than scheduled. The average deviations of the actual times of service from the schedule times given by NSTFn and NSTFo are within 6 seconds and 0.2 second, respectively.

Let us now discuss the performance of the three variants of NSTFo in terms of throughput, waiting times, and unfairness, and then we use only the best performer

Table 1. Violations of Time of Service Guarantees and Average Deviations from these Guarantees (Violations are collected per 1000 requests)

Policy	Model A		Model B	
	Violations	Deviation (sec)	Violations	Deviation (sec)
FCFSg	$11.6 \rightarrow 0.03$	$226 \rightarrow 19.6$	$4.6 \rightarrow 0.09$	$272.9 \rightarrow 26.2$
NSTFn	0	$3.8 \rightarrow 0.29$	0	$6.03 \rightarrow 1.01$
NSTFo-FCFS	0	$0.12 \rightarrow 0.05$	0	$0.14 \rightarrow 0.16$
NSTFo-MQL	0	$0 \rightarrow 0.04$	0	$0 \rightarrow 0.07$
NSTFo-MFQL	0	$0 \rightarrow 0.05$	0	$0 \rightarrow 0.05$

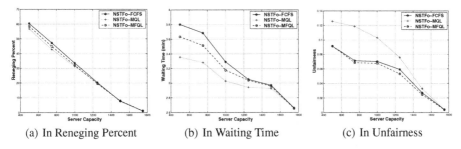

(a) In Reneging Percent   (b) In Waiting Time   (c) In Unfairness

Fig. 1. Comparison among Variants of NSTFo (Model A)

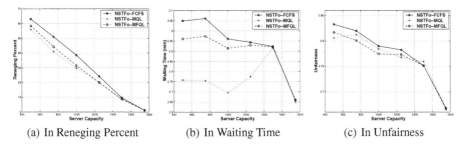

(a) In Reneging Percent   (b) In Waiting Time   (c) In Unfairness

Fig. 2. Comparison among Variants of NSTFo (Model B)

among them in the subsequent analysis. Figures 1 and 2 compare the performance of these variants under Model A and Model B of the waiting tolerance, respectively. The results indicate that NSTFo-MQL performs the best in terms of both throughput and waiting times, followed by NSTFo-MFQL. Despite that NSTFo-MQL is not the fairest, it stands out as the clear winner because fairness is far less important than throughput and waiting times.

Figures 3 and 4 compare the performance of FCFSg, NSTFn, and NSTFo-MQL. The results demonstrate that NSTFo-MQL achieves better throughput and waiting times than NSTFn under both tolerance models, but NSTFn is fairer. Among the three policies, NSTFo-MQL delivers the highest throughput under both tolerance models. We expect the NSTF policies to perform even better in real systems because customers are more likely to defect with FCFSg, which tends to overestimate the waiting times. Unfortunately, the increased likelihood of defection with FCFSg is not captured very accurately by the tolerance models. In both models, the waiting tolerance of customers does not depend on the assigned time of service guarantees if the waiting times (according to these guarantees) may be greater than 5 minutes. This suggests that we are not entirely fair to the proposed policies. NSTFo-MQL also generally achieves the shortest waiting times when the tolerance follows Model B. In the case of Model A, however, FCFSg generally achieves the shortest waiting times, and NSTFo-MQL performs a little worse. Under both tolerance models, FCFSg is the fairest.

Figures 5 and 6 compare the performance of NSTFo-MQL with policies that do not provide time of service guarantees: FCFS, MQL, and MFQL. Note that NSTFo-MQL

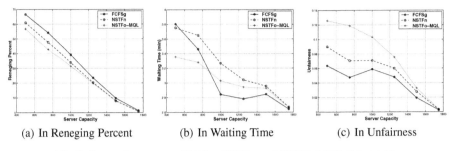

(a) In Reneging Percent   (b) In Waiting Time   (c) In Unfairness

Fig. 3. Comparison among FCFSg, NSTFn, and NSTFo-MQL (Model A)

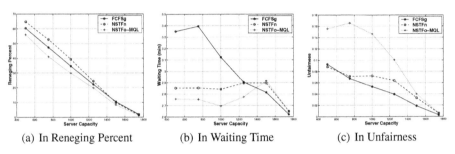

(a) In Reneging Percent   (b) In Waiting Time   (c) In Unfairness

Fig. 4. Comparison among FCFSg, NSTFn, and NSTFo-MQL (Model B)

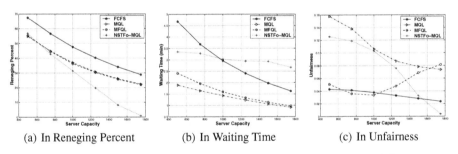

(a) In Reneging Percent   (b) In Waiting Time   (c) In Unfairness

Fig. 5. Comparison of NSTF0-MQL with FCFS, MQL, and MFQL (Model A)

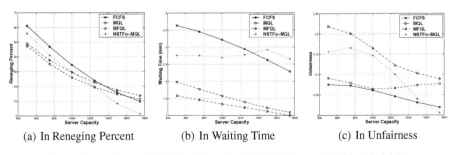

(a) In Reneging Percent   (b) In Waiting Time   (c) In Unfairness

Fig. 6. Comparison of NSTF0-MQL with FCFS, MQL, and MFQL (Model B)

leads to the highest throughput under Model A. It also achieves the highest throughput under Model B but only when the reneging percent is less than 20, which is the most likely operating region as much larger reneging percents would be unacceptable. As expected, MQL and MFQL perform the best in terms of waiting times, and FCFS is the fairest.

5   Conclusions

We have proposed a new class of scheduling policies for VOD servers, called *Next Schedule Time First* (NSTF), which provides customers with hard time of service guarantees and with very accurate schedule times. We have presented two variants of NSTF: *NSTFn* and *NSTFo*. NSTFn assigns freed schedule times to incoming requests, whereas NSTFo assigns them to existing requests. We have presented three variants of NSTFo: *NSTFo-FCFS*, *NSTFo-MQL*, and *NSTFo-MFQL*, which differ in the selection criterion of existing requests that will be assigned better schedule times.

We have demonstrated the effectiveness of NSTF through simulation. We have considered five performance metrics: the number of violations of time of service guarantees, the average deviation of the actual times of service from the time of service guarantees, the overall customer reneging percentage, the average request waiting time, and unfairness. We have studied the impacts of customer waiting tolerance and server capacity (or server load) on the results.

The main simulation results can be summarized as follows. (1) NSTF always meets the time of service guarantees and produces very accurate schedule times. The average deviations of the actual times of service from the schedule times are within 0.2 second (when any implementation of NSTFo is used) and 6 seconds (when NSTFn is used). In contrast, FCFS may violate its time of service guarantees, and these guarantees differ from the actual times of service by 20 seconds to more than 4.5 minutes on the average! (2) NSTFo-MQL is the clear winner among the variants of NSTF when all performance metrics are considered. (3) NSTFo-MQL achieves higher throughput and, in certain situations, shorter waiting times than FCFS that may provide limited time of service guarantees. (4) By motivating customers to wait, NSTFo-MQL outperforms MQL and MFQL (both of which cannot provide time of service guarantees) in terms of throughput for one of the models of waiting tolerance. For the other model, NSTFo-MQL also achieves the highest throughput but only within the most likely operating region of the server. NSTFo-MQL is also fairer than MQL and MFQL for high server capacities because schedule times are assigned on a FCFS basis. As expected, NSTFo-MQL leads to longer waiting times than MQL and MFQL.

NSTF, therefore, not only can provide hard time of service guarantees and very accurate schedule times, but also can deliver outstanding performance benefits.

Acknowledgments

The authors would like to thank the anonymous reviewers and Dr. Dilip Krishnaswamy for their many helpful comments.

References

1. C. C. Aggarwal, J. L. Wolf, and P. S. Yu: The Maximum Factor Queue Length Batching Scheme for Video-on-Demand Systems. *IEEE Trans. on Computers*, Vol. 50, Issue 2, (2001) 97-110.
2. A. L. Chervenak: Tertiary Storage: An Evaluation of New Applications. Ph.D. Thesis, U.C. Berkeley, (1994).
3. A. L. Chervenak, D. A. Patterson, and R. H. Katz: Choosing the Best Storage Systems for Video Service. In *Proc. of the ACM Conf. on Multimedia*, (1995) 109-119.
4. C. Chou, L. Golubchik, J. C .S. Lui: Striping Doesn't Scale: How to Achieve Scalability for Continuous Media Servers with Replication. In *Proc. of the Int'l Conf. on Distributed Computing Systems (ICDCS)*, (2000) 64-71.
5. A. Dan, D. Sitaram, and P. Shahabuddin: Scheduling Policies for an On-Demand Video Server with Batching. In *Proc. of the ACM Conf. on Multimedia*, (1994) 391-398.
6. A. Dan, D. M. Dias, R. Mukherjee, D. Sitaram, and R. Tewari: Buffering and Caching in Large-Scale Video servers. *In Digest of Papers. IEEE Int'l Computer Conf.*, (1995) 217-225.
7. A. Dan, P. Shahabuddin, D. Sitaram, and D. Towsley: Channel Allocation under Batching and VCR Control in Movie-on-Demand Servers. *Journal of Parallel and Distributed Computing*, Vol. 30, Issue 2, (1995) 168-179.
8. R. Flynn, and W. Tetzlaff: Disk Striping and Block Replication Algorithms for Video File Servers. In *Proc. of the Int'l Conf. on Multimedia Computing and Systems*, (1996) 590-597.
9. L. Giuliano: Deploying Native Multicast across the Internet. Online White Paper at `http://www.sprintlink.net/multicast/whitepaper.html`.
10. L. Golubchik, J. C. S. Lui, and R. Muntz: Reducing I/O Demand in Video-On-Demand Storage Servers. In *Proc. of the ACM SIGMETRICS Conf. on Measurements and Modeling of Computer Systems*, (1995) 25-36.
11. K. A. Hua, Y. Cai, and S. Sheu: Patching: A Multicast Technique for True Video-on-Demand Services. In *Proc. of ACM Multimedia*, (1998) 191-200.
12. L. Juhn and L. Tseng: Harmonic Broadcasting for Video-on-Demand Service. *IEEE Trans. on Broadcasting*, Vol. 43, Issue 3, (1997) 268-271.
13. J.-F. Pâris: A Fixed-Delay Broadcasting Protocol for Video-on-Demand. In *Proc. of the Int'l Conf. on Computer Communications and Networks*, (2001) 418-423.
14. A. L. N. Reddy, J. Wyllie: Disk Scheduling in a Multimedia I/O System. In *Proc. of the ACM Conf. on Multimedia*, (1993) 225-233.
15. N. J. Sarhan and C. R. Das: Adaptive Block Rearrangement Algorithms for Video-On-Demand Servers. In *Proc. of Int'l Conf. on Parallel Processing*, (2001) 452-459.
16. N. J. Sarhan and C. R. Das: A Simulation-Based Analysis of Scheduling Policies for Multimedia Servers. In *Proc. of the 36th Annual Simulation Symp.*, (2003) 183-190.
17. N. J. Sarhan and C. R. Das: An Integrated Resource Sharing Policy for Multimedia Storage Servers Based on Network-Attached Disks. In *Proc. of the 23rd Int'l Conf. on Distributed Computing Systems* (ICDCS), (2003) 136-143.
18. S. Sen, L. Gao, J. Rexford, and D. Towsley: Optimal Patching Schemes for Efficient Multimedia Streaming. In *Proc. of the Int'l Workshop on Network and Operating Systems Support for Digital Audio and Video (NOSSDAV)*, (1999) 265-277.
19. P. Shenoy, and V. Harric: Efficient Striping Techniques for Variable Bit Rate Continuous Media File Servers. *Performance Evaluation Journal*, Vol. 38, Issue 2, (1999) 175-199.
20. A. K. Tsiolis and M. K. Vernon: Group-Guaranteed Channel Capacity in Multimedia Storage Servers. In *Proc. of the ACM SIGMETRICS Conf. on Measurements and Modeling of Computer Systems*, (1997) 285-297.
21. H. M. Vin, P. Goyal, and A. Goyal: A Statistical Admission Control Algorithms for Multimedia Servers. In *Proc. of the ACM Multimedia*, (1994) 33-40.

Bandwidth Constrained IP Multicast Traffic Engineering Without MPLS Overlay

Ning Wang and George Pavlou

Center for Communication Systems Research, University of Surrey, UK
{N.Wang,G.Pavlou}@surrey.ac.uk

Abstract. Existing multicast traffic engineering (TE) solutions tend to use explicit routing through MPLS tunnels. In this paper we shift away from this overlay approach and address the bandwidth constrained IP multicast TE directly based on link state IGP routing protocols. The objective is that, through plain PIM-SM shortest path routing with optimized Multi-topology IS-IS (M-ISIS) link weights, the resulting multicast trees are geared towards minimal consumption of bandwidth resources. We apply Genetic Algorithms (GA) to the calculation of optimized M-ISIS link weights that specifically cater for engineered PIM-SM routing with bandwidth guarantees. Our evaluation results show that GA-based multicast traffic engineering consumes significantly less bandwidth resources in comparison with conventional IP approaches, while it also exhibits higher capability of eliminating/alleviating link congestion. The key contribution is a methodology for engineering multicast flows in a pure IP environment, without MPLS explicit routing that potentially suffers from scalability problems in terms of LSP maintenance.

1 Introduction

Traffic Engineering (TE) [1] is an efficient mechanism for improving the service capability of operational IP networks. In literature, traffic engineering approaches can be classified into Multi-Protocol Label Switching (MPLS) based and pure IP-based. With MPLS-based TE, packets are encapsulated with labels at ingress points, which are then used to forward these packets along a chosen explicit Label Switching Path (LSP). In this case, the conventional shortest path based routing infrastructure (e.g., OSPF) is overridden with an MPLS-based explicit routing overlay. While MPLS is a powerful technology for creating overlay networks to support any specific routing strategy, it is also expensive and suffers potentially from scalability problem in terms of LSP state maintenance. On the other hand, the advent of pure IP-based TE solutions challenges MPLS-based approaches in that Internet traffic can also be effectively tuned through native hop-by-hop routing, without the associated complexity and cost of MPLS. Some research works have indicated that OSPF/IS-IS link weights can be intelligently pre-assigned to achieve near-optimal path selections with respect to the expected traffic demand [4], [9].

Despite the progress for unicast services, traffic engineering for multicast flows remains largely a dark area. In the past few years, MPLS-based multicast TE has become a subject of interest, with a number of relevant research works becoming available [2], [5], [6]. In contrast, pure IP-based multicast traffic engineering without MPLS overlay has not yet been explored. The reason for this situation can be summarized as follows. First, the Protocol Independent Multicast – Sparse Mode (PIM-SM)

J. Vicente and D. Hutchison (Eds.): MMNS 2004, LNCS 3271, pp. 140–151, 2004.

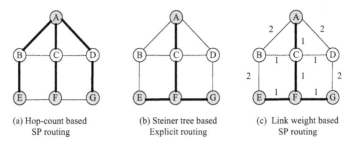

(a) Hop-count based
SP routing

(b) Steiner tree based
Explicit routing

(c) Link weight based
SP routing

Fig. 1. Multicast routing using different approaches.

[3] uses the underlying IP unicast routing table for the construction of multicast trees, and hence it is difficult to decouple multicast traffic engineering from its unicast counterpart. Bandwidth optimization for multicast traffic can be formulated as the directed Steiner tree problem, which is *NP*-complete. The enforcement of Steiner trees can be achieved through packet encapsulation and explicit routing mechanisms such as MPLS tunneling. However, this approach lacks support from hop-by-hop protocols, due to Reverse Path Forwarding (RPF) in the IP multicast routing protocol family. In PIM-SM, if multicast packets are not received on the shortest path through which unicast traffic is delivered back to the source, they are discarded for avoiding traffic loops.

In this paper we investigate the feasibility of engineering multicast traffic based on plain IP routing protocols. Our objective is to minimize the overall network resource consumption with bandwidth constraints, in order to accommodate as many multicast sessions as possible. The enforcement of engineered PIM-SM path selections is via setting optimized link weights for the underlying link state routing protocols. In our proposed approach, PIM-SM follows the shortest path according to the pre-set link weights, whereas the resulting multicast tree is in effect a hop-count Steiner tree with minimum number of links involved, which implies that minimum bandwidth resources are consumed. We demonstrate this with the simple example of Figure 1. We assume that node A is the root of group X that contains member nodes E, F and G. If PIM-SM performs hop-count based shortest path (SP) routing, the total bandwidth consumed is 6 units (1 unit for each on-tree link), as shown in Figure 1(a). In effect, by applying Steiner tree heuristics to this simple example, it is easy to obtain the optimized multicast tree with 4 units of bandwidth consumption, as shown in Figure 1(b). This hop-count Steiner tree can be supported using explicit routing approaches such as MPLS tunnels. For example, in order to deliver multicast packets from node A to E via the engineered path, an LSP tunnel has to be set up along the non-shortest path $A \rightarrow C \rightarrow F \rightarrow E$. On the other hand, by intelligently assigning link weights for the underlying link-state IGP protocol, we can still achieve the same effect in terms of bandwidth conservation, as PIM-SM join requests follow the shortest path in terms of this set of link weights (Figure 1(c)). From this example we can see that hop-count Steiner tree based multicast traffic engineering can be reduced to plain shortest path routing by introducing a set of optimized link weights. The advantage is that, through link weight setting as calculated by off-line network provisioning, IP routers are able to construct optimized multicast trees by simply using Dijkstra's shortest path algorithm. Currently, one difficulty in implementation of this scheme is that most unicast routing protocols such as OSPF and IS-IS do not provide independent set of link weights for different types of flows. Hence it is undesirable to set link weights exclusively for multicast traffic engineering, without considering unicast traffic in the network. In order to decouple multicast from unicast path selection, our approach is based on the Multi-topology extension of the IS-IS protocol (M-ISIS) [7], which is able to populate dedicated Multicast Routing Information Bases (MRIBs, i.e. RPF tables) for PIM-SM routing. This multi-topology routing feature provides a mechanism to separate TE for multicast and unicast flows. A detailed description of the M-ISIS based multicast TE framework will be presented in section 3.

The optimization of link weights through shortest path routing for indirectly obtaining one single Steiner tree in terms of hop-counts is *NP-complete*, since this is an adapted version of the classical Steiner tree problem. In effect, a more practical problem concerning an Internet Service Provider (ISP) for multicast traffic engineering is how to assign a set of unified link weights, such that *all* the multicast trees within the network consume minimum bandwidth resources. At the same time, we consider an additional constraint that the total bandwidth allocated on each link for the overlapping multicast trees should not exceed its capacity. In this paper we adopt a Genetic Algorithm (*GA*) approach as off-line multicast traffic engineering for optimizing overall bandwidth consumption for multiple multicast flows. More specifically, the M-ISIS link weights are adjusted in each *GA* generation so that the overall fitness is geared towards optimized network resource consumption with the constraint of link capacity. The key novelty of this work is that, in a similar fashion to the work in [4], [9] for unicast traffic, multicast flows can also be optimized in hop-by-hop routing based IP networks without relying on MPLS tunneling.

2   Related Work

In [9], the authors proved that, any arbitrary set of *loop-free* routes can be represented with shortest paths with respect to a set of positive link weights. As a typical application to this conclusion, the authors of [4] claimed that by optimizing OSPF/IS-IS link weights for the purpose of load balancing, link congestion can be effectively avoided for unicast services. The key idea of the proposed algorithm is to intelligently adjust the weight of a certain number of links that depart from one particular node, so that new paths with equal cost are created from this node towards the destination. As a result, the traffic originally traveling through one single path can be split into other paths with equal OSPF/IS-IS weights.

Recently, research efforts have also addressed traffic engineering multicast flows, particularly for Quality of Service (QoS) and bandwidth optimization purposes. One common aspect of those schemes is that they are based on explicit routing, typically through MPLS tunneling. The problem of bandwidth optimization in multicast routing is formulated as the Steiner tree problem, which has been extensively studied in the literature, with the TM heuristic [8] being a near-optimal solution. As already mentioned, Steiner trees can be enforced through point-to-multipoint LSPs. In [2], Steiner tree based heuristics are applied for computing multicast path selection only at the edge of MPLS domains, so that multicast TE within the network can be reduced to a unicast problem. In [5], the authors propose an online multicast TE scheme using Steiner tree heuristics, while also attempting to minimize multicast flow interferences.

Despite its flexibility, the explicit routing overlay approach suffers from complexity and cost associated with MPLS deployment. This problem becomes more serious

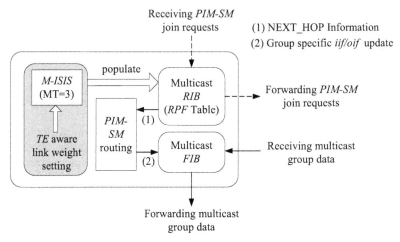

Fig. 2. *M-ISIS* based multicast traffic engineering.

in multicast services, since point-to-multipoint LSPs need to be maintained. Taking these facts into account, we propose a novel scheme for engineering multicast flows in the pure IP based environment, without the deployment of MPLS tunneling.

3   Proposed M-ISIS Based Multicast TE

The traditional OSPF and IS-IS protocols only have uni-dimensional viewpoint on the weight of each link in the network, and this influences path selections for both unicast and multicast traffic. In contrast, M-ISIS provides the original IS-IS protocol with the additional ability of viewing the weight of each link for different logical IP topologies independently. For IPv4 multicast traffic, the field of Multi Topology identifier (MT-ID) with value 3 in M-ISIS is dedicated to the multicast reverse path forwarding topology, i.e., the RPF table for PIM-SM can be populated using a set of independent link weights with MT-ID equal to 3. With this multi-topology capability, it becomes possible that PIM-SM based multicast routing is completely decoupled from the underlying routing table for unicast traffic.

Figure 2 illustrates the basic framework of IP multicast traffic engineering through optimized M-ISIS link weight setting. First, the network topology (e.g., link capacity, edge router information) and the multicast "traffic matrix" are obtained as the input parameters for calculating the optimized link weights over an existing physical network infrastructure. The multicast traffic matrix can be derived through obtaining the following information from each group session: (1) bandwidth demand, (2) root node (i.e., ingress router) and a set of egress routers with potential receivers. An ISP can obtain this information from Service Level Agreements (SLAs) with customers. Here we assume the following business relationship: content providers have SLAs with an ISP and receivers subscribe multicast services offered by the content provider. The latter may pass the necessary information mentioned above to the ISP in order to aid multicast traffic matrix generation. In general, accurate multicast traffic matrix generation is a new research issue that needs further study, and it is outside the scope of this paper. Based on the multicast traffic matrix, the optimized link weights are computed through off-line algorithms (see sections 4 and 5) and configured in the routers that run the M-ISIS routing protocol with MT-ID equal to 3, which is dedicated to the multicast RPF table construction. On receiving Link State Advertisements (LSAs), each M-ISIS aware router computes shortest path trees according to this set of link weights and decides the NEXT_HOP router for a specific IP address/prefix. When a PIM-SM join request is received, the router simply looks up the RPF table and finds the proper NEXT_HOP for forwarding the packet. In this scenario, the delivery of PIM-SM group join requests follows an engineered path, thus the resulting multicast distribution tree from the root to individual members conforms to the TE requirement. In addition, the multicast Forwarding Information Base (FIB) is dynamically updated for the incoming interface (iif) and outgoing interface (oif) list of each group. We can see from Figure 2 that, apart from the offline calculation and setting of link weights, there is no need for any other configuration or extensions to the current M-ISIS and PIM-SM protocols for multicast traffic engineering purposes.

4   Problem Formulation

The following is the integer-programming formulation for computing bandwidth constrained Steiner trees in terms hop counts with the objective of minimizing overall bandwidth consumption. By setting the group-specific *binary* variables $x_{ij}^{g,k}$ and y_{ij}^{g} for each link (i, j), a set of explicit multicast trees with minimum number of links is obtained, which implies that minimum bandwidth consumption is achieved. We first present some definitions below:

G — Total number of active multicast groups;

r_g — Root node of group g ($g = 1, \ldots, G$);

V_g — Multicast member (receiver) set for group g;

D_g — Bandwidth demand for group g traffic on each link;

C_{ij} — Bandwidth capacity of link (i, j);

y_{ij}^{g} — Equal to 1 if link (i, j) is included in the multicast tree for group g;

$x_{ij}^{g,k}$ — Equal to 1 if link (i, j) is on the unique elementary path from the root node r_g of   group g to the group member node k in the multicast tree.

The integer-programming problem of computing a set of bandwidth constrained Steiner trees with minimum overall bandwidth consumption is formulated as:

Minimize

$$\sum_{g=1}^{G} \sum_{(i,j)\in E} D_g \times y_{ij}^{g}$$

Subject to

$$\sum_{h\in V} x_{ih}^{g,k} - \sum_{j\in V} x_{ji}^{g,k} = \begin{cases} 1 & i = r_g \\ -1 & i = k, \quad k \in V_g \\ 0 & i \neq r_g, i \notin V_g \end{cases} \tag{1}$$

$$x_{ij}^{g,k} \leq y_{ij}^{g} \qquad (i, j) \in E, \ k \in V_g \tag{2}$$

$$x_{ij}^{g,k} = 0,1 \qquad\qquad (i, j) \in E, \ k \in V_g \qquad\qquad (3)$$

$$y_{ij}^g = 0,1 \qquad\qquad (i, j) \in E \qquad\qquad (4)$$

$$\sum_{g=1}^{G} y_{ij}^g \times D_g \le C_{ij} \qquad\qquad (i, j) \in E \qquad\qquad (5)$$

The variables to be determined are $x_{ij}^{g,k}$ and y_{ij}^g for every link $(i, j) \in E$. Constraint (1) ensures one unit of multicast flow from r_g to every group member node $K \in V_g$. Constraint (2) guarantees that the amount of flows along link (i, j) must be zero if this link is not included in the multicast tree for group g. Variables $x_{ij}^{g,k}$ and y_{ij}^g are confined to binary values in constraints (3) and (4) for non-splitting of multicast flows. Finally it is required in (5) that the total bandwidth consumption on each link should not exceed its capacity.

As we have mentioned before, the enforcement of the above set of bandwidth constrained hop-count Steiner trees can be achieved through an explicit routing overlay, e.g. through MPLS tunneling, on per group basis. However, the paths in the Steiner tree from r_g to individual group members $K \in V_g$ might not completely overlap with the shortest paths between them. This means that, in case of hop-by-hop routing, multicast traffic flowing on the Steiner tree will be discarded due to the RPF check failure, if the packets are not received from the correct interface on the shortest path back to the source. In order to apply the above programming model to IP layer solutions, we introduce a unified M-ISIS link weight w for each link (i, j), and by properly setting those link weights it is guaranteed that the tree branch from r_g to each receiver $K \in V_g$ is the shortest path according to this set of weights. Put in other words, our strategy is to represent this set of explicit hop-count Steiner trees with shortest path trees through intelligent configuration of a unified set of link weights.

5   A Genetic Algorithm (GA) Based Solution

5.1   Encoding and Initial Population

In our *GA* approach each chromosome is represented by a link weight vector $W = <w_1, \dots w_{|E|}>$ where $|E|$ is the total number of links in the network. The value of each weight is within the range from 1 to *MAX_WEIGHT*. In our experiments we define the value of *MAX_WEIGHT* to be 64 for reducing the search space. On the other hand, the population size is set to 100, with the initial values inside each chromosome randomly varying from 1 to *MAX_WEIGHT*. In addition to these randomly generated chromosomes, we add the solution of using hop-count as the link weight into the initial population (i.e., the weight of every link is set to 1). This is to guarantee that every link can potentially obtain the lowest link weight such that it has the chance to be included into the resulting trees.

5.2   Fitness Evaluation

Chromosomes are selected according to their *fitness*. In our approach, the bandwidth constraint is embedded into the fitness function as a penalty factor, such that the search space is explored with the potential feasible solutions. The fitness of each chromosome can be defined to be a two-dimensional function of the overall network load ($l1$) and excessive bandwidth allocated to overloaded links ($l2$), i.e.,

$$fitness = f(l1, l2) = \frac{\mu}{\alpha \times l1 + \beta \times l2} \qquad (6)$$

where α, β and μ are manually configured coefficients.

In equation (6) $l1$ and $l2$ are expressed as follows:

$$l1 = \sum_{g=1}^{G} \sum_{(i,j) \in E} D_g \times y_{ij}^g \qquad (7)$$

$$l2 = \sum_{(i,j) \in E} \omega_{ij} \times (\sum_{g=1}^{G} D_g \times y_{ij}^g - C_{ij}) \qquad (8)$$

where

$$\omega_{ij} = \begin{cases} 0 & if \ \sum_{g=1}^{G} D_g \times y_{ij}^g \leq C_{ij} \\ 1 & otherwise \end{cases} \qquad (9)$$

We note from fitness function (6) that the objective is two fold: first, chromosomes of the new generations should converge towards a set of Steiner trees in terms of hop counts with the lowest bandwidth consumption, and second, solutions obtained from the offspring should be feasible in that the total bandwidth allocated to the multicast flows traveling through each link should not exceed its capacity. The tuning of α and β can be regarded as a tradeoff between overall bandwidth conservation and load balancing. For example, if we let $\beta = 0$ then the objective is to conserve bandwidth resources only, while setting $\alpha = 0$ infers to minimize link overloading within the network.

5.3 Crossover and Mutation

According to the basic principle of Genetic Algorithms, chromosomes with better fitness value have higher probability of being inherited into the next generation. To achieve this, we first rank all the chromosomes in descending order according to their fitness, i.e., the chromosomes with high fitness (lower overall load) are placed on the top of the ranking list. Thereafter, we partition this list into two disjoined sets, with the top 50 chromosomes belonging to the upper class (UC) and the bottom 50 chromosomes to the lower class (LC). During the crossover procedure, we select one parent chromosome C_U^i from UC and the other parent C_L^i from LC in generation i for creating the child C^{i+1} in generation $i+1$. Specifically, we use a crossover probability threshold $K_C \in (0, 0.5)$ to decide the genes of which parent to be inherited into the child chromosome in the next generation. We also introduce a mutation probability threshold K_M to randomly replace some old genes with new ones. In addition to this type of conventional mutation, we also find the *congested* link with the highest load in the chromosome of the new generation, and we randomly raise its link weight in an ad hoc manner so as to avoid hot spots. In non-congested conditions, this type of mutation the highest loaded link is suppressed.

```
Procedure Computing_fitness(Chromosome i)
begin
      Set the weight of each link according to the gene
        values in chromosome i;
      for each multicast group g
            Compute the shortest path tree T_g rooted at
              r_g, and spanning to all members in V_g;
              for each link (u, v) in T_g
                    Update link load L_uv according to the
                        bandwidth demand D_g of group g;
      end for
      Load1 = 0;    Load2 = 0;
      for each link (u, v) in the network
            Load1 = Load1 + L_uv;
            If L_uv > C_uv
                  Load2 = Load2 + (L_uv - C_uv);
      end for
      return fitness = f(Load1, Load2);
end
```

Fig. 3. Fitness calculation.

```
Procedure Crossover( C_U^i , C_L^i )
begin
      for all genes j = 1 … |E|
            Generate r = random(MAX_WEIGHT);
            if r > K_C
                  C^{i+1}(j) = C_U^i(j);
            else if r > K_M
                  C^{i+1}(j) = C_L^i(j);
            else
                  C^{i+1} = random[1, MAX_WEIGHT];
      end For
      Find gene (link) t with the highest load in C^{i+1};
      if L_t (link load)   > Cap_t (link capacity)
            C^{i+1}(t) = random[C^{i+1}(t), MAX_WEIGHT];
      return C^{i+1};
end
```

Fig. 4. Crossover and mutation.

6 Simulation Results

6.1 Simulation Configuration

In our simulation, we adopt the Waxman's model in GT-ITM topology generator for constructing our network. We generate a random graph of 100 nodes, out of which 50 are configured as Designated Routers (DRs) with attached group sources or receivers. The scaled bandwidth capacity of each network link is set to 10^5 units.

The simulation parameters of the proposed Genetic Algorithm are illustrated in table 1. Apart from the GA approach, we also implemented two non-TE based hop-by-hop routing paradigms and one explicit routing approach: (1) shortest path routing with random link weight setting (Random), (2) shortest path routing in terms of hop-counts (SPH), and (3) Steiner tree approach using the TM heuristic [8]. For this TM Steiner tree algorithm, we use hop count as the link weight, and the resulting trees are group specific, i.e., one Steiner tree is specifically constructed for each multicast group. In the next section we will show that the TM heuristic has the best performance among the four algorithms in terms of bandwidth conservation. Nevertheless, it should be emphasized that, this solution requires the setting up of MPLS tunnels for explicit routing on a per-group basis, and this cannot be directly achieved in a pure IP environment. Hence, the inclusion of the TM algorithm is only to use its performance as a lower bound reference for comparison with the other three hop-by-hop oriented approaches.

Table 1. GA parameter configuration.

Parameter	Value	Parameter	Value
Population size (P)	100	μ	10^7
Maximum generation (M)	500	α	1.0
Maximum link weight (MAX_WEIGHT)	64	β	10
Crossover threshold (K_C)	0.30	Mutation threshold (K_M)	0.01

6.2 Performance Evaluation

We found from our simulation that shortest path routing with hop-counts (SPH) has higher capability in finding *feasible solutions* (i.e., no overloaded links incurred) than random link weight setting approaches (shown later). Hence, we will start from the comparison between GA and SPH in the capability of exploring feasible solutions. Figure 5 presents the ratio of successful instances obtained by GA but failed to be found in SPH. We define the Maximum Link Overload Rate (*MLOR*) as follows:

$$MLOR = \max_{(i,j) \in E} \left(\frac{\sum_{g=1}^{G} D_g \times y_{ij}^g - C_{ij}}{C_{ij}} \right)$$

From this definition we can see that *MLOR* reflects the overloading scale of the most congested link (if any, i.e., *MLOR*>0). In the figure, when the value of *MLOR* computed by SPH is in range of (0%, 5%], GA can obtain feasible solutions (i.e. $MLOR_{GA} \leq 0$) for 65% of these instances. We can also see that, with the increase of

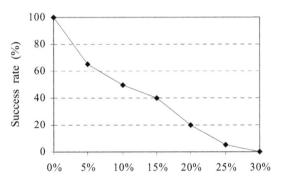

Fig. 5. GA success rate vs. $MLOR_{SPH}$.

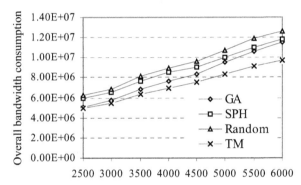

Fig. 6. Total bandwidth consumption vs. Max D_g.

external bandwidth demands, the capability of GA in finding feasible solutions is decreasing. When the *MLOR* value of SPH grows up to 25% due to the higher external traffic demand, the success rate of GA drops to 5%. From this figure, it can be inferred that, when the external group traffic demand is at the brink of causing network congestion, GA has higher capability of avoiding link overloading compared to other approaches. Obviously, it may be the case that no feasible solution exists at all, if external traffic demand exceeds a certain threshold.

Figure 6 illustrates the feature of overall bandwidth conservation capability of individual schemes with the variation of maximum group traffic demand D_g. We see that the GA approach exhibits the best capability in conserving bandwidth among all the hop-by-hop routing schemes. Typically, when the network is under-utilized, our proposed GA approach exhibits significantly higher performance than the conventional IP based solutions without explicit routing. For example when $D_g > 3000$, the overall bandwidth consumption of the Random and SPH solutions are higher than that of GA by 19.3% and 14.9% respectively. Compared with the TM heuristic that needs support from MPLS overlaying, the gap from GA is below 8%. However, when the external traffic demand grows, the performance of GA converges to that of the SPH approach. On the other hand, although the TM algorithm exhibits significant higher capability in bandwidth conservation when the external traffic demand grows ($D_g >$

4000) this does not mean what have been obtained are feasible solutions without introducing overloaded links.

The rest of the simulation evaluates the capability of alleviating network congestions in our proposed solution. Figure 7(a) shows the relationship between the proportion of overloaded links and the maximum group traffic demand D_g in time of congestion. From the figure we can see that there are more overloaded links as D_g increases. The most interesting result is that, through our GA optimization, the percentage of overloaded links is significantly lower than all the other routing schemes. In the most congested situation (D_g =6000), the average rate of overloaded links computed by GA is only 1.4%, in contrast to 12.6% by random link weight setting, 8.6% by the TM heuristic, and 4.4% by SPH respectively. On the other hand, the amount of overloaded bandwidth occurred on the most congested links is another important parameter an ISP is interested in. An ISP should avoid configuring the network resulting in hot spots with high *MLOR*. Through our simulations, we also find that the proposed GA approach achieves the lowest *MLOR* performance. In Figure 7(b), the overloading scale is 45% of the bandwidth capacity on the most congested link in the GA approach with D_g equal to 6000, while this value reaches 110% and 59% in random link weight setting and SPH respectively. Even by using explicit routing TM heuristic, the overloaded bandwidth is 78% of the original link capacity.

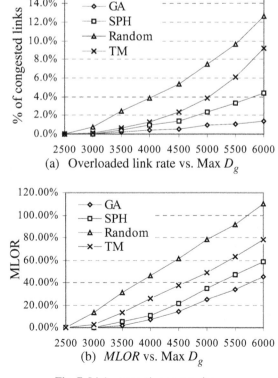

Fig. 7. Link congestion comparisons.

7 Summary

In this paper we proposed an efficient scheme for offline IP layer multicast traffic engineering with bandwidth constraints using Genetic Algorithms. By means of off-line optimizing and pre-configuring M-ISIS link weights, traditional Steiner tree based multicast traffic engineering can be reduced to plain PIM-SM shortest path routing that is widely supported in the current IP routers. Moreover, the GA based approach also exhibits higher capability in finding feasible solutions and reducing network congestion. As far as we know, our proposed approach represents the first attempt to explore effective solutions to multicast traffic engineering based on the hop-by-hop routing semantics. This is in contrast to most of the current multicast traffic engineering schemes that require MPLS support.

Our future work will address the problem of M-ISIS link weight optimization in case of significant traffic dynamics and topology changes (e.g., link failure). Relevant research has been carried out for unicast flows, and we believe that it is equally important to consider this relatively dynamic scenario in IP based multicast traffic engineering semantics.

References

1. D. Awduche et al, "Overview and Principles of Internet Traffic Engineering", RFC 3272, (2002)
2. Baijian Yang et al, "Multicasting in MPLS Domains", Computer Communications, Vol. 27(2), 162-170
3. B. Fenner, "Protocol Independent Multicast - Sparse Mode (PIM-SM): Protocol Specification (Revised)", draft-ietf-pim-sm-v2-new-09.txt, (2004), work in progress
4. B. Fortz et al, "Internet Traffic Engineering by Optimizing OSPF Weights", Proc. IEEE INFOCOM (2000)
5. M. Kodialam et al, "Online Multicast Routing with Bandwidth Guarantees: A new Approach Using Multicast Network Flow", IEEE/ACM Trans. on Networking, Vol. 11, No. 4, (2003), 676-686
6. D. Ooms et al, "Overview of IP Multicast in a Multi-Protocol Label Switching (MPLS) Environment", RFC 3353 (2002)
7. T. Przygienda et al, "M-ISIS: Multi Topology (MT) Routing in IS-IS", draft-ietf-isis-wg-multi-topology-07.txt, (2004), work in progress
8. H. Takahashi, A. Matsuyama, "An Approximate Solution for the Steiner Problem in Graphs", Math. Japonica 6, 533-577
9. Y. Wang et al, "Internet Traffic Engineering without Full Mesh Overlaying", Proc. IEEE INFOCOM (2001)

Weighted Fair RIO (WF-RIO) for Fair AF Bandwidth Allocation in a DiffServ-Capable MPLS Network

Kenji Tsunekawa

NTT Service Integration Laboratories, NTT Corporation,
3-9-11 Midori-cho, Musashino-shi, Tokyo 180-8585, Japan
tune.ken@lab.ntt.co.jp

Abstract. RIO is the primary active queue management technology for handling AF(assured forwarding) class traffic for services that have minimum bandwidth guarantees. However, RIO unfairly allocates the excess AF bandwidth among LSPs(label-switched paths) which have TCP flows aggregated as AF class in a DiffServ-Capable MPLS Network. This issue obstructs the business model in which ISPs promote LSP users to expand the LSP-required bandwidth for enriching the quality of AF traffic. In this paper, we propose a way, called weighted fair RIO (WF-RIO), to resolve this issue. WF-RIO can allocate the excess AF bandwidth among LSPs in proportion to their AF minimum guaranteed bandwidth by multiplying the dropping probability of RIO by an LSP-specific weight which is simply calculated from the traffic rates for the individual LSPs. We evaluate the proposed method by computer simulation and demonstrate its effectiveness.

1 Introduction

1.1 MPLS Supporting Diffserv

In recent years, the systemization of business processes through the use of computer communication technology is rapidly increasing the demands for VPN services that economically provide secure virtual lines connecting geographically dispersed offices to a private company network, using the public Internet as a backbone. MPLS is one of the major technologies employed by ISPs to offer these services. The MPLS protocol resides between the middle of the second layer and the third layer, and it inserts a shim header between these layers. The shim header has two fields, label and exp.

Labels are applied in MPLS to create virtual lines called LSPs (label-switched paths). The LSP required bandwidth is determined beforehand according to a contract between the LSP user and the ISP. An LSP is set up on an appropriate route that can accommodate the required bandwidth. Therefore, each link will likely operate in the over-provisioned case, meaning that the cumulative total demand bandwidth for the LSP is lower than the link speed on each link.

The exp field is utilized by MPLS to support Diffserv classes characterized by different per-hop-behaviors (PHBs) [1]. The exp value of each packet is mapped to a PHB, which is implemented at each MPLS router. The Diffserv architecture defines three classes: EF (expedited forwarding), AF (assured forwarding), and BE (best effort). The EF PHB provides low packet loss, low latency, low jitter, and the maximum guaranteed bandwidth. The EF PHB is usually implemented by applying priority queuing in accordance with the order EF > AF > BE at the output queues of the routers. The EF inflow rate at the edge router must be lower than the EF maximum

J. Vicente and D. Hutchison (Eds.): MMNS 2004, LNCS 3271, pp. 152–163, 2004.

guaranteed bandwidth, which is determined by the contract and is in the range of the LSP required bandwidth.

The AF PHB provides a minimum bandwidth guarantee, as well as efficient utilization of excess bandwidth. The AF minimum guaranteed bandwidth of each LSP is the balance of the LSP required bandwidth that is not consumed by EF traffic. To use this excess bandwidth effectively, AF packets are allowed to inflow at a higher rate than the AF minimum guaranteed bandwidth, as long as they are labeled with a out-of-profile flag specifying a high drop preference at the edge router. An AF packet with the flag "AF_{out} packet" may thus be discarded at the AF output queue of the core router, depending on the availability of resources. Most implementations of AF PHB use RIO (RED with IN/OUT) [2]. RIO is based on RED [3], which drops packets with a certain probability according to the average queue length and avoids the synchronization of TCP flow control caused when many TCP packets overflow together from the buffer. Therefore, this paper assumes that TCP packets with an optional condition belong to the AF class of service.

1.2 Unfair AF Bandwidth Allocation in MPLS Network Supporting Diffserv

RIO employs two probabilities, as shown in Fig.1. One is the probability of dropping an in-profile AF packet (AF_{in} packet), which increases from 0 to ρ_{max_in} as the queue length varies from *min_in* to *max_in*. The second is the probability of dropping an out-of-profile packet (AF_{out} packet), which increases from 0 to ρ_{max_out} as the queue length varies from *min_out* to *max_out*. Accordingly, AF_{in} packets have preference over AF_{out} packets. In the over-provisioned case, in which the cumulative total of the AF minimum guaranteed bandwidth is lower than the link speed, service with the AF minimum bandwidth guarantee is facilitated by RIO discarding AF_{out} packets preferentially at times of AF output queue congestion. It has been reported, however, that RIO has a problem in that the excess AF bandwidth is unfairly distributed among users competing for bandwidth at the AF output queue of the IP router, according to the following parameters: (1) the RTT (round trip time), (2) the number of TCP flows, (3) the target rate, which is the AF minimum guaranteed bandwidth, and (4) the packet size [4].

Usually, an MPLS router has a separate PHB output queue to satisfy the QoS of each PHB [5]. Then the output queue of each class is shared with more than one LSP. As a result, as in the above-mentioned problem, the excess AF bandwidth will be unfairly distributed among the LSPs competing at the AF output queue.

This problem suggests that there is a possibility that the excess AF bandwidth allocated to some LSP with a small AF minimum guaranteed bandwidth is more than that of some LSP with a large AF minimum guaranteed bandwidth, that is, some LSP with a small AF minimum guaranteed bandwidth may have more total AF bandwidth than some LSP with a large AF minimum guaranteed bandwidth. This uncertain excess AF bandwidth allocation without consideration of AF minimum guaranteed bandwidth decreases the desire for each LSP user to contract more LSP-required bandwidth in order to enrich the quality of AF traffic with more AF minimum guaranteed bandwidth. Finally, the issue of the unfair excess AF bandwidth allocation obstructs the business model in which ISPs sell LSP-required bandwidth to LSP users to satisfy the above-mentioned desire.

In this paper, we thus consider a way to resolve the issue of the excess AF band-width being unfairly distributed among LSPs in the over-provisioned case. In other words, this paper presents a method of fair AF bandwidth allocation for aggregated AF class TCP flows on LSPs.

1.3 Related Work

Several methods for improving the unfair AF bandwidth allocation produced by RIO and RED have been proposed [6, 7, 8, 9]. AFC [6] regulates customer traffic with aggregated TCP flows at the edge router in order to evenly share the excess AF bandwidth among competing customers. The edge router, however, must have a traf-fic conditioner function, along with a queue for each customer and feedback conges-tion information from the core router at the edge node. Other methods [7, 8, 9] are mainly intended to lessen the unfairness of bandwidth allocation among TCP flows. For example, RED-PD [7] detects high-bandwidth TCP flows and preferentially drops packets from them. ARIO [8] evenly shares the excess AF bandwidth among the TCP flows. SCALE-WFS [9] allows the flows to share the excess AF bandwidth in a fairly weighted distribution. These technologies, however, are not applicable to fair AF bandwidth allocation for aggregated TCP flows.

1.4 Proposal

In this paper, we propose a method, called weighted fair RIO (WF-RIO), that achieves the fair policy that all LSPs share the excess AF bandwidth in proportion to their AF minimum guaranteed bandwidth. WF-RIO enables a congested router to autonomously provide fair AF bandwidth allocation by applying different discard probabilities for each LSP. WF-RIO obtains the discard probabilities by multiplying the dropping probability of RIO by weights based on the AF bandwidth allocated to the aggregated AF-class TCP flows on each LSP. We show that an effective weight can be calculated from the traffic rates for each LSP and that this weight is independ-ent of the LSP-specific parameters for the aggregated flows.

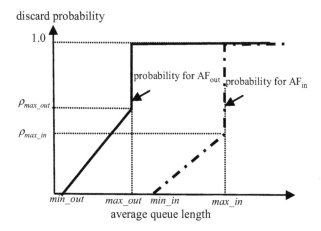

Fig. 1. Probablities of Discard Probabilities in RIO.

2 Analytical Models

In this section, we describe the analytical models we utilized in deriving and evaluating the weighting scheme of WF-RIO. It is well-known that given a random packet loss at a dropping probability P due to a congestion avoidance algorithm like RED or RIO, the average throughput avr of a TCP flow is defined in terms of the RTT, the MSS (maximum segment size) of the flow, and a constant value C which depends on the type of TCP as follows [10]:

$$avr = \frac{MSS}{RTT} \times \frac{C}{\sqrt{P}}. \tag{1}$$

We use the letter i (= 1, 2, …, n) to denote the LSP_i that share the AF output queue. For each LSP_i, we denote the AF-class TCP flow number by f_i, the AF_{in} traffic rate (in bits per second, or bps) by a_i, the AF_{out} traffic rate (bps) by b_i, the packet discard probability per AF-class TCP flow by $\rho^{tcp}{}_i$, and the discard probability of an AF_{out} packet by ρ. We can easily measure a_i and b_i at the router, based on the label and exp fields in the shim headers of each packet. We can then estimate $\rho^{tcp}{}_i$ as follows:

$$\rho_i^{tcp} = \frac{b_i / f_i}{(a_i + b_i)/f_i} \times \rho = \frac{b_i}{(a_i + b_i)} \times \rho. \tag{2}$$

For each LSP_i, we denote the RTT of an AF-class TCP flow by RTT_i, the MSS of the flow by MSS_i and the constant value C of the flow by C_i. Then we estimate avr_i, the average throughput per AF-class TCP flow on LSP_i, as follows:

$$avr_i = \frac{MSS_i}{RTT_i} \times \frac{C_i}{\sqrt{\rho_i^{tcp}}}. \tag{3}$$

From this, we estimate f_i as

$$f_i = \frac{a_i + b_i}{avr_i} = \sqrt{(a_i + b_i) \times b_i \times \rho} \Big/ k_i, \tag{4}$$

$$k_i = \frac{MSS_i}{RTT_i} \times C_i. \tag{4a}$$

Eq. (4) can also be derived from the analytical model that Baines et al. [11] developed for the allocation of bandwidth to aggregated TCP flows in the over-provisioned case.

3 Weighted Fair RIO

We propose a new active queue management technology, called weighted fair RIO (WF-RIO), which can realize a fair policy for allocation of AF bandwidth such that all LSPs sharing the congested AF queue have the same ratio of the allocated AF bandwidth to the AF minimum guaranteed bandwidth, that is, all LSPs share the excess AF bandwidth in proportion to their AF minimum guaranteed bandwidth. Therefore WF-RIO can stimulate the desire for LSP users to buy more LSP-required bandwidth in order to enrich the quality of AF traffic with more AF minimum guaranteed bandwidth, and promote the business model in which ISPs sell LSP-required bandwidth to LSP users to satisfy the above-mentioned desire.

The cause of the unfair AF bandwidth allocation problem lies in the fact that RIO applies the same AF_{out} packet discard probability, ρ, to each LSP. Thus, we propose a fair allocation method that autonomously applies a specific probability, ρ_i, to each LSP_i at each output interface of the MPLS router. The discard probability ρ_i is calculated by multiplying ρ by a weight w_i for each LSP_i. The weights are determined according to the AF bandwidth allocation of each LSP, with an initial value of 1. Before describing this method in detail, we first illustrate its algorithm, with reference to Fig. 2:

1. Each output interface manages the required bandwidth c_i of LSP_i and periodically measures and refreshes the traffic rates (e_i, a_i, b_i) for each service class (EF, AF_{in}, AF_{out}) according to the label and exp values in the shim headers of the packets switched at the interface.

2. If the average length of the AF output queue exceeds *min_out* and WF-RIO–determines the discard probability ρ of an AF_{out} packet based on the average length in the same manner as RIO, the algorithm proceeds to the next step to calculate the weights w_i for each LSP_i. Otherwise, the w_i are reset to 1.

3. Depending on the situation, one of two methods is used to calculate w_i. In the first case, w_i is requested for the first time after the AF bandwidth allocation is judged as unfair at the time of congestion. In the second case, w_i is recalculated after the AF bandwidth allocation is judged as even more unfair as the congestion continues. The situation can be determined from the current value of w_i. Specifically, the first case results when all the w_i equal 1, while the second case results when not all of the w_i are equal to 1. The calculation methods for these two situations are described in the next two subsections.

3.1 Calculating the First Set of Weights w_i

When WF-RIO detects that the average length of the AF output queue exceeds *min_out*, it determines the discard probability ρ of the AF_{out} packet based on the average length in the same manner as RIO. Then, as all the weight w_i equals the initial value of 1 – that is, as all the ρ_i equals ρ, WF-RIO applies ρ to the AF_{out} packets of all LSPs. Later, each time the traffic rate is measured and refreshed; it evaluates the fairness of the AF bandwidth allocation according to a *fairness_index*, which is defined as

$$fairness\_index = \left(\sum r_i\right)^2 \bigg/ \left(n\sum r_i^2\right),\tag{5}$$

$$r_i = af_i / (c_i - e_i) = (a_i + b_i) / (c_i - e_i).\tag{5a}$$

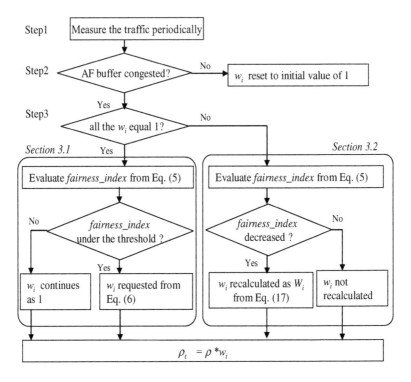

Fig. 2. Algorithm of Weighted Fair RIO.

The *fairness_index* applies Jain's index [12] which quantifies the throughput fairness among flows with the dispersion degree of the ratio of the measured throughput to the fair throughput. As expressed in Eqs.(5) and (5a), the *fairness_index* evaluates the fairness of the AF bandwidth allocation among LSPs with the dispersion degree of the ratio r_i. This value r_i is the ratio of the AF measured throughput af_i, which is the AF_{in} traffic rate a_i plus the AF_{out} traffic rate b_i, to the AF minimum guaranteed bandwidth, which is the required bandwidth c_i minus the EF traffic rate e_i. If all LSPs sharing the congested AF queue have the same ratio r_i of the allocated AF bandwidth to the AF minimum guaranteed bandwidth, that is, all LSPs share the excess AF bandwidth in proportion to their AF minimum guaranteed bandwidth, the *fairness_index* gets the maximum value of 1. As the AF bandwidth allocation increasingly conforms to the fairness policy – that is, as the dispersion degree of the ratio r_i gets smaller – the *fairness_index* gets closer to its maximum value of 1. In the opposite case, the *fairness_index* approaches 0. If the *fairness_index* becomes smaller than a predefined threshold (i.e., the degree of conformance is insufficient), then the weight w_i for each LSP_i is calculated by using Eq. (6):

$$w_i = r_i^2 \times \Sigma \ b_i \Big/ \Sigma \ \left(r_i^2 \times b_i \right). \tag{6}$$

This equation is derived from two conditions. First, after applying the ρ_i, all the expected ratios, r'_i, should be constant. Second, the number of AF_{out} packets discarded by applying the ρ_i should be the same as the number that would be discarded by generically applying ρ.

After applying the discard probability ρ_i to the AF_{out} packets of each LSP_i, the expected average throughput, avr'_i, of the AF-class TCP flow on LSP_i can be predicted from the following equation, which is derived from Eqs. (2) and (3):

$$avr'_i = k_i \times \sqrt{\frac{(a_i + b_i)}{b_i \times \rho_i}} = k_i \times \sqrt{\frac{(a_i + b_i)}{b_i \times \rho \times w_i}} . \tag{7}$$

As it is reasonable to assume that applying the ρ_i doesn't affect the TCP flow number f_i given by Eq. (4), the expected AF bandwidth af'_i of LSP_i can be afterward expressed as follows:

$$af'_i = f_i \times avr'_i = af_i / \sqrt{w_i} , \tag{8}$$

$$af_i = a_i + b_i . \tag{8a}$$

Similarly, as it is reasonable to assume that applying the ρ_i doesn't affect the AF_{in} traffic rate a_i or the EF traffic rate e_i, the expected traffic rates a'_i and e'_i can be expressed as follows:

$$a'_i = a_i , \tag{9}$$

$$e'_i = e_i . \tag{10}$$

The expected ratios r'_i should be equal to some constant g, as expressed from Eqs.(5a), (8), (8a), and(10) by

$$r'_i = \frac{af'_i}{(c_i - e'_i)} = \frac{(a_i + b_i)}{(c_i - e_i) \times \sqrt{w_i}} = \frac{r_i}{\sqrt{w_i}} = g . \tag{11}$$

Thus, the weight w_i can be expressed as follows:

$$w_i = (r_i / g)^2 . \tag{12}$$

In addition, the second condition, that the number of AF_{out} packets discarded by applying ρ_i should be the same as the number discarded by applying ρ, leads to Eq. (13).

$$\left(\sum b_i \right) \times \rho = \sum (b_i \times \rho_i) = \sum (b_i \times \rho \times w_i) . \tag{13}$$

From Eqs.(12) and (13), the square of the constant g can be derived as

$$g^2 = \sum \left(r_i^2 \times b_i \right) / \sum b_i . \tag{14}$$

Equation (6) can be derived from Eqs. (12) and (14). Consequently, as expressed in Eq. (6), we find that the weight w_i of each LSP_i can be calculated from the traffic rates (e_i, a_i, b_i) for each class (EF, AF_{in}, AF_{out}) and the LSP required bandwidth c_i, without considering the values of f_i, RTT_i, and MSS_i for the aggregated AF-class flows.

3.2 Recalculating the Weights w_i

In the case of continuing congestion after the w_i are first requested, the number of TCP flows or the AF minimum guaranteed bandwidth of each LSP may be changing, and thus, the w_i may need to be recalculated. To determine whether this is necessary, each time the traffic rate is measured periodically, the conformance of the AF bandwidth allocation to the fairness policy is evaluated according to the *fairness_index* from Eq. (5). If the *fairness_index* is lower than its most recently calculated value, i.e., if the conformance is judged to be decreasing, the w_i are recalculated to produce new values, W_i, in the following way. Otherwise, the existing w_i are retained.

The current traffic rate measured during a period of congestion may have been influenced by the values of the ρ_i. On the other hand, the AF_{out} traffic rate b_i and the ratio r_i used in Eq. (6) to calculate the w_i correspond to the case in which all the ρ_i equal ρ. Accordingly, to recalculate the w_i, it is necessary to infer b_i and r_i such that all ρ_i equal ρ by utilizing the current traffic rates (e'_i, a'_i, b'_i), the current ratio r'_i, and the w_i. Both b_i and r_i can be inferred from the relation between them and the current traffic rates(e'_i, a'_i, b'_i) ,which are influenced by ρ_i, expressed in Section3.1.

From Eqs.(8) and (9), the AF_{out} traffic rate b_i can be derived as

$$b_i = af'_i \times \sqrt{w_i} - a'_i,$$
(15)
$$af'_i = a'_i + b'_i.$$
(15a)

Then, from Eq. (11), the ratio r_i can be derived as

$$r_i = r'_i \times \sqrt{w_i}.$$
(16)

Consequently, the w_i are recalculated as the following W_i based on the above equations:

$$W_i = r'^2_i \times w_i \times \frac{\sum \left(af'_i \times \sqrt{w_i} - a'_i\right)}{\sum \left\{r'^2_i \times w_i \times \left(af'_i \times \sqrt{w_i} - a'_i\right)\right\}}.$$
(17)

Note that if we assign w_i 1, Eq. (17) becomes the same as Eq. (6).

4 Evaluation Results

In this section, we evaluate the performance of WF-RIO by using the simulation tool, OPNET [13]. For the simulation experiment, we adopted the network model shown in Fig. 3. In this model, all links are 10-Mbps duplex. The link delay time between $user_1$ and ER_1 is fixed at 10 msec, that between $user_2$ and ER_2 is fixed at 40 msec, and that between $user_3$ and ER_3 is fixed at 80 msec. Three LSPs are thus established. The route of each LSP $_{i(=1,2,3)}$ is from $ER_{i(=1,2,3)}$ to ER_4 through the core router, so each has a different RTT. The MSS fields for $user_1$,$user_2$, and $user_3$ select segment lengths of 1500, 1024, and 512 bytes.

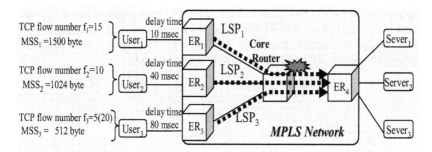

Fig. 3. Experimental network model.

For the AF class of service, several TCP connections for file transfer from user$_i$ to server$_i$ are established through LSP$_i$. At the start of the simulation, the number of TCP connections triggered by user$_1$, user$_2$, and user$_3$ are 5,10, and 15, respectively. The TCP type of user1, user2, and user3 is TCP Reno, TCP Reno and TCP Sack. Then user$_3$ adds 15 TCP connections when the simulation time reaches 34–35 minutes. As the file size is too large for transfer to finish before the simulation ends, each TCP flow continues for the duration of the simulation. For the EF class, video frames are transferred by UDP from user$_i$ to server$_i$ through LSP$_i$ at 0.4 Mbps, which is assumed to be lower than the EF maximum guaranteed bandwidth of 0.5 Mbps. Each LSP is assumed to have a required bandwidth of 1 Mbps. Thus, 0.6 Mbps is available for AF guaranteed-minimum bandwidth traffic from each user. Therefore each LSP has the same bandwidth available for AF traffic in accordance with the fair policy. Congestion occurs at the AF output queue from the core router to ER$_4$. In this scenario, RIO is utilized until a time of 20 minutes; after which the WF-RIO method takes over. In executing WF-RIO, the interval of traffic rate measurement is fixed at 30 seconds and the threshold of the *fairness_index* is fixed at 1.

Figure 4 shows a time chart of the AF$_{out}$ bandwidth b_i allocated to each LSP$_i$. The chart illustrates that the values of b_i were balanced to become equivalent after WF-RIO was initiated. These values were then balanced again soon after b_3 became much larger than the others at the time LSP$_3$ initiated additional AF-class TCP flows.

Figure 5 shows a time chart of the *fairness_index*, while Figure 6 shows a time chart of the weights w_i. These charts illustrate that the *fairness_index* rose after WF-RIO became active, and that the weights w_i differs largely mutually. Then these charts illustrate that all of the w_i changed as soon as the *fairness_index* declined as a consequence of LSP$_3$ initiating the additional flows.

The results show that subtle variation in the AF$_{out}$ bandwidth allocation caused the *fairness_index* to vary even when the number of TCP flows for all LSPs was unchanged. Moreover, we observe that the *fairness_index* increased after a decrease in it caused the w_i to be recalculated. This suggests that WF-RIO attempts to improve the degree of fairness even if the fairness is reduced by a cause other than the number of TCP flows. For example, in the case when the AF minimum guaranteed bandwidth fluctuates due to variations in the EF traffic rate, WF-RIO will attempt to allocate the AF bandwidth to each LSP according to the fair policy.

Figure 7(a) shows a bar graph of the average throughput of each service class through each LSP before WF-RIO became active, while Fig. 7(b) shows a bar graph for the average throughput afterward. We observe from these graphs that WF-RIO eliminated the unfair AF bandwidth allocation due to RIO.

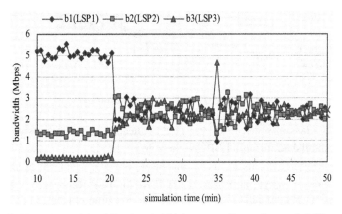

Fig. 4. Time chart of the AF_{out} bandwidth $b_{i(=1,2,3)}$ allocated to each $LSP_{i(=1,2,3)}$.

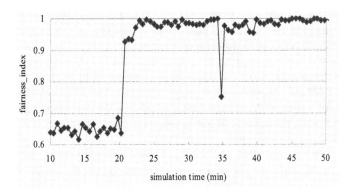

Fig. 5. Time chart of the fairness_index.

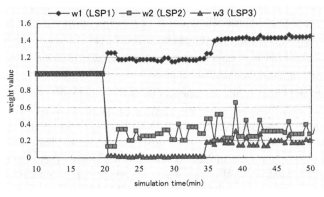

Fig. 6. Time chart of the weight $w_{i(=1,2,3)}$ of each LSP $_{i(=1,2,3)}$.

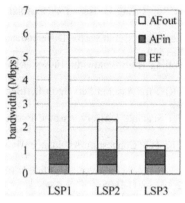

Fig. 7a. Bandwidth allocated by RIO.

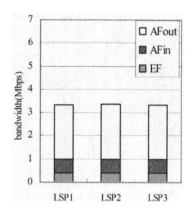

Fig. 7b. Bandwidth allocated by WF-RIO.

5 Conclusion

In this paper we have presented WF-RIO, a new method of fairly allocating AF bandwidth among LSPs competing at a congested AF output queue. WF-RIO achieves the fair policy that all LSPs share the excess AF bandwidth in proportion to their AF minimum guaranteed bandwidth to improve the unfair excess AF bandwidth allocation among the LSPs according to the LSP-specific parameters of the aggregated AF class flows. WF-RIO obtains a per-LSP probability of discarding out-of-profile AF packets by multiplying the dropping probability of RIO by an LSP-specific weight, and then drops packets at that probability. We have shown that the weight of each LSP can be calculated from the traffic rates for each service class (EF, AF_{in}, AF_{out}) and the required bandwidth of the LSP without considering the LSP-specific parameters of the aggregated AF-class flows. Through our evaluation results, we have shown that WF-RIO can eliminate unfair AF bandwidth allocation based on these parameters, and it can thus provide fair AF bandwidth allocation among LSPs sharing a congested AF queue. WF-RIO can stimulate the desire for LSP users to buy more LSP-required bandwidth in order to enrich the quality of AF traffic with more AF minimum guaranteed bandwidth, because WF-RIO can allocate the excess AF bandwidth among LSPs in proportion to their AF minimum guaranteed bandwidth. WF-RIO can promote the business model in which ISPs sell LSP-required bandwidth to LSP users to satisfy the above-mentioned desire.

References

1. RFC3270, Multi-Protocol Label Switching (MPLS) Support of Differentiated Services
2. D. Clark and W. Fang, Explicit Allocation of Best Effort Packet Delivery Service, IEEE/ACM Trans. on Networking, V6, N.4 (1998) 362-373
3. S. Floyd and V. Jacobson, Random early detection gateways for congestion avoidance, IEEE/ACM Trans. on Networking, vol. 1 (1993) 397-413
4. N. Seddigh, et al., Bandwidth Assurance Issues for TCP Flows in a Differentiated Service Network, IEEE GLOBECOM '99 (1999) 1792-1798

5. T. Lee, et al., Implementation of MPLS Router Supporting Diffserv for QoS and High-Speed Switching, IEEE HSNMC'02 (2002) 51-55
6. B. Nandy, et al., Aggregate Flow Control: Improving Assurances for Differentiated Services Network, IEEE INFOCOM'01 (2001) 1340-1349
7. R. Mahajan, S. Floyd, and D. Wetherall, Controlling High-Bandwidth Flows at the Congested Router, IEEE ICNP'01 (2001) 192-201
8. W. Liu, et al., Improve Fairness with Adaptive RIO for Assured Service in DiffServ Networks, IEEE ICCCAS'02, Vol.1 (2002) 680 -684
9. A. Sang, et al., Weighted Fairness Guarantee for Scalable Diffserv Assured Forwarding, IEEE ICC'01, vol.8 (2001) 11-14
10. M. Mathis, et al., The Macroscopic Behavior of the TCP Congestion Avoidance Algorithm, Comput. Commun. Rev., vol. 27, no. 3 (1997)
11. M. Baines, et al., Using TCP Models To Understand Bandwidth Assurance in a Differentiated Service Network, IEEE GLOBECOM'01 (2001) 1800-1805
12. R.Jain, Throughput Fairness Index: An explanation, ATM Forum Contribution 99-0045 (1999)
13. OPNET Technologies, Inc, http://www.opnet.com/home.htm

Sub-network Based Hierarchical Segment Restoration in MPLS Network

Hae-Joon Shin[1], Sang-Heon Shin[2], and Young-Tak Kim[1]

[1] ANT Lab, Yeungnam University,
Gyeongsan Gyeongbuk 712-749, Korea
{fisher,ytkim}@yu.ac.kr
http://antl.yu.ac.kr
[2] Advanced Network Technologies Division(ANTD),
National Institute of Standards and Technology(NIST),
Gaithersburg, MD 20899, USA
shshin@nist.gov

Abstract. In this paper, we propose a segment restoration scheme based on network partitioning to enhance the restoration performance and to manage network efficiently. The proposed restoration scheme divides a large network into several small sub-networks. Since most faults can be restored in a partitioned sub-network or AS(Autonomous System), restoration time is reduced obviously. In this paper, we compare and analyze restoration performance according to the size of sub-networks and restoration schemes. From simulation results, the proposed restoration scheme has high restoration performance compared with other restoration schemes.

1 Introduction

A fault in the high-speed network, such as WDM(Wavelength Division Multiplexing) network and MPLS(Multi-Protocol Label Switching) [1], [2] may cause the massive data losses and degrade the quality of service severely. Therefore fast fault restoration function is an essential requirement in high-speed transport networks.

Any faulty or disconnected working path will severely degrade the end-to-end packet transmission and end-to-end quality of service. So any faulty link/node should be verified as soon as possible, and the user traffic should be rerouted quickly to minimize the possible packet loss. So, fast restoration is essential to increase the reliability of the quality of services of real time multimedia applications. For fast restoration, fast fault detection and fault notification functions are required.

Legacy restoration schemes on mesh network are based on link restoration or path restoration. Link restoration has the advantage of restoration speed but is poor at resource utilization. On the other hand, path restoration is good at resource utilization but poor at restoration speed. So various segment-based restoration schemes [3], [4], [5] are issued to enhance restoration performance.

J. Vicente and D. Hutchison (Eds.): MMNS 2004, LNCS 3271, pp. 164–175, 2004.

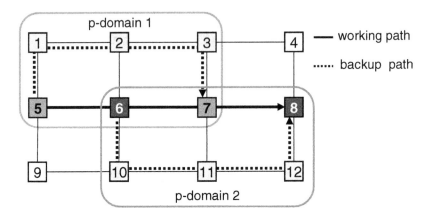

Fig. 1. Shortest Leap Shared Protection (SLSP)

In our previous research [6], [7], we describe basic concepts and principles of segment restoration. In this paper, we propose an enhanced segment restoration scheme based on network partitioning. We also propose provisioning methods of the inter segment backup path and an efficient network partitioning rules for enhanced restoration performance. We analyze restoration performance according to the size of partitioned sub-networks and compare with link-based restoration and path-based restoration.

The rest of this paper is organized as follows. In Section 2, we describe related approaches. In Sections 3 and 4, we propose segment restoration scheme and evaluate its restoration performance, respectively. And we make the conclusion in Section 5.

2   Related Work

2.1   SLSP (Shortest Leap Shared Protection)

SLSP has been proposed to enhance the link- and path-based protection; it partitions an end-to-end working path into several equal-length and overlapped segments [3]. Each segment assigns a protection domain for restoration after a working path is selected. The overlap between adjacent protection domains is designed to protect any boundary node failure along a working path. The SLSP scheme reduces restoration time obviously. In Fig. 1, working path 5-6-7-8 is divided into segments 5-6-7 and 6-7-8, and their backup paths are 5-1-2-3-7 and 6-10-11-12-8. Especially when domain size is 3(a segment consists of three nodes), the restoration time becomes the shortest. But, the SLSP should divide each logical path in a network into several domains(segments) and provide protection domain(segment) for each domain regardless of the hierarchical sub-network configuration of the given network. Therefore, when the number of path in a network increases, the processing complexity also increases.

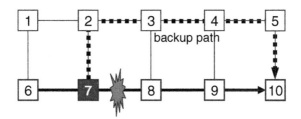

Fig. 2. Sub-path restoration

2.2   Sub-path Restoration

Sub-path restoration [4] patches backup path with a node that detects fault occurrence. When a fault occurs at Link 7-8 as shown in Fig. 2, the upstream node (Node 7) of the failed path does not send an alarm to the source node(Node 6) of the disrupted path; instead, it tries to patch a path by sending a setup message to the destination node(Node 10). Meanwhile, the downstream node(Node 8) sends a teardown message to the destination node(Node 10) of the working path. Since a backup path 2-3-4-5-10 is patched with Node 7, so user traffic is switched at Node 7 and rerouted along 6-7-2-3-4-5-10.

The sub-path restoration scheme reduced restoration time compared with the path restoration scheme relatively. When a fault occurs around an egress node, restoration time is reduced obviously, but when a fault occurs around an ingress node, restoration time similar with the path restoration scheme. Since a backup path is provisioned after a fault occurs, restoration performance is lower than other restoration schemes that use backup path restoration scheme.

2.3   PROMISE (Protection with Multi-segment)

The basic idea of PROMISE [5] is to divide an active path or AP(along which a survivable connection is established) into several possible overlapping active segments(AS) and then to protect each AS with a detour called backup segment or BS(instead of protecting the AP as a whole as in path protection schemes). The BS starts and ends at the same two nodes as the corresponding AS [4].

In Fig. 3, an active path is divided three active segments (AS1, AS2 and AS3) and each active segment has a backup segment (BS1, BS2 or BS3) for

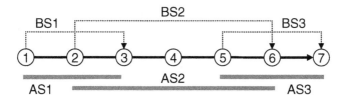

Fig. 3. Illustration of PROMISE

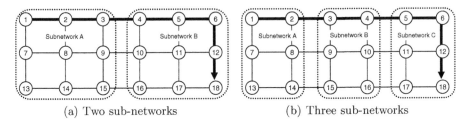

(a) Two sub-networks   (b) Three sub-networks

Fig. 4. Network partitioning

protection respectively. Fault restoration speed is faster than legacy restoration schemes, because a fault can be restored in each segment. The basic idea of path dividing is similar with SLSP. SLSP divides an active path into several equal length segments, but in the PROMISE, the length of active segments is not equal.

3   Proposed Segment Restoration

3.1   Principle of Proposed Segment Restoration

The proposed segment restoration scheme is based on physical network partitioning as shown in Fig. 4. In Fig. 4(a), a network is divided into sub-network A and sub-network B, and an end-to-end path is divided into two segments by physical network partitioning automatically: 1-2-3 and 4-5-6-12-18. So a segment can be a part of an end-to-end whole path. The longest segment is an end-to-end whole path such as 1-2-3-4-5-6-12-18 and a shortest segment is a link such as link 1-2, or link 3-4 as shown in Fig. 4(b). The length of a segment is depends on the number of sub-networks.

To apply the proposed segment restoration scheme to real networks, we should consider two kinds of faults: intra sub-network fault and inter sub-networks faults as shown in Fig. 5. In our research, the detail of two sub-network faults and protection schemes is described.

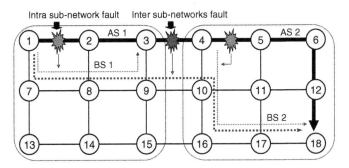

Fig. 5. Intra sub-network fault vs. inter sub-networks fault

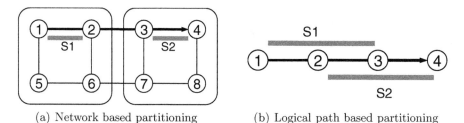

(a) Network based partitioning   (b) Logical path based partitioning

Fig. 6. Path partitioning methods

3.2   Path Partitioning vs. Network Partitioning

Segment restorations are based on path partitioning that is achieved by logical path partitioning and physical network partitioning as shown in Fig. 6. The proposed segment restoration scheme divides a physical network to several sub-networks as shown in Fig. 6(a), while the other approaches [3], [5] are based on logical path partition as shown in Fig. 6(b).

Advantages of logical path based partitioning are: (1) length of segment can be adjusted according to the restoration strategy. The length of segment is very important factor to determine restoration speed. (2) It can provide steady restoration time to fix the segment length by NMS(Network Management System) and so on. Shortcomings are (1) who and how divides a path into several segments? Partitioning is achieved by per-path, so it makes network operation complex. (2) In a network which consists of several AS(Autonomous System) as shown in Fig. 7, if a path is established through several AS, it is impossible or difficult to divide the path into several segments.

The advantages of network-based partition are: (1) a path is divided into several segments by sub-networks automatically. (2) In a network where consists of several AS, when a path is established through several ASs, path partitioning is achieved by AS automatically. So it is easy to apply to various networks without modification of restoration method. (3) In network management perspective, it is easy and efficient to manage small size network rather than large size network. However, it also has shortcoming that proposed segment restoration provides two

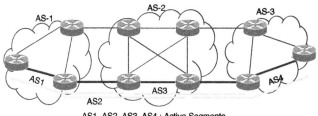

AS1, AS2, AS3, AS4 : Active Segments
AS-1, AS-2, AS-3 : Autonomous Systems

Fig. 7. Network which consists of three AS(Autonomous System)

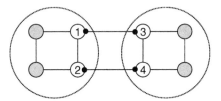

(a) Link-based network partition

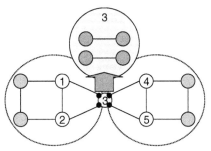

(b) Node-based network partition

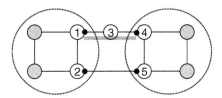

(c) Hybrid network partition

Fig. 8. Path partitioning methods

kinds of backup path (intra sub-network backup path and inter sub-networks backup path) [6], [7].

However, physical network based path partitioning is more useful in both transit network and multi-AS networks. So in this paper, we use network based partitioning method to implement the proposed segment restoration scheme.

3.3 Network Partitioning

Since restoration performance depends on the size and the topology of sub-networks, efficient network partitioning scheme is essential to enhance the restoration performance.

So we make several network partitioning rules as follows:

- Rule 1: Sub-network should have at least two edge nodes for connecting its adjacent sub-networks. This is required for the inter segments fault restoration; if there is just one node that connects two sub-networks, the inter segments fault cannot be restored.

- Rule 2: A link or a node failure within a sub-network must be restored in its sub-network. The link connectivity degree of all nodes within sub-network should be greater than or equal to 2. Mesh topology provides better restoration capability than star or hub and tree topology.

The Rule 1 is an essential requirement to perform the inter segment restoration and the Rule 2 is for the intra segment restoration [6], [7].

Network partitioning is achieved according to above two rules as follows:

- *Link-based network partitioning*: Basic partitioning rule of the proposed restoration scheme. Sub-networks are divided by links as shown in Fig. 8(a). Inter sub-network restoration is triggered when link 1-3 or link 2-4 is broken.
- *Node-based network partitioning*: If it is impossible to divide a network using link-based partitioning, sub-networks can be divided by node as shown in Fig. 8(b). In this case, we assume that a node consists of sub-nodes (ports) and sub-links. So, node-based network partitioning can be concerned a special subset of link-based network partitioning. In this case, inter sub-networks restoration is triggered when a fault occurs in the node 3.
- *Hybrid network partitioning*: When it is impossible to divide using node-based partition or link-based partition, hybrid network partitioning method can be used. In Fig. 8(c), node 3 excludes from two sub-networks; node 3 can be concerned as a link. The hybrid network partitioning is also the extension of link-based partitioning. When a fault occurs at link 1-3, link 3-4, link 2-5 or node 3, inter sub-networks restoration is triggered

Generally, all three partitioning methods can be used in a large size transit network. Basically, link-based partitioning (which is our basic partitioning method) is derived from multi-AS networks.

3.4   Backup Path Provisioning Rules for Inter-segments Restoration

In our segment restoration schemes, faults are classified as intra sub-network fault that occurs in a sub-network, and inter sub-network fault that occurs between two sub-networks. After a working path is established, intra segment backup paths are established in each sub-network for intra segment restoration. Inter segment backup paths are established after each intra segment backup paths are established. We select the path with lowest cost among the four inter-segment backup paths that are calculated by the four bridge methods.

Backup path provisioning methods for inter segment restoration is classified into four types: using two backup nodes, using a backup and a working node, using a working and a backup node, and using two working nodes.

- *B2B(Backup node to Backup node) bridge*: An inter segment backup path is established using two backup nodes as shown in Fig. 9(a).
- *B2W(Backup node to Working node) bridge*: An inter segment backup path is established using a backup node and a working node as shown in Fig. 9(b).
- *W2B(Working node to Backup node) bridge*: An inter segment backup path is established using a working node and a backup node as shown in Fig. 9(c).

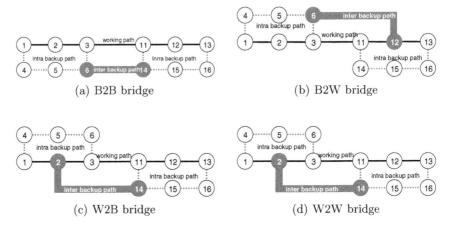

Fig. 9. Bridge methods for inter sub-network restoration

– *W2W(Working node to Working node)bridge*:Fig. 9(d) shows an inter segment backup path using two working nodes, which is the opposite case of using two backup nodes.

4   Simulation and Evaluation

In this section, we analyze and evaluate the performance of the proposed segment restoration scheme for its restoration time and resource requirements compared with other restoration schemes. We measure the average restoration time and backup resource usage for various working paths that have different hop length in two U.S. sample networks as shown in Fig. 10. We make the following assumptions for the simulation.

– All working paths and backup paths are established along its shortest path.
– Backup path should not belong to same SRLG(Shared Risk Link Group) of the working path

4.1   Evaluation of Restoration Time

To compare restoration performance, we use two restoration performance factors: restoration time and backup resource capacity. Restoration time is the most important factor for comparing restoration performance and backup resource capacity is also important to calculate network installation capacity. Restoration time is determined by the sum of fault detection time, fault notification propagation delay time and node processing time as (1) [8].

$$T_{restoration} = T_{detection} + T_{propagation\ delay} + T_{node\ processing} \ . \qquad (1)$$

Here, $T_{restoration}$ is total restoration time, $T_{detection}$ is fault detection time, $T_{propagation\ delay}$ is propagation delay time and $T_{node\ processing}$ is message processing time in a node.

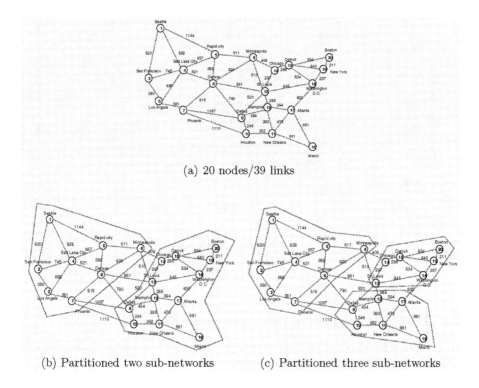

(a) 20 nodes/39 links

(b) Partitioned two sub-networks   (c) Partitioned three sub-networks

Fig. 10. U.S. sample network

For the simulation, we assume $T_{detection}$ sets to 10ms and $T_{node\ processing}$ sets to 1ms per node [9]. $T_{propagation\ delay}$ is calculated using the physical distance of links. So, propagation distance and the number of nodes that are passed by fault notification messages determine restoration time. To reduce restoration time, it is the best way to reduce transfer delay time and the number of nodes that are passed by fault notification messages.

Fig. 11 shows the restoration time according to the size of sub-networks and restoration schemes. In the proposed segment restoration scheme, the restoration time depends on the number of sub-networks. From Fig. 11, we can find that the restoration time of segment x 3 is less than segment x 2. So we can conclude when a network is divided into smaller sub-networks, the restoration performance can be improved

The restoration time of the segment restoration scheme is shorter than the path restoration scheme, but longer than the link restoration scheme. We assume only link failure in this simulation because the link restoration scheme can't restore any node failure and we can't measure the restoration time of the link restoration scheme when a node failure occurs. So the proposed segment restoration has the shortest restoration time in the mixed fault environment such as link failure, node failure and multiple failures.

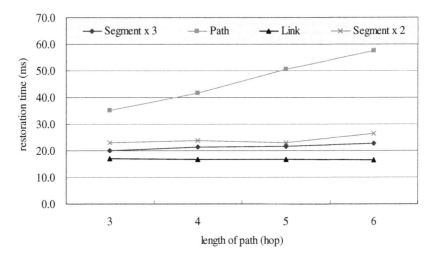

Fig. 11. Restoration time

4.2 Evaluation of Restoration Restoration Capacity

To compare backup resource capacity, we measure the ratio of the required resource of backup paths to working paths using (2).

$$Backup\ resource\ capacity = \frac{total\ bandwidth\ of\ the\ backup\ path}{total\ bandwidth\ of\ the\ working\ path} * 100(\%) \ . \quad (2)$$

Fig. 12 shows backup resource requirement according to the size of sub-networks and restoration schemes. In the proposed segment restoration scheme, the restoration resource capacity is increased when a network is divided into smaller sub-networks.

The path restoration scheme prepares backup resource for a whole path, but the link restoration scheme and the proposed segment restoration scheme prepares backup resource for every link or sub-network respectively; therefore more resource is required compared with the end-to-end path restoration. From the result, we can see that the path restoration scheme requires the least backup resource, while the proposed nt restoration requires more backup resource, but less than link restoration scheme. We summarize restoration performance as a function of the size of sub-network and restoration schemes in Table II.

The link restoration scheme has the shortest restoration time in this simulation, but it can't restore any node failure. So the proposed segment restoration has the shortest restoration time when link and node failure occur. The path restoration scheme has the smallest backup resource capacity compared with other restoration schemes but has the longest restoration time. Path restoration scheme can't guarantee quality of service (QoS) because of slow restoration time, so it is not adequate restoration scheme for high-speed networks such as MPLS and WDM.

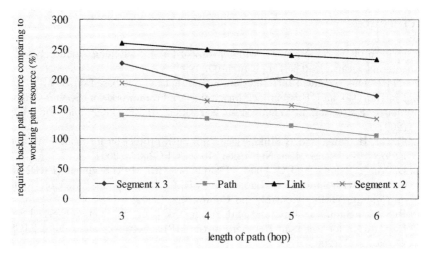

Fig. 12. Required backup resource

Table 1. Comparison of Restoration Performance

		Restoration Time	Required Backup Resource
Proposed restoration	Segment x 2	24.0 ms	162 %
	Segment x 3	21.4ms	198 %
Link Restoration		16.8ms	250 %
Path Restoration		46.2ms	132 %

5   Conclusion

Most restoration schemes for telecommunication network are based on link-based restoration or path-based restoration. The link restoration scheme has short-est restoration time, but lowest backup resource capacity. The path restoration scheme has opposite characteristic. It is difficult to satisfy both fast restoration speed and high resource utilization. But high-speed networks, such as MPLS net-work, require traffic engineering for optimized resource utilization. So restoration schemes for high-speed network must have fast restoration functions and effi-cient backup resource management functions. The proposed segment restoration is based on network partitioning that divides a large network into several small sub-networks. Because most faults are restored in sub-networks, fault restora-tion time is reduced obviously. And backup resource capacity is also less than the link restoration scheme.

From the simulation results, we verified that the segment restoration scheme has advantages in both restoration time and backup resource capacity. The pro-posed segment restoration can provide a good restoration performance for high-speed transport networks.

References

1. IETF mpls working group, "Multi-protocol Label Switching Architecture," IETF Internet Draft, draft-ietf-mpls-arch-05,(1999).
2. ETRI, The Technical Introduction on Internet Service based on ATM, (1999).
3. Pin-Han Ho and Hussein. T. Mouftah, "A Framework for Service-Guaranteed Shared Protection in WDM Mesh Networks," IEEE Communication Magazine, (2002).
4. C. Ou, H. Zang, and B Mukherjee, "Sub-path protection for Scalability and Fast Recovery in WDM Mesh Networks," Proc. OFC2002, (2002).
5. D. Xu, Y. Xiong, and C. Qiao, "Protection with Multi-Segments(PROMISE) in Networks with Shared Risk Link Group(SRLG)," 40th Annual Allerton Conference on Communication, Control, and Computing, (2002).
6. Hae-Joon Shin, Jae-Jun Jang and Young-Tak Kim, "Subnetwork-based Segment Restoration for fast fault Recovery in the MPLS network," Journal of KICS, Vol. 27, No. 11C, (2002).
7. Hae-Joon Shin, Ryung-Min Kim, Young-Tak Kim, "Network Fault Recovery Algorithm based on Segment Automatic Restoration Scheme," Journal of KISS, Vol. 30, No. 3, (2003).
8. ITU-T Recommendation M.495, Maintenance : International Transmission System, (1993).
9. J. Anderson, B. T. Doshi, S. Dravida, and P. Harshavardhana, "Fast Restoration of ATM Networks," IEEE J. Selected Area in Comm., (1994)128-138.

Automated Validation of Service Configuration on Network Devices

Sylvain Hallé, Rudy Deca, Omar Cherkaoui, and Roger Villemaire

Department of Computer Science
Université du Québec à Montréal
C.P. 8888, Succ. Centre-ville
Montréal (Canada) H3C 3P8
{halle,deca,cherkaoui.omar,villemaire.roger}@info.uqam.ca

Abstract. Due to the significant development of network services in the past few years, their validation has become increasingly difficult. The advent of novel approaches to the issue of validation is therefore vital for keeping services manageable, safe, and reliable. We present a model for the validation of service configurations on network devices. A service configuration is modelled by a tree structure, and its properties are described by validation rules expressed in terms of these tree elements. By using an existing logical formalism called TQL, we have succeeded in expressing complex dependencies between parameters, and in automatically checking these dependencies against real-world network descriptions in feasible time.

Keywords: network service management, automated configuration validation

Topic: policy-based management

1   Introduction

The recent years have seen significant development occurring in the domain of network services. In parallel to the creation of new services spreading in increasingly more diverse areas, the networks that support them have become integrated, leading to an increased heterogeneity in topologies, technologies, protocols, and vendors.

Consequent to this booming, the validation of network services has become increasingly difficult: existing validation solutions haven been struggling to keep the pace but barely suffice anymore, and new solutions have been proposed, but are partial. The advent of novel approaches to the issue of validation is therefore vital for keeping services manageable, safe, and reliable.

Some partial validation solutions have been proposed in different areas. For example, the authors in [2], [13] formally verify policy anomalies in distributed firewall rules. [3] develops a set of formal constraints under which a given Virtual Private Network is safe and properly working, but does not mention concrete implementations of the presented approach.

J. Vicente and D. Hutchison (Eds.): MMNS 2004, LNCS 3271, pp. 176–188, 2004.
© IFIP International Federation for Information Processing 2004

In this paper, we present a general-purpose model for the validation of integrity rules in service configurations on network devices. A service configuration is modelled by a tree structure, and its properties are described by validation rules expressed in terms of these tree elements. This allows efficient service validation on the managed network devices, minimises the effort, the errors and the cost for maintenance, consistency checking, and other stages of the service life cycle. Moreover, by using an existing logical tool called TQL [5], we have succeeded in expressing complex dependencies between parameters, and in automatically checking these dependencies against real-world configurations in feasible time.

In sect. 2, we give a brief overview of typical network service properties and of their modelling in tree structures. Section 3 introduces the TQL tree logic and shows how service properties become validation rules expressed in this formalism, while sect. 4 presents the results of the validation of several configuration rules related to the *Virtual Private Network* service on multiple devices. Section 5 concludes and indicates further directions of research.

2   Service Configuration Properties

A service usually requires underlying services or sub-services, such as network connectivity, and has a life cycle starting from the customer's demand and followed by negotiation, provisioning, up to utilisation by the customer and management of the service. Many steps of this life cycle, such as provisioning, entail the manipulation of configuration information in the devices involved in the service offering. The configuration information consists of parameters that can be created or removed and whose values can be changed according to a goal.

The configuration process is hierarchical. Several parameters that logically belong together can be grouped together by means of configuration statements, such as commands or menu windows with buttons and choices. Thus, several parameters can be affected by means of a single command, and conversely, several commands can compose a single feature or a service, in the same way that several services can compose a higher-level service. Consequently, a provider of a higher level service can be a customer of a lower level service.

2.1   Dependencies at Service Configuration Level

The parameters and components of the configuration affected by a service are in specific and precise dependencies. All those dependencies must be studied and captured by the management models, in order to provide effective solutions. We will show some of those dependencies and a methodology for their modelling. For each of the examples presented, we will deduce a configuration rule formalising the dependencies.

Example 1: IP Addresses. The existence or the possible state of a parameter may depend on another such parameter somewhere else in the configuration.

The simplest example of such dependency can be seen in an IP address following the Classless Inter-Domain Routing (CIDR) scheme [10], [16], whose two components, the *value* and the *subnet mask*, are linked by a simple relationship: an address like 206.13.01.48/25, having a network prefix of 25 bits, must carry a mask of at least 255.255.255.128, while the same address with a network prefix of 27 bits must not have a subnet mask under 255.255.255.224.

From this example, we could deduce a simple rule ensuring the validity of all IP addresses used in a given configuration:

> **Example Rule 1** *The subnet mask of an IP address must be consistent with its CIDR network prefix.*

Example 2: Access Lists. Access lists show another example of a generic dependency. Network devices use access lists to match the packets that pass through an element interface and block or let them pass, according to packet information. The configuration of such extended IP access lists has a variable geometry: if the type of protocol used for packet matching is TCP or UDP, the port information (operator, port number or a port number range) is mandatory. If the protocol used is different (e.g. ICMP), there is no port information required.

From this example, we could deduce another rule relating to proper use of access lists:

> **Example Rule 2** *If the protocol used in an access list is TCP or UDP, then this access list must provide port information.*

Access lists illustrate yet another parameter relationship: once an access list is created, an identifier is provided for it. This identifier must then be used to attach the access list to a specific interface.

Example 3: Virtual Private Networks. More complex situations can be encountered, in which the parameters of several devices supporting the same service are interdependent. An example is provided by the configuration of a *Virtual Private Network* (VPN) service [15], [17], [18].

A VPN is a private network constructed within a public network such as a service provider's network. A customer might have several sites, which are contiguous parts of the network, dispersed throughout the Internet and would like to link them together by a protected communication. The VPN ensures the connectivity and privacy of the customer's communications between sites.

The establishment and validation of VPN is a particularly interesting example that has already spawned many books and papers. In particular, [3] develops a set of formal constraints under which a given VPN is safe and properly working. [6] also uses the VPN as an example to present a formal method of validation.

Some part of the connections and communications is realised between the routers at the edge of the provider's network, called *provider edge* or PE-routers, and routers at the edge of the customer's sites (*customer edge routers* or CE-routers). Another part of the connections is made among the PE-routers of the provider's network.

One of the many implementations of the VPN is based on *Multi-Protocol Label Switching* (MPLS), in which the connectivity and communications inside the provider's network are ensured by the Border Gateway Protocol (BGP) processes. A simple way to realise it is by direct neighbour configuration.

Among other requirements of this method, an interface on each PE-router (for example, `Loopback0`), must have its IP address publicised into the BGP processes of all the other PE-routers' configurations using the `neighbor` command [15]. If one of these IP addresses changes the connectivity is lost and the VPN service functioning is jeopardised. Thus,

Example Rule 3 *In a VPN, the IP address of the `Loopback0` interface of every PE-router must be declared as a neighbour in every other PE-router.*

Some of the dependencies might be specific to the vendor implementation of the configuration interface. Such dependencies are of a low level and more difficult to model, because of the diversity of the vendor solutions. For instance, the configuration commands in Cisco's IOS are different from those in Juniper's JunOS, not to mention the different versions of the same vendor's commands. In the following sections, we rather focus on *generic* dependencies.

2.2   Configuration Management Approaches

The International Telecommunications Union (ITU) defines a management model called TMN [12] based on the OSI management framework. Three logical layers of this model are involved in network service management:

- the service-management layer (SML)
- the network-management layer (NML)
- the element-management layer (EML)

The service-management layer takes charge of the connections to the users and the underlying connectivity between users and the provider (e.g. transmitting a video image to the customer).

The network-management layer deals with the topology, the technology (IP, ATM, FR, ...), the protocols (ISDN, BGP, OSP, RIP, ...) and the devices (number, type, and role) used in the network.

The element-management layer deals with the network elements, the configuration parameters (bandwidth, packet size, error rate, IP addresses, routing tables, access lists, etc.) and commands that describe or implement the service.

Network service management can be done by various means: text-based commands, graphical user interfaces, menus, wizards. Routers and switches, like other equipment working in IP networks, are mostly configured by means of commands (around 90%, according to some estimates) running under an operating system, such as NetBSD, Cisco's IOS, and Juniper's JunOS.

In this case, configuration files contain sequences of text commands. Usually, with some exceptions, the default information present in the routers and switches is not recorded in configuration files, but only the alterations of this information.

Configuration files are an important mean for service configuration on network elements. The manipulation of the configuration files contributes to the quick and easy configuring of the routers and switches. Given the important role played by the commands in the service configuration on equipments, it is important to study their properties and particularities in order to draw network element management solutions.

2.3   Modelling the Service Configurations

In this section, we describe how to model service configurations. All properties of a given configuration are described by attribute-value pairs. However, these pairs are organised in a hierarchy that will be represented by a tree structure.

The tree representation is a natural choice, since it reflects dependencies among components, such as the parameters, statements and features. Moreover, trees are simple and handy for defining and performing various operations required by service management tasks. We will see that trees can also be put into direct correspondence with XML files for a better and easier manipulation.

Tree Structures. The basic element of our tree structure is the *configuration node* which implements the concept of attribute-value pairs. A configuration node is in itself a small tree having a fixed shape. Its root is labelled `node`, and it has three children:

- `name`, which itself has a single child of variable label, the name of the attribute
- `value`, which also has a single child of variable label, the value of the attribute
- `child`, which can have as many other `node` structures as desired

Thus, if we are to speak of the IP address of a given component, we use the tree depicted in fig. 1.

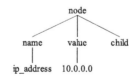

Fig. 1. A simple configuration node

Were we to consider separately the value and the subnet mask of a given address, we could model it in the way represented by fig. 2.

As one can see, our model puts the parameters as children configuration nodes. This approach enables to model simple dependencies among service configuration components, in which the existence of a component is conditioned by the existence of another. These dependencies are modelled by the ancestor-descendent relationship.

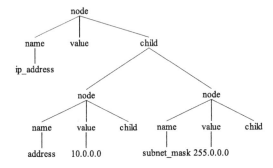

Fig. 2. A configuration node with two children containing additional attributes

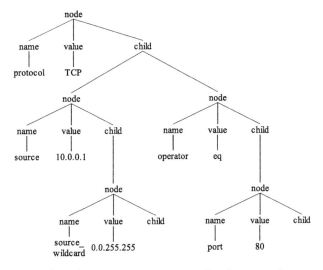

Fig. 3. Partial configuration tree structure for the access list example

To illustrate this concept, let us examine fig. 3, which represents a sample tree for the access list presented in example 2 of section 2.1. In this tree, if the protocol parameter of an extended IP access list has the value TCP or UDP, it is the parent or ancestor node of the associated port node. The standard IP access lists do not have the protocol parameter and thus cannot have the port either. Under some systems, the access list number, stored at the root node of the access list tree, enables us to tell the difference between the two types. If the number is comprised between 1 and 99, the access list is a standard one; if the number is comprised between 100 and 199, the access list is of the extended type.

Taking the concept of hierarchy further, we illustrate in fig. 4 by a larger tree the last example in section 2.1. Each router has a device name, an interface Loopback0 whose address is defined, and some number of neighbor attributes declaring the IP addresses of the neighbouring PE-routers. Figure 4 shows a portion of a tree for a single device named router_1.

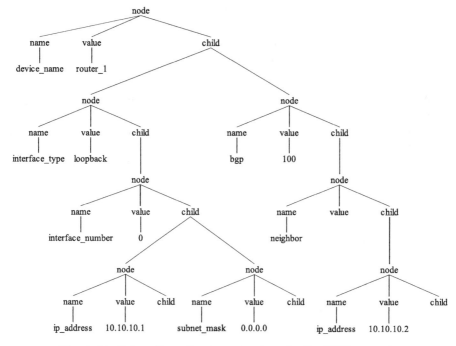

Fig. 4. Partial configuration tree structure for the VPN example

All our Example Rules given in sect. 2 can be translated into the new terminology of trees. Thus, Example Rule 3 becomes the following Tree Rule:

> **Tree Rule 3** *The* value *of the IP address of the interface* Loopback0
> *in the PE* router_i *is equal to the IP address value of a* neighbour
> *component configured under the BGP process of any other PE* router_j.

This "tree-form" acts an an intermediate step between the English-like rules
of sect. 2.1 and the formal syntax that will be introduced in sect. 3. To handle
multiple devices in a same description, we can top all individual trees by a global
common node, called network for instance.

XML Schema Trees. XML (eXtensible Markup Language) is a universal format for structured documents over the web. XML is a widely used standard
developed and maintained by the World Wide Web Consortium (W3C). Over
the years, XML has gained in popularity and is becoming a standard way of
representing virtually any data.

There is a straightforward correspondence between labelled trees like the
ones presented in sect. 2.3 and XML files. Any label in such a tree becomes an
XML "tag", and all children of that label are enclosed between its opening and
closing tag. Hence, one configuration node produces many XML tags. The small
tree of fig. 1 can be easily translated into this piece of XML code:

```
<node>
    <name>ip_address</name>
    <value>10.0.0.0</value>
    <child></child>
</node>
```

We do not include the XML versions of the other trees shown previously, as the translation is direct.

XML is a natural choice of building and manipulating trees, because of its flexibility and the availability of a wide range of features and tools handling XML files.

As shown in the first example of the previous paragraph, some complex dependencies cannot be seized by sole parent-children relationship. We hence need to introduce some kind of formalism and express rules applying to the tree elements (nodes, branches, values, root, etc.). This is what we do in the following section.

3   Modelling the Service Configuration Rules

With configurations described as trees, in order to verify configuration rules, we need a formalism to express properties of trees. Many such formalisms have been developed in recent years [1], [4], [9], [11], [14], [21]. In particular, [5] introduced a logic called TQL (Tree Query Logic), which supports both property and query descriptions. Hence one can not only check if a property is true or false, but also extract a specific subtree that makes that property true or false.

We show in this section how TQL can be used to perform validation tasks on the XML network descriptions modelled in sect. 2.

3.1   A Formalism for Expressing Configuration Rules

Simply put, TQL is a description language for trees. We say that a tree t matches a given TQL expression e and we write $t \models e$ when e is true when it refers to t. We also say that e *describes* t.

The two main constructs in this logic are the edge ([ ]) and the composition (|). Any TQL expression enclosed within square brackets is meant to describe the subtree of a given node. For example, the expression root[child] indicates that the root of the current tree is labelled root, and that this root has only one child, labelled child. The composition operator joins two tree roots; hence, the expression node[name | value] describes a tree whose root is node, and whose two children are the nodes name and value. These operators can be nested at need; thus, the tree depicted in fig. 1 is described by the following TQL expression:

node[name[ip_address] | value[10.0.0.0] | child]

Edge and composition alone can describe any single tree. To express properties about whole classes of trees, other operators are added to the syntax, whose intuitive meaning is given here:

- $\neg A$ (negation): if a tree does not match A, then it matches $\neg\ A$
- $A \vee B$ (disjunction): if a tree matches $A \vee B$, then either it matches A or it matches B (or both)
- $A \wedge B$ (conjunction): if a tree matches $A \wedge B$, then it must match both A and B
- . (existence of a child): $.x$ matches any tree whose root has a child labelled x

These operators allow us to express, for example, the fact that a given access list has a **port** node if its protocol is TCP or UDP:

TQL Query 2
node[name[protocol] | value[TCP $\vee$ UDP] | child[
.node.child.node[.name[port]]]]] $\vee$

It actually tells that the root node of the tree is labelled **node**, whose **name** branch leads to **protocol**, whose **value** branch leads to either TCP or UDP and whose **child** branch spawns another node leading to **port**. If not, then the root node has a **protocol** name different from TCP and UDP.

A similar argument allows us to check that the tree shown in fig. 5 also verifies the property.

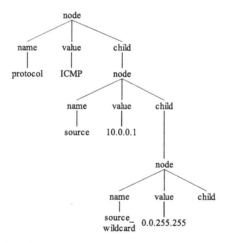

Fig. 5. Another access list tree with no port information

Furthermore, one can extract the protocol name in fig. 3 with the query

$$\text{node}[.\text{value}[\$P]]$$

expressing the fact that the root **node** has a child labelled **value** having its child label assigned to variable \$P. TQL rules are instantiated in a Prolog-like fashion.

Let us also mention that TQL contains a fix-point operator which can be used to recursively express properties at any depth in a tree [4], [5]. This makes TQL suitable for any configuration property.

For more information related to TQL and its syntax, the reader is referred to [4] and [5].

3.2   Applying TQL to Validate Service Configuration File Properties

Each of the Tree Rules to be checked on a given description can be translated into TQL queries by using the operators described above. For example, the VPN Tree Rule 3 now becomes:

TQL Query 3
network[
   .node[.name[device_name] | .value[$N] | .child.node[
      .name[interface_type] | .value[loopback] | .child.node[
         .name[interface_number] | .value[0] | .child.node[
            .name[ip_address] .value[$A]]]]] ∧
   .node[.name[device_name] | .value[¬ $N] ∧¬ .child.node[
      .name[bgp] | .value[100] | .child.node[
         .name[neighbor] | .child.node[
            .name[ip_address] | .value[$A]]]]]]

The first half of the query fetches all tuples of values of `device_name` and `ip_address` for the `Loopback0` interface and binds them to the variables $N and $A. From all these tuples, the second half asks TQL to keep only those for which there exists a device different than $N where $A is not listed as a neighbour. The query returns all addresses of interfaces `Loopback0` not declared as a neighbour in at least one other device. Therefore, if an inconsistency is detected, the set of faulty parameters is returned, thus helping to pinpoint the location of the error in the configuration and eventually correct it. On the other hand, an empty result indicates the property is verified for all addresses and all devices.

The structure and syntax of these rules is straightforward, but cumbersome. However, the advantage of TQL over other tree logics is the availability of a software tool that automatically verifies TQL queries on XML files. This tool is freely available from TQL's site [20].

The TQL tool takes as input an XML file containing the tree we want to check and TQL properties to be verified on that tree. The program performs the verification, and for each of the queries, outputs the portions of the tree that match the given property, if any.

Moreover, once a TQL property is built to check a given rule, it does not need any modification to be checked against any schema tree following the same conventions.

4   Experimental Results

We processed real world XML network descriptions with the following 5 sample properties modelling the MPLS VPN service. Remark that property P4 is the VPN rule we have used as an example throughout this paper.

P1 If two sites belong to a single VPN, they must have similar route distinguisher and their mutually imported and exported route-targets must have corresponding numbers.

P2 The VRF name specified for the PE-CE connectivity and the VRF name configured on the PE interface for the CE link must be consistent.

P3 The VRF name used for the VPN connection to the customer site must be configured on the PE router.

P4 The interface of a PE router that is used by the BGP process for PE connectivity, must be defined as BGP process `neighbor` in all of the other PE routers of the provider.

P5 The address family vpnv4 must activate and configure all of the BGP neighbors for carrying only VPN IPv4 prefixes and advertising the extended community attribute.

All these properties were translated into tree rules, and then into TQL queries in the same fashion as described in sect. 3. These queries were then verified sample XML schema trees of a network composed of 2 to 20 routers. These sample schema trees were automatically generated by a parameterisable script, and then directly fed to TQL. For some of the descriptions we used, one or many of the 5 rules were false. Since rules were processed separately, it was always possible to know which rule failed. The results, summarised in table 1, suggest a validation time roughly polynomial in the size of the configuration to check.

Table 1. Results of TQL query validation for 5 VPN rules

Routers	Config. nodes	XML tags	Checking time (s)				
			P1	P2	P3	P4	P5
2	56	413	0,04	0,04	0,06	0,06	0,04
4	224	1639	0,06	0,12	0,09	0,08	0,12
6	504	3681	0,09	0,24	0,18	0,13	0,20
8	896	6539	0,12	0,38	0,28	0,19	0,32
10	1400	10213	0,15	0,54	0,41	0,29	0,48
20	5600	40823	0,52	2,17	1,52	0,96	1,86

All results have been obtained on an AMD Athlon 1400+ system running Windows XP. As one can see from the previous results, validation time for all rules is quite reasonable and does not exceed 10 seconds for the largest data set. In all these sets, TQL correctly validated the rules that were actually true, and spotted the ones that did not apply.

5   Conclusions

We have shown how network configuration can be modelled first by using tree structures, and then by standard XML files. By using an existing logical formalism called TQL, we have succeeded in expressing complex dependencies between parameters, and in automatically checking these dependencies against real-world network descriptions in feasible time.

The results obtained suggest that this framework could be extended to model all kinds of dependencies in network descriptions for different classes of services. A subset of TQL could even be implemented in existing network management tools to perform background validation tasks and provide insightful messages to an administrator. The ability of TQL to formally detect and prove tautologies and contradictions could also be used to eventually discover conflicting rule sets.

The scalability of our approach over networks of hundreds or thousands of devices must also be assessed. More experiments have to be done to ensure that validation time of larger descriptions remains in practical bounds.

Further work towards a standardisation of descriptions of service configurations is also needed. The Common Information Model (CIM) [8] and Directory Enabled Networking (DEN) [19] initiatives developed by the Distributed Management Task Force (DTMF) [7] are two examples of an XML modelling of all components of network activity that opens the way to a normalisation of their behaviour.

References

1. Alechina, N., Demri, S., De Rijke M.: A modal perspective on path constraints. Journal of Logic and Computation, 13(6) (2003) 939–956.
2. Al-Shaer E., Hamed H.: Discovery of Policy Anomalies in Distributed Firewalls. Proc. IEEE INFOCOM (2004)
3. Bush, R., Griffin, T.: Integrity for Virtual Private Routed Networks. Proc. IEEE INFOCOM (2003)
4. Cardelli, L.: Describing semistructured data. SIGMOD Record, 30(4) (2001) 80–85
5. Cardelli, L., Ghelli, G.: TQL: A query language for semistructured data based on the ambient logic. Mathematical Structures in Computer Science (to appear).
6. Deca, R., Cherkaoui, O., Puche, D.: A Validation Solution for Network Configuration. Communications Networks and Services Research Conference (CNSR 2004), Fredericton, N.B. (2004)
7. Distributed Management Task Force. http://www.dmtf.org/
8. DSP111, DMTF white paper, Common Information Model core model, version 2.4, August 30, 2000.
9. Fournet C., Gonthier G., Lévy J.-J., Maranget, L., Rémy, D.: A Calculus of Mobile Agents. Proc. CONCUR'96 (1996)
10. Fuller, V., Li, T., Yu, J., Varadhan, K.: Classless Inter-Domain Routing (CIDR): an Address Assignment and Aggregation Strategy. RFC 1519 (1993)
11. Gottlob G., Koch, C.: Monadic queries over tree-structured data. LICS'02 (2002) 189–202
12. ITU Recommendation M.3000, Overview of TMN Recommendations. February 2000.
13. Mayer, A., Wool, A., Ziskind, E.: Fang: A Firewall Analysis Engine. Proc. IEEE Symposium on Security and Privacy (2000)
14. Miklau G., Suciu, D.: Containment and equivalence for an Xpath fragment. Proc. PODS 2002 (2002) 65–76
15. Pepelnjak, I., Guichard, J.: MPLS VPN Architectures, Cisco Press (2001)

16. Rekhter, Y., Li, T.: An Architecture for IP Address Allocation with CIDR. RFC 1518 (1993)
17. Rosen, E., Rekhter, Y.: BGP/MPLS VPNs. RFC 2547 (1999)
18. Scott, C., Wolfe, P. Erwin, M.: Virtual Private Networks, O'Reilly (1998)
19. Strassner J., Baker F.: Directory Enabled Networks, Macmillan Technical Publishing (1999)
20. TQL web site, Università di Pisa. http://tql.di.unipi.it/tql/
21. Vitek, J., Castagna, G.: Seal: a framework for secure mobile computations. Internet Programming Languages, LNCS 1686 (1999) 44–77

Agent-Based Mobile Multimedia Service Quality Monitoring

Man Li

Nokia Research Center
5 Wayside Road, Burlington MA 01803
man.m.li@nokia.com

Abstract. An agent-based mobile multimedia service quality monitoring architecture is proposed where agent software is installed on end user mobile phones to monitor service performance, to report measurements to a centralized management server, and to raise alarms if service quality falls below a pre-set threshold. The proposed framework effectively turns thousands of mobile phones into service quality probing stations and provides a cost effective way to obtain true end user experience. Key service performance indicators for service performance evaluation are proposed. Parameters that should be monitored by agents for each service instance are discussed. A procedure to derive the key service performance indicators from service instance measurements is also described. Future researches are then outlined.

1 Introduction

Monitoring end user perceived service quality is a critical step in managing multimedia services over mobile networks. Unlike fixed networks, the air interface in a mobile network has low bandwidth and is subject to higher packet loss and error. As a result, offering multimedia services over mobile wireless networks presents many challenges. On the other hand, multimedia services when offered commercially must meet certain performance standards in order to attract and sustain subscribers. For example, video-streaming services should not have many display interruptions or fuzzy images so that users can enjoy the movies. Furthermore, driven by fierce competitions, mobile operators strive to make sure that the quality of their services is superior to those provided by competitors. As a result, mobile operators have a keen interest in monitoring service quality perceived by end users. In addition, through continuous monitoring, operators can also detect potential performance problems early and make corrective actions in time before large-scale performance problems occur.

Previous studies have produced a good understanding of service performance targets for different services, e.g., web browsing [1]. Impacts of packet loss, delay, and jitter on service performance have also been studied extensively [2], [3], [4], [5], [6]. A current approach for service quality monitoring is to install monitoring tool or software on a dedicated monitoring device such as a laptop. Equipped with a wireless card such as a GSM card, this device can be used for drive-through tests. The monitoring tool would initiate various mobile services from the device and then monitor different aspects of the services, e.g., response time, throughput, etc. The monitoring results are then uploaded to a central management server. Dedicated monitoring devices are reliable but their monitoring results are approximations of the performance

J. Vicente and D. Hutchison (Eds.): MMNS 2004, LNCS 3271, pp. 189–199, 2004.
© IFIP International Federation for Information Processing 2004

perceived by actual customers. The geographic and temporal distribution of the measurements may be quite different from the real user experience. In addition, the application performance on the dedicated devices may be quite different from that on a mobile phone. Further more, deploying thousands of drive-through tests with dedicated monitoring devices can be costly in terms of both hardware and human resources required.

In this paper, we propose an agent-based architecture for monitoring mobile multimedia service quality. It effectively turns thousands of mobile phones into service quality probing stations and provides a cost effective way to obtain true end user experience. The organization of the paper is the following. Section 2 proposes an agent based mobile service quality monitoring architecture. Section 3 discusses the key service performance indicators. Section 4 details what mobile agents shall monitor for each service instance. Section 5 describes the procedure of deriving key performance indicators. Section 6 provides an example for streaming service performance monitoring. Section 7 discusses future researches and Section 8 concludes the paper.

2   Agent-Based Mobile Service Quality Monitoring Architecture

We propose an agent-based architecture for monitoring mobile multimedia services as shown in Figure 1. It is based on the Open Mobile Alliance (OMA) Device Management framework [7]. It consists of mobile agents installed on phones and device management (DM) servers in network operation centers (NOC). The communications between the mobile agents and the device management servers are through the OMA SyncML for device management protocols [9], [8].

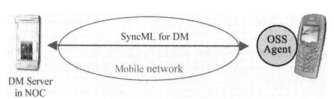

Fig. 1. Mobile agent based monitoring architecture.

Mobile agents are responsible for capturing performance information for each monitored service instance whereas the DM server has the responsibility of collecting measurements from mobile agents and of developing key performance indicators out of the collected measurements. To reduce memory consumption and measurement reporting traffic, a mobile agent can also produce and report performance indicators based on its own measurements. Details of the agent based monitoring architecture are described in the following sections.

2.1   SIPAs and KPIs

We define a *service instance* as an occurrence of a service. For example, the download of a single web page is an instance of a browsing service. A *Service Instance Performance vAlue (SIPA)* contains information that captures a performance aspect of a single service instance. For example, a "status" (success or failure) that is associated with each service instance is a SIPA.

A *Key performance indicator* (KPIs) is a metric that is crucial for evaluating the performance of a service. KPIs are derived from a population of SIPAs. For example, a "service success ratio" is a KPI that is derived from many "status" SIPAs collected by mobile agents.

KPIs provide a high level indication on service performance whereas SIPAs support the derivation of KPIs and are also useful in root cause analysis.

2.2 Mobile Agent

A mobile agent is a piece of software running on a standard mobile terminal. One of the responsibilities of an agent is to collect and report SIPAs. As shown in Figure 1, an agent communicates with a device management server via the SyncML DM protocol. The server controls the agent behavior by loading a monitoring profile. The profile contains the following information:

- Monitoring style. Indicates if the monitoring should be active or passive. For active measurement, a mobile agent executes scheduled tests, e.g., downloads a predefined web page, after checking that enough resources on the mobile phone are available for performing the test. This test activity would have lower priority and can be interrupted if necessary so that real user services are not affected. For passive measurement, the mobile agent starts monitoring calls and service sessions as instructed by this profile. Passive measurement is likely to have little disturbance to real user applications. In both active and passive measurements, an agent records SIPAs associated with each monitored service.
- Schedules. Indicate the start and end of monitoring periods
- User locations. Monitoring can be triggered by user location, i.e., start monitoring when a user is in these cells.
- Bearer types. Instructs the agent to monitor a service only when it uses the specified bearer types. A service may be provided over different bearers, e.g., GSM, Blue tooth, WLAN.
- Service names. The type of services to be monitored
- Servers. For passive monitoring, only when these servers are involved, shall the performance be recorded. For active monitoring, these are the servers to be contacted in order to start services
- Reporting schedule. This dictates when and how agents report results to a management server. Possible choices are: at the end of each service, periodically (e.g., once every hour or every day), or when asked by the server.
- Others, e.g., thresholds for different services. When quality falls below the thresholds, alarms should be raised.

A mobile agent can also pre-process the SIPAs it collects and produce performance indicators (PI) out of these SIPAs. Then the PIs can be reported to the server. For example, instead of reporting the "status" of many web page browsing service instances, the agent can report a single success ratio derived from the SIPAs. We call the indicators derived by a single mobile agent "performance indicators (PIs) ", not KPIs, because they represent only a single end user experience. To further build on this idea, the monitoring profile can also include thresholds for the PIs so that if a threshold is exceeded, the agent will send alarms to the management server. Note, however, that this method needs to be implemented with caution. When many agents in the same cell detect the same performance problem, e.g., service response time is too long, they may all send alarms and introduce a flood of additional traffic into the network that further worsen the situation.

The actual monitoring and recording of SIPAs can be performed in at least two ways. The first approach is to have service applications conduct the measurements. Hence as shown in Figure 2(a) the mobile agent must interface with the service applications. Through the interfaces and based on the monitoring profile, an agent can configure the applications on what, when and how to conduct monitoring of services. When it is time to report measurements, the agent will query the applications for SIPAs and transport them to the server via SyncML. If the DM server instructs the agent to report PI measurements, the agent will query the applications for SIPAs, derive PIs out of the SIPAs, and then deliver the PIs to the server as requested. Periodically, the agent shall query the applications for SIPAs, derive PIs from them, and raise alarms if thresholds are exceeded. This approach employs a relatively simple agent whose responsibility is to collect and report monitoring results. The agent does not need to understand the messages, traffic flows, or logics involved in providing services. On the other hand, this approach does require service applications to implement monitoring interfaces so that they can communicate with an agent. If a third party application does not support a monitoring interface, then that service cannot be monitored.

A second approach is for an agent to snoop the transport layer (e.g., IP packets) as shown in Figure 2(b). The agent then parses the packets to and from applications, and infers SIPAs from them. For example, when the agent sees a HTTP GET request, it records a web service request accordingly. With this approach, the agent is responsible for all the monitoring, recording, and reporting. This approach does not require service applications to support extra interfaces. As a result, any third party developed applications can be monitored. On the other hand, this approach demands a very intelligent and hence complicated agent that understands all the applications. With the limited processing power on current mobile devices, this may not be feasible for the time being. But it may be an option after a few years.

If the speed of growth for memory and processing power of desktop computers could be any predication for the growth of memory and processing power of mobile devices, the consumption of processing power and memory for service performance monitoring may not be a major concern after a few years. On the other hand, the extra reporting traffic introduced into the network may be a concern, given the limited air interface bandwidth and the fact that there may potentially be thousands of mobile agents in a network. There are at least two approaches to reduce reporting traffic. First, compressing the data before transportation in order to save bandwidth. Second, reporting PIs instead of SIPAs.

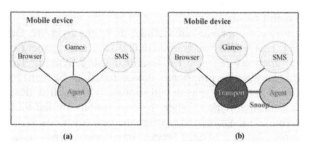

Fig. 2. An agent inside a mobile device.

2.3 Device Management Server

Within the OMA device management framework, a Device Management (DM) server remotely performs mobile device configuration, inventory, diagnostics, software installation, upgrading and configuration. Service quality monitoring can be seen as part of remote diagnostics. The DM server remotely configures monitoring profiles to be used by mobile agents. It also collects or receives SIPA reports from mobile agents and derives KPIs from the SIPAs. Very valuable KPIs can be derived. For example, when location information (e.g., Cell ID) is associated with the measurements, an operator can produce a "service weather report" – how each service is doing in different area. Potential problems may be detected early and diagnosed with the help of the measurements. The measurements can also serve as real time feed back for network optimization.

Specific to the agent based monitoring architecture, the DM server is also responsible for managing the mobile agents, for example, remotely installs and updates agent software, activates or deactivates an agent, pings an agent, if necessary, when the agent has missed multiple scheduled reports.

2.4 SyncML DM Protocols

The protocols used for communications between mobile agents and DM servers are the OMA SyncML Representation Protocol [8] and the SyncML DM protocol [9]. The SyncML Representation Protocol is an XML-based representation protocol that specifies the representation or format of all the information required to perform synchronization or device management. To reduce the data size, a binary coding of SyncML based on the WAP Forum's WBXML is defined. In [9], the use of the representation protocol for device management is specified. It describes how SyncML messages are exchanged in order to allow a device management client and server to exchange additions, deletes, updates and other status information. The SyncML Representation and DM protocols are transport-independent.

2.5 Management Tree

In the OMA DM framework, each device that supports SyncML DM must contain a management tree [10]. The management tree organizes all available management objects in the device as a hierarchical tree structure where all nodes can be uniquely addressed with a URI. Nodes are the entities that can be manipulated by management actions carried over the SyncML DM protocol. The actions include ADD, GET, REPLACE and DELETE. For service performance monitoring, the leaf nodes specify the SIPAs and their properties.

All managed objects or nodes are defined using the SyncML Device Description Framework [11]. OMA DM has been standardizing management objects [12]. Proprietary device functions can also be described using SyncML Device Description Framework. This allows new proprietary device functions be managed before they are standardized. Specifically, device manufacturers will publish descriptions of their devices as they enter the market. When the descriptions are fed into DM servers, the servers will be able to recognize and manage the new functions in the devices.

The above-proposed agent-based service monitoring architecture effectively turns thousands of mobile phones into service quality probing stations. Mobile agents are close to end users and hence can faithfully monitor real end user experience. Drive-through tests are conducted as end users move in mobile networks. Since no additional hardware and manpower are required, it is a cost effective approach for monitoring mobile multimedia service performance.

3 Mobile Service Key Performance Indicators (KPI)

We have described an agent-based monitoring architecture. The next step is to determine a set of key performance indicators (KPI) used by the framework to assess service quality. Mobile multimedia service KPIs shall be able to measure service success ratio, service response time and the quality of the media involved in a service. The recommended service success ratio and response time KPIs are:

- *Service success ratio*: The percentage of service instances that are complete successfully
- *Service response time*: Measures the speed of response to an end user's request for service
- *Bearer Failure Ratio*: The percentage of bearers (e.g., GPRS) that either cannot be established or are established but prematurely disconnected before the end of a service. It indicates how much the network contributes to service failures – a KPI of great interest to mobile operators.

In terms of media quality, there is no single metric that can completely characterize media quality. Instead, we recommend the use of multiple KPIs to evaluate different aspects of media quality. If a service involves multiple types of media (e.g., voice, video), the quality of each media type shall be evaluated separately.

As packets travel through a mobile network, they experience different end-to-end delays. For real time applications, a display buffer is implemented at the receiving end to smooth out the delay jitters so that the media can be displayed continuously. It may happen, for example due to low throughput of the network, that the buffer becomes empty temporally. This causes a display break – a period during which the rendering of streaming data stops. A very short break may not be visible to an end user. However, when a break lasts longer than a threshold, it becomes noticeable performance degradation. Therefore, we propose the following two media KPIs:

- *Display break ratio*: The ratio of the sum of display break durations that are longer than a pre-defined threshold over the service time.
- *Number of display breaks*: The number of media display breaks that last longer than a pre-defined threshold

In addition, the following two KPIs are also necessary for assessing media performance:

- *Packet Loss & Error Ratio: The percentage of packets that are either lost or detected as erroneous. Applicable to media content carried by RTP protocol only*
- *Throughput: Packet throughput of the media involved in the service.*

Many previous studies indicate that packet loss and error ratio has a direct impact on real time media quality [2], [3], [4].

End to end packet delay is also an important performance indicator for media quality. Unfortunately, it is difficult for mobile agents to measure this type of delays because estimating one-way end-to-end delay requires clock synchronization between mobile phones or between mobile phones and servers. Which is difficult to achieve. In addition, monitoring packet delay requires mobile agents to capture and time stamp packets received. Which could potentially consume too much memory and processing power.

4 Mobile Service Instance Performance Values (SIPA)

With the KPIs being specified, we now define the information that must be captured for each service instance, i.e., SIPA, in order to produce KPIs and to help in root cause analysis.

For mobile multimedia services, a service may involve multiple types of media. Therefore, we separate service SIPAs from media SIPAs. Service SIPAs capture the different aspects of a service instance whereas media SIPAs capture the information on media delivery and display. The service and media SIPAs are specified in Table 1 and Table 2. In formal definitions, these SIPAs are arranged in a tree structure and are specified in XML, following the OMA device management framework.

Table 1. Service SIPA.

SIPA	Descriptions
Service Name	The name of a service, e.g., browsing
Application Name	The name of the application used for the service. It identifies the vendor of the application software.
Session ID	A random number that uniquely identifies a service instance on the mobile phone
Setup Duration	The duration to setup a service. Indicate the time required to gain resources that are necessary for the service.
Function Duration	The duration of the time when the service is delivered.
Status	The outcome of a service
Date and Time	The date and time when a user starts to use the service
Location	The location at the end of a completed service or an unsuccessful service attempt.

5 Deriving KPI from SIPA

An agent-based service monitoring architecture shall be able to derive KPIs for a specific service from a pool of SIPA reports. The steps to do so are described below:

1. Filter out the service instances by "Service Name" SIPA. Apply the following calculations on the resulted service instances.
2. *Service success* ratio KPI can be computed as

$$Service\, Success\, Ratio = \frac{Number\, of\, Services\, With\, Status = success}{Number\, of\, recorded\, Services} \quad (1)$$

3. *Bearer failure ratio* KPI for a specific type of media of a service can be computed as

$$Bearer\, Failure\, Ratio = \frac{Number\, of\, Media\, With\, Bearer\, Failure}{Number\, of\, recorded\, Media\, Streams} \quad (2)$$

If a service has bi-directional media delivery, the Bearer Failure Ratio should be calculated for each direction separately.

Table 2. Media SIPA.

SIPA	Descriptions
Session ID	The Session ID of the service to which this media stream belongs
Media ID	A random number that uniquely identifies a media stream within the service instance. This SIPA is applicable when there are multiple media involved in a service.
Server	The address of the server that provides the media delivery. If there is no server involved, this SIPA shall be ignored
Media Type	The type of the media whose quality is being measured.
Direction	The direction (incoming or outgoing) of the measured traffic
Media Setup Duration	The duration to setup this media. Indicate the time required to gain resources that are necessary for the delivery of the media content.
Media Function Duration	The duration of the time when the media content is delivered.
Status	The outcome of a media content delivery
Bearer	Bearer type and if the requested bearer, e.g., UMTS bearer, is established and maintained for the service.
Data Size	The total amount of error free data (in bytes) received (or sent, if monitoring outgoing media stream). This SIPA only applies when the status of the media delivery is success
Packet Counts	The total amount of error free packets received (or sent, if monitoring outgoing media stream). This SIPA only applies when the status of the media is success
Loss & Erroneous Packets	Number of lost or erroneous media packets of the incoming Media. Only applicable for monitoring incoming media
Display Breaks	Number of display breaks that last longer than a pre-set threshold. Only applicable for monitoring incoming real time media
Total Break Length	The sum of all the display breaks (in milliseconds) that are longer than a pre-set threshold. Only applicable for monitoring incoming real time media
Date and Time	The date and time when a user starts to use the media
Location	The location at the end of a completed media delivery or an unsuccessful media delivery.

4. Further filter out the successful service instances by Status = success.

   1. For EACH successful service instance:
- Service response time = Setup Duration
- For EACH media stream associated with the service instance:
  - Number of Display Breaks is directly taken from the Display Breaks SIPA.
  - Display Break Ratio for a media stream instance is calculated as

$$Display\ Break\ Ratio = \frac{Total\ Break\ Length}{MediaFunctionDuration} \tag{3}$$

  - Packet Loss & Error ratio for the media stream instance is computed as

$$Packet\ Loss\ \&\ Error\ Ratio = \frac{Loss\ \&\ ErrorPackets}{PacketCounts + Loss\ \&\ ErrorPackets} \tag{4}$$

- Throughput for the media stream instance is calculated as

$$Throughput = \frac{DataSize}{MediaFunctionDuration} \qquad (5)$$

Note that this estimates the average "good" throughput since the Data Size excludes erroneous and retransmitted data.

2. The *Service Response Time, Number of Display Breaks, Display Break Ratio, Packet Loss & Error ratio, Packet Delay and Throughput* KPIs are obtained as statistics of service instances whose individual performance metrics are computed as described above. For example, 95 percentile of service response time is a Service Response Time KPI.

One may notice that not all SIPAs are used for computing KPIs. This is because that the SIPAs are designed not only for KPI calculations but also for root cause analysis when problems arise.

6 An Example: Streaming Service Quality Monitoring

We use a streaming service to illustrate the monitoring of service quality. Streaming refers to the ability of an application client to play synchronized media streams like audio and video streams in a continuous way while those streams are being transmitted to the client over a data network. As specified in the 3rd Generation Partnership Project (3GPP) [13], [14], [15], a streaming service contains a set of one or more streams presented to a user as a complete media feed. The content is transported with RTP over UDP. The control for the session set up and for the playing of media (PLAY, PAUSE) is via the RTSP protocol [16]. Figure 3 shows streaming service message flows.

When a user starts a streaming service by either clicking a link in a web page or entering a URI of a streaming server and content address, the streaming client on the mobile phone must first obtain a presentation description that contains information about one or more media streams within a presentation, such as encoding, network addresses and information about the content. This presentation description may be obtained in a number of ways, for example, via MMS or RTSP signaling. 3GPP mandates that the description be in the form of a Session Description Protocol (SDP) file [16].

Once the presentation description is obtained, the streaming client goes through a session establishment for each media stream. Specifically, it tries to establish a secondary PDP context for each streaming media and also sends a SETUP request message to the media server in order for the server to allocate resources for the stream. The SETUP reply message contains a session identifier, server port for displaying the media and other information required by a client for playback the media stream.

After all media stream sessions and their required PDP contexts are established, the user may click the play button to start playing the synchronized media. The user can also pause, resume or cancel the streaming service at any time. The RTSP PLAY, PAUSE and TEARDOWN messages are sent to the server for the corresponding action.

A streaming service instance is the setup, delivery and tear down of a streaming service. Applying the SIPA descriptions in Table 1 and Table 2 to a streaming service instance is relatively straightforward. In terms of service SIPA, The Setup Duration is the duration to setup the service. The starting point is when a user clicks a URI from a web page or clicks the return key after entering a URI. The end point is when the user is informed that the streaming service is ready, e.g., the play button is visible. The Function Duration is the duration for the service. The starting point is when the first byte of a media is received. And the end point is when the service is complete, i.e., when all media streams are disconnected. In terms of KPI, service response time in this case is the Setup Duration as shown in the figure.

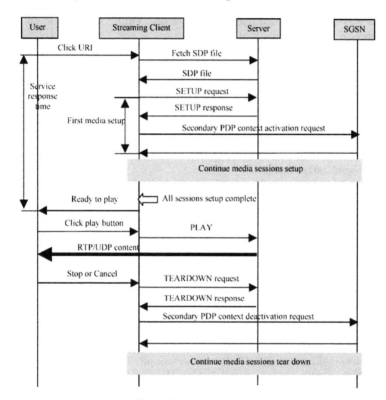

Fig. 3. Streaming Service.

7   Future Investigations

The mobile agents described in this paper can be enhanced with increased intelligence. For example, an agent may also conduct diagnosis. When a user fails to access a service for several times, the agent may be triggered to analyze the situation to decide, for example, if the settings on the phone are correct, if the network is available or if the server is functioning. It can then inform the user on what the problem is and recommend corresponding solutions. Further research is needed on efficient logics to be used by agents for diagnosis, keeping in mind that the memory and processing power are limited on mobile devices.

In order for the agent based monitoring architecture to work with mobile devices from different vendors, the SIPAs need to be standardized.

8 Conclusions

We have proposed an agent-based architecture for monitoring mobile multimedia service quality where agent software is installed on end user mobile phones to monitor service performance, to report measurements to a centralized management server, and to raise alarms if service quality falls below a pre-set threshold. For evaluating service performance, we have also recommended a set of KPIs and SIPAs as well as a procedure of deriving KPIs from SIPAs. The proposed architecture provides a cost effective way to monitor real end user experience. Future research on enhancing the intelligence of mobile agents is also discussed.

References

1. Chakravorty, R., Pratt, I.: WWW performance over GPRS. 4th international workshop on Mobile and Wireless Communications Network (2002)
2. Schlaerth, J., Hoe, B.: A technique for monitoring quality of service in tactical data networks. IEEE MILCOM (1996)
3. Verscheure, O. et al: User-Oriented QoS in Packet Video Delivery. IEEE Network Magazine, November/December (1998)
4. Jassen, J. et al: Assessing Voice Quality in Packet Based Telephony. IEEE Internet Computing, May/June (2002)
5. Kostas, T. et al: Real-Time Voice Over Packet-Switched Networks. IEEE Network Magazine, January/February (1998)
6. Sun, L. et al: Impact of Packet Loss Location on Perceived Speech Quality. Internet Telephony Workshop (2001)
7. ITU-T Recommendation P.862: Perceptual evaluation of speech quality (PESQ), an objective method for end-to-end speech quality assessment of narrowband telephone networks and speech codecs (2001)
8. Open Mobile Alliance™: Enabler Release Definition for OMA Device Management, version 1.1.2 (2003)
9. Open Mobile Alliance™: SyncML Representation Protocol, Device Management Usage, v1.1.2 (2003)
10. Open Mobile Alliance™: SyncML Device Management Protocol, v1.1.2 (2003)
11. Open Mobile Alliance™: SyncML Device Management Tree and Description, v1.1.2 (2003)
12. Open Mobile Alliance™: SyncML DM Device Description Framework, v1.1.2 (2003)
13. Open Mobile Alliance™: SyncML Device Management Standardized Objects, v1.1.2 (2003).
14. 3GPP TS 23.233: Transparent end-to-end packet-switched streaming service, stage 1, v6.3.0 (2003)
15. 3GPP TS 26.233: Transparent end-to-end packet-switched streaming service, general description, v5.0.0 (2002)
16. 3GPP TS 26.234: Transparent end-to-end packet-switched streaming service, protocol and codecs, v5.0.0 (2003)
17. M. Handle et al: SDP: Session Description Protocol, IETF RFC 2327 (1998)

A Performance-Oriented Management Information Model for the Chord Peer-to-peer Framework

Guillaume Doyen, Emmanuel Nataf, and Olivier Festor

The Madyne Research Team
LORIA, 615 rue du Jardin Botanique
54602 Villers-lès-Nancy, France
Guillaume.Doyen@loria.fr

Abstract. In this paper we propose an abstract model dedicated to the performance management of the Chord peer-to-peer framework. It captures information about a Chord community, the associated resources, the participating elements, as well as the global performance of the instantiated services. Our model enables the evaluation of the global health state of a Chord community and to act consequently.

1 Introduction

Chord [1] is a lookup protocol dedicated to Internet applications that need to discover any type of resources (files, CPU, services, ...) maintained by users that form a Chord community. It provides an elementary service: for a given key, Chord returns a node identifier that is responsible for hosting or locating the resource. Chord is deployed in several applications: CFS (Collaborative File System) [2] which is an Internet scale distributed file system, ConChord [3] which uses CFS to provide a distributed framework for the delivery of SDSI (Simple Distributed Security Infrastructure) security certificates and finally DDNS (Distributed DNS) [4] that proposes a P2P implementation of the DNS (Domain Name Service).

Chord offers performance levels in terms of load balancing, consistency and average path length for requests routing. In order to ensure such a performance, it executes dedicated services. However, the performance, as perceived by applications, highly relies on the conditions of the underlying network and the behavior the various and heterogeneous participants. To include these constraints in the evaluation, a performance measurement framework needs to be in place.

In this article, we propose a performance-oriented model for the Chord frameworks. We have chosen this particular P2P system among others (e.g. CAN, Pastry, Tapestry, D2B, Viceroy, ...) mainly because an implementation is available. In a general way, the information model we propose provides a manager with an abstract view of a Chord community, the participating nodes, the shared resources and the different instantiated services. Our model focuses on the performance aspect of the framework and, to reach this objective, we specify a set

J. Vicente and D. Hutchison (Eds.): MMNS 2004, LNCS 3271, pp. 200–212, 2004.

of metrics that feature the Chord framework in terms of service performance, ring consistency and node's equity. This model is built on a previous work that provides a general information model for the management of P2P networks and services [5]. In addition to the embedded features of the Chord framework, having an abstract view of a Chord community, being able to evaluate its global performance, and having the possibility to react consequently, is a major step toward providing a P2P infrastructure aware of Quality of Service (QoS) constraints.

The paper is organized as follows: section 2 provides an overview of the P2P discipline and its management. Then, section 3 presents the Chord P2P framework and its properties. The definition of performance metrics and criteria is addressed in section 4 and the proposed information model is presented in section 5. A summary of the contribution is given in section 6 and future work is outlined.

2   Related Works

Peer-to-peer (P2P) networking is built on a distributed model where peers are software entities which both play the role of client and server. Today, the most famous application domain of this model concerns the file sharing with applications like E-mule, Napster, Gnutella and Kazaa among others. However, the P2P model also covers many additional domains [6] like distributed computing (Seti@Home [7], the Globus Project [8]), collaborative work (Groove, Magi) and instant messaging (JIM [9]). To provide common grounds to all these applications, some middleware infrastructures propose generic frameworks for the development of P2P services (Jxta, Anthill [10], FLAPPS).

While some applications use built-in incentives as a minimal self management feature [11], advanced management services are required for enterprise oriented P2P environments. The latter are the focus of our attention and deserve the availability of a generic management framework.

The first step toward this objective has consisted in designing a generic management information model for P2P networks and services that can be used by any management application as a primary abstraction. The work we have done in this direction has led to a model [5] that aims at providing a general management information model, that addresses the functional, topological and organizational aspects for such a type of application.

We have chosen CIM [12], [13] as the framework for the design of our generic P2P information model because of its richness in terms of classes covering several domains of computing that can be easily reused and extended.

The model we have designed covers several aspects of the P2P domain. First it deals with the notion of peer and its belonging to one or several communities. A particular association class allows the link of peers together in order to establish a virtual topology. One may note that, according to the context, different criteria can be considered to link two peers; for example, it can be based on knowledge, routing, interest or technological considerations. Then, our model features the available resources in a community and especially the ones shared by its composing peers. We particularly address the fact that a resource can be spread in a community and thus (1) we differentiate owners and hosts of shared resources and (2) we split resources into physical (e.g. the chunk of a file on a file system) and logical ones (the aggregation of the different chunks). Moreover, these latter are consumed or provided in the context of services that is the fourth aspect of our model. Indeed, a P2P service is a basic functionality that is distributed among a set of participating peers; thus our model enables the global view of a service as well as the local one. Finally, we have identified particular basic services offered by any P2P framework; it concerns, for example, the way packets are routed in a P2P environment of an overlay type. We have thus modeled routing and forwarding services and the routing tables they generate or use.

In this way, our CIM extension for P2P networks and services provides an abstract view of a P2P network as well as the deployed services located in a manageable environment.

3   Chord

Chord is a framework that aims at providing routing and discovery mechanisms in a P2P environment. It is built on a ring topology in which nodes know their predecessor and successor. A consistent hash method generates a key for each node from its IP address. Then, each node is located in a ring in order to arrange keys in an increasing order. Each Chord node n_i is responsible for the $]predecessor(n_i), n_i]$ range of keys.

Consider a N_T nodes ring. The routing tables maintained by each node n_i will contain about $O((\log_2 N_T)^2)$ entries. Indeed, if the simple knowledge of its predecessor and next node enables the construction of a ring topology, it has poor performance in terms of number of nodes that enter the routing of requests; Figure 1.a illustrates this kind of problem on a ring containing 10 nodes that

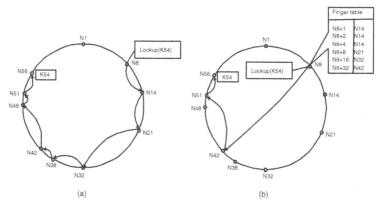

Fig. 1. *Extract from [1].* (a) Request routing by following the ring topology. (b) Request routing through *fingers*

uses a $[0, 64[$ range of addresses. One can see that a request for k_{54} initiated by node n_8 will be routed in 8 hops.

In order to solve this problem, for a key domain comprised in the $[0, 2^m[$ interval, each node n_i maintains a routing entry towards nodes, called *fingers* that own the $successor(n_i + 2^{k-1})$ identifier (with $1 \leq k \leq m$). Thus the number of node involved in a request routing is about $O(\log_2 N_T)$. Figure 1.b shows that with finger tables, the same request for key k_{54} is routed in 3 hops.

4   Metrics for the Chord Performance Monitoring

Chord announces performance guarantees in agreement with its main core principles: the distribution of nodes in a ring topology, the use of a finger table, a consistent hash for nodes and keys, and the regular execution of a stabilization process. These concepts are claimed as providing an embedded way of ensuring a good service operation of the framework.

Nevertheless there is no way to monitor a Chord ring and to know the *health state* of such a P2P community. In order to allow a potential manager to evaluate the current Chord performance, we have defined several metrics. These are: the ring dynamics, the discovery performance, the node's equity and the ring consistency. By enabling a manager to monitor a Chord ring and to react consequently, we aim at providing a P2P framework that can effectively ensure QoS specifications on varying condition in the network.

To express our performance metrics, we introduce the following variables:

N_{MAX}:   The upper bound for identifying nodes and keys. We assume the Chord hash method will generate identifier contained in the $[0, N_{MAX}[$ range. Moreover, all Chord operations are done modulo N_{MAX};

n_i: a node with the i identifier.

N: the set of nodes n_i that are currently present in a ring, with $N = \{n_i\}$.

N_T: the total number of nodes in a Chord ring, with $N_T = Card(N)$.

k_i: a key with the i identifier;

K_i: the number of keys the node n_i is responsible for, with
$K_i = Card(\{k_j\})$ with $id(pred(n_i)) \leq j \leq i$.

K_T: the total number of keys currently stored in the ring, with $K_T = \sum_{i \in N} K_i$.

$\overline{K}$:   the average number of keys per node, with: $\overline{K} = \frac{K_T}{N_T}$

4.1   Measuring the Ring Dynamics

In order to make Chord performance measurements meaningful, we have to present them in their execution context. Indeed, due to dynamic phenomena, performance of Chord may vary strongly. Thus, we have defined metrics for measuring the ring stability.

The two elements that are submitted to dynamics are nodes and keys. Nodes can join and leave a ring in an unpredictable way while keys can dynamically be inserted or removed, or migrate in order to ensure their persistency. Thus for these two elements we have featured (1) their mean time of stability and (2) their change frequency.

Concerning the nodes, we assume that the arrival and departure times are known. For a particular node, all its joining and leaving operations will be stored in a log. Thus we can easily determine its mean time of presence in the ring.

Moreover, in a global way, we propose to evaluate the current arrival and departure frequency with the relations 1 and 2. Whenever a node joins or leaves the ring, the current time is first collected to update the *JoinFrequency* and *LeaveFrequency* indicators and then is stored in the corresponding last time variable.

$$JoinFrequency = \frac{1}{CurrentTime - LastArrivalTime} \tag{1}$$

$$LeaveFrequency = \frac{1}{CurrentTime - LastDepartureTime} \tag{2}$$

Finally, the global presence mean time is calculated by considering a temporal range T. The size of this range is determined according to the context[1]. For all the nodes, all the collected presence times that are contained in this range will be averaged in order to provide a global presence mean time of nodes. Equation 3 calculates it.

$$PresenceMeanTime = \frac{\sum_{i \in N} \sum_{t \in T_i} t}{\sum_{i \in N} Card(T_i)} \text{ with} \tag{3}$$

T: the considered range of time. $T = [T_{Begin}, T_{End}]$.
T_i: the set of presence time records for n_i in range T.
$\quad T_i = \{t \mid t = (T_{Departure} - T_{Arrival}); T_{Departure}, T_{Arrival} \in T\}$

Now concerning the keys, we have collected the same type of values, which allows us to determine the global *InsertionFrequency*, *MigrationFrequency* and *RemovalFrequency* of keys.

To conclude, the metrics defined in this section allow a manager to be aware of the dynamics of a Chord community. This evaluation is crucial because it allows all the following performance measurements to be analyzed in a particular context of dynamics, which gives them all the more sense.

4.2   Measuring the Discovery Performance

One of the core concepts of the Chord framework is the use of finger tables. It provides a good and stable performance on the average number of hops required to route discovery messages. Chord claims that this average is about $O(\log_2 N_T)$.

We have chosen to monitor this crucial value for several reasons. First, it enable the manager to confirm that Chord respects the announced performance. Then, it is a meaningful indicator of the good state of the ring. Indeed, a significant increase of this value will indicate a problem of stability or consistency

---

[1] it may be since the last hour, day, month, ...

that must be due to important join or leave operations of nodes. Thus, for a manager, applying a threshold that can launch an alarm may be useful.

The way we propose to concretely evaluate this value is described in Equation 4. For each node n_i, we define the following metrics:

$NInitiatedRequests_i$:   The total number of discovery requests that the considered node has initiated;

$NForwardedRequests_i$:   The total number of requests that the considered node has received and forwarded to another node;

$NReceivedRequests_i$:   The total number of requests destined to the considered node.

Then, we sum each of these metrics and deduce the real average number of hops per request. This value may be compared to the theoretical $\frac{1}{2} \log_2 N_T$.

$$AveragePathLength = \frac{\sum_{i \in N} NReceivedRequests_i + \sum_{i \in N} NForwardedRequests_i}{\sum_{i \in N} NInitiatedRequests_i}$$

(4)

By this way, we are able to monitor the performance of the discovery service that is the main function provided by the Chord framework and the only visible to a user.

4.3   Measuring the Nodes Equity

Contrary to the client/server model, the P2P one is a model where resources are distributed. This feature improves the load-balancing and enables the equity between all the participants. Moreover, it avoids any bottleneck that would concentrate the traffic and stand for central points of failure. In the case of Chord, ensuring a well balanced distribution of the keys among the different participating nodes is essential to guaranty a good performance of the system. In the opposite case, if some nodes host the major part of the keys, the Chord performance would collapse due to the too strong solicitation of these nodes; finally, the ring would tend to operate in a client/server way with nodes that are not dedicated to this task.

From this point, we have established a metric that can evaluate the distribution of the keys among the nodes. Chord claims that each node will be responsible for no more that $(1+\epsilon)\overline{K}$ keys and we propose to monitor this value. As shown in Equation 5, it consists in evaluating the variance of the key repartition in a ring. For each node n_i, we consider difference between the current hosted number of keys and the ideal average value and average this value on the whole ring.

$$NodesEquity_\% = 1 - \frac{1}{K_T} \sum_{i \in N} \lfloor \mid K_i - \overline{K} \mid \rfloor$$

(5)

The node's equity measurement is a useful indicator of the keys distribution in a Chord ring. This knowledge, added to the average number of keys per node and the effective number of keys a node hosts, indicates precisely any ring unbalance and we may imagine that, in this case, a manager could assign new nodes identifier and so redistribute the keys in order to improve the ring balance.

4.4   Measuring the Ring Consistency

The performance guarantees announced by Chord concerning the lookup service are respected if the ring is consistent. In case of an inconsistency, performance will collapse and the number of hops involved in request routing may increase from $O(\log_2 N_T)$ to $O(N_T)$. To monitor the ring consistency, we have used the constraints defined in [1]. These are:

- **Constraint 1** *Consistence of the immediate successor relations. This constraint is completed if, given the current presence of nodes in the ring, each node is effectively the predecessor of its successor.*
- **Constraint 2** *Consistence of the successors lists. Each node maintains a list of the k first successor in the ring. The constraint is completed if, given the current presence of nodes in the ring, (1) the lists maintained by each node effectively contain the immediate successors and (2) these successors are available.*
- **Constraint 3** *Consistence of the finger tables. This constraint is completed if, given the current presence of nodes in the ring, for each node n_i, a finger (1) matches the following relation $successor(n_i + 2^{k-1})$, where $1 \leq k \leq m$ and (2) is available.*

We consider a Chord ring is consistent if each of the above constraints are completed. In order to enable a manager to evaluate the consistency of a ring, each node must make information about its successor, its successor list and its finger table, available.

Concerning the management data, we have defined several elements to indicate the ring consistency. Locally, we have defined four boolean values that can inform the node of the consistency of its information. These boolean values will be evaluated by a manager and pushed in the MIB of the concerned node. Consider a node n_i. The first value, named $IsConsistent_i$, deals with the global consistency of the node; it is true if the constraints 1, 2 and 3 are completed. The next three, named $SuccessorIsConsistent_i$, $SuccessorListIsConsistent_i$ and $FingerTableIsConsistent_i$ inform about the respect of constraints 1, 2 and 3 respectively.

Now, considering the global consistency of a ring, we have defined the *IsGloballyConsistent* boolean value that indicates if the ring is consistent, with:

$$IsGloballyConsistent = \bigwedge_{i \in N} IsConsistent_i \qquad (6)$$

Then, as shown in Relation 7, to have a more precise estimation of the ring consistency, we have defined a percentage value that indicates the consistency level. The *valueOf* function returns 1 when the $IsConsistent_i$ value is set to true and 0 otherwise.

$$GloballyConsistencyLevel_\% = \frac{1}{N_T} \sum_{i \in N} valueOf(IsConsistent_i) \qquad (7)$$

Lastly, in order to help a manager to locate a consistency problem, we have defined, for each node, a counter that references the number of times the considered node is badly referenced by others ones.

To conclude, the different local and global consistency indicators enable a manager to be aware of the good state of a ring. From this point, in case of inconsistency one may envisage several management actions like stopping the current forwarding of requests, forcing the execution of the stabilization process on some nodes that present obsolete knowledge and finally let the stopped request go on.

5   A Chord Information Model

Given our objective of Chord global model and the preceding performance measurement definitions, we propose a management model for Chord that is performance-oriented. It lies on a generic model for P2P networks and services that we have designed. The following sections present our Chord model and the way we have applied the preceding theoretical metrics to it.

5.1   Chord Node, Chord Ring and Virtual Topology

In the Chord framework, nodes are organized in an ordered ring. In this way, we consider that a Chord ring represents a community of peers. The model we propose is represented on Figure 2. In order to model a Chord ring, we have designed the ChordRing class that inherits from the Community class. The

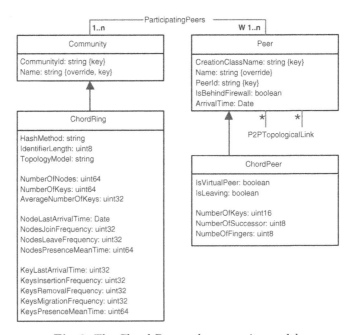

Fig. 2. The Chord Peer and community model

properties of the ChordRing are divided into two sets. the first one provides general information about the ring and the second one contains performance data, according to the metrics defined above.

Chord nodes are modeled through the ChordPeer class. This class inherits from the Peer one and defines several properties. The first set of properties contains general information about the node and the second one informs about the load of the node. It deals with the total number of keys hosted by a node, and the size of its routing informations expressed for the successor list and the finger table.

Concerning the topology, each Chord node knows its predecessor and its successor. Thus, by extending this mutual local knowledge to all the nodes of a ring, Chord establishes a virtual ring topology. In our model, we use the P2P-TopologicalLink association class to represents these links. The Description attribute allows us to distinguish links toward a successor or toward a predecessor. We use this knowledge among others to estimate the ring consistency.

5.2 Keys and Resources

In the Chord framework, a node is responsible for a set of keys that represent resources. Nevertheless, the nature of the resources can be of several types. For example in CFS [2] it can be a file or a pointer toward a remote file. On the other hand in DDNS, a key will represent a DNS entry. This is why we have chosen to represent keys with the ChordKey abstract class that inherits from the PeerResource one. This way, we let an application build over Chord inheriting from it in order to represent any concrete resources. Figure 3 presents this specialization. The LastMigrationTime property is a local indicator of the key movement that is used to determine the global dynamics of a ring.

5.3 Chord Services

The Chord framework is composed of two services. The first one is the lookup service. It represents the main functionality of Chord. The second one is the stabilization service. As described in [1] this process is executed in the background and checks the consistency of the ring.

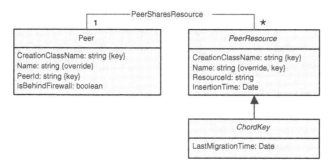

Fig. 3. The Chord resources model

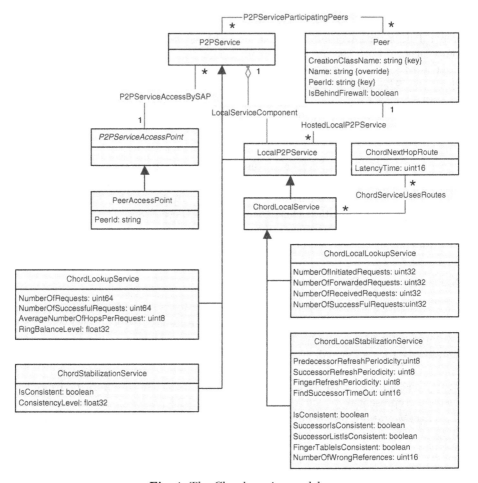

Fig. 4. The Chord service model

Chord Global Services. In the P2P model we have previously designed [5], we have defined a P2P service as being the aggregation of local instances. In this section, we address the Chord services in a global way.

The Chord service model is represented on Figure 4. The lookup and stabilization services are captured through the ChordLookupService and ChordStabilizationService classes. These classes inherits from the P2PService class of our P2P model.

First, the ChordLookupService class aims at providing information about the lookup service behavior. Thus, we have defined properties that match the metrics defined for the lookup service performance measurement. These are the total number of requests, the number of successful requests (that is another ring efficiency criterion) and the average path length involved in requests routing. Finally, the ring balance level provides a global estimation of the distribution of keys among nodes. These values are not directly accessible but are the result of the aggregation of nodes'local information.

Now, concerning the ChordStabilizationService we have just two properties to represent its global features. The IsConsistent boolean property stands for the global stability of the ring and the ConsistencyLevel deals with the average percentage of nodes that are in a consistent state.

Chord Local Services. As explained above, P2P services are the result of local instances. This is why we have designed the LocalChordLookupService and LocalChordStabilizationService classes.

First, the LocalChordLookupService class contains several properties that are involved in the calculation properties of the ChordLookupService class properties. The NumberOfInitiatedRequest represents the number of lookup requests the local node has started. Then, the NumberOfForwardedRequests informs about the number of requests the local node has relayed. Finally, the NumberOfReceivedRequests informs the number of requests the local node has received as a destination. Finally, the NumberOfSuccessfulRequests represents the total number of requests the node has honored.

Then, the LocalChordStabilizationService class deals with the execution of the stabilization process on a particular node. Its attributes are split into two sets. The first set represents information collected by the considered node and provided to the manager. That is to say, the frequency of the predecessor, successor and finger refreshment. As for the second set of properties, it is computed and provisioned by the manager in the nodes. The NumberOfSuccessor property provides the size of the successor list. Then, the FindSuccessorTimeOut informs on the maximum time a node waits for a response from a node that can be a successor. This timeout is used in the stabilization process during the update of the successor list. Finally, the NumberOfWrongReferences deals with the number of times a node is badly referenced by other ones.

In addition to these services, we have modeled the routing tables of nodes. Nevertheless, this modeling aspect doesn't address the performance issue of the Chord framework and it is described in [5].

6   Conclusions and Future Works

Chord is a framework dedicated to the resources discovery in a P2P environment; given a key, Chord associates a node that is responsible for hosting or locating it. Its core principles lie on the use of a consistent and well balanced hash function for nodes and keys, a distribution of nodes on a ring topology, the use of finger tables and the regular execution of a stabilization process. Chord offers several performance guarantees in terms of average path length, load balance and information consistency. Nonetheless, in case of a real Chord deployment, additional behaviors influence the performance of the framework and a management infrastructure is necessary.

To effectively monitor the performance of a Chord community, we presented an abstract model that is performance-oriented. This work is based on a previous one directed towards the design of a generic information model for P2P networks and services. Globally, our model enables a manager to have an abstract view of a Chord community and to feature its operation performance. We have defined several metrics that evaluate the ring dynamics, consistency and balance as well as the lookup performance. Our goal is to provide a manager with tools that will help him to be aware of a Chord ring state and to react consequently. Our opinion is that these feedback data are essential for the deployment of the Chord framework in manageable P2P applications that can respect QoS agreements and deal with phenomena that cannot be captured by analytic models. Concerning the metrics we have defined, we consider them as basic indicators of a Chord community. Moreover, we assume that, in order to provide more advanced estimators, they can be combined and even enter the definition of policy rules. This way, given a Chord community, a manager could be able to act on participating elements in order to ensure service levels.

Our future works will first consist in deploying our model in a Chord implementation to (1) establish the validity of our theoretical model and (2) estimate the cost of our management infrastructure. To do that, we will first have to define a management architecture and a dedicated protocol for P2P networks, that is one of our current work. Indeed, we are thinking about the notion of manager in a P2P context, and the way peers collaborate to perform management tasks. Then, in conjunction to this first direction, we are extending this work toward the design of a generic performance information model for DHTs. This model would aim at featuring the performance of existing DHT like D2B, CAN or Pastry among others.

References

1. Stoica, I., Morris, R., Karger, D., Kaashoek, M.F., Balakrishnan, H.: Chord: A scalable peer-to-peer lookup service for internet applications. In: Proceedings of the 2001 conference on applications, technologies, architectures, and protocols for computer communications, ACM Press (2001) 149–160
2. Dabek, F., Kaashoek, M., Karger, D., Morris, R., Stoica, I.: Wide-area cooperative storage with CFS. In: Proceedings of the 18th ACM Symposium on Operating Systems Principles (SOSP '01), Chateau Lake Louise, Banff, Canada (2001)
3. Ajmani, S., Clarke, D.E., Moh, C., Richman, S.: ConChord: Cooperative SDSI certificate storage and name resolution (2002) Presented at the International Workshop on Peer-to-Peer Systems.
4. Cox, R., Muthitacharoen, A., Morris, R.: Serving dns using chord. In: Proceedings of the 1st International Workshop on Peer-to-Peer Systems (IPTPS), Cambridge, MA (2002)
5. Doyen, G., Festor, O., Nataf, E.: A cim extension for peer-to-peer network and service management. (In: *to appear in* Proceedings of the 11th International Conference on Telecommunication (ICT'2004))
6. Oram, A., ed.: Peer-to-peer: Harnessing the Power of Disruptive Technologies. O'Reilly & Associates, Inc. (2001)
7. Anderson, D.: SETI@Home. Number 5. In: (in [6]) 67–76

8. Foster, I., Kesselman, C.: Globus: A metacomputing infrastructure toolkit. The International Journal of Supercomputer Applications and High Performance Computing **11** (1997) 115–128

9. Doyen, G., Festor, O., Nataf, E.: Management of peer-to-peer services applied to instant messaging. In Marshall, A., Agoulmine, N., eds.: Management of Multimedia Networks and Services. Number 2839 in LNCS (2003) 449–461 End-to-End Monitoring Workshop 2003 (E2EMON '03).

10. Babaoglu, O., Meling, H., Montresor, A.: Anthill: A framework for the development of agent-based peer-to-peer systems. In: The 22th International Conference on Distributed Computing Systems (ICDCS '02), IEEE Computer Society (2002)

11. Mischke, J., Stiller, B.: Peer-to-peer overlay network management through agile. In Goldszmidt, G., Schönwälder, J., eds.: Integrated Network Management VIII, Kluwer Academic Publisher (2003) 337–350

12. Bumpus, W., Sweitzer, J.W., Thompson, P., R., W.A., Williams, R.C.: Common Information Model. Wiley (2000)

13. Distributed Management Task Force, Inc.: Common information model v2.7. (www.dmtf.org/standards/standard_cim.php)

Real-Time Analysis of Delay Variation for Packet Loss Prediction

Lopamudra Roychoudhuri and Ehab S. Al-Shaer

School of Computer Science, Telecommunications and Information Systems,
DePaul University, 243 S. Wabash Ave., Chicago, IL-60604, USA

Abstract. The effect of packet loss on the quality of real-time audio is significant. Nevertheless, Internet measurement experiments continue to show a considerable variation of packet loss, which makes audio error recovery and concealment challenging. Our objective is to predict packet loss in real-time audio streams based on the available bandwidth and delay variation and trend, enabling proactive error recovery for real-time audio over the Internet. Our preliminary simulation and experimentation results with various sites on the Internet show the effectiveness and the accuracy of the Loss Predictor technique.

1 Introduction

Quality of an audio communication is highly sensitive to packet loss [4],[17]. Majority of packet loss in the Internet occurs as the result of congestion in the links. Packet loss for audio is normally rectified by adding redundancy using Forward Error Correction (FEC) [11]. However, unnecessarily high degree of FEC can actually be detrimental rather than beneficial to the ongoing communication because of the excessive traffic. Here the challenge is to ensure a bandwidth-friendly transmission with an effective degree of loss recovery by dynamically changing the degree of FEC. In this paper, we present the investigations to develop a mechanism to predict packet loss in real-time audio streams based on delay variation and trend, which will enable proactive error recovery and rate control for real-time Internet audio.

The basic idea of our proposed on-line loss prediction method is to successfully track the increase and decrease trends in one way delay, and accordingly predict the likelihood of packet loss due to congestion leading to lack of available bandwidth. However, this task becomes difficult due to the unpredictable and dynamic nature of cross traffic in the Internet. In this paper we attempt to formalize a framework to express the likelihood of loss in the next packet train in terms of (1) changes in the available bandwidth, manifested as end-to-end delay variations, and (2) near-past history of congestion in terms of short-term and long-term trends in delay variation. The value returned by the Predictor indicates the current degree and severity of congestion and lack of available bandwidth, hence the likelihood of packet loss, created by cross traffic bursts. The predictor value is fed back from the receiver to the sender in order for the sender to take proactive FEC actions and rate control.

J. Vicente and D. Hutchison (Eds.): MMNS 2004, LNCS 3271, pp. 213–227, 2004.

In our approach, we designate the minimum delay of a path as the baseline delay, signifying the delay under no congestion. We also identify the delay at the capacity saturation point of a path as the loss threshold delay, after which packet loss is more likely. We track the increase patterns or trends of the delay as an indication of congestion causing packet loss. We have seen in our experiments that each site shows a consistent minimum baseline delay. We also observe a range of loss threshold delay values after which loss is observed more often. The loss threshold delay shows a variety of ranges and behaviors due the unpredictable nature of the cross traffic in the network at that time. To measure these path delay characteristics, we propose certain measurement metrics classified in three categories – Delay Distance, Short Term Trend and Long Term Trend. Delay Distance gives an absolute ratio of the delay value in relation to the baseline and loss thresholds. The Short-term Trend and the Long-term Trend metrics give indications of sharpness and consistency of upward and downward delay trends in short and long term window of past packets. In the Loss Predictor approach we determine these metrics from the ongoing traffic and combine them with different weights based on their importance in order to estimate of the packet loss likelihood.

Subsequent sections are organized as follows. Section 2 contains references to the related work. Section 3 presents the Predictor approach, with subsections describing the delay-loss correlation model and the Predictor formalization. We present the evaluation results in Section 4, and conclusion and future work in Section 5.

2   Related Work

Paxson examined the delay-loss correlation issue in his PhD thesis [16]. But he concluded that the linkage between delay variation and loss was weak, though not negligible. In contrast with Paxson's observations, we predict packet loss based on the observed patterns of delay variation, rather than depending on the overall amount of delay variation as indicator of congestion.

Moon's Technical Report and PhD thesis [13] explored this issue to a certain degree. They reported a quantitative study of delay and loss correlation patterns from offline analysis of measurement data from the Internet. But they did not attempt to take a further step of real-time prediction of packet loss from the delay variation data of an ongoing communication.

The researchers measuring performance of Mbone, a virtual Internet Backbone for multicast IP, observed that there is a correlation between the bandwidth used and the amount of loss experienced [5],[6].

Pathload [10] uses the delay variation principle to measure available bandwidth. They send streams of increasing rate till the stream saturates the available bandwidth and starts showing distinct increase in delay. The same principle is used in TCP Vegas [3], which exploits RTT variation to measure the difference between the actual and the expected sending rate to provide better congestion detection and control. Packet loss is highly probable when the available bandwidth is low and is consumed by the ongoing cross traffic. Our research methods and experiments are based on this premise.

Sender based Error and Rate Control mechanisms for audio, such as by Bolot & Garcia [2], Bolot & Fosse-Parisis [1], Padhye, Christensen, & Moreno [15], Mohamed et al. [12] adapt to packet loss using RTCP feedback from the receiver – thus these mechanisms react to packet loss. In contrast, we predict packet loss and take FEC actions based on the nature of the prediction; hence our approach handles packet loss proactively based on the current loss likelihood.

3 Loss Predictor Approach

3.1 Analysis of Delay-Loss Correlation Model

Here we formalize a number of propositions which constitute our framework based on baseline, loss threshold delay and trends.

Let the path from the sender to the receiver consist of H links, $i = 1, \ldots, H$. Let the capacity of the link be C_i . If the available bandwidth at link i be A_i, the utilization of link i is $u_i = (C_i - A_i)/C_i$. We assume that the links follow FCFS queuing discipline and Droptail packet dropping mechanism. Let the sender send a periodic stream of K packets, each of size L bytes, at rate R_0, to the receiver. Hence a packet is sent in $L/R_0 = T$ time interval. Also there are $(C_i - A_i)T$ (in other words, $u_i C_i T$) bytes of cross-traffic, in addition to the source stream, arriving at link i in interval T. It has been shown in [10] that the One-Way Delay (OWD) D^k of the k-th packet is:

$$D^k = \sum_{i=1}^{H} \left(\frac{L}{C_i} + \frac{q_i^k}{C_i} \right) = \sum_{i=1}^{H} \left(\frac{L}{C_i} + d_i^k \right) \tag{1}$$

and the OWD difference between two successive packet k and $k + 1$ is

$$\Delta D^k = D^{k+1} - D^k = \sum_{i=1}^{H} \frac{\Delta q_i^k}{C_i} = \sum_{i=1}^{H} \Delta d_i^k \tag{2}$$

where q_i^k is the queue size at link i upon arrival of packet k (not including the kth packet), and d_i^k is the queuing delay of packet k at link i, and $\Delta q_i^k = q_i^{k+1} - q_i^k$, $\Delta d_i^k = d_i^{k+1} - d_i^k$. Clearly, the minimum OWD a packet can have is when there is no queuing delay, denoted as the baseline delay. From (1):

$$D_{baseline} = \sum_{i=1}^{H} \frac{L}{C_i} \tag{3}$$

Proposition 1. Δd^k *increases as the available bandwidths at the tight links decrease, and vice versa.*

Let a set of 'tight' links be the set of links in the path that contribute to the majority of the queuing delay. Over the interval T, the link i receives $(R_{i-1}T +$

$u_i C_i T$) bytes (stream and cross traffic) and services $C_i T$ bytes, where R_{i-1} is the exit-rate from link $i-1$. As shown in [10], we can express R_i as follows:

$$R_i = \begin{cases} R_{i-1} \frac{C_i}{C_i + (R_{i-1} - A_i)} & \text{if } R_{i-1} > A_i \\ R_{i-1} & \text{otherwise} \end{cases} \qquad (4)$$

The change in queue size Δq_i^k can be expressed as the difference of the arrival rate (packet and cross-traffic) at i-th link and service rate at i-th link: $(R_{i-1}T + u_i C_i T) - C_i T = (R_{i-1} - A_i)T > 0$ if $R_{i-1} > A_i$. Thus,

$$\Delta d_i^k = \begin{cases} \frac{(R_{i-1} - A_i)}{C_i}T > 0 & \text{if } R_{i-1} > A_i \\ 0 & \text{otherwise} \end{cases} \qquad (5)$$

Suppose there are k 'tight' links, i.e. for links $m_1, m_2, \ldots m_k, R_{i-1} > A_i$. Then from (2) and (5),

$$\Delta D^k = \sum_{i=1}^{H} \Delta d_i^k = \frac{R_{m_1-1} - A_{m_1}}{C_{m_1}}T + \ldots + \frac{R_{m_k-1} - A_{m_k}}{C_{m_k}}T \qquad (6)$$

Hence ΔD^k will increase if the available bandwidths at the tight links A_{m_1}, $A_{m_2}, \ldots, A_{m_k}$, decrease, and vice versa. Thus D_k will show steeper rate of increase if there is lesser available bandwidth at the tight links, i.e. if there is higher rate of cross traffic through the tight links.

Suppose in particular, m-th link is the considerably narrow link, s. t. $C_m \ll C_i, i = 1, \ldots H, i \neq m$. For the sake of simplicity, let us also consider that (i) m-th link is the most tight link (bottleneck link), i.e. the available bandwidth at this link $A_m = (1 - u_m)C_m$ is the minimum available bandwidth of the path, and (ii) $R_{i-1} > A_i$ only for $i = m$, since m-th link is much narrower than others. Then from (4), $R_{m-1} = R_{m-2} \ldots = R_0$. Then (6) can be simplified as:

$$\Delta D^k = \frac{R_{m-1} - A_m}{C_m}T = \frac{R_0 - A_m}{C_m}T \qquad (7)$$

Hence ΔD^k increases if the minimum available bandwidth at the bottleneck link decreases, and vice versa. $\square$

Thus under simplified conditions, D^k will show steeper rate of increase if there is lesser available bandwidth at the tightmost link, i.e. if there is higher rate of cross traffic through the tightmost link.

Proposition 2. *There exists a range of OWDs in which packet loss is likely.*

In this proposition we show the existence of a range of delays in which loss is likely, that is, we establish a range of loss threshold delays. Since $C_m < C_i$, hence $1/C_m > 1/C_i, i = 1, \ldots H, i \neq m$. Then $M/C_m \geq q_i/C_i, i = 1, \ldots H$, where M is the queue capacity at m-th link, assuming that the queue capacities at each link are same. When the queue at m-th link is filled up, the OWD is given by:

$$D_{ObservedLoss} = \sum_{i=1, i \neq m}^{H} \left(\frac{L}{C_i} + \frac{q_i^k}{C_i}\right) + \frac{L+M}{C_m} \qquad (8)$$

$D_{ObservedLoss}$ is the observed loss threshold delay (OTD). Delay values higher than this value indicate that loss of the next packet is likely. From (3) and (8),

$$D_{ObservedLoss} > D_{baseline} \tag{9}$$

In particular,

$$\sum_{i=1}^{H} \frac{L}{C_i} + \frac{HM}{C_m} \geq D_{ObservedLoss} \geq \sum_{i=1}^{H} \frac{L}{C_i} + \frac{M}{C_m}$$

Thus OTD is bounded by the minimum loss threshold delay (lower bound), $D_{minOTD} = \sum_{i=1}^{H} \frac{L}{C_i} + \frac{M}{C_m}$, when only one link is the bottleneck, and the maximum loss threshold delay (upper bound) $D_{maxOTD} = \sum_{i=1}^{H} \frac{L}{C_i} + \frac{HM}{C_m}$ when all H links are bottlenecks. In particular, if $\frac{M}{C_m} \geq \sum_{i=1}^{H} \frac{q_i^k}{C_i}$, i.e. the occupied queue size at the tight link is larger than the sum of queue sizes at the rest of the links, which is possible when there is a single bottleneck considerably narrower than the rest of the links,

$$D_{ObservedLoss} = \sum_{i=1}^{H} \frac{L}{C_i} + \frac{M}{C_m} \geq \sum_{i=1}^{H} (\frac{L}{C_i} + \frac{q_i^k}{C_i}) \tag{10}$$

In that case the observed loss threshold delay is equal to the maximum observed delay. □

Thus the likelihood of loss of the packet k at m-th link can be expressed as a combination of the following delay factors: (1) the current total queuing delay relative to the worst queuing delay (from (1), (3), (8) and (9)),

$$= \frac{D^k - D_{baseline}}{D_{ObservedLoss} - D_{baseline}} = \frac{\sum_{i=1}^{H} d_i^k}{\sum_{i=1,i\neq m}^{H} d_i^k + \frac{M}{C_m}} \tag{11}$$

which is a value between 0 and 1, and (2) rate of delay increase, (from (7))

$$= \frac{\delta D^k}{\delta T} = \frac{R_0 - A_m}{C_m} \tag{12}$$

3.2   Loss Predictor Formalization

The challenges of implementing the above model and deriving the likelihood of packet loss from network delay measurements are as follows: (1) to establish a range of delays that can be considered as the baseline delay for a particular path, (2) to determine a range of delays for a loss threshold, (3) to measure the delay increase ratio and trends, and (4) to find a likelihood of loss from the combining the above factors.

These challenges lead us to develop the Loss Predictor metrics - (1) Delay Distance, (2) Short-term Trend and (3) Long-term Trend. Delay Distance is

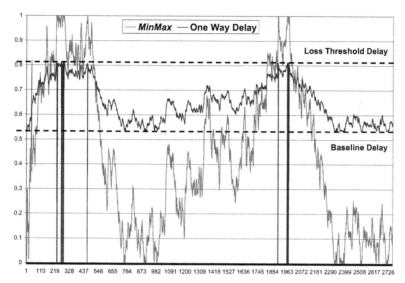

Fig. 1. Behavior of *MinMax*

derived from equation (11). It gives an absolute ratio of the delay value in relation to the loss threshold. The Short term Trend and the Long term Trend metrics are derivations of equation (12). They indicate the sharpness and consistency of upward and downward delay trends over a short and long term window of past packets. Short term trend metric tracks sharp changes in the delay, due to sudden burst of high degree of cross-traffic, which is more critical for loss if the delay is close to the loss threshold. In contrast, the long-term increasing trend tracks gradual rising trends due to persistent decrease in bandwidth, signifying gradual congestion build-up leading to packet loss. By considering the rate of increase, the short-term and the long-term metrics prevent Delay Distance metric from over-reacting to the absolute value of the delay. Thus these metrics work complementary to one another. We formalize the Loss Predictor as a weighted function of these three metrics. The Loss Predictor can be expressed as the following:

$$0 \leq f(DelayDist, ShortTermTrend, LongTermTrend)$$
$$= w_1 * DelayDist + w_2 * ShortTermTrend + w_3 * LongTermTrend \leq 1$$
$$\text{and } w_1 + w_2 + w_3 = 1$$

The Predictor uses dynamic weights that depend on the current delay situation and congestion level. This is described later.

Delay Distance (*MinMax*). This metric gives an absolute ratio of the current delay value above the baseline in relation to the loss threshold. This can be expressed as the following:

$$MinMax = min\left(1, \frac{D^k - base}{thr - base}\right) \tag{13}$$

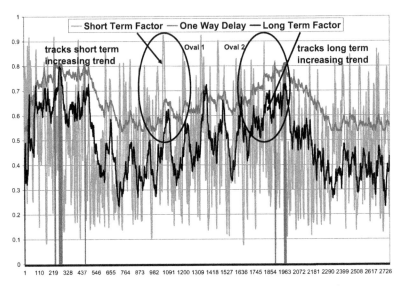

Fig. 2. Behavior of Long Term and Short Term Trends

where, $base$ = the most observed delay so far, considered to be the baseline delay, D^k = the delay value of the k-th packet, thr = the threshold delay at which a loss is observed.

The value of this metric lies between 0 and 1. The minimum of the linear increase ratio and 1 is taken, since we have observed that the maximum delay in a session can increase much higher than the threshold delay, and thus D_k can be larger than thr.

This metric is computationally simple. Fig. 1 shows the behavior of the metric. This value of the metric lies between 0 and 0.2 when the delay is close to the baseline, but rises up consistently to high values (0.8 to 1.0) when the delay reaches the loss threshold. Thus it is a good indicator of the absolute delay increase or decrease between the baseline and the loss threshold, and hence is an important component of loss prediction.

Long Term Trend Metrics. These metrics are required to measure long-term trends in the delay increase, indicating if an over all increasing trend is evident for a large number of preceding packets. The length of this packet window is adjusted dynamically based on the delay mean deviation observed so far, and is typically 20 to 50 packets. The following metrics indicate consistency in increasing trends, i.e. how consistently the delay is increasing for every measured packet pair, and are useful to measure this trend.

Long Term Consistency Measures (Spct/Spdt). We use variations of PCT (Pairwise Comparison Test) and PDT (Pairwise Difference Test) presented in [10]. Both of them are indicators of consistent increasing trends in a packet train. *Spct* is smoother in showing the long-term trends, whereas *Spdt* reacts with larger degree of increase or decrease over a packet train length of Γ. The range of *Spct* is [0,1] and of *Spdt* is [-1,1], scaled to [0,1]. We use Exponential Weighted Average [9] with gain 0.9 to smooth out undesired oscillations.

$$Spct = \frac{\sum_{k=2}^{\Gamma} I(D^k > D^{k-1})}{\Gamma - 1}, \quad I(X) = 1 \text{ if X holds, 0 otherwise}$$

$$Spdt = \frac{D^\Gamma - D^1}{\sum_{k=2}^{\Gamma} |D^k - D^{k-1}|}$$

We also use the average of *MinMax* for a long term packet window, which provides a long-term trend of the relative increase in delay magnitude. We consider an average of above three measures to calculate the long-term factor. In Fig. 2 oval 2 this metric successfully tracks consistent increasing and decreasing trends of one way delay over 20 to 50 packets.

Short Term Trend Metrics. These metrics are required to measure short-term trends in the delay increase, signifying how fast the delay is increasing over last small window of packets. The length of this packet window is adjusted dynamically based on the mean delay deviation observed so far, and is typically 5 to 10 packets. As the delay gets close to the loss threshold, more weight should be given to these metrics, because a sharp change in the delay will become more critical for loss. We present *SI* as an indicator of sharpness of increase (the 'slope' of the increase), and *SpctST/SpdtST* as indicators of the consistency of increase.

Sharpness Indicator (SI) This metric determines how fast the delay is approaching the loss threshold by measuring the slope of the line joining the delay values of the current packet and the previous packet.

$$SI = max(-1, min(1, (D^k - D^{k-1})/(t^k - t^{k-1})))$$

Under a sudden burst of high congestion, the slope is observed to be steeper. Thus higher degree of slope indicates higher congestion, and hence higher likelihood of packet loss. The range of this metric is truncated from $[-\infty, +\infty]$ to [-1,1] and scaled to [0,1].

We also use *SpctST* and *SpdtST*, which are short term versions of *Spct* and *Spdt*. As *SpdtST* is more sensitive to sudden changes to delay, we choose the short-term trend to be the average of *SI* and *SpdtST*. This metric fluctuates considerably from packet to packet, but successfully tracks the short term increasing and decreasing trends (Fig. 2 oval 1).

3.3 Predictor Weight Factor Formalization

Here we describe the intuitions behind the selection of the metric weights w_1, w_2 and w_3 described in 3.1. Since *MinMax* is the best indicator of the delay increase in terms of the baseline and loss threshold, w_1 is chosen higher than the short term and the long term trend weights w_2 and w_3. We divide the range of possible values [0,1] of *MinMax* into three zones 'Yellow', 'Orange' and 'Red', signifying the levels of criticality in regard to packet loss likelihood.

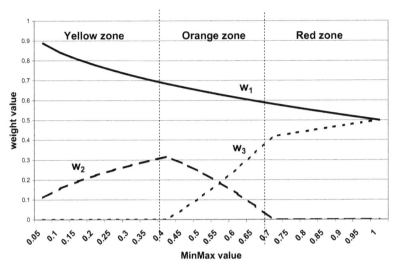

Fig. 3. Weight Function Set

Yellow Zone (0 ≤ MinMax ≤ 40%): The low value of *MinMax* is not important in this zone, neither are short-term fluctuations. The long-term metric indicates if there is an over all increasing trend, and thus is a significant factor to consider. Thus we choose $w_2 = 0$, and an increasing w_3.

Orange Zone (40% < MinMax ≤ 70%): This is the critical alert period where we see the signs of delay increase which is of concern, and any sign of sharp increase, showed by the short-term trend, should be considered with increasing weight. Thus we choose an increasing w_2, and a decreasing w_3.

Red Zone (70% < MinMax ≤ 100%): In this zone the delay is high enough to be close to the loss threshold. Here every possible sign of short term increasing trend should be taken into account along with the high *MinMax* value. The long term is ignored here. Thus we choose an increasing w_2, and $w_3=0$.

In the following prototype function we use functions w_1, w_2 and w_3 as weights for *MinMax*, *STermTrend*, *LTermTrend* and a fourth function w_4 to control the behaviors of *STermTrend* and *LTermTrend* following the weight control 'rules' in different zones.

$$predictor = w_1 * MinMax + w_2 * STermTrend + w_3 * LTermTrend$$
$$w_1 = 1 - \sqrt{MinMax}/2, w_2 = \sqrt{MinMax}/2 * w_4, w_3 = \sqrt{MinMax}/2 * (1 - w_4)$$

$$w_4 = \begin{cases} 1 & \text{in Yellow zone} \\ 1 - (MinMax - 0.4)/0.3 & \text{in Orange zone} \\ 0 & \text{in Red zone} \end{cases}$$

In Fig. 3 w_1, w_2 and w_3 follow the weight 'rules', with proper increasing and decreasing behaviors in different zones. We give more appreciation to *LTermTrend* by selecting an increasing w_2 in the Yellow zone. But as *Min-*

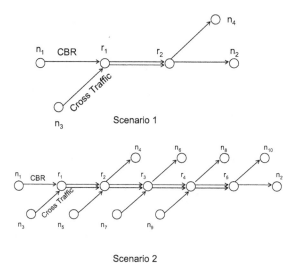

Fig. 4. Simulation Scenarios

Max approaches Orange and Red zones, *STermTrend* is given more priority by choosing an increasing w_3. This enhances the importance of the trend factors and incorporates the zones in the predictor calculation.

4   Predictor Evaluation: Simulation and Experiment Results

In this section we present the simulation and experiment results that evaluate the Predictor algorithm in terms of *accuracy* and *efficiency*. Ideally the predictor should behave accurately, that is, the predictor should report high values for the majority of packet loss occurrences. The predictor should also be efficient by not over-estimating when there is no loss.

We used the network simulator ns-2 [14] to evaluate the Predictor algorithm simulating congestion under a range of cross-traffic and intermediate hop scenarios. We created two scenarios described in Fig 4. We assumed FCFS queuing and Droptail packet dropping for the links. In scenario 1, a CBR stream of 64kbps flowed from n1 and n2 through two intermediate hops, r1-r2 being the bottleneck link (capacity 700kbps) and four Pareto cross traffics with shape parameter=1.9 (meaning infinite variance) flowed from n3 to n4 via r1-r2. In scenario 2, a CBR stream of 64kbps flowed from n1 and n2 through five intermediate hops (r1, r2, r3, r4 and r5), and four Pareto cross traffics flowed through the intermediate hops as shown in the figure. In both cases we gathered a large number of data by introducing a varied number of transient cross traffics of different packet sizes (100 bytes to 1000 bytes) and rates (200kbps to 900kbps) at dispersed points in time, causing different degrees of congestion resulting in stream packet loss at the intermediate links.

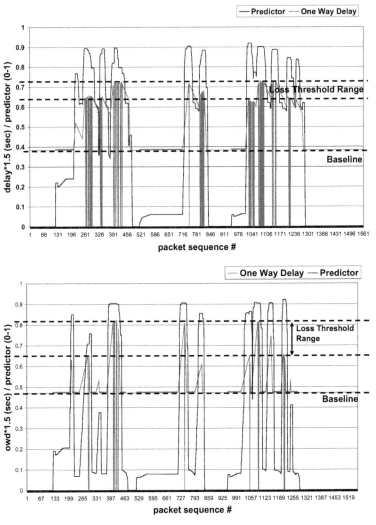

Fig. 5. (a) & (b): OWD, loss threshold and Predictor (Simulation Scenarios 1 and 2)

For the Internet experiments we conducted two sets of experiments on RON/ NetBed [7], and PlanetLab [8], two wide-area network testbeds consisting of sites located around the Internet. A "Master" program from a US site sent a 1 minute speech segment to various sites across the world and received it back recording statistical information. The packet size varied between three sizes (256 bytes, 512 bytes, 1K) and the send rate varied among two values (1ms gap, 10ms gap), generating streams of high rates ranging from 204Kbps to 8Mbps in order to create temporary congestion in the path and observe the effects manifested as packet loss. We ran this experiment every 4 hours for a period of seven days.

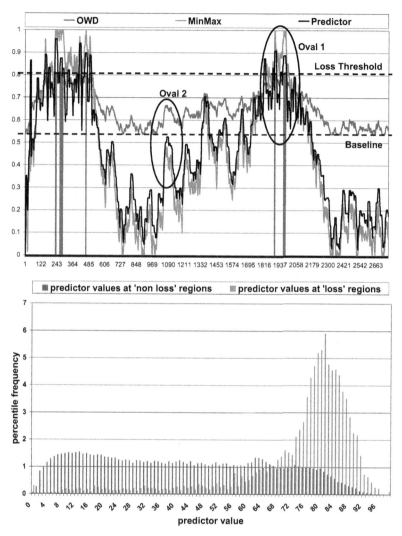

Fig. 6. Predictor behavior in Internet Experiments: (a) Loss Threshold and Predictor: USA-Korea (b) Predictor Accuracy and Efficiency

Predictor Behavior in Simulation and Internet Experiments. In Figs. 5(a) and (b) we present examples of simulation results from scenarios 1 and 2. Both these figures show an identifiable baseline delay. The loss thresholds on the other hand, vary from one another considerably. Scenario 2 has increasingly wider loss threshold range and delay variation compared to scenario 1. This is due to variable and random degrees of cross traffic flowing through multiple links causing unpredictable congestion at different parts of the path. In contrast, congestion at one bottleneck link, though created by various degrees of cross traffic, produces more predictable results in scenario 1. In both scenarios,

Table 1. Predictor Accuracy in Simulation Scenarios

	Predictor Value Percentage Ratio	
Predictor value in 'around loss' region	Scenario 1	Scenario 2
> 0.6	78%	59%
0.4 to 0.6	20%	22%
≤ 0.4	2%	19%

predictor value lies consistently between 0.75 and 0.92 around the loss regions, denoting high likelihood of packet loss, but decreases to low values in the range of 0 to 0.2 when the delay decreases close to the baseline. Thus the predictor successfully reacts to the baseline, loss threshold and increasing and decreasing trends of the delay in a wide variety of congestion situations.

Figure 6(a) shows the Predictor for a selected example from an Internet experiment. We see that around the loss regions the predictor value lies consistently between 0.8 and 0.9, denoting high likelihood of packet loss, but decreases to low values in the range of 0.1 to 0.3 when the delay decreases close to the baseline. Thus the predictor successfully reacts to the baseline, loss threshold and increasing and decreasing trends of the delay. Fig 6(a) also shows the effect of the Short-term and Long-term Trend on the Predictor. In Oval 1, marking a Red zone (*MinMax* value larger than 0.70), the short-term trend accentuates the Predictor based on immediate sharp increase of delay. In Oval 2, the Long-term trend pulls up the Predictor value based on the long-term increasing trend in the Yellow and Orange zones, even when *MinMax* value is not very high.

Predictor Accuracy. We ran the Predictor algorithm against all the data we collected. The data is presented in Figure 6(b) as a summary of the Predictor efficiency and accuracy for Internet experiments. We divided the data into 'around loss' and 'no loss' regions - an 'around loss' region being -20 to +20 packets around a loss, and packets outside 'around loss' regions being in 'no loss' region. We took predictor values for the packets in the 'around loss' regions to determine the predictor accuracy. Ideally, the predictor should predict accurately, that is there should not be any loss at low values of the predictor. We see that there is about 10% loss at low values (values smaller than 0.6).

The accuracy for the simulation is shown in Table 1. Around loss regions, the predictor value is greater than 0.6 78% of the times in scenario 1 vs. 59% in scenario 2. Only 2% of the times the predictor value has been under 0.4 in loss regions, compared to 19% for scenario 2. In scenario 2 we simulate more variable and random degrees of congestion at different parts of the path compared to scenario 1, resulting in less accuracy for the predictor. This motivates us into refining the predictor for better accuracy under such variable conditions.

Predictor Efficiency. Here we study the other side of the same coin, that is, how efficient the predictor is by not over-estimating when there is no loss. Both the simulation scenarios show very small percentages (5% for Scenario 1, 2% for scenario 2) of predictor value larger than 0.7 in the 'non loss' region. Figure 6(b) shows a small percentage (about 16%) of high predictor value (value larger than 0.7) in the non loss region for Internet experiment sites.

The efficiency is a critical input to the Predictor. As part of our future work, we shall use the efficiency factor as a self-feedback to the Predictor mechanism in order for it to evaluate and refine its prediction on an ongoing basis.

5   Conclusion and Future Work

This paper presents a framework of a Packet Loss Predictor: a novel mechanism to predict packet loss in real-time audio streams by observing the delay variation and trends. Loss Predictor approach is based on (i) determining certain metrics for measuring the delay variation characteristics from the ongoing traffic, (ii) combining them with weights based on their importance, and (iii) deriving a predictor value as the measure of packet loss likelihood. The Predictor value, fed back to the sender, indicates current degree and severity of congestion and likelihood of packet loss, and can be a vital component in sender-based error and rate control mechanisms for multimedia. The proactive predictor feedback makes the framework superior to mechanisms with static and reactive feedbacks, and a viable technique for majority of network conditions.

We present simulation and experiment results showing the accuracy and efficiency of the algorithm achieved so far. The results of the Predictor under simulation scenarios and experiments show 60%-90% accuracy and 85%-98% efficiency. As future work, we need to refine the metrics and the weight factors to improve the accuracy and efficiency of the Predictor. This will enable us to use the Predictor more reliably in proactive error and rate control mechanisms. Various packet window sizes introduced in this paper also need to be tuned. Formalization is also necessary for sender initiated proactive FEC and rate control actions, which depend on the Predictor feedback values. Also, we would like to extend the concepts of the Loss Predictor to paths with Random Early Detection (RED) packet dropping mechanisms and apply the Loss Predictor to DiffServ, Overlay and Multicast frameworks.

References

1. Bolot, J.,Fosse-Parisis, S.,Towsley, D.: Adaptive FEC-Based Error Control for Internet Telephony. IEEE Infocom (1999)
2. Bolot,J., Vega-Garcia,A.: Control Mechanisms for Packet Audio in the Internet. Proceedings IEEE Infocom, San Francisco (1996) 232-239
3. Brakmo,L.S., O'Malley,S. W., Peterson,L.: TCP Vegas: New Techniques for Congestion Detection and Avoidance. ACM SIGCOMM Conference(1994) 24-35
4. Cole,R.G., Rosenbluth,J.H.: Voice over IP Performance Monitoring. ACM SIGCOMM (2001)
5. Handley,M.: An examination of Mbone performance. USC/ISI Research Report: ISI/RR-97-450
6. Hermanns,O., Schuba,M.: Performance investigations of the IP multicast architecture. Proc. IEEE Global Internet Conference (1996)

7. https://www.emulab.net/index.php3

8. http://www.planet-lab.org/

9. Jacobson,V.: Congestion avoidance and control. Proc. ACM SIGCOMM Conference, Stanford (1988) 314-329.

10. Jain,M., Dovrolis,C.: End-to-end Available Bandwidth: Measurement Methodology, Dynamics and relation with TCP Throughput. SIGCOMM (2002)

11. Lin,S., Costello,D.J.: Error Correcting Coding, Fundamentals and Applications, Prentice Hall, Englewood Cliffs, NJ (1983)

12. Mohamed,S., Cervantes-Perez,F., Afifi,H.: Integrating Network Measurements and Speech Quality Subjective Scores for Control Purposes. IEEE Infocom (2001)

13. Moon,S.B.: Measurement And Analysis Of End-To-End Delay And Loss In The Internet. PhD Thesis, Department of Computer Science, University of Massachussets, Amherst (2000)

14. The Network Simulator: ns-2: http://www.isi.edu/nsnam/ns/

15. Padhye,C., Christensen,K., Moreno,W.: A New Adaptive FEC Loss Control Algorithm for Voice Over IP Applications. Proceedings of the 19th IEEE International Performance, Computing, and Communication Conference (2000) 307-313

16. Paxson, V.: Measurements and Analysis of End-to-End Internet Dynamics. PhD Thesis, Computer Science Division, University of California, Berkeley (1997)

17. Roychoudhuri,L., Al-Shaer,E., Hamed,H., Brewster,G.B.: Audio Transmission over the Internet: Experiments and Observations. IEEE International Conference on Communications (ICC), Anchorage, Alaska (2003)

18. Roychoudhuri,L., Al-Shaer,E., Hamed,H., Brewster,G.B.: On Studying the Impact of the Internet Delays on Audio Transmission. IEEE IP Operations and Management (IPOM), Dallas, Texas (2002)

SLA-Driven Flexible Bandwidth Reservation Negotiation Schemes for QoS Aware IP Networks

David Chieng[1], Alan Marshall[2], and Gerard Parr[3]

[1] Faculty of Engineering, Multimedia University,
63100 Cyberjaya, Selangor D.E., Malaysia
htchieng@mmu.edu.my

[2] School of Electronic & Electrical Engineering, The Queen's University of Belfast,
Ashby Bld, Stranmillis Rd, BT9 5AH Belfast, Northern Ireland, UK
a.marshall@ee.qub.ac.uk

[3] School of Computing and Information Engineering, University of Ulster,
BT52 1SA Coleraine, Northern Ireland, UK
gp.parr@ulster.ac.uk

Abstract. We present a generic Service Level Agreement (SLA)-driven service provisioning architecture, which enables dynamic and flexible bandwidth reservation schemes on a per-user or a per-application basis. Various session level SLA negotiation schemes involving bandwidth allocation, service start time and service duration parameters are introduced and analysed. The results show that these negotiation schemes can be utilised for the benefits of both end user and network provide such as getting the highest individual SLA optimisation in terms of Quality of Service (QoS) and price. A prototype based on an industrial agent platform has also been built to demonstrate the negotiation scenario and this is presented and discussed.

1 Introduction

In today's complex network environment, QoS provisioning for real-time applications over IP-based networks is a great challenge. Firstly, service and network providers will have to deal with a myriad of user requests that come with diverse QoS or Service Level Agreement (SLA) requirements. The providers will then need to make sure that these requirements can be delivered accordingly. To address these issues, we propose a unique Service Level Agreement (SLA)-driven service provisioning architecture that enables flexible and quantitative SLA negotiations for network services. In this paper we focus on bandwidth reservation and management on a per-user, per-application or per-flow basis. Software agents are employed to assist the service provider in guiding, deciphering and responding quickly and effectively to users' requests. These satisfy the two most important performance aspects in SLA provisioning; availability and responsiveness.

This paper is organised as follows: Section 2 first presents the service provisioning architecture and a set of associated SLA parameters. Section 3 and 4 introduce the respective SLA utilities and prototype system. Section 5 presents the SLA negotiation schemes enabled by the proposed architecture and section 6 describes the simulation environment. The simulation results and evaluations are then discussed in section 7. Finally the related work, the overall analysis and conclusions are drawn in section 8 and 9 respectively.

J. Vicente and D. Hutchison (Eds.): MMNS 2004, LNCS 3271, pp. 228–240, 2004.

2 SLA Driven Service Provisioning Architecture

In general, many end users/customers and service or network providers are still unable to specify SLAs in a way that benefits both parties. For example, the network providers may experience service degradation by accepting more traffic than their networks can handle. On the contrary, they may fail to provide services to the best of their networks' capabilities. In this work, bandwidth reservation is emphasized since it is the single most important factor that affects the QoS. The limits for delay, jitter and buffer size can be determined by the bandwidth reserved for a flow [1]. The architecture not only provides immediate reservation, it also allows bandwidth resource to be reserved in advance. The high-level service parameters that can be negotiated are summarized in table 1 as follow:

Table 1. SLA Parameters.

SLA Parameters	Description
Price (P)	Maximum price for this connection per transaction or price per unit bandwidth ($/b).
Start Time (Ts)	Reservation start time or activation time.
Session Length (T)	Reservation session duration or reservation enforcement duration.
Guaranteed BW (b)	The amount of bandwidth guaranteed/reserved.
Option (Ω)	Priorities setting and preferences

The generic architecture as shown in figure 1 is proposed [2][1]. The Domain Manager (DM) generally manages the network domain. It communicates with the policy server that administrates policies, rules and actions for different services stored in a policy repository. In these policies, various limits such as maximum bandwidth that a user can reserve at a time, maximum or minimum reservation duration, etc, can be specified and enforced through other elements in our architecture. The Path Table (PT) stores the logical 'reservable' path or route ID info. The Resource (bandwidth) Reservation Table (RRT) comes in the form of a resource/time table. This allows the network provider to lookup and allocate network resources (bandwidth) at present and also in the future. The User Service Database (USD) stores individual customer's SLA information such as service ID, the respective bandwidth allocation (b), agreed service activation time (Ts), session duration (T), path ID or routing option, billing option, and also other rules and policies bound to this particular user. After an SLA is accepted, the DM maps the required configurations down to the Policy Enforcement (PEP) layer where the appropriate QoS control is performed.

The policies can be enforced in such a way that when the duration of resource reservation T expires, the connection will automatically revert to best effort mode. Alternatively, the allocated bandwidth will be sustained until it is needed by other incoming non-preemptable sessions. The advance reservation facilities are desirable for services are such as Video on Demand (VoD) and news broadcast where service start time are known in advance. In a situation where the desired session time cannot be specified or it is not known a priori such as in IP voice calls, an alternative scheme is

---

[1] The generic architecture shown in figure 1 has been presented in [2]. Current paper provides a more refined architecture and extended [2] with a prototype implementation and some additional results.

necessary. Agents can be employed to optimise resource usage bilaterally such as performing dynamic resource negotiations. Here, autonomous agents also play an important role in enhancing service discovery process i.e. via advertisement. This is essential in today's heterogeneous network environments where not all networks offer services with QoS options. Various admission control schemes or policies can then be enforced to control and optimise resources, and at the same time maximising user satisfaction and network provider's profit.

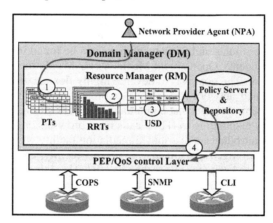

Fig. 1. Generic SLA Architecture.

3 SLA Utilities

We extend the SLA management utility model proposed by [3]. It gives both end user and network provider a unified and computationally feasible approach to perform session request/admission control, quality selection/adaptation, resource request/allocation decisions, etc. In this work, a user request i for a guaranteed service session can be represented by:

$$u_i (b_i, Ts_i, T_i, P_i, \Omega_i) \tag{1}$$

After translating to a resource usage function in terms of reserved bandwidth, this can be represented by:

$$r_i (b_i, Ts_i, T_i) \tag{2}$$

In order to make the request more elastic, tolerances or variation levels are introduced and so that the probability of a request being rejected can be reduced. For example, a video subscriber might not mind waiting for another 1 or 2 minutes until the requested resources become available. Alternatively, if this is not possible, the subscriber may opt for a slightly lower video quality at some discounted price. The service provider may on the other hand propose an alternative if the demanded service cannot be granted.

Occasionally, the provider may want to propose a higher quality higher bandwidth video session with a cheaper price in order to maximize network utilization. On another occasion, a provider may propose a higher bandwidth with shorter session rather than lower bandwidth with longer session. The utility can be represented by equation (3) as follows:

$$u_i\left(b_i \pm a, Ts_i \pm b, T_i \pm c, P_i \pm d\right) \qquad (3)$$

Where a, b, c and d are the tolerance limits acceptable by the user. These tolerance parameters can be embedded as part of user policies or preferences (Ω) as shown in equation (1).

4 System Prototype

To demonstrate the agent-enhanced SLA brokering and negotiation scenarios, a system prototype that consists of a real agent system environment has been developed. More detailed case studies and implementations can be found in [4]. In this work, we used the Fujitsu Phoenix Open Agent Mediator (OAM) platform to build the service provisioning system. The goal was to develop highly flexible, robust and dynamically extensible distributed network service broker prototype. In this platform, agents are realised using Phoenix servlets that communicate via HTTP over TCP/IP. Agent servlets are invoked by responding to HTTP calls from browsers or other agent servlets.

Phoenix OAM introduces a distributed mediation facility where the agents' execution flows can be arranged dynamically. With this facility, an agent is known by its "functions" i.e. offered services rather than its URI. This information is registered at a mediation table through advertisement. Hence, multiple servlet agents registered under the same "function" can be accessed in parallel. In addition, servlet agents can be dynamically loaded and unloaded at run-time (service plug and play can be realized). When a mediator agent receives a request, it will find the desired agents by collaborating with other mediators that reside in other network domains.

The prototype demo illustrates the SLA brokering and negotiation scenario. Here, the network stakeholders involved are the end user, the access service provider, the network/connectivity provider and some content providers. When a User Agent (UA) is first invoked by an end-user, it downloads a page from the Access Service Provider Agent (ASPA). The page offers a range of network services as shown in figure 2. The ASPA will broker the request to the target Content Provider Agent (CPA) that represents the VoD service provider. The agent then replies to the user with a VoD service subscription page as shown in figure 3. The subscription page allows the user to select the movie title, the desired quality, the desired movie start time, the tolerance parameters, the maximum price he or she is willing to pay, etc.

Fig. 2. Service Brokering Page.

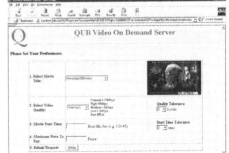

Fig. 3. VoD Service Subscription Page.

Assuming the user wants to watch the movie "Hannibal" that requires a duration of 180mins; the desired video quality is "Premium"; the desired movie start time is at 13:00; and the maximum acceptable price for this service is 300 pence. The maximum quality tolerance is 1 level, i.e. from premium (10 Mbps, q_i) to high (8 Mbps, q_{i-1}) if the requested quality cannot be provided. Alternatively, if the requested quality cannot be honoured at the specified start time, the user may be willing to accept a tolerance of maximum ±5 minutes. The resulting SLA utility is therefore:

$$u_i(b_i = 10 - 2, Ts_i = 1300 \pm 5, T_i = 180, P_i = 300\text{max})$$

Once the "Setup" button is clicked, the UA then proceeds to encode these preferences into Phoenix's URLEncoded parameters and sends it to the ASPA. In order to setup a network connection with the required SLA, the ASPA needs to negotiate with the Network Provider Agent (NPA). If the requested SLA can be satisfied, the service will be granted.

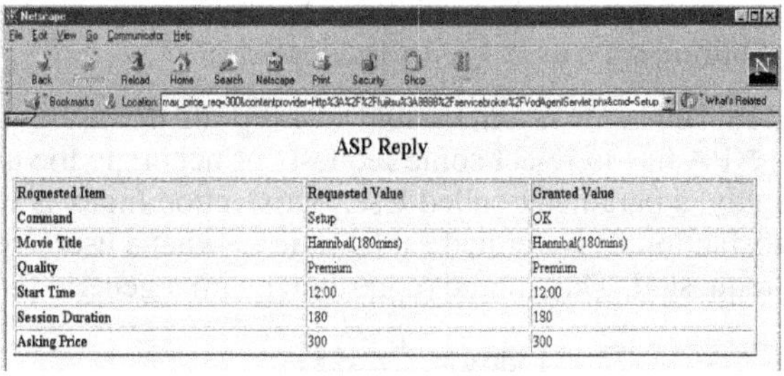

Requested Item	Requested Value	Granted Value
Command	Setup	OK
Movie Title	Hannibal(180mins)	Hannibal(180mins)
Quality	Premium	Premium
Start Time	12:00	12:00
Session Duration	180	180
Asking Price	300	300

Fig. 4. Reply from ASPA.

Figure 4 shows the reply if all the requested SLA parameters are granted. If the requested SLA (with the tolerances) cannot be honoured, the ASPA may issue a "Reject" or initiate a new phase of negotiation.

5 SLA Negotiation Schemes

With the proposed service provisioning architecture, dynamic SLA negotiations can take place i.e. between a User Agent (UA) and a Network Provider Agent (NPA). We introduce four novel session level SLA negotiation schemes i.e. *Bandwidth Negotiation at Resource Limit (BNRL), Guaranteed Session Duration Negotiation for both Session Cut Short (SDN-CS)* and *Temporary Session Bandwidth Drop Off (SDN-TBD)*, and *Guaranteed Session Start Time Negotiation with Delay (STN-D)*. The impact of these negotiation schemes on service availability, network utilisation or revenues and mean user satisfaction are analysed. In this work, three SLA performance metrics are introduced.

Rejection Probability (p_{rej}). This parameter directly reflects the service availability. It is vital for most service/network providers to maintain a minimum level of service availability as part of their SLAs. We define the overall rejection probability as:

$$\rho_{rej} = \frac{N_{rej}}{N_{rec}} \tag{4}$$

Where N_{req} = Total number of SLA requests rejected and N_{rec}= Total number of SLA requests received.

Percentage Mean Utilisation or Mean Reservation Load ($\%\overline{R}_s$). It is defined as the percentage of total mean reserved bandwidth in Resource Reservation Table (RRT) in relative to its total bandwidth capacity (C). This is represented by:

$$\%\overline{R}_s = \frac{\left(\dfrac{\sum_{t=t_1}^{t_2} R(t)}{t_2 - t_1 + \tau}\right)}{C} \cdot 100\% = \frac{\overline{R_{T_{col}}}}{C} \cdot 100\% \tag{5}$$

Where $t = t_1, t_1 + \tau, t_1 + 2\tau, \ldots t_2$ and $t_1 \leq t \leq t_2$. $R(t)$ is the reservation load in the RRT at minimum 'reservable' timeslot t, $\%\overline{R}_s$ is the mean RRT utilisation measured during a period of time, T_{col}. $T_{col} = t_2 - t_1 + \tau$ where t_1 (inclusive) is the start collecting data period, and t_2 is the stop collecting data period. $\%\overline{R}_s$ reflects the revenue earned if a usage-based billing such as in GPRS is adopted.

User Satisfaction Index. It is impossible to keep all the users happy all the time. Sometimes, the NPA has to reject some requests or negotiate the users' SLA requirements. In this study, a parameter called User Satisfaction Index is introduced to represent a user's satisfaction. It is defined as the ratio of what a user is granted to what the user originally requested. This can be represented with a generic function as follows:

$$\text{Index} = \frac{\theta_{granted}}{\theta_{requested}} \tag{6}$$

The NPA needs to ensure that the average user satisfaction index does not fall below a certain threshold.

6 Simulation Environment

A network model using Block Oriented Network Simulator (BONeS) [5] has been developed to study the negotiation schemes above. The logical capacity of the links in terms of 'reservable' bandwidth across the network is fixed at C bps. The minimum and maximum limits for bandwidth requested per user (b_r) are set 1 and 156 units respectively where one unit may represent 64kbps. The offered load $\%\overline{R}_q$ (same definition as $\%\overline{R}_s$) is defined as percentage mean load requested in relative to the total bandwidth capacity of the link (C). The b_r distribution profile with the above parameters is shown in figure 5. The idea is to create a distribution that generates more requests for lower bandwidth, i.e. voice calls. The average b_r for this distribution is measured at 58.32 units or 3.73Mbps if 1 unit = 64kbps.

Figure 6 was generated by scanning through the RRT at a particular instance with C set at 1562 units and with 20% of incoming requests were requesting bandwidth resource in advance. It is shown that at t=5000s, some future resources have already been reserved.

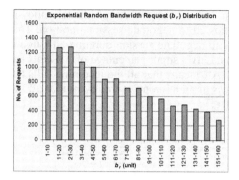

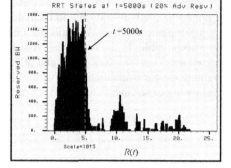

Fig. 5. b_r Request Distribution.

Fig. 6. 20% Advance Reservation.

7 SLA Negotiation Schemes Evaluation

The following experiments were simulated over 200,000s or 55.55 hours simulation time. To ensure the simulation is in a stable state, t_1 is set at 100,000s and t_2 is set at 200,000s. In the following experiments, each simulation was run using different random number generator seeds in order to investigate the deviation caused by the simulation model. The data are then used to plot the confidence intervals i.e. mean, maximum and minimum values of the results. Due to the limited space however, only the results from the three session level SLA negotiation schemes i.e. *Guaranteed Session Duration Negotiation for both Session Cut Short (SDN-CS)* and *Temporary Session Bandwidth Drop Off (SDN-TBD)*, and *Guaranteed Session Start Time Negotiation with Delay (STN-D)* and are presented in this paper. The results for *Bandwidth Negotiation at Resource Limit (BNRL)* negotiation scheme can be found in [2].

7.1 Guaranteed Session Duration Negotiation

This section investigates the scenario when the end users are willing to negotiate the guaranteed session duration. Logically, this is only applicable to those applications whose bandwidth does not need to be guaranteed throughout the session such as web browsing, FTP, or other less critical real-time applications. Here, two schemes are proposed namely the *Session Duration Negotiation with Session Cut Short* and *Session Duration Negotiation with Temporary Session Bandwidth Drop Off*.

Session Duration Negotiation – Cut Short (SDN-CS)

In this scheme, if the requested session T_r (from Ts to $Ts+T_r$) is not available, the maximum available 'continuous' session duration will be proposed to the end users. A user's duration tolerance T_{tol} is defined as the percentage of T_r when the bandwidth is not guaranteed or $T_{tol} = \left(\dfrac{T_r - T_g}{T_r}\right) * 100\%$, where T_g is the guaranteed session duration granted. The service request utility function with session duration negotiation can be represented by $u_i(b_i, Ts_i, T_i - T_{tol} * T_i, P_i)$. This only happens if the required bandwidth has already been booked by other Advanced Reservation (AR) calls. In other words, without AR calls, session negotiation will not happen. An additional policy is applied here where only the immediate is allowed to negotiate session duration. This is a fair assumption as AR calls are unlikely to negotiate session duration although it is also possible. In the following experiments, only a small percentage of AR calls are considered i.e. 0%, 10%, 20% and 30%. 0% AR means that all the incoming calls are requesting for immediate reservation. It is worth mentioning at this point that all the following experiments were carried out at $90\%\overline{R}_q$.

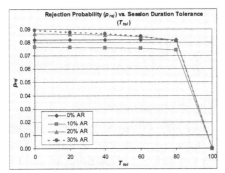

Fig. 7. ρ_{rej} vs. T_{tol}.

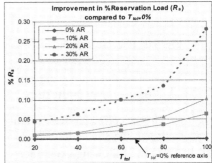

Fig. 8. $\%\overline{R}_s$ Improvement with T_{tol}.

From figure 7, generally the drop in p_{rej} is not significant from $T_{tol} = 0\%$ to $T_{tol} = 80\%$. For 0% AR, T_{tol} has no effect on p_{rej} since no negotiations take place. When there is 10% AR calls, the users experience lower p_{rej}. This is because the chance of requests being blocked by prescheduled AR calls is low. However p_{rej} increases when there are 20% and 30 % of AR calls because more immediate reservation calls are being blocked by the existing AR sessions. The chance of a prescheduled AR session blocking new AR calls is negligible. In fact none has been recorded for 20% and 30% AR.

Figure 8 shows that $\%\overline{R}_s$ generally improves if session duration is negotiable (compared to $0\%T_{tol}$). The effect is more significant if the percentage of AR calls is high. However the degree of improvement is quite small with this scheme ($<0.3\%\overline{R}_s$ even with 100% T_{tol}). It also proves that without AR call, SDN-CS basically has no effect on $\%\overline{R}_s$. In terms of revenue, if 1 Mbps of guaranteed bandwidth is priced at is $2 per hour, only around $0.10 extra revenue per hour is earned with $T_{tol} = 20\%$ at AR calls=30%.

In this experiment, the Session Duration Index (SDI) is used to represent overall users' satisfaction. It is defined as the mean ratio of session duration granted over session duration requested or mean (T_g/T_s). The simulation result shows that the difference in SDI is almost negligible. The reason is very few negotiations are actually successful with this scheme. Therefore, an alternative session negotiation scheme was introduced.

Session Duration Negotiation – Temporary Bandwidth Drop off (SDN-TBD)

In this scheme, rather than having the guaranteed session duration being cut short, the users may be willing to tolerate intermittence drop off in bandwidth. This is used if the total duration or total number of time slots $\tau(T_u)$, when b_r cannot be granted, is not larger than the tolerance level, T_{tol}. Therefore $T_{tol} = (T_u/T_r)*100\%$ for this scheme. However at each T_u time slot, the maximum available bandwidth will be granted. In other words, 'Best Effort Reservation' is performed at each T_u time slot. In this experiment, $\%\overline{R}_q$ is also set at 90% but the percentage of AR calls is fixed at 20%. Figures 9-11 compare the two schemes (SDN-CU and SDN-TBD).

As shown in figure 9, SDN-TBD scheme suffers a higher p_{rej} when T_{tol} is <50% but yields a lower p_{rej} when T_{tol} exceeds 50%. This is because $\%\overline{R}_s$ improves significantly with SDN-TBD scheme even with small T_{tol} (figure 10).

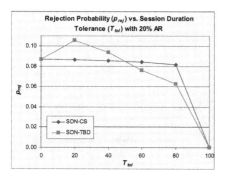

Fig. 9. ρ_{rej} vs. T_{tol}.   **Fig. 10.** $\%\overline{R}_s$ Improvement vs. T_{tol}.

The sudden increase in RRT utilisation leaves less bandwidth for future requests and therefore causes p_{rej} to increase suddenly. p_{rej} can only be reduced by further increasing the T_{tol}. These results are expected since SDN-TBD scheme offers 'best effort reservation' when the requested bandwidth at certain RRT time slots are not available. Whereas SDN-CS scheme just provides the session guarantee up until the instance when the first 'bandwidth not available' time slot at RRT is encountered. In terms of revenue, even with only 20% T_{tol}, SDN-TBD yields an extra ~5.6 $\%\overline{R}_s$ as compared to SDN-CS. This is extremely significant as if, for example, 1 Mbps of guaranteed bandwidth is priced at $2 per hour, then this represents an increase of ~$11.20 per hour for a 100 Mbps link.

Figure 11 compares the SDI between these two schemes. For SDN-TBD, SDI is defined as mean $[(T_r - T_u)/T_r]$. Here, SDN-TBD drops significantly with T_{tol} as compared to SDN-CS. This is expected as more negotiations have been taking place.

7.2   Guaranteed Start-Time Negotiation with Delay (STN-D)

This scheme can be applied if the user does not mind delaying the guaranteed service start time (Ts) if the requested bandwidth is not available at the desired service or session start time, Ts_r. Rather than asking the user to request again in the future, a network provider can allocate an alternative session start time that is within the user's tolerance limit, Ts_{tol}. Ts_{tol} is defined in unit(s) of time slot, τ (where τ is 1 second). This can be represented by the service request utility function, $u_i(b_i, Ts_i + Ts_{tol}, T_i, P_i)$. In this experiment, different percentages of the advance reservation (AR) calls are considered and the offered load, $\%\overline{R}_q$ is fixed at 90%:

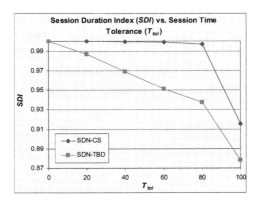

Fig. 11. SDI vs T_{tol}.

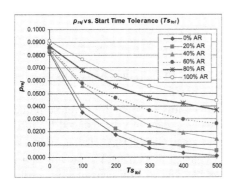

Fig. 12. ρ_{rej} vs. Ts_{tol}.

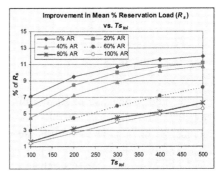

Fig. 13. $\%\overline{R}_s$ Improvement vs. Ts_{tol}.

The STN-D scheme produces a significant drop in ρ_{rej} as shown in figure 12. The effect is less significant if the percentage of AR calls is high because the incoming IR and AR requests are likely to be blocked by other prescheduled AR sessions. Figure 13 shows that $\%\overline{R}_s$ generally improves when session start time is negotiable. The improvement is most significant when all the calls are requesting for immediate reservation or 0%AR. Here, extra $7.08\,\%\overline{R}_s$ is obtained with 0%AR series when Ts_{tol} =100s. From the figure, it can also be deduced that the $\%\overline{R}_s$ improvement drops as the percentage of AR calls increases. This is due to higher blocking probability experienced by new immediate and AR calls if the number of prescheduled sessions is high.

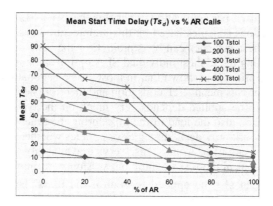

Fig. 14. Mean Ts_d (in second) vs. % AR calls.

Figure 14 shows that in general, users experience shorter mean start time delay $\overline{T}_{sd}$ as the percentage of AR calls increases. This is because the session start time of the AR calls falls within a given range, $Ts_{min} \leq Ts \leq Ts_{max}$. Therefore these calls have higher chances to get their desired Ts. In a way this figure also corresponds to the users' satisfaction level where the longer the $\overline{T}_{sd}$, the lower the satisfaction. On average, $\overline{T}_{sd}$ stays lower than 15s when Ts_{tol} = 100s.

8   Related Work

The frameworks for specifying and managing policies related to programmable networks [6] and DiffServ-based network [7] are complementary to our work. The proposed SLA notations, object-oriented methodologies, conflict management methods, etc, can be adopted to enhance our architecture.

The concept of resource reservation in advance has also been addressed in [8], [9], [10], [11], etc. To our knowledge however, none of the above work provides a detailed analysis on session level SLA negotiations. Work by [11] focuses on the design, implementation and evaluation of their Resource Reservation in Advance (ReRA) mechanism by extending the existing RSVP protocol on ATM. The authors also address best-match alternative reservation scenarios similar to that offered by our SLA negotiation schemes. However, in the paper no experimental work was presented.

[12] proposes an agent-based reservation system for immediate and AR calls. In their work, a call 'lookahead' time is applied to decide the admission of immediate reservation calls. The effects on rejection probability, pre-emption probability and overall RRT utilisation are studied. We extend their work by looking into session-level negotiation issues involving guaranteed bandwidth, session duration and session start time.

9   Overall Analysis and Conclusions

This paper has presented an SLA-driven service provisioning architecture that facilitates quantitative bandwidth, session duration, session start time preferences negotiations, etc. on a per user, per application or per flow basis via SLA. Four novel session level SLA negotiations schemes based on this architecture have been evaluated. The results show that these schemes can be exploited for the benefits of both negotiating parties such as getting the highest individual SLA optimisation in terms of Quality of Service (QoS) and price. It is shown that in most cases, negotiation reduces rejection probability and improves mean RRT utilisation and therefore network's revenues. The choice of scheme to be applied depends very much on the type of applications, the user's preferences and also the load of the link during the time of negotiation. It also depends on the network provider's strategies or policies whether to maximise reservation load (RRT utilisation) or to maximise service availability. Various policies can also be applied to control the session duration, session start time (Ts_{min} or Ts_{max}), etc. Pricing strategies can also be applied to control the users' behaviours. Indirectly, these are seen as a means to manage bandwidth resource [14].

Acknowledgement

The authors gratefully acknowledge Fujitsu Telecommunications Europe Ltd for funding this work and Fujitsu Teamware Finland for the software support.

References

1. Q. Ma, P. Steenkiste: Quality of Service Routing for Traffic with Performance Guarantees, IFIP International Workshop on Quality of Service (IWQoS'97), New York, May (1997), 115-126
2. David Chieng, Alan Marshall: A Policy-Based Bandwidth Resource Provisioning Architecture, IFIP/IEEE Net-Con'2002, Paris, FRANCE, 23-25 Oct (2002)
3. S. Khan, K. F. Li, E. G. Manning: The Utility Model for Adaptive Multimedia Systems, International Conference on Multimedia Modelling, Singapore, Nov (1997)
4. David Chieng, Alan Marshall: Dynamic Network Service Brokering with Open Agent Mediators, International Symposium on Information and Communications Technologies (M2USIC) 2003, Petaling Jaya, Malaysia., 2 - 3 Oct (2003)
5. BONeS DESIGNER Ver 4.01, Alta GroupTM of Cadence Design Systems, Inc
6. Morris Sloman, Emil Lupu: Policy Specification for Programmable Networks, Proceedings of First International Working Conference on Active Networks (IWAN'99), Berlin, June (1999)
7. L. Lymberopoulos, E. Lupu, M. Sloman: An Adaptive Policy Based Management Framework for Differentiated Services Networks, Proceedings of 3rd IEEE Workshop on Policies for Distributed Systems and Networks (Policy 2002), Monterey, California, June (2002).
8. M. Karsten, N. Beries, L. Wolf, R. Steinmetz: A Policy-Based Service Specification for Resource Reservation in Advance, Proceedings of the International Conference on Computer Communications (ICCC'99), Tokyo, Japan, Sept (1999), 82-88
9. D. Ferrari, A. Gupta, G. Ventre: Distributed Advance Reservation of Real-Time Connections, NOSSDAV'95, New Hampshire, USA, April (1995). (Springer Verlag LNCS Vol.1018)
10. L. Wolf, R. Steinmetz: Concepts for Resource Reservation in Advance, Special Issue of the Journal of Multimedia Tools and Applications on The State of The Art in Multimedia, Vol. 4, No. 3, May (1997)

11. Alexander Schill, Frank Breiter, Sabine Kuhn: Design and Evaluation of an Advance Reservation Protocol on top of RSVP, IFIP 4th International Conference on Broadband Communications, Stuttgart, March (1998) 23-24
12. O. Schelen, S. Pink: Resource sharing in advance reservation agents, Journal of High Speed Networks: Special issue on Multimedia Networking, Vol. 7, No. 3-4, (1998) 213-218
13. David Chieng, Alan Marshall, Ivan Ho, Gerald Parr: A Mobile Agent Brokering Environment for The Future Open Network Marketplace, Seventh International Conference On Intelligence in Services and Networks (IS&N2000), Athens, 23-25 Feb (2000), (Springer Verlag LNCS Vol. 1774) 3-15
14. David Chieng, Alan Marshall, Ivan Ho, Gerald Parr: Agent-Enhanced Dynamic Service Level Agreement In Future Network Environments, *IFIP/IEEE MMNS 2001*, Chicago, 29 Oct - 1 Nov (2001), (Springer Verlag LNCS Vol. 2216) 299-312

An Enhanced Virtual Time Simulator for Studying QoS Provisioning of Multimedia Services in UTRAN

David Soldani, Achim Wacker, and Kari Sipilä

Nokia Networks, System Technologies,
P.O. Box 301, FIN-00045 Nokia Group, Finland
{david.soldani,achim.wacker,kari.sipila}@nokia.com

Abstract. This paper describes an enhanced virtual time simulator for studying the provisioning of new services throughout the UMTS Radio Access Network (UTRAN). Several simulations were run to verify the feasibility of the tool and to investigate the effectiveness of the supported QoS mechanisms. The radio resources utilization is analyzed in terms of cell throughput and transmission power. The quality of experience is assessed separately for each of the offered services by tailored combinations of performance metrics, which determine the degree of satisfaction of the user of the services. The simulation results show the proposed simulator to be an appropriate tool for studying several aspects of radio network management, such as service planning and QoS provisioning.

1 Introduction

In UMTS only a layered bearer service architecture and QoS attributes are defined: Implementation and planning aspects of the actual QoS management functions are left to vendors' and operators' choice [1]. Hence, due to the complexity of the system and infrastructure costs, any practical deployment of radio resources management (RRM) algorithms and offered services in UTRAN needs to be validated a priori by means of static or dynamic simulations, depending on the desired level of time resolution and accuracy. For this purpose, several tools were presented in the literature, e.g.: A *static simulator* for WCDMA radio network planning was presented in [2], and an advanced WCDMA *dynamic simulator* for detailed analyses of RRM functions was described in [3]. Evaluation of the suitability and accuracy of such tools, as well as a comparison of thereof can be found in [4] and [5]. However, none of the published solutions was designed for an effective QoS provisioning. Radio network planning tools are mainly based on circuit switched (CS) communications, analyze snap shots of the system status, and do not include the possibility of handling radio resources based on QoS and/or quality of experience (QoE) requirements. Conversely, dynamic system level simulators typically run with far too high time resolution and require lengthy simulation times to design networks and/or analyze thoroughly the deployment of application services. This paper describes a virtual time simulator that overcomes the limitations of the static tool presented in [2], and the complexity of the dynamic simulator discussed in [3]. The tool enhances the version described in [6] with multi-cell propagation scenarios and realistic RRM functions as implemented in [2] and [3], respectively. Also, for more accurate analyses, the simulator includes: User definable traffic models for packet switched streaming, Push to Talk over Cellular (PoC), See What I See (SWIS, or real time video sharing, RTVS), Multimedia Messaging (MMS), WAP

J. Vicente and D. Hutchison (Eds.): MMNS 2004, LNCS 3271, pp. 241–254, 2004.
© IFIP International Federation for Information Processing 2004

and Dialup connections [7]; and the possibility of monitoring system and service performances as recommended in [8].

Section 2 describes the simulator architecture, the currently supported traffic and propagation models, QoS management functions and metrics for assessing service and network performances. Section 3 presents the simulated environment and parameters. Section 4 examines the outputs of the simulator and discusses the performance results. Section 5 summarizes the key issues and conclusions upon the simulator utilization.

2   Simulator Structure

The simulator consists of a modular structure with clear interfaces. Each module is implemented independently so that each entity may be straightforwardly replaced by an alternative solution. The tool includes the following functions: Traffic and path loss generators, Admission Control (AC), Load Control (LC), Packet Scheduler (PS), Power Control (PC), Process Calls (PrC) and Performance Monitoring (PM). AC, LC and PS are cell-based algorithms, whereas PC, PrC and PM are system-based functions. The statistically large enough amount of User Equipments (UEs) in the system does not make it necessary to have them really moving: The mobility effects may be taken into account by e.g. speed dependent E_b/N_0 requirements. Soft handover (SHO) affects mainly AC and PS. In the former, diversity (DHO) branches are processed first, followed by the main branches. In the latter, the bit rate assigned to the radio link set (UE) is the minimum of the bit rates allocated separately (for each cell) to all radio links of the active set. SHO gains may be taken into account in the E_b/N_0 requirements based on SHO condition. Since the system in high traffic situations is downlink capacity limited [5], the presented simulator supports only this direction. The structure to simulate the uplink could be easily implemented using exactly the same concept except that the transmission power levels at base station (BS) would need to be replaced by the received ones. The maximum resolution of the tool is one radio resource indication period (*RRI*), i.e. the time needed to receive the power levels from the base stations. A simulation flowchart is illustrated in Fig. 1.

2.1   Traffic Generator, Models and Mix

Call and session arrivals are generated following a Poisson process [8], and mapped onto the appropriate QoS profiles [1], depending on the carried type of traffic. Circuit switched (CS) speech and video calls are held for an exponentially distributed service time, and their inter-arrival periods follow exactly the same type of distribution [8]. Packet switched services are implemented as an ON/OFF process with truncated distributions [9]. The duration of the ON period depends mainly on the allocated bit rate and object size, which is modeled differently depending on the carried application [10]. Different distributions are also used to model the related OFF time behaviors and session lengths. The utilized traffic models and the adopted traffic mix (in *share of calls*) in this work are listed in Table 1.

All calls/sessions (generated at the beginning of each simulation) are subsequently processed (played back) taking into account the corresponding arrival times, service activities and priorities, hence the name *virtual time* simulator.

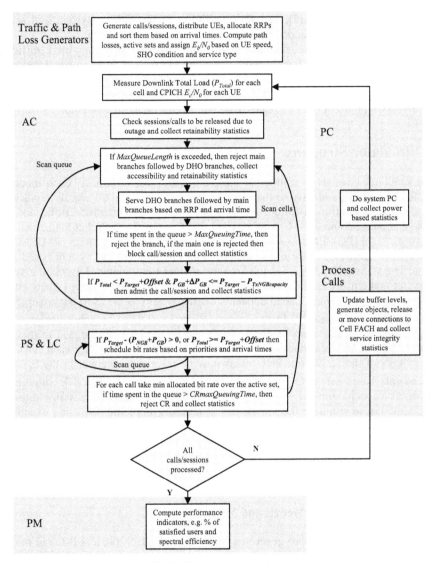

Fig. 1. Simulation flow chart.

2.2 Path Loss Generator

Across the simulation area, each call gets assigned a random position, but also other particular mobile distributions are possible. For each mobile location, the received power levels from all cells are calculated first and then the cells satisfying the SHO conditions are assigned as active. Each cell can be configured separately. For the path loss calculations, the Okumura-Hata model described in [11] and the models defined in [12] are supported. By implementing an appropriate interface it is also possible to import the propagation calculated by another radio network planning tool. Correlated slow fading can be overlaid as described in [8]. Fig. 2 (a) and (b) show the path losses

Table 1. Adopted traffic models and mix.

Service	Data rate (kb/s)	Buffer size (s)	Object size (kB)	Off time (s)	Session length (Objects)	Mix (%)
PoC	8	1	Exponential 6 mean, 0.5 min, 40 max	Exponential 60 mean, 1 min, 1200 max	Geometric 8 mean, 1 min, 30 max	18
Streaming	64	8	Uniform 160 min, 3200 max	-	1	12
MMS	Best Effort	-	Exponential 20 mean, 3 min, 200 max	-	1	5
Dialup	Best Effort	-	Log-normal ($\mu=5$, $\sigma=1.8$) 0.1 min, 20000 max	Pareto ($k=2$, $\alpha=1$) 2 min, 3600 max	Inv. Gaussian ($\mu=3.8$, $\lambda=6$) 1 min, 50 max	15
SWIS	64	1	Exponential 80 mean, 32 min, 2400 max	-	1	10
WAP	Best Effort	-	Log-normal ($\mu=2$, $\sigma=1$) 0.1 min, 50 max	Exponential 20 mean, 1 min, 600 max	Geometric 3 mean, 1 min, 50 max	13
Speech	12.3	-	-	-	Exponential 90 s	20
Video	64	-	-	-	Exponential 120 s	7

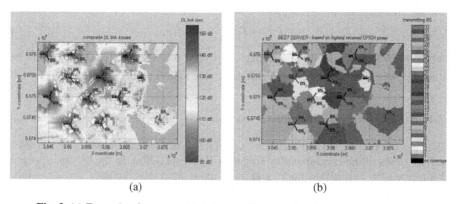

(a)   (b)

Fig. 2. (a) Example of supported link losses; (b) example of cell dominance areas.

and the cell dominance areas for the simulation scenario (downtown Helsinki, Finland) adopted in this work.

2.3 Admission Control Function

When a connection is set up, AC assigns to the bearer in question a *Resource Request Priority (RRP)* value based on its QoS profile. (The lower the RRP value the higher the priority.) New radio link requests are arranged into a queue and served following the strict priority principle (branch additions have top priority) and, at a given priority, based on their arrival times (FIFO). Resource requests are rejected if either the *queue length* or the corresponding *maximum queuing time* is exceeded. Except for the over-load situation, defined by

$$P_{TxTotal} = P_{NGB} + P_{GB} > P_{TxTarget} + \textit{Offset} \qquad (1)$$

where $P_{TxTotal}$ is the total transmission power in the cell due to guaranteed (GB) and non guaranteed bit rate (NGB) traffic and $P_{TxTarget}$ + *Offset* is the overload threshold, NGB bearers are always admitted; whereas GB traffic is blocked if either (1) or the following inequality is satisfied:

$$P_{GB} + \Delta P_{GB} > P_{TxTarget} - P_{TxNGBcapacity} ,$$ (2)

where $P_{TxNGBcapacity}$ is the capacity optionally dedicated to NGB traffic and ΔP_{GB} is the estimated power increase in the best serving cell if the bearer in question is admitted. ΔP_{GB} is calculated using (3), which is a modified version of the formula used in [5] to estimate the initial power when a radio link is established for the first time:

$$\Delta P_{Tx} = \frac{\rho R}{W} \left(\frac{P_{tx,CPICH}}{\rho_c} + (1 - \alpha) P_{TxTarget} - P_{TxTotal} \right),$$ (3)

where ρ and R are the required E_b/N_0 and maximum bit rate of the bearer in question, $P_{tx,CPICH}$ is the power of the common pilot channel, ρ_c is the received CPICH E_c/N_0, W is the chip rate (3.84 Mchip/s), and α is the DL orthogonality factor ($\alpha = 1$ means perfect orthogonality). Ultimately, during SHO, diversity branches are not set up if the following condition is satisfied:

$$P_{GB} + \Delta P_{GB} > P_{TxTarget} + Offset ,$$ (4)

where P_{GB} is the actual non-controllable power in the target cell and ΔP_{GB} is the estimated power increase in the same cell due to the radio link in question.

2.4 Packet (Bit Rate) Scheduler Function

Bit rates of admitted NGB bearers are scheduled based on their actual *RRP* values and arrival times of the corresponding Capacity Requests (CRs). In the bit rate allocation, PS follows the best effort model and relies upon the power budget $P_{NGB,Allowed}$ left by the GB and NGB active (a) and inactive (i) connections, i.e.

$$P_{NGB,Allowed} = P_{TxTarget} - (P_{GB}^a + P_{GB}^i + P_{NGB}^a + k \cdot P_{NGB}^i) .$$ (5)

The power of inactive GB traffic, P_{GB}^i, takes into account the needs of the bearer services just admitted, but not yet on air; whereas the NGB inactive power, P_{NGB}^i, is the one reserved for the bearer services in discontinuous transmission (DTX). k is a weighting factor, which allows the user to specify the amount of total power for inactive NGB connections to be taken into account in the power budget; k ranges from 0 to 1, 1 being the most conservative value. Bit rates are allocated every *scheduling period* by matching the estimated transmission powers to sum up to (5). Power estimates are based on (3). In the case of SHO, the allocated bit rate is the minimum of the bit rates scheduled for each of the links of the radio link set. Capacity requests are rejected if they queue longer than the corresponding *CR maximum queuing time*. Allocated bit rates may be rescheduled only if the ongoing communication has lasted more than the related *granted minimum allocation time*. The bit rate allocation method for the dedicated channel is based on the *minimum and maximum allowed bit rates*, which define, respectively, the lower and upper limits of the allocated Transport Format Set (TFS). In the current implementation, only dedicated transport channels (DCHs) are available for packet data transmission. Bearers that were longer in DTX than the corresponding *inactivity timer* are moved to Cell FACH (Forward Access Channel). In this state, the transmission is temporarily interrupted. When new data arrives at the radio network controller (RNC) buffer, a new CR is sent to PS and subsequently another DCH is allocated to the bearer in question, as explained above.

2.5 Load Control Function

The only load control action supported by the simulator is the reduction of bit rates of NGB bearer services when (1) is satisfied. The bit rate may be downgraded only when the allocation time of the carried service lasted longer than the corresponding *granted overload minimum allocation time*. The bit rates are reduced starting from the bearers with lowest priority and, at given priority, based on their arrival times (FIFO). Power estimates in the bit rate decrease algorithm are based on (3).

2.6 Process Calls Function

All active calls in the system are processed at once each radio resource indication period, as illustrated in Fig. 1. If the ongoing connection is CS, the simulator collects its throughput, increases the active connections counter, and releases the call in the case it lasted longer then the corresponding call duration period (see Table 1). For each packet switched connection, we check first whether either the RNC buffer or the source buffer is not empty. Then, if there is data to transmit, the active session throughput is collected and the active connections counter accordingly increased. Besides this, the status of the corresponding buffer in the UE is monitored and updated. If during the ON period the buffer gets empty, the re-buffering procedure is activated and the user of the service is considered unsatisfied. When the user is reading (or the connection is in idle mode, in the case of PoC), the transfer delay of the delivered object is calculated, the connection is marked as inactive and the inactivity period monitored. If the dwelling time of the DCH in question lasted longer than the corresponding *inactivity timer*, the terminal is moved to Cell FACH state, and the corresponding allocated resources are released. When the reading time is over, either a new object to be downloaded and the corresponding reading time are regenerated, or the ongoing packet communication is released, depending on the corresponding session length (see Table 1). In the former case, if the time needed to fill up the buffer in the terminal is more than the corresponding *buffering delay*, the user of the service in question is recorded as unsatisfied.

2.7 Power Control Function

The simulator supports an ideal power control function that includes the effects of a large-scale propagation channel (see Section 2.2), but not fast fading. Multi-path fading and SHO effects are taken into account in the service E_b/N_0 requirement. The interference is realistically modeled: At any simulation time step, the received power from all cells except from the best server is counted as interference, and hence the corresponding coupling effect is fully taken into account. (Note: Form the best server only the fraction of the power determined by the non-orthogonality is considered as interference.)

The power control system of equations can be written as:

$$\frac{Wp_{i_m} / L_{m,i_m}}{R_{i_m} P_m / L_{m,i_m} (1 - \alpha_{i_m}) + \sum_{n,n \neq m} P_n / L_{n,i_m} + N_{i_m}} = \rho_{i_m},$$

$$i_m \in I(m), \quad m = 1, ..., M \tag{6}$$

where the symbols in (6) are explained in Table 2.

Table 2. Symbols in the PC system of equations.

Symbol	Explanation
I_m	Index of a UE served by BS m
m, n	Indices of BSs
$I(m)$	Set of UE indices served by BS m
M	Number of cells
p_{i_m}	BS transmitted power for UE i_m
P_m, P_n	Total transmit power of BS m and BS n
L_{m,i_m}	Pathloss from BS m to UE i_m served by BS m
L_{n,i_m}	Pathloss from BS n to UE i_m served by BS m
R_{i_m}	Bit rate used by UE i_m
α_{i_m}	Orthogonality factor for UE i_m
N_{i_m}	Noise power (thermal plus equipment) of UE i_m
ρ_{i_m}	Required E_b/N_0 for UE i_m

Equation (6) simply equates the received E_b/N_0 with given transmission powers to the required E_b/N_0 for sufficient quality of the connection. Taking into account that:

$$P_m = \sum_{i_m \in I(m)} p_{i_m} + p_{c,m}, \tag{7}$$

where $p_{c,m}$ is the sum of common channel powers from BS_m, (6) can be rewritten in the compact form as an M times M linear system of equations of the type $Ax = b$, where the unknowns are the total BS powers. During the simulations, we first resolve this linear system and then from (6) we derive the individual radio link powers. The solutions are then used to estimate the transmission powers of GB and NGB services in (1)-(5). AC and PC ensure that the BS total transmission power is kept below its maximum and the WCDMA pole capacity is not exceeded. The existence of solutions to the type (6) of equations was studied e.g. in [13]. The power of common channels is a cell based management parameter (see Section 3).

2.8 Performance Monitoring Function

Several performance indicators can be collected during the *measurement period*, e.g. *call block ratio* (CBR) caused by queuing and/or buffer overflow, *call drop ratio* (CDR) due to power outage, *active session throughput* (AST), *capacity request rejec-*

tion ratio (CRRR) for NGB traffic, *object transfer delay* for Browsing, MMS and Dialup connections, and *re-buffering* for streaming, PoC and SWIS applications. *Link and cell based powers*, as well as CPICH E_c/N_0 values are also computed during the simulated time. From such measurements is derived the *geometry factor* (G), defined as the ratio between the received power from the serving cell and the power received from the surrounding cells plus noise [5].

System and service performances can be assessed as recommended in [8], and for this purpose tailored *user satisfaction* criteria can be input to the simulator. In this work, a speech or video user is satisfied if the call neither gets blocked nor dropped. In addition to this criterion, for PoC, SWIS and streaming users no re-buffering is allowed during the communication, and the time to fill up the related buffer needs to be reasonably short; for Dialup (http, emails, ftp, etc...), WAP browsing, and MMS, the AST has to be higher than 64 kb/s, 32 kb/s and 8 kb/s, respectively. Furthermore, none of the capacity requests of NGB services must be rejected. The *spectral efficiency* is computed as the system load (cell throughput normalized with respect to the chip rate, 3.84 Mchip/s) at which a certain percentage of users of the worst performing service are satisfied. Different thresholds can be set for the distinct bearers, though 90% is the default value for all applications.

3   Simulation Environment and Assumptions

Speech, video and SWIS were offered with guaranteed bit rate, and all other services were run on the best effort. Speech and video calls were served as CS-Conversational, whereas SWIS was carried on PS-Streaming class. PoC, streaming and WAP/MMS were mapped onto PS-Interactive. Dialup connections, which comprised, for example, ftp, emails and http traffic, were carried on PS-Background class. The RRP values were set such that speech calls had top priority, followed by video and SWIS calls. Within the Interactive class, using different traffic handling priorities (THPs), PoC was handled first, followed by streaming and WAP/MMS. Dialup was served in the end. The differentiated parameter values, which further improve PoC and streaming performance at the expenses of lower priority services, and the mapping of the services onto distinct QoS profiles are illustrated in Table 3. Performance results were analyzed using a macro cellular network located in the downtown of Helsinki (see Fig. 3), where terminals were uniformly randomly distributed, but not on the water. The simulation was performed over a period of 2 hours using a time step of 200 ms (RRI period), and all statistics were collected over the entire simulation period. The traffic mix and the traffic intensity were held constant, i.e. 2 call/session attempts per second. The corresponding offered traffic was about 750 users per cell over the all simulated time. Table 4 reports the most important network parameters.

Table 3. Mapping of services onto QoS classes and parameter values.

QoS Profile	Service	Bit Rate (kb/s)	RRP	Min. All. Bit Rate (kb/s)	AC Max. Queuing Time (s)	Granted Min. DCH Alloc. Time (s)	Granted Min. DCH Alloc.Time in Overload (s)	Buffering Delay (s)	Inactivity Timer (s)	CR Max. Queuing Time (s)
CS-conv.	Speech	12.2	1	GB	5	-	-	-	-	-
	Video	64	2	GB	10	-	-	-	-	-
PS-stream.	SWIS	64	3	GB	10	-	-	5	-	-
PS-int. THP1	PoC	0, 8	4	8	15	15	10	4	60	4
THP2	Streaming	0, 64	5	64	15	10	5	16	5	10
THP3	WAP/MMS	0, 16, 32, 64, 128, 144, 256, 384	6	32	15	5	0.2	-	10	10
PS-backg.	Dialup	0, 16, 32, 64, 128, 144, 256, 384	7	16	15	1	0.2	-	5	5

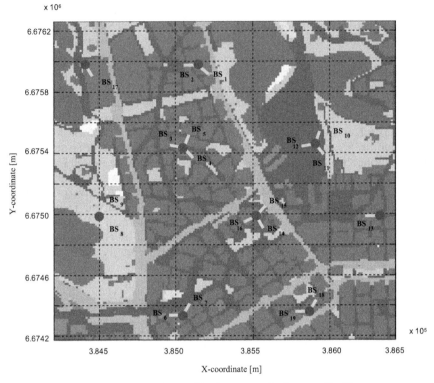

Fig. 3. Simulation scenario used in the case study discussed in this paper.

Table 4. Most important system based parameters.

Parameter	Value
Call/session mean arrival rate	0.5 s
Radio resource indication period (*RRI*)	0.2 s
Simulation time (s)	7200 s
Power target for DL AC	3 dB below BTS total power
Overload offset for DL AC	1 dB above power target
Orthogonality (α)	0.5
Period for load control actions	0.2 s (1 RRI)
Period for Packet Scheduling	0.2 s (1 RRI)
E_b/N_0 requirements	
Speech	7 dB
SWIS	6 dB
Streaming	6 dB
PoC	7 dB
MMS/WAP	5/5.5 dB
Dialup	5.5 dB
Maximum BTS Tx power	43 dBm
P-CPICH Tx power	33 dBm
Sum of all other CCH Tx powers	30 dBm
Length of AC queue	10 Radio bearers
Dedicated NGB capacity	0 dB, i.e. not used
Power weight for inactive NGB traffic (k)	0.5

4 Simulation Results and Discussion

The simulation results of the case presented in the previous section are shown through Fig. 4 to Fig. 8 and in Table 5. The offered traffic mix over the all simulated period is illustrated for each of the simulated cells in Fig. 4 (a). Fig. 4 (b) illustrates the average cell throughput as a function of the deployed cells and services. From these graphs, taking into account the traffic models and mix reported in Table 1, we conclude that the *traffic generator works as planned*.

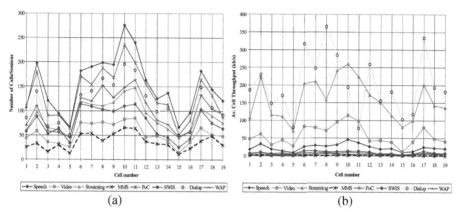

Fig. 4. Traffic distribution over the 19 cells: (a) Offered load in call arrivals; (b) average cell throughputs (service based values in kb/s for each of the simulated cells).

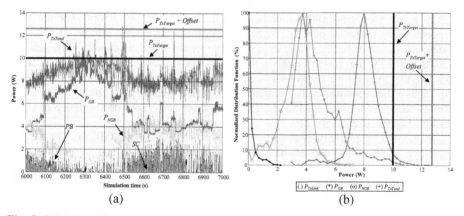

Fig. 5. Cell 11: (a) Snapshot of the simulation period; (b) normalized distribution functions of the radio link (.), GB (*), NGB (o), and total (+) downlink transmission power.

A snapshot (1000 s) of the load status in Cell 11 (see Fig. 3), where most of the users resulted unsatisfied, is depicted in Fig. 5 (a). The values plotted against the simulation time are the transmission powers, the power budget (*PB*) and scheduled capacity (*SC*). From this figure, we can notice that *all supported QoS management functions work as intended*. In fact, the power budget for NGB traffic, defined in (5) and denoted by *PB* in the figure, is properly scheduled, i.e. at a given NGB traffic volume and available bit rates, the curve of the allocated bit rates (*SC*) closely follows the *PB* one. Hence, the scheduling algorithm presented in Section 2.4 turns out to perform as well as expected. Besides this, when the total load in the cell ($P_{TxTotal}$, i.e. $P_{GB} + P_{NGB}$) reaches the overload threshold, denoted by $P_{TxTotal}$ + *Offset*, the NGB allocated bit rates are accordingly reduced by LC and in turn immediately resumed when the P_{GB} decreases and the system backs off to its normal state of operation. Furthermore, the measured GB load (P_{GB}) hardly ever trespasses the target threshold ($P_{TxTarget}$) defined in (2), which confirms the accuracy of (3) in the power estimates during the admission control and bit rate allocations. Ultimately, following the input traffic mix, $P_{TxTotal}$ preserves its point of equilibrium ($P_{TxTarget}$), which thus validates the supported AC and PC functions.

The normalized distribution functions of the transmission powers in Cell 11 are shown in Fig. 5 (b). The radio link power (P_{TxLink}), GB transmission power (P_{GB}), NGB transmission power (P_{NGB}) and total downlink transmission power ($P_{TxTotal}$) distributions reflect exactly the load status in the cell previously discussed, the input parameter values reported in Table 4, and the constraints in the RRM functions defined in Section 2.3, 2.4, 2.5 and 2.7.

None of the calls/sessions was rejected due to buffer overflow and almost none of the speech, video and SWIS calls was blocked due to the time spent in the AC queue, as shown in Table 5 in terms of call block ratio (CBR). This is in line with the offered traffic, which hardly ever exploited the available cell capacity. As a result, almost all users of the GB services resulted satisfied.

The effects of the prioritization between GB services can be noticed in Fig. 6 (a), where the percentage of satisfied users for each of the deployed services is illustrated as a function of the simulated cells. In Cell 10 and 11, the quality experienced by speech users, in terms of CBR, is better than the accessibility offered to SWIS and video users. As expected, more evident in the figure is the differentiated treatment of NGB traffic, which reflects exactly the provisioned discrimination between real time (RT) and non-real time (NRT) services of Interactive and Background classes. In fact, in each of the simulated cells, the percentage of satisfied users of Dialup is the lowest, followed by WAP and MMS; and for the RT services, PoC performance is always better than the streaming one.

A more detailed analysis upon the reason why the users of NGB services were not satisfied is possible based on the raw performance indicators illustrated in Fig. 6 (b), Fig. 7, and in Fig. 8 (a). In these figures, the intended differentiation between services in terms of the metrics characterizing the QoE of each of the deployed services is also visible. In particular, Fig. 6 (b) and Fig. 7 (a) show, respectively, the 10th percentile of the average active session throughput (AST) and the capacity request rejection ratio (CRRR) collected for each of the above services during the measurement period, as a function of the deployed cells. The throughput experienced by Dialup users is lower than the corresponding one offered to WAP/MMS users, which underwent the same treatment. Conversely, the accessibility offered to PoC and streaming services, while requesting capacity to PS, is better than the corresponding blocking experienced by WAP/MMS and Dialup users. Fig. 7 (b) reveals how the throughput deterioration adversely affects the PoC and streaming performance in terms of re-buffering in the UE. As expected, the re-buffering ratio is higher for streaming, whereas the dissatisfaction due to "too long time to refill up the buffer" depicted in Fig. 8 (a) is higher for PoC. This is due to the fact that the tolerance for streaming users (up to sixteen seconds) was higher than for PoC ones, which were not supposed to wait for more than four seconds (see Table 3).

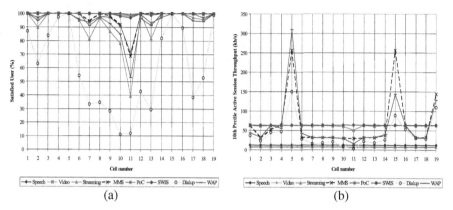

(a)   (b)

Fig. 6. Service based indicators for each of the simulated cells: (a) Percentage of satisfied users; (b) 10th percentile of the average active session throughput during the simulated time.

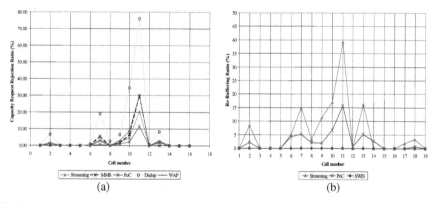

(a)   (b)

Fig. 7. Service based performance indicators for each of the simulated cells: (a) Capacity request rejection ratio; (b) re-buffering ratio.

The differentiation between WAP/MMS and Dialup connections and the benefit of thereof is also shown in Fig. 8 (b) and Table 5, where the transfer delays of the WAP, MMS and Dialup objects during the simulation period are presented. The measured metrics reflect exactly the calculated object delay from the median of the AST and object size, which is an additional evidence that the process call and performance monitoring functions (see Fig. 1, Section 2.6 and 2.8) work as intended.

5   Conclusions

An effective solution to study the provisioning of QoS before the deployment of new services throughout UTRAN was presented. As a part of this framework, the currently supported QoS management functions were investigated in terms of: Offered traffic mix, transmission powers, throughput, queuing time, object transfer delay, call block ratio, call drop ratio, capacity request rejection ratio, and percentage of satisfied users. Simulation results showed the proposed *virtual time* simulator to perform as expected and to be a good trade off between the complexity of an advanced *dynamic* simulator and the straightforwardness of a *quasi-static* tool. Thus, the described solution has the potential for investigating any QoS management algorithm and multimedia service provisioning in UTRAN, before its deployment throughout a real WCDMA network. Furthermore, the simulator may be used to find an optimum trade-off between service quality, capacity and coverage requirements for any of the services in a 3G mobile network operator's service portfolio.

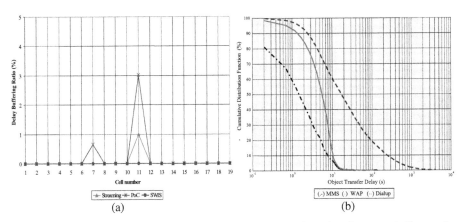

Fig. 8. (a) Too long time needed for re-buffering ratio (service based performance indicators for each of the simulated cells); (b) MMS, WAP and Dialup object transfer delays (system based statistics upon all simulated time).

Table 5. System based measurement results.

Service type	CBR (%)	CDR (%)	CRRR (%)	RBR (%)	DBR (%)	Median AST (kb/s)	Median Object Size (kB)	Calculated Object Delay (s)	SU (%)
Speech	0.05	0.00	-	-	-	12.2	-	-	99.95
Video	0.16	0.00	-	-	-	64.0	-	-	99.84
Streaming	0.00	0.00	1.93	6.35	0.05	63.4	1682	212.2	91.67
MMS	0.00	0.00	2.29	-	-	70.5	15	1.7	97.55
PoC	0.00	0.03	1.08	2.49	0.19	8.0	4	4.0	96.31
SWIS	0.32	0.00	-	0.00	0.00	64.0	89	11.1	99.68
Dialup	0.00	0.00	8.44	-	-	51.4	120	18.7	59.94
WAP	0.00	0.05	2.57	-	-	66.0	48	5.8	94.24

Note: RBR = Re-Buffering Ratio, DBR = Delay Buffering Ratio; SU = Satisfied Users

References

1. 3GPP, TS 23.107: QoS Concept and Architecture
2. Wacker, A., Laiho, J., Sipilä, K., Jäsberg, M.: Static Simulator for Studying WCDMA Radio Network Planning Issues. Proceedings of VTC, IEEE, Vol.3. Spring (1999) 2436–2440
3. Hämäläinen, S., Holma, H., Sipilä, K.: Advanced WCDMA Radio Network Simulator. Proceedings of PIMRC, IEEE. Aalborg, Denmark (1999) 509–604
4. Holma, H., Toskala, A. (eds.): WCDMA for UMTS. John Wiley & Sons, Revised Edition (2001) 313 p
5. Laiho, J., Wacker, A., Novosad, T. (eds.): Radio Network Planning and Optimization for UMTS. John Wiley & Sons (2002) 484 p
6. Soldani, D., Laiho, J.: A Virtual Time Simulator for Studying QoS Management Functions in UTRAN. Proceedings of VTC, IEEE, Vol. 5. Fall (2003) 3453–3457
7. Halonen, T., Romero, J., Melero, J. (eds.): GSM, GPRS and EDGE Performance. John Wiley & Sons, Second Edition (2003) 615 p
8. ETSI, TR 101 112 (UMTS 30.03) v.3.2.0: Selection Procedures for the Choice of Radio Transmission Technologies of the UMTS
9. Shankaranarayanan, N., Jiang, Z., Mishra, P.: User-Perceived Performance of Web-Browsing and Interactive Data in HFC Cable Access Networks. Proceedings of ICC, IEEE, Vol. 4. (2001) 1264–1268
10. Klemm, C.L., Lohmann, M.: Traffic Models for Characterization of UMTS Networks. Proceedings of GLOBECOM, IEEE, Vol. 3. (2001) 1741–1746
11. COST 231, TD(91)73: Urban Transmission Loss Models for Mobile Radio in the 900 and 1800 MHz Bands
12. ITU-R M. 1225: Guidelines for Evaluation of Radio Transmission Technologies for IMT-2000. (1997)
13. Hanly, S.V.: Information Capacity of Radio Networks. Ph.D. Dissertation, Kings College, University of Cambridge (1993) 225 p

Event-Based Programming Structures for Multimedia Information Flows

Kaliappa Ravindran[1] and Ali Sabbir[2]

[1] City College of CUNY and Graduate Center,
Department of Computer Science,
Convent Avenue at 138th Street,
New York, NY 10031, USA
ravi@cs.ccny.cuny.edu

[2] CUNY Graduate Center, Computer Science,
365 Fifth Avenue,
New York, NY 10016, USA
asabbir@hotmail.com

Abstract. In this paper, we propose a programming model based on 'timed event dissemination' for structuring a distributed real-time multimedia presentation. In this model, event notifications capture program-generated actions and/or user-level object accesses on a multimedia window. A coherent effect of these actions requires enforcing deadlines on the event processing over prescribed time intervals. To meet this requirement, the paper advocates an integration of the 'flow of time' as part of the semantics of data presentation on a multimedia window. The paper explores a programming paradigm for event processing: *causal ordering* of timed messages, to realize multimedia data presentations. This yields simplicity and uniformity in the programming structure of multimedia applications. The presentation specifications in our model can be easily and accurately mapped onto system-level QOS parameters (such as network delays and play-out buffer delays) for scheduling purposes. This in turn may lead to an optimal use of the system resources by a multimedia presentation protocol. The generality of our event-oriented programming interface also allows reducing the multimedia system development costs through software reuse.

1 Introduction

A real-time presentation system (RPS) collects the data of various source entities, transports the data through the underlying network, and delivers the data at destination entities for consumption [1]. During a processing of data, maintaining the required temporal association between the data of various streams is necessary in the presence of system induced delays and asynchrony (e.g., multimedia synchronization). This is possible, from the RPS perspective, by segmenting the data streams into application perceivable distinct units along the real-time axis and exercising *temporal presentation control* on these data segments at users. In a multimedia document access for example, a user activity may possibly consist

J. Vicente and D. Hutchison (Eds.): MMNS 2004, LNCS 3271, pp. 255–268, 2004.
© IFIP International Federation for Information Processing 2004

of graphic input from a menu using mouse click to highlight a certain portion of the document and text input from a keyboard and audio input from a voice phone to annotate an update on the document. Here, the text input may need to be presented at a user station after the mouse click within, say, 2-3 seconds (*sec*). Thus a temporal presentation involves extracting the timing relationship between various data segments collected at sources and determining the delivery times of these data segments at receivers for processing.

The above temporal presentation control depicts a *user-level view* of synchronizing the occurrence of multiple types of data. To support this view, the RPS should embody an application-level specification of temporal presentation control requirements on data. Using this specification, an underlying protocol may implement a set of network level and end-system level mechanisms to meet the data presentation requirements.

The presentation control information is typically made available to the RPS in the form of *quality of service* (QOS) parameters that indicate the various temporal characteristics of data presentation. For instance, how long the processing of a data x at a user can be deferred with respect to that of another data y is specifiable as a QOS parameter. The end-system mechanisms deal with generating real-time *presentation schedules* that control the processing times of data units at various system elements in the path to receivers, so that the QOS parameters specified can be met (by buffering and sequencing the data across the transport-application layer interface). If, for instance, the data x is scheduled for processing at time T but arrives at a receiver at time $(T - t)$, it is buffered by the end-system protocol for a duration of t before presentation to the user. As can be seen, the QOS specification and the underlying presentation protocols form essential parts of a RPS.

This paper provides a flexible and canonical specification model for presentation QOS that can be transcribed onto a communication system. The model is based on application specifiable segmentation of data streams, and playing out data segments in a certain order and in a timely manner, based on the temporal relationships between them.

A key feature of our model is the integration of real-time constraints into a *causal ordering* of data segments (or messages) that flow between end-systems to manipulate user-level objects. In this notion, the messages exchanged between various objects flow in a prescribed order and within prescribed intervals inducing 'state changes' in them (e.g., generation of visual cues in human mind by a video clip that annotates a graphics image display). The application-specific enforcement of presentation control allows flexibility in generating play-out schedules of data and optimizes the usage of system resources to application needs. The paper provides methods to derive the system-level QOS requirements from application-specified information (through APIs) and to parameterize the protocol procedures with this QOS.

The paper is organized as follows: Section 2 describes our model of causal ordering based real-time data presentation. Section 3 describes the specification construct that incorporates the presentation model. Section 4 describes the protocol procedures to derive network QOS parameters from presentation specifications. Section 5 compares our notion of causal ordering with extensions made to Lamport's 'logical clock'-based message ordering. Section 6 concludes the paper.

2   Model of Timed Data Presentation

A real-time data stream may be segmented into application-specific units for end-to-end transport and synchronization (e.g., a voice clip in multimedia lecturing). The presentation-level processing of a data segment (or message) involves the generation and/or dissemination of device-specific information elements carried in the message over a prescribed time interval. In this section, we describe a temporal characterization of the data presentation problem, which will allow us to determine the structure of presentation-level primitives.

2.1   Sensory Perception of Data

If t'_m and t_m indicate the time of generation of a message m by the data source (i.e., server) and the start time of play-out of m at a receiver respectively, then $t_m \geq t'_m + \overline{D}$, where $\overline{D}$ is the delay suffered by m in various system elements implementing the message path (such as the network and play-out scheduling buffers). Where multiple inter-stream messages are involved, the play-out of m may be additionally delayed pending the play-out of one or more other messages.

Fast responsiveness and improved cohesiveness at user level requires that the effects of m be seen: i) before the deadline imposed by the timeliness requirements of m, and   ii) after the persistence effects message(s) prior to m have already ceased. The timeliness condition may be expressed in terms of the maximum allowed *latency* β_m between the generation and dissemination of m:

$$t_m \leq (t'_m + \beta_m). \tag{1}$$

As example, the layout diagram of a construction building may need to be presented within, say, 1-2 *sec* after requesting the multimedia server, with video and voice illustrations of the diagram timed in a way to enable a virtual tour of the building. If we assume that the designer should see a layout display on the local workstation in response to a point-and-click action within 0.5 *sec* and the upstream delay in network paths is 50 *msec*, we can set $\beta_m \approx 0.45$ *sec*. When $\overline{D} < \beta_m$, the presentation of m can start sooner than the deadline set by β_m. The play-out time of message m should satisfy the following relation:

$$t_m > t_{m_x} + \delta_{m_x} + \zeta_{m_x}, \tag{2}$$

where m depicts the next action upon seeing message m_x, δ_{m_x} is the play-out time of m_x (i.e., the time over which the data units of m_x are delivered to the end-device for processing) and ζ_{m_x} indicates how long the effects of m_x persist in the application. The choice of t_m needs to account for any user-level 'thinking time' required after the sensing of m_x that will allow generation of the context for m. The 'thinking time' requirement imposes a minimum separation between the occurrence of a set of successive messages. The relation (2) models the passage of real-time with intervals of duration large enough to accommodate the data persistence and user-level thinking effects. In an example of displaying text sequences in a workstation window, δ_m may be 2 *sec* and ζ_m may vary, say, from 1 *sec* to 3 *sec*. From equations (1) and (2), the 'thinking time' and the allowed latency of messages may be related as:

$$(t_{m_x} + \delta_{m_x} + \zeta_{m_x}) < (t'_m + \beta_m). \tag{3}$$

Overall, a data stream is representable by a timed sequence of messages $[\cdots, m_x, m, \cdots]$, with the inter-message separation determined by the user-level 'thinking time' required on m and the persistence duration $(\delta_m + \zeta_m)$.

2.2 'Real-Time Persistence' Based Causal Ordering

The temporal relationships among activities on a user-level object prescribe the order and the real-time intervals in which the messages depicting these activities are presented to users. How these relationships are captured and processed by the RPS is the focus of our paper.

Given two messages y and x describing actions on an object, the relation '$y \succ x$' denotes that x should occur after the persistence duration of y has elapsed and within a certain time limit T^{max}. The meaning is that the state change in the object caused by y persists over a real-time interval $[t_y, t_y + \delta_y + \zeta_y]$ providing the context for a state change by x, where $T^{max} \geq [t_x - (t_y + \delta_y + \zeta_y) + \delta_x + \zeta_x]$. In the earlier example, voice clip may (say) be presented 2 *sec* after the icon highlighting, and persist for a 3 *sec* duration. We refer to the relationship $y \succ x$ as 'x causally depends on y', which depicts a schedule $t_x > t_y + \delta_y + \zeta_y$. When neither $x \succ y$ nor $y \succ x$ is specifiable, y and x are said to be concurrent, denoted as $\| \{x, y\}$. Here, it does not matter whether an object executes x followed by y or vice versa, or simultaneously, as long as the actions are executed within the time limit T^{max}, i.e.,

$$T^{max} \geq max(\{(\delta_y + \zeta_y), (t_x - t_y + \delta_x + \zeta_x)\}) \text{ for } t_y \leq t_x$$
$$T^{max} \geq max(\{(\delta_x + \zeta_x), (t_y - t_x + \delta_y + \zeta_y)\}) \text{ for } t_x \leq t_y.$$

Causal ordering of messages allows solving the data presentation problem in an application-specific manner. The underlying program structure is uniform across applications: namely, the synchronization of user operations on an object by a temporally ordered processing of the messages. For use with RPS however, the current notions of message causality – defined over 'logical time' – need to be extended for integrating the 'flow of real-time'.

2.3 Temporal Intervals

A presentation activity can generate multiple messages, such as a video clip, text information and cursor marker, as part of a single update action on a document[1].

---

[1] A 'video clip' is treated as a single message for presentation purposes. A lower level system layer may however treat the 'video clip' as consisting of a timed sequence of picture data frames to be delivered at presentation entities.

Accordingly, we need to treat the various component messages as bundled together by the temporal relationships between them. A temporal interval is the real-time duration over which the effects of all messages generated by a presentation activity can persist, given as T^{max}. An interval basically indicates the granularity of real-time meaningful to the application, and hence constitutes the unit of segmentation of real-time axis. See Figure 1.

Since a message is the basic unit supported by the RPS in terms of which presentation activities are constructed, the ordering relationship among various activities is transcribed directly onto the corresponding messages. In the earlier example, the highlighting mark on the city map and the text and voice annotation by a user are deemed to occur over a single temporal interval. These messages cannot be interleaved with messages of other activities, since user attention on the map pertains to one activity at a time. On the other hand, messages pertaining to activities on unrelated objects can be interleaved in different ways.

PRESENTATION SYSTEM IN A WORKSTATION

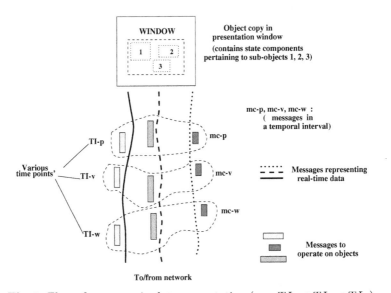

Fig. 1. Flow of messages in data presentation (say, $TI_p < TI_v < TI_w$)

Thus, temporal intervals provide an elegant framework for distributed programming of functions to access and manipulate user-level objects.

2.4   Synchronization Specifications

The temporal ordering relationship between presentation activities on an object determines the extent of concurrency possible in their execution. To reap this concurrency, we need to be able to specify and enforce the required order of occurrence of the corresponding messages, so that they may interleave with one another in many possible ways.

Many existing techniques to determine these requirements are based on time-stamps, whereby a message with a time stamp T is declared to occur after all messages with a time stamp lower than T [2]. These techniques are less suitable for use by RPS, because the human-oriented nature of data presentations allows synchronization constraints that can be weaker [3] than what the RPS is able to infer bottom-up from the message flows incident on it. Precisely extracting the constraints in turn allows exploiting the concurrency more effectively, and hence offers an increased performance potential of the RPS.

Accordingly, we need a programming interface that allows extracting the intended synchronization requirements at the user level. For example, a text annotation to a document update may need to occur after a voice annotation. As another example, a text annotation and a video clip describing a scene can occur in parallel, even though they may be sent one after the other by the source. Such requirements, extracted during execution of a data presentation, can then be used by a protocol in the RPS to determine the scheduling required on messages to move them through various system elements in the path leading to clients (such as network links and play-out buffers).

3   Object-Level Message Ordering

The specification of causal dependency relations between messages needs to be embedded into programming primitives that allow the presentation of messages at user entities. The synchronization related features we embed into the primitives are described below.

3.1   Specification of Causal Relationships

The application provides a declarative specification of message ordering dependencies. A user entity specifies the temporal ordering of a message z relative to a message y (i.e., $y \succ z$) with the following primitive:

$$((z, p_z),\ Occurs\_After(y, l_z, u_z)),$$

where $p_z = (\delta_z + \zeta_z)$, l_z is the minimum time that should elapse since the occurrence of y, and u_z is the maximum time that can elapse. The parameter l_z is based on the user-level 'thinking time' required when the action y occurs so that the context for processing a next action z can be generated. The parameter u_z captures the maximum allowed user-level 'responsiveness time' in disseminating the action z once y is seen to have occurred. Given that $u_z > l_z > 0$, the time interval over which z can be played-out is determined from $t_z \in [t_y + \delta_y + l_z, t_y + \delta_y + u_z]$ and δ_z. When $Occurs\_After$(NULL) is specified, z can be processed without any constraint, i.e., immediately upon arrival from the network.

In the earlier example, the concurrent delivery of text and voice annotations to the highlighting mark on a city map, as captured by the causal relation 'highlight $\succ \|\{\text{text}, \text{voice}\}$', may be specified as (times are in seconds):

$$((\text{text}, 5),\ Occurs\_After(\text{highlight}, 2, 4))$$
$$((\text{voice}, 4.5)),\ Occurs\_After(\text{highlight}, 3, 5)),$$

with, say, $\delta_{\text{highlight}} = 1.25$. The time intervals for these messages are given by: $[t_{\text{highlight}} + 1.25 + min(\{2,3\}),\ t_{\text{highlight}} + 1.25 + max(\{4+5, 5+4.5\}))]$.

The *Occurs_After* is basically a programming notation to explicitly construct the causal ordering relation ($\succ$). The causal order constraints are carried in messages for use by the underlying protocols to enforce play-out of the messages in an appropriate sequence and over specified real-time intervals. In this aspect, the persistence parameter p_z may correspond to the 'explicit time duration' allowed in SMIL (the WWW Consortium's S̲ynchronized M̲ultimedia I̲ntegration L̲anguage [4]).

3.2   Dependency on Multiple Messages

An extended form of the *Occurs_After* construct allows a user to specify complex ordering relationships with AND and OR 'logical connectives' on causally precedent messages. For instance, the AND connective for 2 messages takes the form:

$$((z, p_z),\ Occurs\_After(y_1 \land y_2, l, u)),$$

which indicates that z be processed after both y_1 and y_2, with l and u being relative to the latest of y_1 and y_2 (note that $\|\{y_1, y_2\}$). In the previous example, the user may display, say, an annotation on the graphics image to give visual cues for the text and voice information. This may be specified as:

$$((graphics, 3.25),\ Occurs\_After(\text{text} \land \text{voice},\ 2.5,\ 3.5)).$$

The time interval for occurrence of 'graphics' message is:

$$[max(\{t_{\text{text}} + 5, t_{\text{voice}} + 4.5\}) + 2.5,\ max(\{t_{\text{text}} + 5, t_{\text{voice}} + 4.5\}) + 3.5 + 3.25].$$

See Figure 2 for an illustration. The '$\land$' operator linking z to $y_1, y_2, \cdots$ has a stronger semantics than the 'par' construct allowed by SMIL, in that the '$\land$' prescribes a concrete parallel composition of operations relative to z.

A causal dependency based on OR 'logical connective' is similar to the 'switch' element of SMIL. Again, in a 2-message case, it takes the form:

$$((z, \delta_z),\ Occurs\_After(y_1 \lor y_2, l, u)),$$

indicating that z be processed after either y_1 or y_2 (or both), with l and u being relative to whichever occurs the earliest during execution. In one scenario for example, user annotation on a graphics image may be generated right after the text or voice information, specified as:

$$((graphics, 3.25),\ Occurs\_After(\text{text} \lor \text{voice},\ 2.5,\ 3.5)).$$

The '$\lor$' operator can induce non-determinism in a program execution, with non-reproducible event sequences. The non-determinism may however be restricted to within the current temporal interval.

For brevity, we consider only AND dependencies.

Various points along time-axis for
$((z, p_z),\quad Occurs\_After\,(\,y,\,l_z\,,\,u_z\,))$

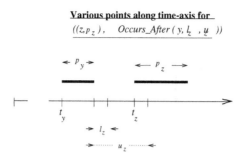

Time-points for sample scenario of text, voice, graphics and highlighting data presentation

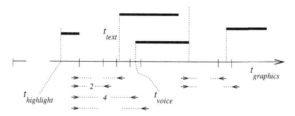

Fig. 2. Illustration of $Occurs\_After$ specifications

3.3 System Delay Specifications

The message-level asynchrony captured by causality behavior is incorporated in a 'quality of service' specification QOS_{pres}. The parameters specified in QOS_{pres} may be used to: i) generate a specification of the system delay behavior, and ii) generate a play-out schedule for data segments arriving through system elements. These functions are incorporated as distinct elements in a synchronization protocol. See Figure 3.

A main feature of delay specification is the allowed end-to-end latency $\overline{D}_q$ on media messages. For interactive multimedia applications (e.g., multi-player video game), $\overline{D}_q$ is set low – say, less than 100 $msec$. For applications with less user-level interactivity (such as 'multimedia lecture presentation' to an audience), $\overline{D}_q$ can be high. Given a set of messages to be presented in a temporal interval, the presentation protocol in the RPS sifts through the $Occurs\_After$ specifications on various messages for determining $\overline{D}_q$. Since the user-specified parameter $(u_z - l_z)$ indicates the variability allowed in the presentation times of a message z relative to its causally precedent message (i.e., the extent of asynchrony), $\overline{D}_q$ has a direct relationship to this user-level parameter.

A higher value of $\overline{D}_q$ allows sending a message over a transport path with longer message queues and/or containing lower bit-rate communication links. Consider, for example, the sending of a 15 sec MPEG-1 video clip followed by a 10 sec 'thinking time'. The message carrying the video clip consists of 4.05 $mbytes$ of data, generating a bit rate of 2.16 $mbps$ over the 15 sec duration (obtained from trace analysis experiments). When sent over a 1.8 $mbps$ link, the

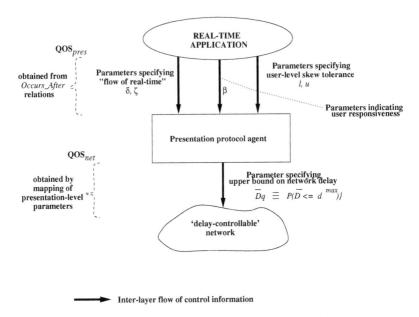

Fig. 3. Mapping of application parameters to network delay behaviors

presentation at a receiver has to start about 3 *sec* later, in comparison to sending over a 2.16 *mbps* link. So choosing a 1.8 *mbps* link (against a 2.16 *mbps* link) is possible only when $\overline{D}_q > 3$ *sec*. In general, message-level asynchrony captures the user tolerance to latency in data presentations.

$\overline{D}_q$ may often be specified in terms of a bound on the message delays incurred by the network. Another aspect is whether a delay bound is enforced by the network deterministically or probabilistically, with the former requiring a higher allocation of resources in data paths through the network than the latter. In general, the delay specification on the network may be expressed in terms of a delay bound d^{max} in the form:

$$\overline{D}_q \equiv \{(X, P(\overline{D} \leq X))\}_{\forall X \in (d^{min}, d^{max}]}$$

for $d^{max} > d^{min} > 0$, where d^{min} is the minimum delay suffered by messages flowing through system elements and $P(\overline{D} \leq X)$ depicts the probability distribution of the actual message delay incurred. $P(\overline{D} \leq d^{max}) = 1.0$ and $P(\overline{D} \leq d^{max}) < 1.0$ refer to a deterministically delay-bounded path and a probabilistically delay-bounded path respectively. Note that it is the 'data path' from a multimedia server to clients that is subject to delay specification $\overline{D}_q$ (we assume, without loss of generality, that the 'control path' from a client to the server incurs negligible delay).

The media level concurrency prescribed through *Occurs_After* relations translates into message-level asynchrony. The latter in turn can be mapped to the allowed variability in network delays incurred on messages (i.e., a specification of $\overline{D}_q$). Refer to Figure 3.

4   Specifying Delay Controllability

The underlying presentation protocol should take into account the message deadlines prescribed by applications and the resource demands imposed on networks, when specifying a value for d^{max}. The tradeoffs to be considered are as follows (see Figure 4):

- Specifying a large value of d^{max} will reduce the amount of resource demands imposed on the network but may result in some of the messages missing their presentation deadlines;
- Specifying a smaller value of d^{max} will increase the amount of resource demands on the network, but can eliminate the likelihood of messages missing their deadlines.

Also, a higher probability of enforcing a given delay bound places larger resource demands on the network, with a deterministic enforcement of the bound imposing the maximum resource demands[2].

4.1   Presentation Skew Due to Delays

Given a set of messages $\{m\}$, the condition $d^{min}+p_m < \beta_m$ will ensure a non-zero probability of presenting a message m. Assuming that messages are not generated ahead of time (as in many live presentation settings), the condition $d^{max}+p_m < \beta_m$ is necessary to avoid a non-presentation of m due to an insufficient life-span of m. As can be seen, the delay specification is relative to the life-span of messages prescribed through β parameters.

Messages can miss their deadlines under two circumstances: when probabilistic delay bounds are specified for network paths (i.e., $P(\overline{D} \le d^{max}) < 1.0 \ \forall \ d^{max} \in \mathcal{R}^+$) or when lax bounds are specified (i.e., d^{max} is set to a value higher than that prescribed by the β parameters). A higher degree of laxity in message delivery, specified through a lower probability of enforcing a given delay bound, may result in more messages missing their presentation deadlines. This in turn may increase the frequency of *glitches* seen by users when accessing the object. So the level of user tolerance to presentation glitches has a bearing on the extent to which delay bounds need to be enforced. Since a probabilistic delay bound imposes less demand on network resources in comparison to a deterministic bound, a lax user tolerance can be mapped to a reduced resource allocation.

4.2   Handling of Missed Deadlines

A presentation skew may sometimes exceed the application-level tolerance limits (as set by the u parameter), manifesting as a glitch in the presentation of messages to the application. As an illustrative analysis of the problem of presentation misses, we map the probability distribution governing the network delay

---

[2] See [5] for a quantitative study of the underlying message scheduling mechanisms to realize 'parameterizable delay' networks.

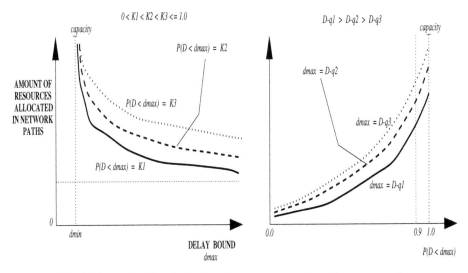

Fig. 4. Network delay behaviors from resource allocation perspective

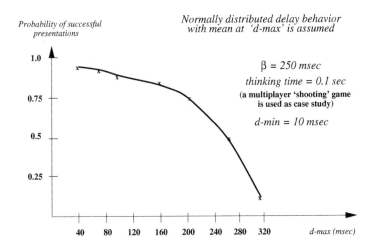

Fig. 5. Presentation probability versus network delay behaviors

behavior on individual messages (in terms of d^{max}) into a probability that one or more messages from a set of concurrently generated y_j's will meet their deadlines. Figure 5 shows an analysis of the likelihood of successful presentations for a network that enforces probabilistic delay bounds.

Recovery from a glitch may often depend on how long the glitch effects persist and how tolerant the application is to these effects. In a multimedia lecture for example, a glitch is observable as the absence of, say, a video clip to annotate the lecture. The effect of missed visual cues may persist in the minds of the human viewer for a few seconds. When the tolerance limits are exceeded, a recovery from the glitch may manifest in activating an application specified 'exception handler'. The absence of a video clip may however be handled by delivering only the voice clip corresponding to the missed video clip, which may be acceptable due to the slow varying nature of the visual and aural cues at the human viewer [6]. In general, various levels of tolerance to skew among messages are specifiable in QOS_{pres}, with hooks into application-supplied exception handlers.

5   Existing Notions of Message Causality

We argue that the notion of 'message causality' is the right basis for structuring of data presentations in distributed real-time systems for two reasons. First, a synchronization construct based on 'message causality' is readily incorporatable into a distributed programming system since this notion has been well-studied by the distributed systems research community. Second, user-level actions in an interactive setting can be more flexibly expressed through 'cause-and-effect' relationships. In this light, we compare our extended notion of 'message causality' with both the classical approaches that do not support the notion of 'real-time' and the 'add-on' approaches that are tailor-made to fit 'real-time' into the classical approaches.

5.1   Logical Time-Stamp Based Approaches

Currently available causal order primitives [7],[8] infer message causality based on the 'logical time stamps' internally generated by the communication system ('implicit' approach to extracting concurrency in the application). If, for instance, messages m_1 and m_2 are sent in that sequence by a user U, these primitives treat m_2 as causally dependent on m_1. This may not however be the intention of U, such as m_1 and m_2 being concurrent because they are update requests on different (unrelated) documents. Thus existing primitives are at a lower level and do not precisely extract the concurrency in an application, resulting in less message-level asynchrony (i.e., more synchronization latency), in comparison to our 'explicit' approach[3] [9].

Also, the above primitives do not directly incorporate 'real-time' into message-level causality. Even though a 'real-time support' layer can be introduced on top of such causal order based communication systems, this additional layer cannot compensate for the lost concurrency and hence the lost ability to prescribe lax delays when moving the messages through lower level system elements. The only advantage of such a 'real-time' layer will be in lax scheduling of messages at the time of presentation.

---

[3] An underlying protocol that enforces causal delivery with only implicit information will incur more synchronization latency. In the earlier scenario, buffering of m_2 pending a subsequent arrival of m_1 may increase the time of completion of processing m_1 and m_2, viz., '$> \delta_{m_2} + \delta_{m_1}$' instead of '$> max(\{\delta_{m_1}, \delta_{m_2}\})$'. The performance problem arises due to lack of knowledge in the system that m_1 and m_2 are concurrent.

5.2   Causality Augmented with Time Deadlines

The[4] notion of 'Δ-causality' proposed in [10] prescribes an upper bound 'Δ' on the delivery time of a message m' relative to its causally precedent message m. This corresponds to our parameter $u_{m'}$ underlying the relation: $m \succ m'$. Though useful for designing real-time transfer protocols in the network with a message delivery bound 'Δ', the 'Δ-causality' notion does not capture the 'flow of real-time' in a distributed computation, because there is no lower bound on the time of delivery of m'. In contrast, our notion allows prescribing a persistence duration p_m of m and a lower bound $l_{m'}$ on the delivery time of m' relative to m, viz., $t_{m'} > (t_m + p_m + l_{m'})$. So our notion is at a higher level, easily employable in distributed programming environments.

The work of J. P. Courtiat and et al [11] uses the notion of 'causality' to realize synchronization. But the specification model treats the 'causality' and 'real-time flow' notions separately, which necessitates more complex programming constructs. However, our work integrates these notions in the specification model, whereby a concise set of programming constructs suffices to generate presentation schedules. Likewise, the work of P. Amer [12] deals with specifying a partial order based transport service for multimedia data. The service specification method is oriented towards developing validation models for temporal specifications of distributed multimedia applications. Such a transport service first needs to be incorporated into distributed programming primitives before use in developing applications.

As can be seen, our *Occurs_After* construct allows explicit specification of message causality, using an 'object-oriented programming' framework that transforms the processing of causally ordered messages into object-level 'state changes' occurring over specific real-time intervals.

6   Conclusions

The paper presented a model for synchronizing real-time data during presentation to the application. The basic premise in our approach is that the user level component of the communication system takes the burden of synchronization, instead of the network. This introduces flexibility in the message transport protocols and allows optimizing the usage of network resources to application needs.

The temporal properties of real-time presentation are specifiable in the form of a *causal ordering* on the data segments, i.e., messages, flowing across application entities. In this notion, application entities are modeled as objects, with the messages exchanged between various objects in a prescribed order and within prescribed intervals inducing 'state changes' in them. Since causal ordering of messages is amenable for easier implementation in a distributed system, our model may be viewed as generating a transport-oriented QOS description that is mappable into a specification on the required delay behavior of the underlying

---

[4] Our concurrency enhancements are manifestations of multimedia object partitioning in the form of 'spatial subparts' and 'temporal subparts' as allowed in SMIL [4].

system. Such a mapping is more directly usable in an implementation of presentation protocols than the higher level petrinet based specifications typically employed.

Our model of causal ordering allows application characteristics to be mapped into a set of data delivery procedures composed in the form of data presentation protocol. A possible relaxation of the data delivery constraints and the network delay requirements, as allowed by the model, offers a potential for optimal usage of system resources. The specification method is itself independent of how the client and server modules are separated in applications, which allows easier construction of programming models of real-time applications for analysis and verification, and a uniform implementation of communication systems. Furthermore, our specification model can be recursively employed in a hierarchically decomposed real-time presentation system.

References

1. G. Blair, G. Coulson, M. Papathomas, P. Robin, J. S. F. Horn, and L. Hazard. A Programming Model and System Infrastructure for Real-time Synchronization in Distributed Multimedia Systems. IEEE Journal on Selected Areas in Communications, vol.14, no.1, (1996), 249-263.
2. L. Lamport. Time, Clocks and Ordering of Events in Distributed Systems. Communications of the ACM, (1978).
3. R. D. Hill. Supporting Concurrency, Communication, and Synchronization in Human-Computer Interaction – The Sassafras UIMS. ACM Transactions on Graphics, vol.5, no.3, (1986), 179-210.
4. Worldwide Web Consortium. Synchronized Multimedia Integration Language (SMIL) 1.0 Specification. P. Hoschka (ed.), W3C Recommendation, (1998).
5. B. Field, T. F. Znati, and D. Mosse. V-NET: A versatile Network Architecture for Flexible Delay Guarantees in Real-time Networks. IEEE Transactions on Computers, vol.49, no.8, (2000), 841-858.
6. R. Steinmetz. Synchronization Properties in Multimedia Systems. IEEE Journal on Selected Areas in Communications, vol.SAC-8, no.3, (1990), 401-412.
7. K. Birman and T. A. Joseph. Exploiting Virtual Synchrony in Distributed Systems. 11-th Symp. on Operating System Principles, ACM SIGOPS, (1987).
8. L. L. Peterson, N. C. Buchholz and R. D. Schlichting. Preserving and Using Context Information in Interprocess Communication. ACM Transactions on Computer Systems, vol.7, no.3, (1989), 217-246.
9. K. Ravindran and A. Thenmozhi. Extraction of Logical Concurrency in Distributed Applications. Proc. Intl. Conf. on Distributed Computing Systems, IEEE-CS, Pittsburgh (PA), (1993).
10. R. Yavatkar. MCP: A Protocol for Coordination and Temporal Synchronization in Multimedia Collaborative Applications. Proc. Intl. Conf. on Distributed Computing Systems, IEEE-CS, Yokohama (Japan), (1992), 606-613.
11. J. P. Courtiat, L. Carmo, and R. Oliviera. A General-Purpose Multimedia Synchronization Mechanism Based on Causal Relations. IEEE Journal on Selected Areas in Communications, vol.14, no.1, (1996), 185-195.
12. P. Amer, C. Chassot, T. J. Connally, M. Diaz and P. Conrad. Partial-order TRansport Service for Multimedia and Other Applications. IEEE/ACM Transactions on Networking, vol. 2, no. 5, (1994), 440-455.

SIPC, a Multi-function SIP User Agent

Xiaotao Wu and Henning Schulzrinne

Columbia University, Department of Computer Science,
New York, New York 10032, USA
{xiaotaow,hgs}@cs.columbia.edu

Abstract. Integrating multiple functions into one communication user agent can introduce many innovative communication services. For example, with networked appliance control, a user agent can turn off the stereo when receiving an incoming call. With location sensing, a user agent can automatically reject a call if it knows the location preference is 'quiet'. Multi-function interactions enable services that are otherwise impossible. In this paper, we first present the new services introduced by the integration, then introduce our SIP user agent, SIPC, which handles these new services in a programmable way. SIPC integrates multimedia call setup, networked appliance control, presence handling, Internet TV, instant messaging, location sensing, networked resource discovery, third-party call control, real-time multimedia streaming, emergency call handling, and conference floor control into one application. We analyze the relationship among these functions and propose different approaches for function integration. SIPC uses the Session Initiation Protocol (SIP) for multimedia call setup and the Language for End System Services (LESS) for service programming.

Keywords: multi-function integration; SIP; SAP; networked appliance control; location-based services; SLP; RTSP; SIP event notification; floor control; LESS

1 Introduction

One of the most important advantages of Internet telephony is its ability to provide innovative services. In Internet telephony systems, traditional telephony services, such as call transfer, can be enhanced by the integration of Internet services, such as email, web, instant message, presence notification and directory lookups. The enhancements require Internet telephony end systems to perform more functions in addition to audio and video communications.

Some instant messaging applications, such as MSN Messenger, have integrated on-line/offline indication, instant messaging, email, and web browsing into one application. In our SIP [1] user agent, SIPC [2], in addition to the functions mentioned above, we also support networked appliance control, real-time multimedia streaming, networked resource discovery, third-party call control, Internet TV, location sensing, emergency call handling, and conference floor control. Multiple functions may interact with each other and introduce many new services that are otherwise impossible. For example, SIPC can automatically turn off the stereo in the user's room when receiving an incoming call. A SIPC user can share an Session Announcement Protocol (SAP) session with his friends by putting the session information in a SIP INVITE request. SIPC can base call decisions on location information. In Section 2, we detail the new service examples.

J. Vicente and D. Hutchison (Eds.): MMNS 2004, LNCS 3271, pp. 269–281, 2004.

Too many functions in one application may make the application too complicated to maintain. In Section 3, we analyze the relationship among all the functions in SIPC. Based on the analysis, we discuss the practical integration approaches that can minimize the overall application complexity, while still providing convenient ways for function interaction.

SIPC handles multi-function interaction in a programmable way. We have defined a service creation scripting language called the Language for End System Services (LESS) [3]. In Section 4, we describe how SIPC uses LESS scripts to perform multi-function interaction.

In Section 5, we briefly introduce the implementation details of SIPC. Section 6 concludes the paper and discusses our future work.

2 New Services Introduced by Multi-function Integration

In traditional telephony systems, communication services are provided by the switches in communication networks. The services are performed based on very limited information, such as the address and the busy status of the caller and the callee, allowing only a small set of actions, in most cases, to route calls.

In Internet telephony systems, services can be implemented in both network servers and intelligent end systems. With the integration of Internet services, such as presence indication, Internet telephony services have access to much richer information, and offer a richer set of service actions, not limited to call routing, the actions can also be networked appliance control, instant messaging, email and web browsing. We describe a few of the new services below.

2.1 Setup Preferable Communication Environment

Communication quality is not only determined by the quality of audio/video streams transmitted between endpoints, but also affected by the communication environment where the talkers are in. For example, background noise may affect audio conversation and brightness of lights may affect video conversation. In a networked home with network controllable appliances, the integration of networked appliance control into a communication agent may help to setup environment conducive to communication. In our lab environment, SIPC can automatically pause the stereo through a Slink-e controller [4] when receiving an incoming call. If the call requires video communication, SIPC can also automatically adjust the brightness of the lamp in our lab through an X10 controller. SIPC uses the SIP DO [5] method to perform networked appliance control.

2.2 Call Handling Based on Presence Information

The integration of presence information handling can help to make call decisions. In traditional telephony systems, a caller usually knows nothing about a callee's status before making a call. In Internet telephony, a caller can know not only the online/offline status, but also other information, such as the location privacy preference, of the callee. SIPC can generate many new services based on the status information, for example, automatically calling a friend when the friend is online, or starting a conference only when all the essential participants are online.

2.3   Use Networked Resources

The integration of location sensing, networked resource discovery, networked appliance control, and third-party call control enables a portable end system to use networked resources for better communication quality. Usually the capability of an end system is in inverse proportion to its portability. A portable end system usually has a small display, low-quality audio, and inconvenient input devices. However, if there are networked devices with good multimedia I/O capabilities in the communication environment, user agents with the support of Service Location Protocol (SLP) [6] and SIP third-party call control architecture (3pcc) [7] can control the networked devices for communication.

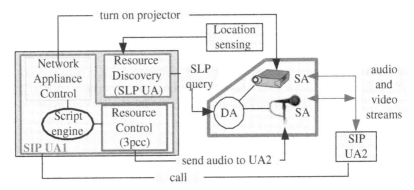

Fig. 1. Using networked resources for better communication quality

We have proposed an architecture [8] [9] that allows end systems to use available resources in the environment, such as displaying video on a wall-hanging plasma display or getting audio from an echo-canceling microphone. To support such an architecture, an end system needs to find out available resources and control them. As shown in Figure 1, with location sensing, SIPC may retrieve location information and find available resources in the communication environment by including location information in the SLP query [6]. SIPC can then use networked appliance control and SIP third-party call control (3pcc) [7] to control the resources.

2.4   Location Sensing and Location-Based Services

Many applications used in the Internet today benefit from using location information. In Internet telephony systems, location information may help to make call decisions or trigger automatic communication actions. For example, when receiving an incoming call, SIPC can be programmed to check its own location and then play a loud ring tone if the place-type is street, or flash its icon if the privacy of the place is quiet. SIPC uses location information in three ways: it becomes part of outgoing requests sent to remote parties, it triggers automatic actions, and it governs communication behaviors.

Location information can be revealed to remote parties for location tracking as part of the presence notification or encoded in MIME [10] with other content. Location information could be room (name or function information), civic (street and community), categorical (such as movie theater), activity (such as travel) and privacy preference (such as quiet). SIPC can convey location information, for example, in a SIP NOTIFY request in RPID format [11] or GEOPRIV Location Object Format [12], to the parties explicitly showing interests in the information. SIPC can also include the location information in SIP REGISTER or PUBLISH [13] requests to upload the location information to a location server. When sending an emergency call, SIPC will encode its location information in MIME in a SIP INVITE request. The emergency call taker can conveniently track the caller with the location information.

When SIPC gets location information, it may invoke a service script, such as a LESS [3] script, to perform automatic actions. The location information can be the user's own location or remote buddy's location. The service script can handle absolute location information or relative location information between two people. For example, when SIPC gets its own room number, it can automatically turn on the light of the room. When it gets its buddy's location and find the distance to the buddy is less than a certain value, it can automatically send an instant message to the buddy.

Integrating location information with call control services can help to govern appropriate communication behavior. For example, in a movie theatre with a movie playing, the Bluetooth device in the movie theatre may broadcast its location information as 'quiet', when SIPC gets the location information, its service scripts may automatically block incoming calls unless the priority of the call is emergency.

2.5   Internet TV Session Sharing

The Session Announcement Protocol (SAP) [14] advertises multicast multimedia sessions and their parameters to prospective participants. Integrating a SAP user agent into SIPC allows users to easily share an interesting program with their friends. If a user finds an interesting program and wants to ask his friends to watch the same program, the user needs to convey the program information to his friends. Since both SIP and SAP use the Session Description Protocol (SDP) [15] to describe session information, SIPC can get the SDP content of the SAP packets and put the content in a SIP INVITE request. This way, the user can simply call his friends with the SDP content without having to know the session details.

2.6   Voicemail Handling

The integration of web, email and SIP message waiting indication [16] provides various ways for handling voicemail. A voicemail can be sent as an email attachment, or as a HTTP [17] URL or a Real Time Streaming Protocol (RTSP) [18] URL in an email. The voicemail information can also be in SIP message waiting indication[16] notification. SIPC can dial into the voicemail server to get the voicemail, or play the email attachment, or start a web browser to retrieve the voicemail.

2.7 Conference Floor Control with Active Talker Indicator

During a conference, floor control [19] helps to assign talking rights. Only the floor holders' voice gets delivered to each participant. In a classroom environment, when a student gets the floor, turning on the light on the student's desk, or adjusting the video camera to face the student may help to find the talker. The integration of networked appliance control with conference floor control in SIPC can handle this task gracefully.

3   How to Integrate Multiple Functions

The above service examples show that multi-function integration may bring many innovative services. However, integrating too many functions in one application may make the application too complicated and may confuse users if the application contains functions users don't need. Since SIPC directly interacts with users, any confusion from users may impair its usability. It is very important to choose an appropriate integration method to enable the new services in SIPC but without making it too complicated and without adding too much implementation efforts. Before discussing the integration methods, we first list the functions integrated in SIPC, and investigate the relationship among these functions.

3.1 Functions Integrated in SIPC

SIPC can support a range of media types, such as audio, video, whiteboard and desktop sharing and can perform functions beyond multimedia calls. SIPC uses the SIP DO [5] method to perform networked appliance control, uses the SIP event notification architecture [20] to perform presence notification, uses the Session Announcement Protocol (SAP) [14] to retrieve multicast multimedia session information, uses RTSP to retrieve voicemail, uses DHCP Options for Civic Addresses [21] and GEOPRIV Location Object Format [12] for location sensing, uses the Service Location Protocol (SLP) [6] to find available networked resources, uses SIP for third-party call control [7] to control networked resources. SIPC uses external applications to handle email and web browsing. SIPC integrates a SIP CGI [22] and a LESS [3]/CPL [23] engine to handle service script. Section 5 provides more details on the implementation.

When integrating all these functions into SIPC, we noticed that many functions overlap each other, and the functions may interact with each other in different ways. Below we analyze the relationship among these functions and propose the integration approaches based on this analysis.

3.2 Overlap Among SIPC Functions

Many of the functions mentioned in Section 2 overlap with each other. Because of the overlap, integrating a new function into SIPC will not increase the overall complexity too much. As shown in Figure 2, SAP user agents, RTSP user agents and SIP [1] user agents all use SDP [15] for session description and RTP [24] for real time media stream transmission. The presence status, conference status, location information, and emergency event can all be transmitted by the SIP event notification architecture [20]. All of

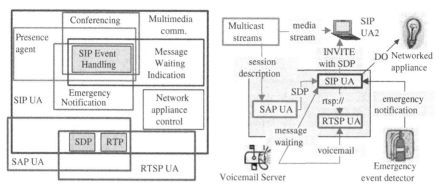

Fig. 2. Overlap among SIPC functions   **Fig. 3.** Interaction among SIPC functions

the SIP event notification, SIP multimedia session setup and SIP networked appliance control can share the same SIP stack.

3.3 Interaction Among SIPC Functions

In the service examples described in Section 2, we noticed that multi-function inter-action introduces new services. As shown in Figure 3, the SAP user agent passes the session description information to the SIP user agent so the SIP user agent can invite another SIP user agent, SIP UA2, to watch the same multicast media session. When the SIP user agent gets the message waiting indication from voicemail server, it can instruct the RTSP user agent to retrieve the voicemail. When the SIP user agent gets an emer-gency notification [25], it can control networked appliances for emergency handling.

Based on the investigation on the overlap and interaction among SIPC functions, we present the approaches on multi-function integration below.

3.4 Approaches for Multi-function Integration

The integration methods can be build-in and interprocess-control. The build-in method is to hardcode functions into a user agent so the user agent can invoke the functions by using API calls. The functions integrated by the build-in method are tightly coupled with each other. They can share code with each other and easily interact with each other by API calls. The interprocess-control method puts functions outside the user agent. The functions integrated by the interprocess-control method may interact with each other via interprocess communication, such as Dynamic Date Exchange (DDE [26]) and Message Bus (MBUS [27]). When adding a new function, three criteria may help to choose an appropriate integration method. First, the build-in method is more applicable if the new function shares many components with the existing functions. Second, if the new function interacts with the existing functions extensively, the build-in method is preferable. Third, if there are existing popularly used applications supporting the new function, the interprocess-control method is more appropriate. Below we illustrate how we apply the criteria in integrating the function set of SIPC.

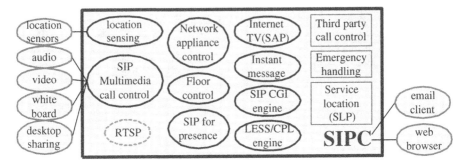

Fig. 4. Function set in sipc

Figure 4 shows the function set of SIPC. The functions inside the big thick-line-rectangle are integrated into the SIPC core, others are running in separate processes and controlled by the core by interprocess communication.

In SIPC's function set, all SIP related functions, such as SIP call setup, SIP DO method for networked appliance control, SIP event notification, SIP for instant messaging, SIP third-party call control, and SIP emergency call handling, share the same SIP stack and are tightly related to each other. These functions should be integrated in build-in way and put into one application. If we choose to use SIP and SOAP [28] for conference floor control [19], the floor control function should also be put into the same application.

To support the Session Announcement Protocol (SAP) and the Real Time Streaming Protocol (RTSP), based on the investigation in the Section 3.2 and 3.3, and the service examples in Section 2, we consider the best way is to integrate them in build-in way with the SIP functions. Both SAP and RTSP sessions use SDP for session description, and RTP for multimedia transmission, the same as SIP multimedia sessions, so code sharing is possible. Using external SAP and RTSP applications requires communication interfaces between SIP functions and SAP and RTSP functions. The communication interface is not trivial to build to handle function interactions.

The Service Location Protocol (SLP) support can be either build-in or interprocess-control because there is not much code sharing between SLP support and other functions. The communication interface between an SLP client and a SIP user agent can be simple. We choose to build an SLP client into SIPC because the implementation effort is not much but it is easier to perform function interactions.

There are two modes for location information retrieval. In the first, a user agent determines its own location, and announces it to other system components that need the information. We name this active location sensing. For example, the user agent can use GPS or measure the field strength of wireless access points [29] to get the location information. Active location sensing may involve different kinds of location sensors. Instead of building all the location sensing technologies into SIPC, we use the interprocess-control method to integrate active location sensing functions. When SIPC starts, it listens on a TCP port for location information. Location sensors can send location documents in GEOPRIV Location Object Format [12] to that port.

The other mode is passive location sensing. In passive mode, a user's profile is put in a small device, such as an IR/RF programmable badge or an i-Button [30]. The device reader in a context can read the user's profile and send the information to a location server. The user needs to subscribe to the location server to get his own location information. SIPC implements the SIP event notification architecture [20] to handle location subscriptions and notifications.

In terms of function support for email and web browsing, we noticed that there are many existing email and web browsing applications. Instead of implementing email and web functions into SIPC, the preferable way is to integrate email and web browsing functions in the interprocess-control way. For example, on a Windows platform, by setting proper Windows Registry values, people can invoke SIPC from a web browser, or invoke a web browser from SIPC.

4   Program Multi-function Interactions

In Section 2, we presented some new services but without describing how to perform these services. Instead of hardcoding these services one by one, it is more convenient to make the services programmable by service scripts and customizable. We defined a service creation script language named Language for End System Services (LESS) [3]. LESS is extended from the Call Processing Language (CPL) [23], but with more emphasis on end system service creation. We choose to use LESS as the service creation language for SIPC because it is designed to be simple, easy to understand, and safe for end users to use. The simplicity and the tree-like structure of LESS make the graphical description of a LESS script and its XML document fully exchangeable. Any valid LESS scripts can be converted into graphical decision trees, and vice-versa. Though general purpose programming languages, such as C/C++ and Java, may also have graphical development environment, a graphical interface of an arbitrary program written in C/C++ or Java is extremely unlikely to be able to do anything more than represent the language constructs in the most basic manner. We did an in-depth analysis of the simplicity and safety of LESS [31] and developed a graphical service creation environment (SCE) for LESS, which is presented in Section 5.4.

The script below shows a LESS service script performing stereo control based on the caller's address. With the script, if the call is from sip:boss@example.com, the script will turn off the stereo.

```
<less>
  <incoming>
    <address-switch field="origin">
      <address is="sip:boss@example.com">
        <device:turnoff device="sip:stereo@room1.example.com"/>
      </address>
    </address-switch>
  </incoming>
</less>
```

A more complicated LESS service script below requires the integration of presence information handling, location sensing and instant messaging. When a SIPC instance equipped with the script receives an event notification showing that Bob, whose SIP URI is `sip:bob@example.com`, is online, it will check the location relation between the script owner and Bob. If they are at the same floor and close to each other, the script generates an instant message to Bob.

```
<less>
  <EVENT:notification>
    <address-switch> <address is="sip:bob@example.com">
      <EVENT:event-switch> <EVENT:event is="open">
        <location-relation-switch uri1="sip:bob@example.com">
          <location-relation distance="10" same="FLR">
            <location url="sip:bob@example.com">
              <IM:im message="Hi, I'm next to you"/>
            </location>
          </location-relation>
        </location-relation-switch>
      </EVENT:event> </EVENT:event-switch>
    </address> </address-switch>
  </EVENT:notification>
</less>
```

To incorporate all the new functions, we need to extend LESS with new packages, such as networked appliance control, presence information handling, SAP session handling, and location information handling. For example, in the above service scripts, we have the action `device:turnon` defined for networked appliance control. Defining a new LESS package is covered in [3] and [23].

5   Implementation

SIPC [2] is a SIP user agent written in Tcl/Tk and C/C++. It is originally developed to handle Internet telephony calls. Figure 4 shows SIPC's function set. The functions circled in solid have already been implemented, the functions circled in dotted line are under development, the functions in rectangle are partially implemented. As we integrated more and more functions into SIPC, we found many new services introduced by multi-function integration, some examples as we described in Section 2. Below, we briefly introduce the main user interface, the service creation environment, the functions for location sensing, and emergency call handling in SIPC.

5.1   The Main User Interface of SIPC

Figure 5 shows the main user interface of SIPC. By clicking on different function buttons, users can manually invoke different functions. In the service frame, a user can program new services to automatically handle multi-function interactions. We detail the service creation environment of SIPC in Section 5.4. In the 'presence information' frame, the user can see not only the buddies' presence status, but also their locations. If the user click the 'location map' button, the buddies' locations can be pinpointed in location maps.

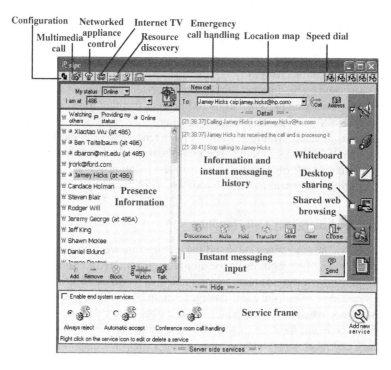

Fig. 5. Main user interface of SIPC

5.2 Location Sensing and Location-Based Services in SIPC

Figure 6 shows the location map in SIPC. Buddies' locations are pinpointed on the map. In the map, a room can be a communication target. As shown in the figure, right click on a room, a user can easily broadcast instant messages or conference call invitations to all his buddies in the room.

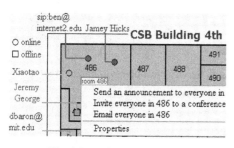

Fig. 6. Location map in SIPC

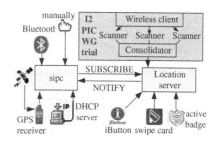

Fig. 7. Location sensing in SIPC

As shown in Figure 7, SIPC supports both active location sensing and passive location sensing. In active mode, SIPC can get its civil location encoded in DHCP options for civic addresses [21] from a DHCP server, or get its geospatial location by reading the serial port connected to a GPS receiver. It can also get its location information from the Bluetooth beacon sent by a location server. In passive mode, users can use iButton, swipe card (such as university ID card), or active badge to generate location information and store the location in our location server. The location server can then NOTIFY SIPC about the location changes.

SIPC was used by the Internet2 Presence Integrated Communication working group (PIC WG) for their rich presence trials in Internet2 member meeting in Fall 2003 and Spring 2004. SIPC used passive location sensing in the trials. The gray area in Figure 7 shows the trial setup. Multiple scanners gathered signal strength from the wireless client on which SIPC was running. The consolidator calculated the location based on the signal strength information and sent it to the location server. The location server sent the location information to SIPC by SIP NOTIFY requests.

5.3 SIPC for Emergency Call Handling

Figure 8 shows the emergency call handling architecture we are developing using SIPC. At the caller side, SIPC acquires its location, e.g., from DHCP options. Since different countries may have different emergency numbers, SIPC will send a NAPTR [32] request to the DNS server to get the local emergency numbers. When a user dials a number, SIPC will check whether it is an emergency number or not. If it is an emergency call, SIPC will encode the location in MIME in the outgoing SIP INVITE request. At the emergency call taker side, SIPC can pinpoint the caller on a map based on the location encapsulated in the INVITE request. In the figure, the SIP proxy server helps to route emergency calls to an appropriate emergency communications center.

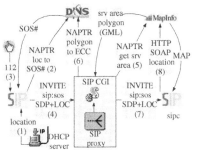

Fig. 8. Emergency call handling using SIPC

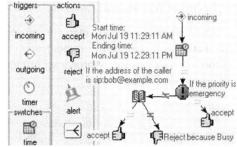

Fig. 9. Service creation environment in SIPC

5.4   Service Creation Environment in SIPC

We have developed a graphical service creation environment for SIPC. As shown in Figure 9, a user can simply drag a trigger events, such as *incoming* call, into the drawing area, then put different switches, such as *location-switch* and *address-switch*, for condition matching, then put different actions, such as *accept* or *reject* a call, into the drawing area. The user can connect these elements into a decision tree. The decision tree can be translated into a LESS script. SIPC can then handle calls based on the LESS script.

6 Conclusion and Future Work

In this paper, we described how to integrate multiple Internet-oriented functions in our SIP user agent, SIPC, and presented the new services facilitated by the multi-function integration. The integration is not simply putting all the functions together but run them separately, instead, a careful design is required to minimize the overall complexity of the application, and enable function interactions. Multi-function interactions enable many innovative services that are otherwise impossible. We use LESS service scripts to automate the interactions. We also briefly introduced the implementation details of SIPC. We will investigate more Internet services, such as conference control, quality of service handling, and user profile management, for integration and define more LESS packages for new services.

References

1. Rosenberg, J., Schulzrinne, H., Camarillo, G., Johnston, A.R., Peterson, J., Sparks, R., Handley, M., Schooler, E.: SIP: session initiation protocol. RFC 3261, Internet Engineering Task Force (2002)
2. Wu, X.: (Columbia university SIP user agent (sipc)) http://www.cs.columbia.edu/IRT/sipc.
3. Wu, X., Schulzrinne, H.: Programmable end system services using SIP. In: Conference Record of the International Conference on Communications (ICC). (2003)
4. Nirvis Inc.: (Slink-e) http://www.nirvis.com/slink-e.htm.
5. Moyer, S., Maples, D., Tsang, S.: A protocol for wide-area secure networked appliance communication. IEEE Communications Magazine 39 (2001) 52–59
6. Guttman, E., Perkins, C.E., Veizades, J., Day, M.: Service location protocol, version 2. RFC 2608, Internet Engineering Task Force (1999)
7. Rosenberg, J., Peterson, J., Schulzrinne, H., Camarillo, G.: Best current practices for third party call control (3pcc) in the session initiation protocol (SIP). RFC 3725, Internet Engineering Task Force (2004)
8. Berger, S., Schulzrinne, H., Sidiroglou, S., Wu, X.: Ubiquitous computing using SIP. In: ACM NOSSDAV 2003. (2003)
9. Shacham, R., Schulzrinne, H., Kellerer, W., Thakolsri, S.: An architecture for location-based service mobility using the SIP event model. In: Mobisys Workshop on Context Awareness. (2004)
10. Borenstein, N., Freed, N.: MIME (multipurpose Internet mail extensions) part one: Mechanisms for specifying and describing the format of Internet message bodies. RFC 1521, Internet Engineering Task Force (1993)
11. Schulzrinne, H.: RPID – rich presence information data format. Internet draft, Internet Engineering Task Force (2003) Work in progress.
12. Peterson, J.: A presence-based GEOPRIV location object format. Internet Draft draft-ietf-geopriv-pidf-lo-01, Internet Engineering Task Force (2004) Work in progress.
13. Niemi, A.: Session initiation protocol (SIP) extension for event state publication. Internet Draft draft-ietf-sip-publish-02, Internet Engineering Task Force (2004) Work in progress.
14. Handley, M., Perkins, C.E., Whelan, E.: Session announcement protocol. RFC 2974, Internet Engineering Task Force (2000)
15. Handley, M., Jacobson, V.: SDP: session description protocol. RFC 2327, Internet Engineering Task Force (1998)

16. Mahy, R.: A message summary and message waiting indication event package for the session initiation protocol (SIP). Internet draft, Internet Engineering Task Force (2003) Work in progress.
17. Fielding, R., Gettys, J., Mogul, J.C., Frystyk, H., Berners-Lee, T.: Hypertext transfer protocol – HTTP/1.1. RFC 2068, Internet Engineering Task Force (1997)
18. Schulzrinne, H., Rao, A., Lanphier, R.: Real time streaming protocol (RTSP). RFC 2326, Internet Engineering Task Force (1998)
19. Schulzrinne, H., Wu, X., Koskelainen, P., Ott, J.: Requirements for floor control protocol. Internet Draft draft-ietf-xcon-floor-control-req-00, Internet Engineering Task Force (2004) Work in progress.
20. Roach, A.B.: Session initiation protocol (sip)-specific event notification. RFC 3265, Internet Engineering Task Force (2002)
21. Schulzrinne, H.: DHCP option for civil location. Internet draft, Internet Engineering Task Force (2003) Work in progress.
22. Lennox, J., Schulzrinne, H., Rosenberg, J.: Common gateway interface for SIP. RFC 3050, Internet Engineering Task Force (2001)
23. Lennox, J., Wu, X., Schulzrinne, H.: CPL: a language for user control of Internet telephony services. Internet draft, Internet Engineering Task Force (2003) Work in progress.
24. Schulzrinne, H., Casner, S., Frederick, R., Jacobson, V.: RTP: a transport protocol for real-time applications. RFC 3550, Internet Engineering Task Force (2003)
25. Schulzrinne, H., Arabshian, K.: Providing emergency services in Internet telephony. IEEE Internet Computing 6 (2002) 39–47
26. Netscape corporation: (Netscape's DDE implementation) http://developer.netscape.com/docs/manuals/ communicator/DDE/index.htm.
27. Ott, J., Perkins, C.E., Kutscher, D.: A message bus for local coordination. RFC 3259, Internet Engineering Task Force (2002)
28. World Wide Web Consortium: (Simple object access protocol (soap) 1.1) http://www.w3.org/TR/SOAP/.
29. Niculescu, D., Nath, B.: Ad hoc positioning system (APS). In: GLOBECOM (1). (2001) 2926–2931
30. Dallas Semiconductor: (iButton) http://www.ibutton.com.
31. Wu, X., Schulzrinne, H.: The simplicity and safety of the language for end system services (LESS). Technical report, Department of Computer Science, Columbia University (2004)
32. Mealling, M., Daniel, R.W.: The naming authority pointer (NAPTR) DNS resource record. RFC 2915, Internet Engineering Task Force (2000)

Optimizing Continuous Media Delivery by Multiple Distributed Servers to Multiple Clients Using a Genetic Algorithm

Gerassimos Barlas and Khaled El-Fakih

Department of Computer Science,
American University of Sharjah, P.O.B. 26666, UAE
{gbarlas,kelfakih}@aus.ac.ae

Abstract. In this paper we explore the potential of a VoD system that is based on a paradigm that has been recently proposed: that of combining many distributed servers to handle the delivery of each requested media. When faced with a system comprised of N servers and M clients, the problems to be addressed are: (i) how to split the delivery task among different servers and (ii) how to pair clients and servers, the objective being to minimize the access time of the clients.

To this end, we present an analytical framework that enables the division of the delivery process for each client in a distributed manner. This framework is coupled with a genetic algorithm that enables an optimal or near-optimal solution to the problem of pairing clients and servers, in a small number of generations.

The paper is concluded by a rigorous study of a N-servers, M-clients system that answers a number of important questions like, what is the quality of service achieved and how our proposed system behaves under increased load.

Keywords: multiple servers, multiple clients, genetic algorithms, video on demand, divisible load.

1 Introduction

VoD presents a number of significant problems that have limited the scope and clientele of most deployed systems to-date. The size of the data involved, even with the latest codecs available (MPEG4), presents serious challenges to the video servers and the carrier network. Multicasting [6] and other technologies like simulcasting [7] permit the shift of the bottleneck from the servers themselves. Alas, these delivery approaches also "shift" control away from the end-user which is ultimately the main allure of the VoD paradigm.

Keeping up with the user demands, puts hefty requirements on the servers. Parallel video servers and intelligent disk scheduling has the potential needed, but more-often-than-not they offer a localized solution. Clients with a slower connection to a server have to wait for a very long time before the playback can commence (a.k.a. Access Time - AT).

J. Vicente and D. Hutchison (Eds.): MMNS 2004, LNCS 3271, pp. 282–294, 2004.
© IFIP International Federation for Information Processing 2004

A recently proposed approach to the delivery of continuous documents is to employ multiple *distributed* servers to deliver a requested document. The framework needed for scheduling such a delivery has been originally presented in [20] and further expanded and refined in subsequent publications [3] for the case of a single client. In this paper we address the problem of how a system with multiple clients and servers behaves and what are the characteristics of the services offered. Our contribution also lies in the proposal of a genetic algorithm for solving the server-client mapping problem under the constraint of minimizing the average access time.

As a first step we describe the mathematical framework that enables the calculation of a multi-server delivery schedule for a single client. Both single and multi-installment strategies are described, the latter offering better utilization of available resources, smaller AT and better suitability to adaptive strategies. The genetic algorithm works by randomly producing a population whose individuals are possible solutions to the client-server mapping problem. The algorithm produces optimal (or near optimal) mappings without suffering from intractability. Our genetic algorithm is hybridized, i.e. departs from classical GA techniques, by employing procedures for finding feasible schedules and for avoiding premature convergence to local optima. We have used a GA since we do not have an exact solution for the delivery strategies and since GAs were successfully used in solving a variety of optimization problems [8][15].

Our simulation study shows that the proposed solution offers a vastly improved level of service from the traditional single server/per client approach. Not only are average AT substantially lower, but even under extreme loads that would cause denial of service to some clients, our system deteriorates gracefully. Please note that the term server is used here to refer to server sites and not particular machines. Each site could be a parallel server farm.

The paper is organized as follows: Section 2 presents related work in the field. Section 3 holds a formal definition to the problem followed in Section 4 by the mathematical framework needed for computing how to service a single-client's request. The genetic algorithm used to compute a near-optimum schedule for a battery of clients is presented in Section 5. A simulation study concludes the paper by comparing our work to the classical single-server per client approach.

2   Related Work

The idea of combining multiple geographically distributed servers for video data delivery was originally introduced in [20]. The idea of using multiple connections to geographically distributed mirror sites has been also suggested by Rodriguez et.al. for minimizing FTP download times [18]. In similar premises, the GridFTP protocol extension and associated tools facilitate speedier object replication/mirroring in high-performance computational grids [19]. GridFTP supports both parallel and stripped transfers, the latter being closer to the technique utilized by our multiserver distribution strategy. In this paper we assume only single connections for each client-server pair, although multiple connections can be supported without modifications to the partitioning framework of section 4.

Most of the work on VoD has been focused on parallel video servers. A good introduction on the subject is given by J. Lee in [14]. Jung et.al [12] have also proposed the use of a data partitioning scheme among servers that resembles data-interleaving in disk arrays (RAID).

Multicasting [6] can maximize network utilization while at the same time minimize the server load. Patching has been proposed by several researcher as a way of accommodating clients with different playback-starting times - a major obstacle in the use of multicasting for VoD. Patching minimizes communication overheads by retransmitting only the parts of the movie that a client has missed [5]. The problem with multicasting is that it requires infrastructure changes like special routers, etc.. Also, traffic localization is needed in order to cope with network errors and communication delays. Not to mention of course, that each movie should be requested by many clients at the same or close-enough time.

The simulcast protocol [7] has been proposed as an alternative to multicasting. The advantage is that no modification or special treatment by the network is required. Simulcasting uses the clients as repeater nodes. The problem is that asymmetrical connections like ADSL are not designed to efficiently support such operations, making simulcast a choice only for low bit-rate content.

Rejaie et.al. [17] proposed a layered video format and associated mechanism for tuning data volume to network capacity. Pejhan et.al. [16] have demonstrated a similar technique adapted to the MPEG standard. By storing a single video along with the motion vectors needed for encoding it at smaller frame rates can be efficiently used for quality adaptation. Both techniques allow the adaptation of the QOS to network congestion and/or different communication speeds. However, compromising quality can be a downside to a commercial service.

3   Problem Description

The architecture examined in this paper consists of N servers connected to M clients by generally non-uniform connections via the Internet. Each server holds complete copies of the movies that could be requested.After a client requests a particular movie, a number of servers $\leq N$ are devoted to serving this request, by sending *disjoint* parts of the requested movie to the client.

Each server S_i devotes $bw_{i,j}$ bandwidth for servicing client C_j. The number of connections that can be simultaneously activated to a client are limited by the client's available bandwidth bw_{C_j}. Similarly, a server cannot accept connections that would exceed its total bandwidth bw_{S_i} (see section 4.3). In the remaining sections bandwidth is expressed in time-per-data-transferred units (e.g. sec/MB)

The arrangement described above for the distribution of the media files is a proxy-at-client architecture [14], i.e. each client has to merge the individual server streams prior to playback. An alternative approach could be to have the proxy implemented by an ISP, thus making the client totally agnostic to the details of the implementation and thus far simpler.

In order to build a model of the whole process, we assume that an affine model dictates the communication costs. Thus, sending a part m of a movie from server

S_i to client C_j requires $bw_{i,j}$ m $L_j + o$, where o is a constant overhead that can be associated with setup activities or the cost of establishing a connection etc., and L_j is the length of the movie requested by client C_j. In this paper we assume that o is incurred only once for each request and that it is the same for all servers.

The problem of a single client with multiple servers has been examined before in the literature [20], where a thorough comparison of single and multi-installment strategies is available. The derivations presented in subsections 4.1 and 4.2 are simplifications of work presented in [3]. In this paper we focus on examining the behavior of a large scale system involving many clients and servers using a multi-server delivery strategy. Such a system can offer improved customer service while maximizing server utilization. Our model simplifications may introduce a level of inaccuracy as far as real systems are concerned (for example data losses are ignored) but these issues can be addressed in the future.

In the remaining sections we also use these notations: R represents the inverse of the movie playback rate (expressed in sec/MB). R is assumed to be constant for each movie, i.e. we have Constant Bit-Rate media. $m_{j,i}$ represents the document part that is delivered by server S_i during installment j. For the next subsection only, m_i is used instead of $m_{0,i}$ for simplicity.

4   Scheduling Document Delivery

4.1   The Single Installment Case

If we assume that the clients don't share any communication links apart from the ones originating from the servers, then the delivery schedule can be found for each individual client separately.

To simplify notation, in this subsection we remove the index related to client identification from our parameters. If $k \leq N$ servers upload content to a client, continuity of the playback is ensured if the following hold:

$$AT + m_0 \; R \; L \geq m_0 \; L \; bw_0 + o \tag{1}$$
$$AT + (m_0 + m_1) \; R \; L \geq m_1 \; L \; bw_1 + o \tag{2}$$

$$\dots$$

$$AT + R \; L \sum_{i=0}^{k-1} m_i \geq m_{k-1} \; L \; bw_{k-1} + o \tag{3}$$

In order to minimize the AT, the equality sign should be used in the above inequalities. By doing so, and by subtracting successive inequalities, we get $m_{i+1} = \frac{bw_i \; m_i}{bw_{i+1} - R}$ for $i = 0, \dots, k - 2$. Or in general

$$m_{i+1} = \frac{m_0 \prod_{l=0}^{i} bw_l}{\prod_{l=1}^{i+1} (bw_l - R)} \tag{4}$$

Since the sum of all m_is should be equal to 1 (also referred to as the normalization equation), then we can compute m_0 from:

$$\sum_{i=0}^{k-1} m_i = 1 \Rightarrow m_0 = \left(1 + \sum_{i=1}^{k-1} \frac{\prod_{l=0}^{i-1} bw_l}{\prod_{l=1}^{i}(bw_l - R)}\right)^{-1} \tag{5}$$

and the access time from:

$$AT = L\,(bw_0 - R)\,m_0 + o \tag{6}$$

In the case of uniform connections $bw_i \equiv bw$, the above equation can be used for estimating the number of servers that would be needed given a desired AT:

$$(5), (6) \Rightarrow \left(\frac{bw}{bw - R}\right)^k = \frac{R\,L}{AT - o} + 1 \Rightarrow k = \lceil \frac{log(\frac{R\,L}{AT-o} + 1)}{log(\frac{bw}{bw-R})} \rceil \tag{7}$$

4.2   The Multi-installment Case

Server utilization can be substantially improved by splitting the document delivery into several installments, as each server stays idle for less time. Using a multi-installment approach means that each server uploads disjoint document parts in sequence (see Figure 1).

The continuity of the playback given N servers and W installments, is ensured by satisfying the following $N \cdot W$ inequalities for each j installment, i server pair:

$$AT + R\,L\,\left(\sum_{l=0}^{i} m_{j,l} + \sum_{k=0}^{j-1}\sum_{l=0}^{N-1} m_{k,l}\right) \geq L\,bw_i \sum_{k=0}^{j} m_{k,i} + o \tag{8}$$

In order to minimize the AT, the equality sign should be used in the above inequalities. By subtracting successive equalities for the parts delivered during the first installment it can be shown similarly to the single installment case, that

$$m_{0,i+1} = \frac{m_{0,0} \prod_{l=0}^{i} bw_l}{\prod_{l=1}^{i+1}(bw_l - R)} \tag{9}$$

Using the same approach for installments $j = 1, \ldots, W - 1$, we can show that:

$$m_{j,i} = \begin{cases} \frac{bw_{N-1}\sum_{k=0}^{j-1} m_{k,N-1} - bw_0 \sum_{k=0}^{j-1} m_{k,0}}{bw_0 - R}, & i = 0 \\[2ex] \frac{bw_{i-1}\sum_{k=0}^{j} m_{k,i-1} - bw_i \sum_{k=0}^{j-1} m_{k,i}}{bw_i - R}, & i = 1, \ldots, N - 1 \end{cases} \tag{10}$$

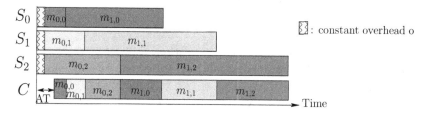

Fig. 1. Example of a multi-installment delivery by 3 servers employing 2 installments.

Equations (9) and (10) define each $m_{j,i}$ as a linear function of parts that precede it in the play-back order. Since (9) to (10) represent linear relationships between each $m_{j,i}$ and $m_{0,0}$, computing the latter can be done by assuming that $m_{0,0}$ is a constant, i.e. 1. This is equivalent to multiplying all parts by a constant $C \geq 1$ which can be estimated by the normalization equation:

$$\sum_{k=0}^{W-1}\sum_{l=0}^{N-1} m_{k,l} = 1 \qquad (11)$$

since the sum of the computed parts will equal C. The above constitutes a $O(N\,W)$ process that can yield very quickly the desired movie partitioning/schedule.

4.3   The General Case

In the general case, we have M distinct clients C_j, each requesting a different movie of L_j length and with a playback rate of R_j. The additional problem that needs to be addressed is that of determining which servers should be allocated to each client in order to minimize the average AT. To solve this mapping problem we employ a genetic algorithm that is shown to converge to a solution in a small number of generations.

All requests are assumed to be simultaneous and have to be serviced concurrently. Despite this being an unrealistic assumption, it is not without merit as it allows us to investigate the steady-state of the system. Also, the genetic algorithm we present, can be employed in an adaptive system, where the network conditions constantly change and the pairing of clients-servers has to change in response. An incremental GA [1] might be appropriate for solving this problem. In this case, the genetic algorithm could be employed for revising the distribution plan at regular intervals. The new schedule would take effect for each client at the beginning of each new installment, hence the benefit of using multiple installments. Such a modification could be easily incorporated in our algorithm.

The objective function that has to be minimized is the following:

$$Z = \overline{AT} = \frac{AT_1 + AT_2 + \ldots + AT_M}{M} \qquad (12)$$

All the above are subject to the following constraints:

- Each server allocates only one slot to each client, i.e.:

$$k_j \leq N \quad \forall\, j = 0, \ldots, M - 1 \qquad (13)$$

where k_j are the number of servers/connections utilized by C_j.
- The total bandwidth consumed should not exceed the servers' capacity:

$$\sum_{j=0}^{M-1} bw_{i,j}^{-1} \leq bw_{S_i}^{-1} \qquad (14)$$

$\forall\, i = 0, \ldots, N - 1$. If a server S_i is not employed by a client C_j, $bw_{i,j} = \infty$.

– Each client's bandwidth should not be exceeded:

$$\sum_{i=0}^{N-1} bw_{i,j}^{-1} \leq bw_{C_j}^{-1} \ \forall \ j = 0, \ldots, M-1 \tag{15}$$

5   A Genetic Algorithm for the Mapping Problem

Genetic algorithms have been adopted for solving a variety of engineering, science, and operations research problems [8][15]. In the following subsection, we give background information on the genetic paradigm and subsequently we describe how a GA can be adapted for solving the mapping problem.

5.1   Background

Genetic algorithms are based on the mechanics of natural evolution [9]. Throughout their artificial evolution, successive generations each consisting of a population of possible solutions, called individuals (or chromosomes, or vectors of genes), search for beneficial adaptations to solve the given problem. This search is carried out by applying the Darwinian principles of "reproduction and survival of the fittest" and the genetic operators of crossover and mutation which derive the new offspring population from the current population.

Reproduction involves selecting, in proportion to its fitness level, an individual from the current population and allowing it to survive by copying it to the new population of individuals. The individual's fitness level is usually based on the cost function given by the problem under consideration. Then, crossover and mutation are carried on two randomly chosen individuals of the current population creating two new offspring individuals. Crossover involves swapping two randomly located sub-chromosomes (within the same boundaries) of the two mating chromosomes. Mutation is applied to randomly selected genes, where the values associated with such a gene is randomly changed to another value within an allowed range. The offspring population replaces the parent population, and the process is repeated for many generations. Typically, the best individual that appeared in any generation of the run (i.e. best-so-far individual) is designated as the result produced by the genetic algorithm.

In the following subsections, we describe how genetic algorithms can be adapted for solving the mapping problem. We present the components of a hybrid genetic algorithm (GA) for minimizing the function Z defined in Eq. (12). The algorithm is hybridized by procedures and design choices that account for both the likelihood of producing infeasible individuals as a result of crossover and mutation, and for the premature convergence to a local optima. An outline of the algorithm is given in Fig. 2.

5.2   Population, Chromosomal Representation and Feasibility

GAs population is an array of POP number of individuals. An individual in the population is encoded as an $(N \times M)$-element vector $[X_{1,1}, X_{1,2}, \ldots X_{1,M},$

```
Generation of initial population, Size POP
Set rates for genetic operators
Evaluate fitness of individuals
Repeat
    Rank individuals & allocate reproduction trials
    for(i=1 to POP step 2) do
            Randomly select 2 parents from list of reproduction trials
            Apply crossover & mutation
    Endfor
    Evaluate fitness of offspring's
    Check feasibility of individuals
    Do hill-climbing
    Preserve the fittest-so-far (elitism)
Until (termination criterion is satisfied)
Solution = Fittest.
```

Fig. 2. Hybrid Genetic Algorithm for the Mapping Problem.

$X_{2,1}, X_{2,2}, \ldots X_{2,M}, \ldots X_{N,1} X_{N,2}, \ldots X_{N,M}]$ where N is the number of the servers and M is the number the clients, and it corresponds to a candidate solution to the allocation of servers to clients that provides a candidate solution to the optimization problem. The sub-vector $X_{1,1}, X_{1,2}, \ldots X_{1,M}$ corresponds to the clients allocated to server 1, sub-vector $X_{2,1}, X_{2,2}, \ldots X_{2,M}$ the clients allocated to server 2, and so forth. An element (gene) $X_{i,j} = 1$ (or 0), for $i \in [1\ldots N]$ and $j \in [1\ldots M]$, indicates the allocation (or deallocation) of server i to customer j.

The initial population of individuals is usually randomly generated. However, in our case, a random generation of individuals introduces too many infeasible individuals to the population. An individual is considered *infeasible*, if it does not satisfy the given constraints (14) and (15). In other words, an individual is infeasible if it is not able to service all the clients because the sum of the active links to each server from a client is greater than the maximum bandwidth of that client, or the sum of the links to each client from a server is greater than the maximum bandwidth of that server. The constraint set (13) is by default satisfied by the above described chromosomal representation of an individual.

In order to reduce the infeasibility problem, the initial individuals generator was written in such a way that it assigns at random one of the servers to a client. Then, it tries to assign another server, if the second server does not make the individual infeasible (too much bandwidth for the client). This method is good in decreasing the infeasibility in the population. It only generates feasible solutions, unless the servers are too slow or overloaded.

5.3   Objective Functions Evaluation and Reproduction Scheme

Using the genes of an individual, the fitness Z of an individual is evaluated as described in (12). Henceforth, the minimal average access time of all clients corresponds to the minimum value of the fitness Z of all feasible individuals.

In GA, the whole population is considered a single reproduction unit within which random selection is performed. Our reproduction scheme involves elitist ranking, followed by random selection of mates from the list of reproduction trials (or copies) assigned to the ranked individuals. In the ranking scheme [2], the individuals are sorted by their fitness value. After sorting, each individual is assigned a ′rank based on a scale of equidistant values for the population. The ranks assigned to fittest and least-fit individuals are 1.2 and 0.8, respectively. Individuals with ranks greater than 1 are first assigned single copies. Then, the fractional part of their ranks and the ranks of the lower half of individuals are treated as probabilities for random assignment of copies.

It has been found that ranking based selection with a maximum rank of 1.2 produces individual survival percentage of 92 to 98% in different generations[2]. This helps in maintaining population diversity and controlling premature convergence. Elitism is used to exploit good building blocks and to ensure that good candidate solutions are saved if the search is to be truncated at any point. Preservation of the fittest individual is done by replacing the least-fit individual by the fittest-so-far individual if the latter is better than the current-fittest.

5.4 Genetic Operators, Hill-Climbing and Termination Criteria

The genetic operators employed in GA are crossover and mutation. Pairs of individuals are randomly selected from the mating pool. Each pair of these strings undergoes crossover as follows: an integer position k along the individual is selected at random between $[1..(N * M)]$, where $N * M$ is the individual length. The two new individuals are created by swapping all characters(genes) between $k + 1$ and $N * M$ inclusively. In our case, a random selection of the crossover point (i.e. k) produces two infeasible individuals. In order to solve this problem, a smarter mode of crossover was implemented. Rather being totally random, the crossover point is taken only at the end of a client. In this way, we preserve each client's feasibility. Moreover, in order to preserve servers feasibility, many crossover points are tried in order to select a point that produces two feasible individuals. The standard mutation operator is employed. Individuals and gene positions where the alteration of the value is going to occur are selected randomly. A mutation rate of 0.02 and crossover rate of 0.7 [10] are used in our implementation.

To refine the solution quality, a simple problem-specific hill-climbing procedure which may decrease the individual's fitness values is incorporated. Our GA determines how many individuals to "hillclimb" by computing the function $numHill$ that starts with tightened hillclimbing rate and increases this rate as the run progresses. We have experimented with different hillclimbing functions and we have found that the following one yields the best solution quality:

$$numHill = \begin{cases} 0.5 \times NumFeasible \; if \; 0 < t \leq 100 \\ 0.7 \times NumFeasible \; if \; t > 100 \end{cases} \quad (16)$$

where t is the current generation and $NumFeasible$ is the number of feasible individuals in the current population. Our GA randomly selects $numHill$ feasible solutions formed in each generation and applies to each of them the following hill-climbing procedure that searches the space nearby an individual solution using a simple "add link" methodology. The procedure randomly selects (N*M)/3 genes and then applies the following to each one: If the value of the gene is 0, then it is provisionally incremented to 1. If the resulting solution is feasible, the provisional change is made permanent and the new solution becomes the incumbent. This means that a link between a certain client and a server is established. This decreases this client's access time, and thus decreases the average access time of the individual. However, if the resulting solution is infeasible, the provisionally incremented gene is restored to its original value. This hill-climbing procedure enables individuals to rapidly climb the peaks, speeding up the evolution process.

The termination criterion is satisfied when we converge to a solution. In this work, convergence is indicated when the best-so-far string does not change its Z value for 15 consecutive generations. We experimented with different values of POP size, and it was found that POP=20 yields the best solution quality.

6   Simulation Study

In order to test the effectiveness of the proposed scheme over a traditional single-server approach, we run rigorous simulation tests estimating how each of the problem parameters reflects on the quality of the delivered service, measured by the AT. It should be noted that although other objective functions could be employed as well, e.g. service costs, client buffer-space, AT variability, etc., these are going to be treated in future extensions of this work.

The parameters that were used in the simulations are listed below:

- N : the number of servers ranged between 2 and 5
- M : the number of clients ranged in $[100, 500 \cdot N]$, targetting a wide variety of loads, including ones that cause server saturation.
- W : the number of installments ranged between 1 and 5
- bw_S : the servers' bandwidth was fixed at $0.08s/MB$ (equiv. to $100Mb/s$)
- bw_C : to represent the variety of clients that could use the service, each client's available bandwidth was randomly selected from 3 possible values:
  - 16 s/MB: equivalent to a 500 kbps ADSL, with a probability of 30%
  - 21 s/MB: equivalent to a 384 kbps ADSL, with a probability of 60%
  - 63 s/MB equivalent to a 128 kbps ISDN, with a probability of 10%
- $bw_{i,j}$: the connection speed between client C_j and server S_i was uniformly selected from $\left[bw_{C_j}, 125s/MB\right]$, the upper limit corresponding to $64kbps$.
- L_j : movie sizes were chosen from a uniform distribution in the $[500, 1000]$MB range, which is typical for MPEG-4-coded feature-length movies.
- R_j : playback rates were chosen randomly from a uniform distribution in the $[600, 1200]\,kbps$ range, again typical MPEG-4 rates for high-quality media.

As a benchmark, we calculated the AT that the clients would enjoy if they were serviced by a single server only. In this "sequential" approach, each client C_j connects to the fastest available server, i.e. the non-saturated one that exhibits the smallest $bw_{i,j}$.

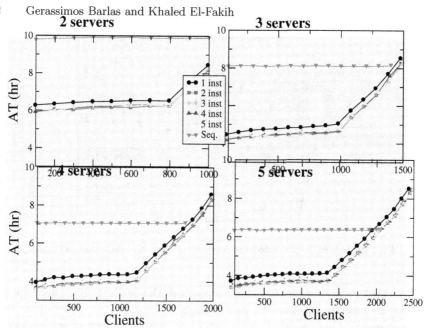

Fig. 3. AT vs the number of clients, for different number of servers and installments.

For each combination of N, M and W values, a total of 100 runs were performed. The average AT versus the total number of clients is shown in Figure 3. As can be clearly observed, increasing the number of servers acts favorably in improving the offered service. The shape of the curves is dictated by the availability of server resources. As the number of clients grows, some of them may settle for slow connections, or even for just a single server. As a result, the average AT increases but the success of our multi-server GA-based scheme is that the clients can be continuously served even when the sequential scheme begins to fail, as indicated by the absence of data points for high M in the corresponding curves of Figure 3. In these situations a large number of clients is denied service.

It should be noted that the clients are examined in a non-specific order, i.e. they are not sorted prior to pairing them with a server in the sequential scheme. Although a sorting step could possibly extend the viability of the sequential scheme to more clients, it is unlikely that this would improve the exhibited AT which is consistently above the one provided by our multi-server scheme.

Figure 3 also shows that increasing the number of installments improves the average AT. Performance gains are however scant after 2 or 3 installments. More installments might offer an edge for the deployment of an adaptive (responding to connection-state changes) delivery scheme.

The ratio of the bandwidth a server uses for uploading movies over its total bandwidth can be used as a metric of a server's saturation. We refer to this ratio as "server occupancy". Figure 4 shows the number of generations required for the GA to converge, versus the server occupancy. The generations needed take a sharp decline following a slight increase as the server occupancy increases. The

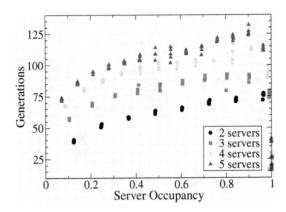

Fig. 4. Generations needed for convergence versus the server occupancy.

reason for this is that the GA fails to improve the original solutions generated, giving up after exceeding the preset threshold for passed generations before improvement. Also, as expected, an increase in the number of servers leads to slightly slower convergence rates due to the expansion of the solution space.

7   Conclusion

In this paper we present a novel approach for optimizing the delivery of movies to multiple clients by multiple servers. We present a genetic algorithm that can generate an optimum or near-optimum mapping of servers to each client request, in an effort to minimize the average AT.

The proposed delivery scheme and mapping algorithm manage to outperform a traditional sequential delivery in every respect, yielding far superior AT while at the same time maintaining normal operation under severe loads that would otherwise cause a denial of service.

Future extension of our work could include:

– Offering different classes of service. Apart from the financial benefits that such an extension would provide, it is only natural that faster and slower clients should be not treated in the same fashion in many different levels.
– Extending the genetic algorithm to handle arbitrary request arrival times. Delivery schedules and mappings could be refined periodically in response to the changing network conditions and/or servers' state (e.g malfunction).

References

1. Awad M., Mansour N., El-Fakih K.: Incremental genetic algorithm. Proc. CSITeA'02, Foz do Iguazu, Brazil, June 6-8 (2002) 24-29.
2. Baker J.E.: Adaptive Selective Methods for Genetic Algorithms. Proc. Int. Conf. on Genetic Algorithms (1985) 101-111.

3. Barlas G., Veeravalli B.: Optimized delivery of Continuous-Media Documents using Distributed Servers. ISCA PDCS 2002 Proceedings, Louisville, USA (2002) 13-19.
4. Boyce J.M., Gaglianello R.: Packet Loss Effects on MPEG Video Sent Over the Public Internet. Proc. ACM Multimedia, Bristol (1998) 181-190.
5. Cai Y., Hua K.A.: An Efficient Bandwidth-Sharing Technique for True Video on Demand Systems. Proc. ACM Multimedia, Orlando (1999) 211-214.
6. Eriksson H.: MBONE: The Multicast Backbone. Comm. of the ACM, Vol. 37, No. 8 (1994) 54-60.
7. Furht B., Westwater R., Ice J.: Multimedia Broadcasting over the Internet: Part I. IEEE Multimedia, October-December (1998) 78-82.
8. Gen M., Cheng R.: Genetic algorithms and engineering optimization. Wiley, New York (2000).
9. Goldberg D.E.: Genetic Algorithms in Search, Optimization and Machine Learning. Addison-Wesley (1989).
10. Grefenstette J.J.: Optimization of Control Parameters for Genetic Algorithms. IEEE Trans. on Systems, Man, and Cybernetics, Vol. 16, No. 1 (1986) 122-128.
11. Gringeri S., Egorov R., Shuaib K., Lewis A., Basch B.: Robust Compression and Transmission of MPEG-4 Video. Proc. ACM Multimedia, Orlando (1999) 113-120.
12. Jung G.S., Kang K.W., Malluhi Q.: Multithreaded Distributed MPEG-1 Video Delivery in the Internet Environment. Proc. ACM Symp. on Applied Computing, Como, Vol.2 (2000) 592-597.
13. Kuhne G., Kuhmunch C.: Transmitting MPEG-4 Video Streams over the Internet: Problems and Solutions. Proc. ACM Multimedia, Orlando, Vol.2 (1999) 135-138.
14. Lee J.Y.B.: Parallel Video Servers: A tutorial. IEEE Multimedia, Apr-Jun, (1998) 20-28.
15. Miettinen K. et al.: Evolutionary algorithms in engineering and computer science. McGraw-Hill, New York (1999).
16. Pejhan S., Chiang T.H., Zhang Y.Q.: Dynamic Frame rate Control for Video Streams. Proc. ACM Multimedia, Orlando (1999) 141-144.
17. Rejaie R., Handley M.: Quality Adaptation for Congestion Controlled Video Playback over the Internet. Proc. ACM SIGCOMM, Cambridge (1999) 189-200.
18. Rodriguez P., Kirpal A., Biersack E.W.: Parallel-Access for Mirror Sites in the Internet. Proc. of Infocom, Tel-Aviv, Israel (2000).
19. Stockinger H., Samar A., Allcock B., Foster I., Holtman K., Tierney B.: File and Object Replication in Data Grids. J. Cluster Computing, 5(3) (2002) 305-314.
20. Veeravalli B., Barlas G.: Access Time Minimization for Distributed Multimedia Applications. Multimedia Tools & Applications, Kluwer Academic Publishers, Vol. 12 (2000) 235-256.

Providing Seamless Mobility
with Competition Based Soft Handover Management

Johan Kristiansson and Peter Parnes

Department of Computer Science & Electrical Engineering, Media Technology
Luleå University of Technology,
971 87 Luleå, Sweden
{Johan.Kristiansson,Peter.Parnes}@csee.ltu.se

Abstract. As host mobility and radio interference in wireless networks cause packet losses and delays, it is difficult to develop useful mobile real-time media applications. This paper describes a new handover strategy for end-to-end mobility called Competition based Soft Handover Management (CSHM). During a handover, redundant packet streams are sent through multiple connections which are later merged into one stream when received by the other end-point. As each network connection competes with other connections in contributing to the merged packet stream, the handover process can be viewed as a competition.

As a proof of concept, CSHM has been implemented in Resilient Mobile Socket, RMS, an application-layer mobility scheme and used together with Marratech Pro, which is a commercially available e-meeting application. By using this prototype, the paper shows that it is possible to minimize redundant packets as well as decrease packet losses during handovers.

1   Introduction

The rapidly growing number of Wi-Fi hotspots and worldwide deployment of new wide-area networks, such as UMTS have made it possible to develop new wireless multimedia services that can be used anywhere and anytime using any available carrier or operator. Mobile e-meeting applications that are running on portable devices with multi-access capabilities will for example allow users to stay connected and participate in virtual communities by using wide-area cellular networks or inexpensive high performance Wi-Fi connections.

Even if multi-access gives users more flexibility in communication, it also imposes new demands on network management and interoperability. When users move between different physical locations, it may become necessary due to limited coverage or bad network performance to make a handover to another network. Similarly, if a better network becomes available, a handover should automatically be initialized to the network offering the best price/performance ratio subject to the user's need.

Today, users must normally take an active part in the handover process and are often required to manually select which network to use. Moreover, during or immediately after a handover it is very common that packet losses and delays occur due to signaling propagation of new location updates. For most applications, such as HTTP or FTP, handover delay is not of vital importance, e.g. waiting one or two second extra when

J. Vicente and D. Hutchison (Eds.): MMNS 2004, LNCS 3271, pp. 295–307, 2004.

downloading a web page is not critical. For real-time media on the other hand, delays and packet losses are extremely important and even a small disturbance can make a media stream unintelligible.

Research about mobility management has so far mainly focused on how to preserve communication and manage location updates. Handover management however, i.e. making fast and low delay handover decisions is still a challenging problem. A handover algorithm must for example be able to evaluate all available networks and select the best performing network as fast as possible in order to avoid interruptions in communications. This is particularly difficult as wireless performance can fluctuate rapidly due radio interference, especially if the coverage is bad.

Oscillations are another problem with handover management. If it takes time to complete a handover and if the performance of a network fluctuates, then there is always a risk that handovers are triggered back and forth between two or more networks causing instability and seriously degraded performance.

These problems raise the question of whether or not it is possible to design a handover algorithm that can:

1. Automatically select the network that is the most suitable for real-time media, i.e. the network with the least packet losses and end-to-end delay.
2. Make a handover to that network without the users perceiving interruptions in real-time media flows.
3. Make handover decisions without the users perceiving degraded performance due to oscillations.

This paper presents a new handover decision algorithm called *Competition based Soft Handover Management* CSHM, that solves these problems. In the paper it is assumed that mobile hosts have access to at least two connections simultaneously. It can also be worth to point out that handover decisions are only based on network performance. Decisions based on financial costs, such as dynamic charge models (none flat-rate) is left for future work.

The rest of the paper is organized as follows. Section 2 gives a brief introduction to previous work related to handover management. In section 3, the RMS is briefly described followed by a more extensive presentation of CSHM. In section 4, the algorithm is evaluated using the Marratech Pro prototype and in section 5, the paper is finally concluded with discussion and future work.

2   Background and Related Work

There have been numerous proposals for providing lossless handovers and minimizing the handover delay to support wireless multimedia. Several micro-mobility schemes have for example been proposed to complement Mobile IP [14]. Cellular IP [18] provides improved handover support in limited geographical areas by incorporating cellular principles found in traditional telecommunication networks. Another micro-mobility scheme, Hierarchical Mobile IP [15], tries to reduce the home network registration time by using a hierarchical network management structure. A difference between the work presented in this paper and research related to Mobile IP, is that CSHM is completely implemented in the application-layer and requires no support from the networks. As mobility is managed end-to-end, CSHM can provide seamless handovers between any network (e.g. a handover between a Wi-Fi network and a UMTS network) and not only seamless handovers within a Mobile IP or Cellular IP enabled network. Another difference is that the paper focus on handover control, i.e. how to trigger handovers, rather than describing how to implement handover support.

A common way to trigger handovers is to monitor the signal strength to the base-stations and use some sort of dwell-timers, hysteresis or threshold based control algorithm [3, 13, 19]. One problem with these handover strategies is that they tend to increase the handover delay, which makes them unsuitable for real-time media.

To make more accurate handover decisions, several location-aided handover strategies have been proposed in the literature [6, 8]. These studies have shown that user movements can be fairly predicted by using a history of recorded user movements, current direction and velocity of the user. However, it has been discussed that mobility prediction algorithms in general are incapable of adapting to new situations and that a small random variation can cause many mobility prediction algorithms to fail [4]. Besides, it is unclear if current technologies, for example the 802.11b can provide sufficient positioning precision [10] to make handover decisions fast enough to support real-time media.

Clearly, if packet loss during handovers could be avoided completely, it would be possible to perform speculative handovers without degrading the quality. To provide lossless handovers between heterogeneous networks, some work has recently been done to add soft handover support in layers above the network layer. RMS [11] provides for example soft handover support by allowing simultaneous use of multiple UDP sockets for data communication. Similar functionality is provided by the ADD-IP [16] mechanism in the Stream Control Transmission Protocol (SCTP) [7].

The major contribution of this paper is a new type of handover management strategy for end-to-end based soft handovers. In contrast to other IP based soft handovers schemes such as [9], CSHM is designed to use multiple IP connections simultaneously. Rather than using redundant connections only as passive backup links, the paper shows how redundancy can be used to improve network performance and how to evaluate end-to-end performance during handovers.

CSHM can also be compared with other multi-link streaming protocols, for example the work presented in [5] or the Multimedia Multiplexing Transport Protocol [12]. However, it is important to point out that the purpose of CSHM is not to increase the throughput, but rather to minimize packet delay during handovers.

3   Competition Based Soft Handover Management

There is a strong relationship between handover management and mobility management. While the later provides the fundamental architecture that is needed to execute handovers, handover management controls and initializes handovers. To understand how CSHM works, it is necessary to first explain how handover support is implemented in the RMS.

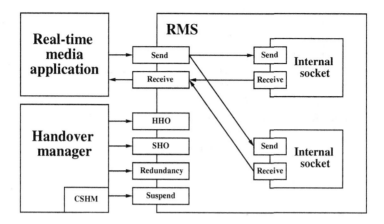

Fig. 1. An overview of the RMS architecture.

3.1   Resilient Mobile Socket

RMS is an application layer mobility scheme for streaming real time media, developed at the division of Media Technology at Luleå University of Technology. The primary purpose of the RMS is to preserve the communication and provide a more robust platform by allowing applications to suspend connections and then resume them using another (or the same) IP address.

An application that sends and receives packets over the Internet normally uses a socket, representing an end-point of a communication link to another application running on the Internet. By encapsulating multiple sockets into a new socket abstraction (RMS), any encapsulated or internal socket can fail without disturbing the applications. As each internal socket represents an entry point to each connected network, running applications will still be able to communicate if the current active internal socket becomes disconnected and another internal socket is available. In this way, a handover process in RMS refers to migrating data flows between different internal sockets.

Figure 1 shows an overview of the RMS architecture and how internal sockets are encapsulated. Note, that RMS besides functionality to send and receive packets also provides methods to control which internal sockets that should be used.

The *SUSPEND* procedure is used to hibernate on-going communication and is automatically called when all network connections are lost, i.e. no internal sockets can be used.

The *HHO* (hard handover) procedure provides the opposite operation and is used to recover from a disconnection or to initiate a handover to another network. During a hard handover, the currently active internal socket is first removed before a new internal socket is created. A hard handover is typically a reactive or an unplanned operation and occurs when something unexpected happens to the system, for example when a connection is suddenly lost. Managing handovers in this case is quite simple as there is usually only one connection to choose from.

The *SHO* (soft handover) procedure provides in contrast to hard handovers, functionality to use redundancy during handovers by using multiple internal sockets simultaneously to send and receive packets. This technique eliminates handover delay and prevents packets from getting lost, but must be proactively initiated to be effective, i.e. initiated before the currently active internal socket becomes disconnected. Because the RMS now has access to multiple connections, a handover management algorithm must be able to evaluate and select the best available connection.

An important component in the RMS architecture is the *Handover Manager*, which can be seen to the left in figure 1. The Handover Manager is responsible for monitoring the system and triggering handovers by calling the procedures mentioned above. A difference between RMS and other mobility management schemes such as Mobile IP, is that handover decisions are always made per packet stream rather than for the whole system. This makes it possible to apply different handover strategies for different media. Audio packets can for example be sent over a Wi-Fi connection while video packets are sent over a UMTS network. Moreover, for none real-time media it may be sufficient to only use hard handovers as soft handovers usually waste bandwidth. From a handover management point of view, this kind of flexibility is extremely important as it relieves the Handover Manager from resolving conflicting handover requirements.

3.2   Competition Based Handover Management

To be able to use soft handovers efficiently several new problems must be solved. The perhaps most difficult problem is how to decide when to initialize soft handovers. As mentioned before, soft handovers must always be initialized proactively, i.e. triggered when at least two internal socket are available. A soft handover management scheme must consequently be able to predict when a connection is going to be lost.

Another difficult problem with soft handovers is how to minimize redundancy. As redundancy wastes resources, both in terms of bandwidth and computer resources, an efficient soft handover management algorithm should strive to minimize redundant packets and in the same time keep the network performance as good as possible.

The rest of this section discusses how CSHM addresses these problems and how handover decisions can be made by using a competition based evaluation between internal sockets.

3.3   Making Proactive Handover Decisions

Even if it would be possible to make proactive handover decision based on mobility prediction, it is important to point out that real-time media such as Voice-over-IP requires that handover decisions are made within a couple of hundreds of milliseconds, before the playout buffer is exceeded. Considering the precision of current technologies and how much the network performance can fluctuate during a couple of hundreds of milliseconds, location-aided handovers do not seem to be a very promising approach. Besides, it is very likely that the performance of a radio network gets degraded even if the user is not moving at all, e.g. somebody closes a door or the user touches the radio antenna.

A more realistic alternative to location-aided handover is to make handover decisions based on jitter interruptions in media streams. When radio conditions are bad it is very common that packets get lost over the air interface. Link-layer approaches such as automatic repeat request (ARQ) attempt to hide channel losses from the network layer by re-transmitting lost packets. However, as it takes time to retransmit lost packets, i.e. ARQ will increase packet delay, and since packets cannot be retransmitted forever some packets will still get lost.

When a user moves away from a network physically, it is very likely due to limited coverage that packet losses and delay occur just before a connection is completely lost. This information is used by the CSHM algorithm to proactively initialize a soft handover.

When an RMS end-point receives a packet stream from another RMS, it calculates a packet delay based on the arrival time of the current packet and the previous packet. If the packet delay exceeds a threshold value, Φ, it will send a *SHO request* to the other end-point, asking it to initialize a soft handover. In this way, the receiver sends feedback[1] to the sender, which makes the final handover decision. If an RMS is both sending and receiving packets, it will take at least two handover decision rounds before both incoming and outgoing packets are duplicated. Note that CSHM does not make any difference between a severely congested network and a network with bad radio performance. If an access network becomes congested somewhere, it may also be reasonable to initiate a handover to another network, assuming that the congested network is not shared with the other available access networks. In this case, there is a risk that redundancy makes the congestion even worse, which will negatively affect the performance of all internal sockets.

It is important to point out that triggering handovers based on interruptions in media streams can only be applied if packets are sent with regular intervals, i.e. packets are sent in a specific pattern. To manage handovers for other (none real-time) media, the Handover Manager periodically scans the routing table for changes. In case a soft handover has not already been initialized, the Handover Manager will for example trigger a hard handover if the currently used network adapter disappears from the routing table. Similarly, to determine if a new network adapter performs better than the current one, the CSHM algorithm can be configured to automatically trigger a soft handover when a new network adapter appears in the routing table.

3.4 Filtering out Duplicate Packets

If packets are not lost over the network, the receiver will get duplicate copies of each packet when redundancy is enabled. Even if many multimedia applications are designed to handle forward error correction (FEC) and duplicate packets, it can dramatically decrease the performance of the applications. In group communication applications, like Marratech Pro, it is very common due to lack of ubiquitous multicast to use a server/reflector to re-distribute packets to other participants. Hence, sending multiple copies of each packet will undesirably increase the load on the server.

To prevent this from happening, a mechanism is needed to filter out duplicate packets and automatically turn off redundancy when performance becomes satisfactory again. By encapsulating all redundant packets into a new packet containing a sequence

---

[1] RMS provides an in-band signaling protocol, which can be used to exchange control information between peers.

number, the first packet received for a given sequence number is forwarded to the application and all other copies are dropped. One advantage of using this *first-come-first-serve* scheme is that it can significantly improve the network performance during a handover. If for example two networks are performing badly, it may still be possible to merge the bad networks into one good network.

Algorithm 1 Competition based Soft Handover Management.

Ensure: the best performing internal socket is always used
1: $dwellTimer \Leftarrow 0$
2: **loop**
3:     **if** $packetDelay > \Phi$ **then**
4:         enableRedundancy()
5:         $dwellTimer \Leftarrow 0$
6:     **end if**
7:     **if** $dwellTimer > \Delta$ **then**
8:         $isocket_{default} \Leftarrow selectWinner(Contribution_{isocket_1}, .., Contribution_{isocket_N})$
9:         disableRedundancy()
10:    **end if**
11:    increase($dwellTimer$)
12: **end loop**

3.5 Selecting a New Default Internal Socket

To minimize redundant packets, CSHM uses a dwell-timer that expires after a predefined amount of time, Δ. Assuming that a new SHO request has not been received, i.e. the dwell-timer has not been reset, redundancy will be disabled after the dwell-timer has expired.

The CSHM algorithm is summarized in algorithm 1. One important difference between CSHM and other handover algorithms [3, 13, 19] is that the new default connection is not decided before the handover. During the handover, each receiver calculates in percent how much each duplicated stream (internal socket) contributes to the merged stream. This new metric is called *packet contribution* and can be viewed as a combination of packet losses and delay in respect to all other duplicated streams. The internal socket that got the highest packet contribution is selected as the new default internal socket after the dwell-timer has expired.

The whole handover process can be viewed as a *competition* where the threshold, Φ, determines when the competition starts, the dwell-timer, Δ, when the competition ends, and packet contribution who the winner is. A competition may not necessarily result in a handover as it is possible that the currently selected internal socket wins. This means that CSHM can also be used to improve network performance without actually switching networks.

4 Evaluation

To evaluate CSHM, a working prototype has been built by integrating RMS with Marratech Pro [1], a commercially available e-meeting software providing tools for synchronous interaction by combining audio, video, chat and a shared white-board.

Extensive use of Marratech Pro has shown that audio is the most sensitive of all involved real-time media [17]. This evaluation has therefore focused on exploring the relationship between different Φ and Δ settings and the effect on GSM audio quality. The following sections describes the prototype, the experimental test-bed and present the results.

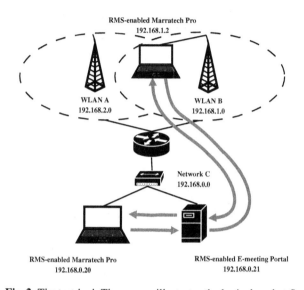

Fig. 2. The test-bed. The arrows illustrates the logical packet flow.

4.1   Implementation

The main part of the RMS is implemented in Java JDK 1.4 under Microsoft Windows XP. The Java Native Interface was used to implement functionality not supported by the Java platform. The IP Helper API [2] available in Windows was used to access the routing table and to detect new or disconnected network adapters.

Marratech Pro was modified by replacing the standard Java DatagramSocket with the RMS. Since Marratech Pro clients either uses IP-multicast or a media gateway called the e-meeting Portal to distribute packets, it was also necessary to replace the standard Java DatagramSocket in the e-meeting Portal. The CSHM algorithm was implemented as a part of the Handover Manager mentioned in section 3.1.

4.2   Methodology

The Marratech Pro based prototype has been tested and used together with a commercial GSM/GPRS network and several 802.11b Wi-Fi networks. Unfortunately, as the GSM/GPRS network performed badly[2], it was impossible to transmit real-time media over it. Besides, as the network was shared with other users, it was hard to interpret the

---

[2] The round-trip time was larger than one second.

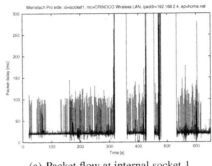

(a) Packet flow at internal socket 1

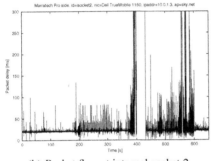

(b) Packet flow at internal socket 2

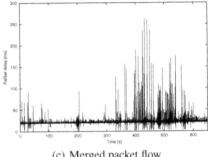

(c) Merged packet flow

Fig. 3. Packet flows during the experiment.

results and make repeatable experiments. It was even difficult to repeat the experiment by moving around between purely isolated 802.11b networks as it was impossible to move exactly the same in each experiment. One solution to this problem would be to repeat the experiment until a statistical certainty is obtained. However, as this can be very time consuming, it was decided to use some other method.

Another possibility would be to use a network simulator, but as this would require a re-implementation of both CSHM and RMS in the simulator it was finally decided to emulate different traffic flows instead. By saving a trace file for each internal socket and then replay the trace files it was possible to test how different Φ and Δ settings affected the merged stream. It was particularly interesting to investigate packet losses and how many redundant packets that were received as well as how many times the playout buffer[3] was exceeded.

Figure 2 illustrates the test-bed that was used to generate the trace files. The test-bed consists of three hosts and two partly overlapping Wi-Fi networks connected to a shared network. Wi-Fi connectivity was provided by two Apple AirPort with built-in NAT routing and two Lucent Orinoco Wi-Fi adapters attached to a laptop. Each Wi-Fi adapter was associated with different Wi-Fi network. The E-meeting Portal was run on a AMD Athlon 1.2 GHh computer and the others were run on Intel Pentium III 1.2 GHz

---

[3] Marratech Pro uses a dynamic playout buffer between 0 and 125 ms.

Table 1. Data from the experiment at the Marratech Pro end-point.

	Internal socket 1	Internal socket 2	Merged stream	Emulated
Packets received	23448	27699	30557	30557
Total packet contribution	26.5%	73.5%	–	–
Packet delay ≥ 50 ms	286	290	114	132
Packet delay ≥ 125 ms	57	53	22	22
Lost packets	7468	3217	359	359

Table 2. Data from the experiment at the Portal end-point.

	Internal socket 1	Internal socket 2	Merged stream	Emulated
Packets received	24867	29319	30909	30909
Total packet contribution	5.1%	94.9%	–	–
Packet delay ≥50 ms	350	280	166	166
Packet delay ≥125 ms	68	27	27	27
Lost packets	6049	1597	7	7

computers. Microsoft Windows XP Professional was used as the operating system on all computers.

4.3   Results

The trace files were generated by moving around physically with one laptop in the testbed and sending GSM audio between the two Marratech Pro clients. By disabling the CSHM algorithm temporarily and using redundancy during the whole experiment, it was possible to get full trace files for both internal sockets.

Figure 3 shows the packet delay for each internal socket at the Marratech Pro side as well as the packet delay for the merged packet stream. Similar results were obtained for the Portal end-point.

As can be seen in figure 3(a) and 3(b), *internal socket 1* lost connectivity three times while *internal socket 2* lost connectivity only one time. Since all disconnections occurred at different times, it was possible to merge *internal socket 1* and *internal socket 2* to one packet stream without the user noticing any disconnections at all. Moreover, note that the packet delay for the merged stream is significantly reduced compared with *internal socket 1* and *internal socket 2*. Apparently, all copies of a specific packet were not always lost even if the packet loss rate was high for both internal sockets.

Table 1 and table 2 summarize statistics from the experiment for the Marratech Pro and the Portal end-point. At the Marratech Pro side, *internal socket 1* contributed in total with 73.5% of all packets received and at the Portal side *internal socket 1* contributed with 94.9% of all packets sent to the Portal end-point. Note that the Portal end-point only had one network connection during the experiment and hence only one internal socket. The result presented in table 2 shows how the *internal socket 1* and the *internal socket 2* located at the Marratech Pro side were perceived at the Portal side.

Table 3. Relationship between Φ, duplicated packets and lost packets. $\Delta = 100$ ms.

	Φ=Infinity	Φ=21 ms	Φ=25 ms	Φ=50 ms	Φ=100 ms
Packets received	30909	30885	30868	30862	30799
Packet delay $\geq$125 ms	22	22	22	22	22
Lost packets	7	31	48	54	117
SHO requests	0	2498	1924	1104	541
Duplicated packets	23306	3103	1882	870	363

Table 4. Relationship between Δ, duplicated packets and lost packets. $\Phi = 50$ ms.

	Δ=Infinity	Δ=50 ms	Δ=100 ms	Δ=200 ms	Δ=0.5 s	Δ=2 s
Packets received	30909	30725	30862	30871	30868	30891
Packet delay $\geq$125 ms	22	22	22	22	22	22
Lost packets	7	191	54	45	48	25
SHO requests	0	1131	1104	1078	1075	1016
Duplicated packets	23306	237	870	1653	2519	11873

As can be seen in table 1 and table 2, the emulated stream corresponds quite well with the merged stream obtained from the experiment. The merged stream can also be viewed as the base case or the optimal case as redundancy was always used. Ideally, a Φ and Δ setting should result in a similar stream, but with less redundant packets.

4.4 CSHM Performance

The CSHM parameter space was explored by locking one parameter, either Δ or Φ and tuning the other parameter. The goal with this investigation was not to obtain an optimal parameter setting, but rather to get a better understanding of the CSHM algorithm.

Table 3 and 4 show the relationship between, Δ, Φ, lost packets and duplicated packets for the Marratech Pro end-point. Similar results were obtained at the Portal end-point. The numbers presented in table 3 and 4 are average values from six test runs. As can be seen in table 3, a small Φ value resulted in many SHO requests, which consequently resulted in more duplicated packets and hence less lost packets. Each GSM packet was sent with approximately 20 ms delay and setting Φ close to 20 ms resulted in 2498 SHO requests. When Φ was set in the range between 0 and 100 ms, the playout buffer was exceeded 22 times, which is exactly the same performance as the base-case, i.e. the optimal performance.

The relationship between Δ, lost packets and duplicated packets was investigated by locking Φ to 50 ms and adjusting the Δ parameter. As expected, a large Δ value resulted in more duplicated packets and hence less lost packets. Since redundancy improved the performance during the experiment, a large Δ also resulted in fewer SHO requests.

By studying the trace files it was observed that if the packet arrival jitter was low and packet losses were concentrated in terms of time, it was efficient to use a low Φ value and a big Δ value. If on the other hand the packet arrival jitter was high, then it made more sense to use a higher Φ value to prevent the CSHM algorithm from always being active.

5   Discussion

In the introduction it was asked whether or not it is possible to develop a handover decision algorithm that can:

1. Automatically select the network that is the most suitable for real-time media, i.e. the network with the least packet losses and end-to-end delay.
2. Make a handover to that network without the users perceiving interruptions in real-time media flows.
3. Make handover decisions without the users perceiving degraded performance due to oscillations.

In brief, the key to solve all these problems is to utilize multiple network connections simultaneously. The first problem is for example solved by using redundancy to compare each network connection and automatically select the connection with the least packet losses and end-to-end delay. As the use of a new internal socket does not affect the performance of the currently used socket, there is no risk that the performance gets degraded because of a handover. As an implication, it is no longer important to reduce the handover frequency, i.e. the users will not perceive any performance degradation when trying a new network.

The second problem is solved by merging multiple packet streams into one stream. This technique can also be used to decrease packet delay and reduce packet losses without performing a handover to another network. The results presented in the paper indicate that CSHM can be used to merge badly performing networks to one good network. However, if redundancy is going to be used as proposed in the paper, it is important to be able to control and minimize redundant packets. The results suggest that CSHM can be used to solve this problem or at least to reduce redundant packets for GSM audio traffic.

Regarding the oscillations, i.e. the third problem, the CSHM algorithm does not directly eliminate the oscillations as it is still possible that handovers are triggered back and forth between several networks, i.e. multiple SHO requests are triggered. However, the users will not perceive degraded performance due to the oscillations as the host receives packets from both the old and the new network during the handover. Rather than repeatedly switching between two badly performing networks, CSHM uses redundancy to improve the performance until some of the networks become stable again or until there is only one working connection left.

Acknowledgment

This work was done within the VITAL project, which is supported by the Objective 1 Norra Norrland – EU structural fund programme for Norra Norrland. Support was also provided by the Centre for Distance-spanning Technology (CDT) and Mäkitalo Research Centre (MRC).

References

1. Marratech AB. , 2004. <http://www.marratech.com>.
2. Microsoft IP Helper API. , 2003. <http://msdn.microsoft.com>.
3. S. Aust, D. Proetel, N. A. Fikouras, and C. Görg. Policy based Mobile IP Handoff Decision (POLIMAND) using Generic link Layer Information. In *IEEE 5th International Conference on Mobile and Wireless Communication Networks (MWCN'02)*, 2003.
4. R. Chellappa, A. Jennings, and N. Shenoy. A Comparative Study of Mobility Prediction in Fixed Wireless and Mobile Ad Hoc Networks. In *IEEE International Conference on Communications (ICC 2003)*, 2003.
5. S. Dhananjay and P.T. Goff. Multiple IP Links for Improving Throughput and Reliability in Mobile Environments. In *INFOCOM*, 2002.
6. F. Erbas, J. Steuer, K. Kyamakya, D. Eggesieker, and K. Jobmann. A Regular Path Recognition Method and Prediction of User Movements in Wireless Networks. In *VTC Fall 2001, Mobile Technology for Third Millennium*, 2001.
7. R. Stewart et al. Stream Control Transport Protocol, 2001. IETF RFC2960.
8. F. Feng and D.S. Reeves. Explicit Proactive Handoff with Motion Prediction for Mobile IP. In *IEEE Wireless Communications and Networking Conference (WCNC'04)*, 2004.
9. S. Kashihara, K. Iida, H. Koga, Y. Kadobayashi, and S. Yamaguchi. End-to-End Seamless Handover using Multi-path Transmission Algorithm. In *Internet Conference 2002 (IC'02)*, 2002.
10. C. Komar and Ersoy C. Location Tracking and Location Based Service Using IEEE 802.11 WLAN Infrastructure. In *The Fifth European Wireless Conference Mobile and Wireless Systems beyond 3G*, 2004.
11. J. Kristiansson and P. Parnes. Application-layer Mobility support for Streaming Real-time Media. In *IEEE Wireless Communications and Networking Conference (WCNC'04)*, 2004.
12. L. Magalhaes and R. Kravets. MMTP: Multimedia Multiplexing Transport Protocol. *ACM SIGCOMM Computer Communication Review*, 31(2):220–243, 2001.
13. Y. Min-hua, L. Yu, and Z. Hui-min. The Mobile IP Handoff Between Hybrid Networks. In *IEEE 13th International Symposium on Personal, Indoor and Mobile Radio Communication (PIMRC'02)*, 2002.
14. C. Perkins. IP Mobility Support, 1996. IETF RFC2002.
15. H. Soliman, C. Castelluccia, K. Malki, and L. Bellier. Hierarchical MIPv6 Mobility Management, 2002. Internet Draft, IETF. Work in progress.
16. R. Steward and et al. Stream Control Transmission Protocol (SCTP) Dynamic Address Reconfiguration, 2003. Internet Draft, IETF. Work in progress.
17. Kåre Synnes, Peter Parnes, and Dick Schefström. Robust Audio Transport using mAudio. Research Report, ISSN 1402-1528, ISRN LTU-FR–99/04–SE, Luleå University of Technology, 1999.
18. A. Valkó. Cellular IP: A New Approach to Internet Host Mobility. *ACM SIGCOMM Comp. Commun. Rev.*, 29(1):50–65, 1999.
19. H.J. Wang. Policy-Enabled Handoffs Across Heterogeneous Wireless Networks. Technical Report CSD-98-1027, 1998.

Large-Scale Mobile Multimedia Service Management in Next Generation Networks[*]

Daniel Negru[1], Ahmed Mehaoua[1], Anastasios Kourtis[2], and Eric LeBars[3]

[1] CNRS-PRiSM Lab., University of Versailles,
45, avenue des Etats-Unis 78035 Versailles, France
{dan,mea}@prism.uvsq.fr
[2] Institute of Informatics and Telecommunications NCSR "DEMOKRITOS",
Agia Paraskevi Attikis, 15310 Athens, Greece
kourtis@iit.demokritos.gr
[3] Thales Broadcast & Multimedia
1, rue de l'Hautil, zone des Boutries, 78700 Conflans Ste Honorine, France
Eric.lebars@thales-bm.com

Abstract. Last decade has seen a tremendous growing interest in wireless and mobile multimedia IP networking. As a consequence, the number and variety of devices allowing an Internet access has grown impressively and easily-transportable mobile devices have received an enormous success. More and more, new products are launched with an Internet access possibility and the trend now is the ability to get connected anywhere, anytime, anyhow. But, achieving such a task implicates an increasing complexity of the networking and service management. The fundamental multimedia applications, for which multicasting is the predominant delivery technique, need to be provided in a mobile environment. In this paper, we investigate the issues arising from the interoperation of mobile and multicasting mechanisms, focusing on specific multimedia constraints. From then, we propose an innovative protocol for an efficient delivery of multimedia services to desired mobile terminals. A solution for an anywhere, anytime, anyhow connection is hence presented.

1 Introduction

For many years now, there has been a sensational increase in the number and variety of devices connected to the Internet. Consequently, this has caused a lack of available IP addresses, one of the main issues addressed in Internet Protocol version 6 (IPv6) [1], the new version of the Internet Protocol, which is expected to be the leading standard for next generation networks. Above all, with the emergence of mobile devices such as laptops and PDAs, the number of mobile users, who expect to access services and applications the same way they did in wired networks, became larger and larger. The IETF proposed the *Mobile IPv6* [2] approach to deal with this emerging network service requirement.

In the meantime, there has been a tremendous growing interest in multimedia applications. Demand for multimedia group communication, audio and video streaming, videoconferencing, distributed games or Internet TV has rapidly increased. The inher-

---

[*] This work has been partially performed within the context of the European research project IST ATHENA (http://www.ist-athena.org). The authors would like to thank the participants for their contributions.

J. Vicente and D. Hutchison (Eds.): MMNS 2004, LNCS 3271, pp. 308–319, 2004.

ent nature of most multimedia applications is that a communication may include a large number of participants. They are considered as one-to-many or many-to-many, where one or multiple sources are sending to multiple receivers. Multicasting is the technique that most efficiently supports this type of transmission.

The combination of mobility and multicasting for the delivery of large-scale multimedia applications, in IPv6 networks, represents an important challenge. The principal objective is to enable users to access the desired multimedia program with sufficient Quality of Service anywhere, anytime and anyhow, hence through any kind of mobile device. There exists some techniques designed to multicast mobility, the most famous being IETF's ones based on *Mobile IPv6* [2]: *Bi-directional Tunneling (BT)*, which builds a tunnel between the *home network* and the *foreign network* of the mobile node, and *Remote Subscription (RS)*, which reconfigures the multicast tree by considering the new location of the mobile node. Several others have been elaborated but none has really addressed the problem focusing on IPv6 networks and specific multimedia constraints.

In this paper, we propose a novel approach for the management of IPv6 mobile terminals whishing to receive multicast multimedia services. We essentially focus on multimedia specific constraints and try to provide the best mechanism with the least delivery delays and service interruption periods. The result is a called Mobility for Multicast Multimedia Applications in IPv6 Networks (*M3IP6*), based on MIP6 with enhanced messages and addition of special entities. This protocol has been fully evaluated and will be deployed at a large-scale, thanks to the European research project ATHENA, for which it has received strong support.

The article is constructed as follows. First, we present related works, including *Mobile IPv6*'s based solutions. Next, we focus on our proposal, by first stating the problem and then explaining the design and description of the *M3IP6* protocol. After that, the evaluations of our solution, along with protocols' comparisons, are exposed. Finally, the large-scale deployment thanks to the ATHENA European project is presented.

2 Related Works

Some researches exist on the convergence of multicasting and mobility but they mainly focus on IPv4 networks. Besides *Mobile IPv6* and its two extended approaches: *Remote Subscription (RS)* and *Bi-directional Tunneling (BT)*, there aren't many applicable to IPv6 networks.

2.1 Mobile IPv6

The first approach to multicast mobility in IPv6 networks would be to extend IETF's *Mobile IPv6* protocol. In *Mobile IP* [3], each mobile node has a permanent *home address* (HoA), and receives a transient *care-of address* (CoA) when visiting a foreign network. The mobile node registers its current CoA with its *home agent* (HA), which is located in its home network. The home agent intercepts and tunnels to the CoA all packets destined to the mobile node. *Mobile IPv6* integrates new features: no more foreign agents needed, stateful or stateless autoconfiguration, route optimization, HoA Destination Option. Further information can be found in [2]. It appears that MIP6 is lighter and more efficient than MIP4.

The current IETF's *Mobile IPv6* specification proposes two approaches for supporting multicast services to mobile hosts: *Remote Subscription* (RS) and *Bidirectional Tunneling (BT)*.

In Remote Subscription, the Mobile Node joins the multicast group each time it enters a foreign network. The main advantage of this approach is that multicast data are delivered on the shortest path. On the other hand, the multicast delivery tree must be frequently updated. This generates significant signaling overhead, and might result in unnecessary bandwidth consumption. Nevertheless, multicast traffic keeps flowing, until soft-state multicast group management information expires. Another major drawback of this proposition would be the join latency, which could be much too significant for multimedia real-time applications.

In Bi-directional Tunneling, the Home Agent forwards multicast packets to the Mobile Node through a unicast tunnel. This approach has the advantage that the multicast delivery tree is not updated every time the Mobile Node moves to a different network. On the other hand, the data delivery path is not optimal because of triangular routing and redundancy may occur in case of several Mobile Nodes willing to receive the same multicast flow, in the same foreign subnet: *Tunnel Convergence Problem*.

2.2 Mobile Multicast Protocol (MoM) and Range-Based (RB)MoM

Mobile Multicast Protocol (*MoM*) [4] solves the *Tunnel Convergence Problem* by using a *Designated Multicast Service Provider* (DMSP). This solution allows to provide at most once multicast delivery. It does solve the problem for IPv4 networks but not for IPv6 ones, since there are no foreign agents in IPv6. Also, a long DMSP handoff can occur if the FA has to reselect its DMSP, and multicast delivery may be disrupted, which is unacceptable for real-time communications.

The *Range-Based MoM* (*RBMoM*) [5] solution is a trade off between the shortest delivery path and the overhead induced by the multicast delivery tree reconfiguration. It uses *Multicast Home Agents* (MHA) with a limited service range to alleviate the problem of a long handoff. As for *MoM*, *RBMoM* uses FA and thus cannot be directly extended to IPv6. Also, the performance of *RBMoM* is controlled by the selection of service range and, still, handoffs may occur when moving fast from high-distant networks. Other similar approaches can also be found, dedicated exclusively on IPv4, such as *Mobility by Multicast Agent* (MMA) [6].

3 Proposal of an Efficient Protocol for Mobile Multicast Multimedia Applications in IPv6 Networks

Our solution for an efficient management of terminal mobility for multicast multimedia applications in IPv6 networks is now depicted. First, the problem of an efficient handling of multimedia communications in a mobile environment is stated through exposing the constraints of those specific services. Next, the architectural scheme of our solution is explained.

3.1 Multimedia Services Constraints

As presented above, no efficient solution exists for handling mobility for multicast applications in IPv6 networks, especially concerning multimedia sessions, which have their own constraints. Several proposals may achieve some parts of these. Nevertheless, they are not suitable to multimedia applications since they do not overcome multimedia constraints and especially in next generation's based IPv6 networks. Those constraints mainly include:

- Packet loss. Losses of multimedia packets can severely hamper the quality of the stream and damage the perception of the media at the end user;
- Delay and error resilience. Especially streaming video must reconcile the conflicting constraints of delay and error resilience. In order to maintain a high level of user interactivity, delay must remain relatively small (200ms);
- Delay variation or network jitter. An important delay variation would cause problems for applications that want to play out received data at a constant rate, such as streaming applications;
- Bandwidth variation. Available bandwidth varies with time and the streaming system should adjust its sending rate as well as the quality of the transmitted bitstream in accordance with these changes. This constraint cannot be overcome through our work. It is dedicated to the multimedia source.

The proposal described herein takes highly into consideration the first three constraints. Their evaluation will be processed trough two special metrics: service interruption period and delivery delay.

3.2 Mobility for Multicast Multimedia Applications in IPv6 Networks (M3IP6)

The proposed solution is called *Mobility for Multicast Multimedia Applications in IPv6 Networks* (M3IP6). It is based on IETF's *Mobile IPv6* approach and is not dependent of any multicast protocol, as long as *MLD* messages are used for registration, de-registration, and other important features at a LAN level. The different phases of the protocol will now be described.

First, a new Home Agent (HA) entity has to be considered for multicast sessions, in addition to the original HA, which task is dedicated to unicast flows. This Multicast Home Agent, MHA, will be in charge of retransmitting multicast flows to the Mobile Node when it is away from its home subnet. This is considered as phase 1 of the protocol. The MHA is dynamic; it depends on the previous location of the MN and changes accordingly.

The MHA and the HA are the same when the MN moves away from its home subnet, for the first time. But next, if the MN starts moving again to another foreign network, the new MHA will then not be the same entity as the HA. For most convenience, it should be the Designed Router (DR) of the last visited network but, it could also be another node of this network as well. The only imperative point is that the MHA has registered to all the multicast groups the MN has, so that it can retransmit the flows to the MN without having to register again – that's why the DR is certainly the most appropriate one. Therefore, when moving to foreign subnets, there's no significant latency at the MN side concerning multicast flows, essential feature for multimedia applications.

Also, while at a foreign network, a MN will subscribe to desired multicast groups by sending appropriate *MLD* report messages onto the foreign network link, as described by remote subscription solution. After this phase is completed and multicast flows arrive from the DR of the link the MN is actually on, the MN will deregister from its MHA (which was on the previous visited link). Phase 2 of the *M3IP6* protocol is then initiated. We can see that the advantages of remote subscription are still present in our solution, without the drawback of long-lasting time wasting for the joining to (a) delivery tree(s).

We could have chosen not to specify a new entity, the MHA, and to make all the traffic (unicast and multicast) pass through the HA. Even though this approach would have seemed simpler, the HA being constantly considered as the multicast forwarding entity, it has too important drawbacks. Above all, this method is not efficient enough in case of multimedia streams. Concerning disruption, it is acceptable since the MN will only stop receiving multicast data for a short period of time, which corresponds to the delay introduced by the MN for sending the appropriate instructions to the HA and to trigger the resumption of multicast forwarding. Though, there still remains a huge problem in the case of many multicast registrations of Mobile Nodes. The HA will have to support all of these and thus congestion in the node can occur, especially with multimedia streams, which are usually very heavy. The HA would be over-loaded. Therefore, this method is not adapted at all to large-sized mobile nodes environment and high-consuming bandwidth applications.

3.3 M3IP6 Protocol Description for Terminal Mobility

The *M3IP6* protocol is based on extensions of *Mobile IPv6* and *MLD* proposals.
New messages are added to the *Mobile IPv6*'s ones:

- Multicast Binding Update (MBU) from the MN to its MHA, to notify that it has moved;
- Multicast Binding Acknowledgement (MBA), return message from the MHA after receiving a MBU;
- Deregistration MBU (lifetime=0) and MBA, messages between the MN and its MHA to cease the retransmitting of multicast flows through this way.

Some additional lists will be implemented into the nodes:

- Multicast Home Agents list for MNs, similar to the Home Agents list for unicast flows;
- Multicast Binding Cache for MHAs, similar to the Binding Cache for unicast flows.

For *MLD* extensions, only a special message is added to inform the Designed Router that it should not stop receiving the multicast flow, provided the MN is the last one willing to receive it and it is away: MLD Listener Hold. Here is a detailed description of how this protocol works for terminal mobility:

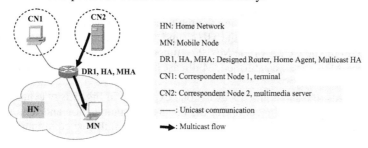

Fig. 1. MN at Home Network.

First, the MN is at home (Fig. 1). It establishes an unicast communication with the terminal CN1 and it receives a multicast flow from the multimedia server CN2. The Designed Router is also determined as the HA of the MN.

Next, the MN moves to a foreign network (Fig. 2). Concerning the unicast communication between the MN and CN1, classic *Mobile IPv6* messages are sent to establish the tunnel MN-HA: Binding Update and Binding Ack. The same mechanism is used for the multicast flow from the multimedia server CN2, to which the MN is registered: Multicast BU, from the MN to the MHA (which is the same entity as the HA at this moment) and Multicast BA, from the MHA to the MN. Then, the Multicast Binding Cache of the MHA is updated consequently with the Care-of-address of the MN and a Multicast MHA-MN tunnel is established. In this first move case, we consider the tunnel as the same as for unicast communication. This represents phase 1.

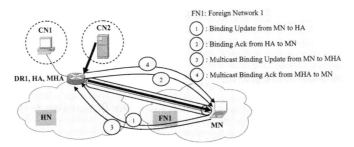

Fig. 2. First Move of the MN.

After the reverse tunnels are established between the HA or MHA, and the MN for the unicast and multicast applications, packets are being encapsulated and transmitted through this way. Next (Fig. 3), for the unicast communication, route optimization is established according to the *Mobile IPv6* specifications. Concerning the multicast flow, the MN registers to the DR2 of the foreign network it is actually in. When the registration process is done and the MN may receive the multicast flow from DR2, it informs its MHA that it does no longer need to receive these packets through the tunnel: Multicast Deregistration BU from the MN to the MHA (1), Multicast Deregistration Back from the MHA to the MN (2). Then, the multicast MN-MHA tunnel is destroyed; the MN-HA tunnel for unicast communications remains still (as described in *Mobile IPv6*'s draft). The MHA is no longer DR1 but it switches to DR2. From now on, phase 2 of the mechanism is activated.

Now, the MN starts moving again to another foreign network FN2 (Fig. 4). The same process as above is initiated (phase 1) but at this point, the MHA and the HA are not the same anymore. Concerning the multicast flow between CN2 and the MN, first a MBU is sent from the MN to the MHA, updating consequently its Multicast Binding Cache with the new CoA of the MN. The tunnel between the MHA and the new location of the MN is then established. Multicast packets from CN2 are encapsulated and transmitted this way.

Afterwards, the same process as the one explained in Fig. 3 is executed again. The MN enables Route Optimization for the unicast communication and remote subscription to the multicasting flow through the new DR for multicast communications. With this solution, MNs will always act this way when switching from a subnet to another, even when they come back home.

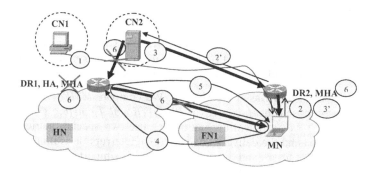

○1 : Route Optimization Establishment for Unicast Communication

○2 ○2' : Multicast Registration Procedure through DR2 (MLD and PIM messages)

○3 ○3' : Multicast Flow reception through DR2

○4 : Multicast De-registration BU from MN to MHA

○5 : Multicast De-registration BAck from MHA to MN

○6 : Suppression of the Multicast Flow from the MN-MHA tunnel, suppression of MN-MHA tunnel and establishment of DR2 as the new MHA for MN.

Fig. 3. Optimization of Mobile O7perations.

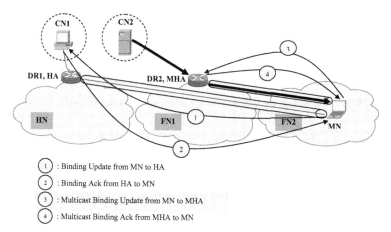

○1 : Binding Update from MN to HA

○2 : Binding Ack from HA to MN

○3 : Multicast Binding Update from MN to MHA

○4 : Multicast Binding Ack from MHA to MN

Fig. 4. MN's Next Moves Process.

4 Evaluation and Demonstration

Our solution is well-adapted for supporting multimedia applications since it signifi-cantly reduces disruption and insures optimal multicast routing and low system over-load. The *M3IP6* protocol has been fully evaluated when dealing with terminal mobil-ity through specific metrics, comparison, and simulation. The implementation and demonstration stage has found support in the European project ATHENA.

4.1 Protocol's Evaluation

The evaluation of our protocol has been performed first through a theoretical evaluation based on metrics, then based on a comparison to other mobile multicast protocols. There is also a simulation process and deeper looks that can be found in [10].

Theoretical Evaluation Based on Metrics. We compare *M3IP6* with the two solutions already proposed in *Mobile IPv6*: *Bi-directional Tunneling (BT)* and *Remote Subscription (RS)*. For efficient evaluation, we use two special metrics: the service interruption period and the delivery delay. Service interruption is fundamental for the evaluation of packet losses and disruptions, one of the important constraints of multimedia applications. Delivery delay also highly concerns real-time applications, for which important delays imply loss of quality. Hence, we suppose the followings: $d(a,b)$: Distance between node a and node b, in number of links; S: The multicast source; Del_{prop}: Propagation delay on a link, assuming it is the same on each link of the network for each kind of message and neglecting processing and queuing delays; $Int(MN)$: Service interruption or the time interval during which the mobile node looses multicast connectivity, when it moves from its home network to a foreign one; $Del(MN, S)$: Delivery delay or the time interval necessary to deliver a multicast packet from the source S to the mobile node. *JDel(MLD)*: The Join Delay, experienced by *MLD* timers. This value could be set to a lower one but this may have repercussions (overflow of signalization). By default, it is of 125s.

Service Interruption Period. Concerning the Service Interruption Period, we compare the three solutions by neglecting agent discovery and we reach the following conclusion. All details can be found in [10]. We obtain the shortest service interruption period with our protocol:

$$\mathrm{Int}_{\mathrm{M3IP6}}(\mathrm{MN}) < \mathrm{Int}_{\mathrm{BT}}(\mathrm{MN}) << \mathrm{Int}_{\mathrm{RS}}(\mathrm{MN})$$
$$\text{if } d(\mathrm{MN}_{\mathrm{CoA}}, \mathrm{MHA}) < d(\mathrm{MN}_{\mathrm{CoA}}, \mathrm{HA}). \tag{1}$$

Or at least, the same as for *BT* in some cases (when the MN moves for the 1st time):

$$\mathrm{Int}_{\mathrm{M3IP6}}(\mathrm{MN}) \sim \mathrm{Int}_{\mathrm{BT}}(\mathrm{MN}) << \mathrm{Int}_{\mathrm{RS}}(\mathrm{MN}). \tag{2}$$

Delivery Delay. We now consider and compare the Delivery Delays of the three solutions. We neglect processing and queuing delays of the messages.

In *BT*, there is the establishment of a tunnel between the HA and the MN. We will not consider the encapsulation and decapsulation time of the packets:

$$\mathrm{Del}_{\mathrm{BT}}(\mathrm{MN}, \mathrm{S}) = \mathrm{Del}_{\mathrm{prop}}[d(\mathrm{S}, \mathrm{HA}) + d(\mathrm{HA}, \mathrm{MN}_{\mathrm{CoA}})]. \tag{3}$$

The packets do not have a direct path, as shown Fig. 5 (a), consequently a delay occurs in the delivery mechanism. In *RS*, there is no tunnel and therefore, the delivery is achieved directly, no delay is induced; it can be seen in Fig. 5 (b):

$$\mathrm{Del}_{\mathrm{RS}}(\mathrm{MN}, \mathrm{S}) = \mathrm{Del}_{\mathrm{prop}}d(\mathrm{S}, \mathrm{MN}_{\mathrm{CoA}}). \tag{4}$$

However, in *M3IP6*, it is a bit more complex to estimate the Delivery Delay. The first phase of the *M3IP6* mechanism consists of the establishment of a bi-directional tunnel between the MHA and the MN. The Delivery Delay could be compared to the one of *BT*, with the difference that it is not the HA but the MHA that retransmits the multicast flow:

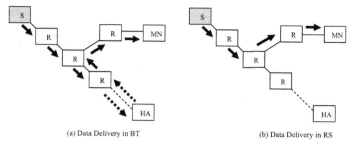

(a) Data Delivery in BT   (b) Data Delivery in RS

Fig. 5. Data Delivery Mechanisms in BT and RS.

1ˢᵗ phase: $Del_{M3IP6}(MN, S) = Del_{prop}[d(S, MHA) + d(MHA, MN_{CoA})]$.   (5)

Thus, since the MN's movement will not be, in most cases, further than one network away at a time, only one (or at most two) router(s) will generally separate the two networks, as shown Fig. 6.

Consequently, on the first stage of the mechanism, the delivery delay is more optimal for *M3IP6* than for *BT* (and of course, a bit less optimal than *RS*), in most cases:

1ˢᵗ phase: $Del_{RS}(MN, S) < Del_{M3IP6}(MN, S) \ll Del_{BT}(MN, S)$.   (6)

When reaching the second phase, the MN is registered to multicast flows through the DR of the visited network, exactly identical to the *RS* mode. Therefore, the delivery of the packets is direct:

2ⁿᵈ phase: $Del_{M3IP6}(MN, S) = Del_{prop}d(S, MN_{CoA})$.   (7)

We then obtain, for the second phase, the best delivery delay possible with our protocol:

2ⁿᵈ phase: $Del_{M3IP6}(MN, S) = Del_{RS}(MN, S) \ll Del_{BT}(MN, S)$.   (8)

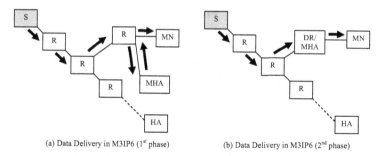

(a) Data Delivery in M3IP6 (1ˢᵗ phase)   (b) Data Delivery in M3IP6 (2ⁿᵈ phase)

Fig. 6. Multicast Data Delivery Mechanism in M3IP6.

In conclusion, our *M3IP6* protocol is the most efficient one, considering the two most important metrics for multimedia applications: the Service Interruption Period and the Delivery Delay. The shortest interruption period is obtained, as well as the best delivery delay, compared to *RS* and *BT*.

Comparison to Other Mobile Multicast Protocols. The main advantage of our solution is that it is entirely designed to support for the best multimedia applications, focusing on their constraints. Even if it may increase the bi-directional tunnel duration, it absolutely minimizes the multicast tree complexity while still meeting the delay constraints (i.e. a short handoff for services continuity). The use of a Multicast Home Agent (MHA) reduces significant disruption and the establishment of the multicast subscription at the visited network side assures optimal multicast routing and low system overload. Moreover, this distinct location of MHA and HA allows processing of multicast flows by a QoS differentiation scheme, for which solutions already exist. Minimum latency, short join delay, routing optimality are among the important features the proposal has been based on. System load has also been taken into account, as well, in this evaluation process.

The following table (Table 1) shows the advantages and drawbacks of most of the proposals in this area: *Remote Subscription (RS)*, *Bi-directional Tunneling (BT)*, *Range-Based MoM (RBMoM)*, *MMA*, and ours, among different criteria.

Table 1. Comparison of Mobile Multicast Protocols.

	RS	BT	RBMoM	MMA	M3IP6
Join Delay	High	Optimal	Short	Short	Optimal
Multicast Routing	Optimal	Non-Optimal	Sub-Optimal	Sub-Optimal	Sub-Opt.->Opt.
Handoff Occurrence	High	Optimal	Sub-Optimal	Low	Optimal
Tunnel Convergence	No	Yes	No	No	No
IPv6 Support	Yes	Yes	No	No	Yes
Add. Signalisation	No	No	Yes	Yes	Yes
Add. Support at FN	Low	No	No	Low	Yes
System Load	No	Yes	Low	Low	Low
Source Mobility	Possible	Possible	Not Specified	Not Specified	Possible

4.2 Demonstration on ATHENA Platform

The EU-funded IST Project ATHENA (ATHENA - Digital Switchover: Developing Infrastructures for Broadband Wireless Metropolitan Area Network Access [9]), which started in January 2004, takes into consideration mobility concepts and technology interoperation between DVB-T and IP. ATHENA proposes the use of the DVB-T in regenerative configurations and exploits the networking capabilities of the television stream for the creation of a powerful backbone that interconnects distribution nodes within a city. Fig. 7. shows an overall representation of the networking aspects of the project.

Among its objectives, the ATHENA European project is conducting research activities in DVB-T system and mobility. One of the goals of this research project is to set the proposed architecture described above and make feasible scenarios of mobility, with proper solutions and enhancements. In this particular environment, we can distinguish several mobility issues, either on the concern of access networks behind CMNs (WLAN and UMTS devices), or switching between CMNs and experiencing layer-3 handovers and finally, at a larger scale between broadcasting areas. Concerning access networks behind CMNs, such as WLAN and UMTS, solutions for achieving mobility in those cases are known and exploited. The first challenge is to support the mobility case when a mobile user equipped with a DVB-T receptive device switches from one broadcasting area to another or inside the same broadcasting area from a frequency to another. A second objective is to permit the accessibility of IP services by no DVB-T receivers, located behind CMNs and able to perform mobility actions from one CMN to another. This point is covered by our proposed protocol: *M3IP6*. In this broadcasting context, there will essentially be multicast multimedia IP services, which will be transmitted between users. The intention is to provide wide access to mobile users, permitting them to switch instantly from an area to another.

Therefore, the ATHENA project consists of a perfect support for integrating and developing at a large scale, mobility aspects, issues and, thus, our proposed solution.

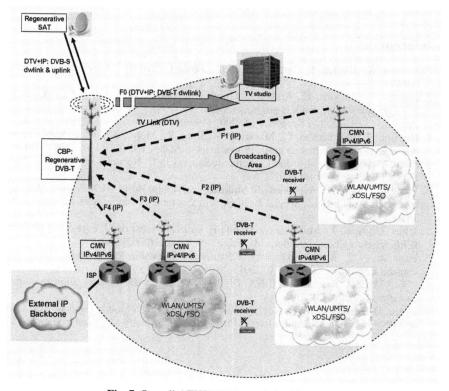

Fig. 7. Overall ATHENA Network Architecture.

5 Conclusion

The establishment of an efficient handling of mobility for multicast multimedia applications becomes a need nowadays, especially given the tremendous growing demand for these kinds of services and the steady increase in the number of mobile wireless devices connected to the Internet. Over the last few years, there have been several interesting proposals to achieve the interoperation of Mobility and Multicasting, but none explicitly focused on IPv6 networks. The IETF's *Mobile IP* Working Group proposes *Remote Subscription* and *Bi-directional Tunneling* but they both have important drawbacks, inadequate to the specific QoS required by multimedia applications.

We introduced a novel approach for an efficient mobility management for Multicast Multimedia Services in IPv6 Networks and proposed the *M3IP6* (Mobility for Multicast Multimedia Applications in IPv6 Networks) protocol. Our solution provides a simple and efficient method, based on *Mobile IPv6*, for transparently handling multicast receivers' mobility. *M3IP6* advantages are to reduce data delivery delays and achieve almost a no service interruption period. Therefore, it overcomes most of the important multimedia constraints. Above all, it appeared to be designed to fully comply with multimedia communications. Its integration into the European project ATHENA will provide a perfect context for the deployment at a large scale of *M3IP6*'s proposal.

References

1. Deering, S., Hinden, R.: Internet Protocol, Version 6 (IPv6) – Specification. RFC 2460 (1995)
2. Johnson, D., Perkins, C., Arkko, J.: Mobility Support in IPv6. Internet Draft, draft-ietf-mobileip-ipv6-24.txt, work in progress (2003)
3. Perkins, C.: IP Mobility Support. RFC 2002 (1996)
4. Harrison, T., Williamson, C., Mackrell, W., Bunt, R.: Mobile Multicast (MoM) Protocol: multicast support for mobile hosts. Proceedings of ACM MOBICOM '97 (1997) 151–160
5. Lin, C.R., Wang, K.-M.: Mobile Multicast Support in IP Networks. Proceedings of IEEE INFOCOM'00 (2000) 1664-1672
6. Wang, Y., Chen, W.: Supporting IP Multicast for Mobile Hosts. ACM/Kluwer Mobile Networks and Applications, Special Issue on Wireless Internet and Intranet Access, vol. 6, no. 1 (2001) 57-66
7. Jelger, C., Noel, T.: Multicast for Mobile Hosts in IP Networks: Progress and Challenges. IEEE Wireless Communications Magazine, vol. 9, no. 5 (2002) 58-64
8. Feamster, N.G.: Adaptive Delivery of Real-Time Streaming Video. Ph.D. Thesis, Massachusetts Institute of Technology (2001)
9. IST ATHENA Report: ATHENA Digital Switchover: Developing Infrastructures for Broadband Access (2003)
10. Negru, D., Mehaoua, A.: Deploying Multimedia Services to Mobile Users in Next Generation IPv6 Networks. Technical Report PRiSM Lab., University of Versailles, France (2004)

Mobility Prediction in Wireless Networks Using Neural Networks

Joe Capka and Raouf Boutaba

School of Computer Science, University of Waterloo
200 University Ave. West, Waterloo, Ontario, N2L 3G1, Canada
{jcapka,rboutaba}@uwaterloo.ca

Abstract. Wireless network resource use depends in large part on the mobility of network users. The ability to predict this mobility at least in part enables the network to anticipate resource use in the future and take precautionary measures if necessary. This work presents a neural network prediction system that is able to capture some of the patterns exhibited by users moving in a wireless environment and can then predict the future behaviour of these users. These predictions can then be used in a multitude of ways to ensure proper and predictable resource use.

1 Introduction

The popularity of wireless voice communication grew explosively during the end of the last century. The next anticipated step in wireless communication is the delivery of data services, specifically internet services to mobile users. It is anticipated that mobile users in the near future will not only be concerned with the availability of these wireless services, but also with the quality of these services.

One mechanism proposed to aid in providing a certain quality of service is limiting the number of users accessing the network resources at a given point in time. This is known as Admission Control (AC). Many types of AC mechanisms have been proposed for wireless networks [2], [6], [7]. This paper introduces a mobility prediction mechanism that can be used by AC mechanisms to better anticipate the future state of the network and thus make better call accept/reject decisions.

The rest of this paper is organized as follows: Section 2 introduces some background concepts, section 3 provides an overview of current research status, section 4 describes the design of the neural network predictor, section 5 discusses the simulations used to evaluate the predictor performance, section 6 presents the results and section 7 concludes the paper.

2 Background

2.1 Distributed Call Admission Control

Distributed Call Admission Control is a type of AC that uses information from more than the network access point (NAP) the user is currently connected to, and deals with the granularity of calls. One of the crucial decisions for any dCAC scheme is deciding which of the NAPs will be involved in the admission decision. This decision is not trivial since the group of NAPs that result in the best admission decision can vary

J. Vicente and D. Hutchison (Eds.): MMNS 2004, LNCS 3271, pp. 320–333, 2004.

according to many factors. These factors can include global data such as the average congestion level in the network, time of day and day of week. It is not difficult to see however that the optimal group of NAPs will be different for each call that is being admitted to the network, and thus more important to determining this optimal group of NAPs is local NAP data as well as specific call data. Local NAP data is data such as traffic patterns observed at a specific NAP, or the congestion of the network in the neighbourhood of the NAP. Data specific to the call being admitted is data such as the resource requirements of the call and the expected call duration.

In trying to devise a way to determine the optimal group of NAPs to involve in a distributed admission decision, it quickly becomes evident that the question being asked is how to best predict which NAPs the MT requesting admission will visit during the lifetime of the call. Therefore the problem has been reduced to one of mobility prediction.

2.2 Mobility Prediction

Intuitively mobility prediction would be the determining of a mobile terminal (MT)'s future location. Although this is the general idea, there are many details that must be specified in order to truly understand what is being described.

The first item that needs further definition is 'location'. The location of the user carrying the MT is primarily thought of as their geographic coordinates. It has been noted however that there are problems with associating the MT's location directly with the user's geographic location. [11], [13] It is better to consider the motion of the MT through the network as the successive list of connections that the MT experiences. What this means exactly is that the MT location is always one of a finite set of locations representing one of the possible access points in the network (NAP). This is illustrated in Figure 1 where the dashed line represents the user mobility and the location of the MT changes as the connection to the network changes from one access point to another. In this particular example, the MT starts at NAP 2, moves through NAPs 5, 6, 7, 11 and ends at NAP 13. It is evident that the idea of a MT's location is greatly simplified by adopting this abstraction from the user's location. The second item worth mentioning is the notion that a prediction is usually based on some previous knowledge. The exact specification of what knowledge is used to make a prediction is very crucial in determining the appropriateness of that prediction scheme. If a prediction is based on data that is simply not available in a given situation, that prediction scheme is useless in that scenario regardless of how well it performs in other scenarios. An example of this is a requirement of privacy. If the prediction scheme has to respect the privacy of users and is only allowed to query their MTs for a very short mobility history, it may not be able to function properly. The data it requires may be present in the system but simply not accessible.

The third item to consider is the classification of the prediction as one that predicts the *time of an event* or one that predicts the *event at a time*. The *time of an event* type of prediction is one that is presented with an event that is expected to occur and is required to predict the time of this event. An example of this is a prediction mechanism required to predict the time at which a given MT will handoff from one NAP to another. The *event at time* type of prediction is one that is required to predict the state of a system at a given time in the future. An example of this type of prediction scheme is one that is asked what NAP an MT will be connected to at a time t in the future.

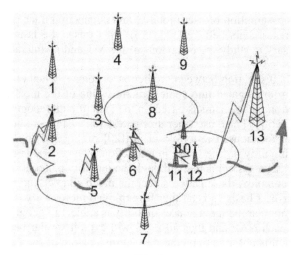

Fig. 1.

The fourth and last item requiring discussion is the granularity of the prediction. If the prediction mechanism is predicting the time of an event, to what accuracy is the time predicted? Seconds, minutes etc. If the prediction mechanism is on the other hand predicting the event at a time, this event is most likely defined at least in part by a location and thus the granularity of the location needs discussion. This means that a location can be specified in geographical coordinates, a single NAP, a group of NAPs etc.

3   Mobility Prediction Mechanisms

There are many ways of attempting to solve mobility prediction which, result in many prediction mechanisms. Each is unique and developed in order to solve a specific problem or specific type of problem but they are all related and many can be used in scenarios other than those they are proposed for.

There are two main types of wireless networks where mobility is important. These would be a system supported by infrastructure, such as a cellular system supported by base stations, etc. and a system that has no supportive infrastructure, such as ad-hoc networks. The main difference is that an infrastructure supported system can refer to fixed NAP for location while an infrastructure-less system needs an abstract location reference.

Mobility prediction research has mainly focused on supporting the next expected handoff. [1], [3], [10], [12], [15], [16] In reality, MTs will be able to move throughout the network and experience multiple handoffs during the lifetime of a call. It may therefore be necessary to predict more than just the next location the MT visits or the next event the MT will experience. [7],[17],[21]

A large portion of recent research still assumes that user mobility and the connection trace for an MT are strongly dependent. There are a large number of prediction systems that have been proposed which attempt to measure or capture some regularity of the user's mobility in order to extrapolate from this knowledge about the future behaviour of the user's MT [1], [3], [12], [15], [16]. Real life mobility traces have shown that this assumption of user mobility and connection trace of the MT is not as valid as most researchers believe [11], [13]. This raises the issue that it will most likely be necessary to study the behaviour of the MT and its interaction with the network directly.

Another main distinction between prediction systems is whether data is stored on a per user basis or aggregated into some structure. One of the most common per-user types of prediction mechanisms is based on the idea of path recognition [1], [9], [16]. Aljadhai and Znati [17] also use a per user prediction system predicting a user's most likely cluster of locations. Biesterfeld et al. [20] propose a neural net scheme that learns a user's mobility profile to use in prediction. The general argument when using a per-user prediction system is that although the mobility patterns seen in the network as a whole are complex, these patterns become much simpler and more regular when viewed on a per-user basis and can thus be exploited more easily. Prediction schemes that use aggregation argue that the user mobility is subject to geographical constraints at the place of each NAP and thus all users will exhibit similar behaviour at a given NAP. Therefore it is possible to predict the future location of such a user knowing the aggregate behaviour of all or similar users at that NAP. Soh and Kim [5] introduce a prediction technique that uses a road topology database that stores the probability of transfer from one road segment to another.

Another difference in the approaches to solve the problem of mobility prediction seen in current work is whether the prediction produced is based on measurement of user or MT behaviour or matching the pattern of this behaviour with previous behaviour. A measurement based approach will typically compute a probability of events occurring, depending on the value of some parameters. [17] Pattern matching techniques on the other hand attempt to match the observed user behaviour with some previously observed behaviour and forecast the future based on the observed patterns. [1], [9], [16], [17], [18] This distinction is most evident in the per-user type of prediction mechanisms, since most of the schemes that use aggregation will attempt to capture patterns in an overall sense but perform each individual prediction using a measurement of some kind. [10], [12]

4 Predictor Design

We propose a mobility prediction system that uses a neural network to capture connection trace patterns in wireless networks in order to predict future behaviour of MTs. While there has been some research that uses neural networks for similar purposes [19], [20], [21], our approach is novel in that our predictor learns general patterns present at NAPs as opposed to user specific patterns. As proposed in [5], [10], there is good reason to believe that mobility patterns will be influenced in a significant way by the geographic limitations and trends present at the location of a NAP. We also note that although user mobility may be quite regular, there is a significant amount of independence between this regularity and regularity in the connection trace of an MT belonging to such a user [12], [14]. MT connection traces are influenced by the state of the network and there may be regularity in how a network behaves at particular locations which is a regularity of the network as opposed to a regularity of user mobility. This regularity is impossible to extract from user behaviour. This is best illustrated with a simple example in Figure 2, where a user, represented by the dashed line, initiates a call and connects to either NAP 5 or NAP 2 depending on the state of the network. The handoffs then proceed as illustrated, either from even numbered NAP to even numbered NAP or odd numbered NAP to odd numbered NAP due to some property of the network. Knowing the exact mobility of the user will not determine exactly the behaviour of the MT connection since each time this route is taken, there are two possible connection traces. Studying the MT connection directly, the network regularity present can be observed. As a consequence, our prediction system trains a separate neural network at each NAP using short connection trace histories of MTs that connect to that NAP. The aim is to capture general patterns in local connection behaviour and use these to predict future behaviour of MTs that connect to this NAP. There are a number of advantages to using a generalized pattern recognition mechanism as opposed to a user specific one. First there is no need for each user to build up an individual history since there is an expectation that MT traces for users traveling along similar paths will share localized patterns. Second, a general pattern predictor is better able to handle erratic behaviour by a single user. In a per-user prediction system, a user that behaves in a way he/she never has before will cause the predictor to perform poorly since this type of behaviour is not incorporated into the knowledge the predictor has about that user. In a general pattern predictor, there is at least a chance that some other user has behaved in a way similar to the erratic user and thus the predictor is somewhat prepared for such behaviour. Third, there is an issue of privacy that may arise when keeping track of individual user travel patterns. This issue is not present when only immediate history is used to train a neural network and thus aggregate the individual user travel patterns into more general ones.

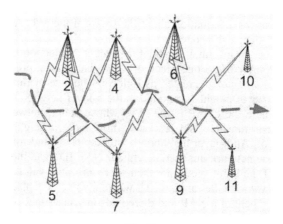

Fig. 2.

The complete predictor consists of a number of components built around the neural network classifier. Initially it is necessary to collect and convert MT connection traces into data that can be used to train the neural network. The neural net is then trained with this data and ready to predict. The predictions from the neural net are not however of a form directly understandable and have to be translated into a set of NAPs that the MT is expected to move to in the future. Also, the neural net is trained to predict only the near future, so there is an external mechanism that allows for a recursive prediction farther into the future. Before these components are described in detail, some terminology must be introduced and a few concepts defined.

4.1   Concepts

The predictor views MT connection traces on a discreet time scale of a chosen time unit *t*. This time unit is known as a *time step*. The time step scale needs to be small enough such that MT connection traces are approximately continuous.

A network only experiences handoffs if there is more than one NAP present. NAPs that can handoff to each other are considered direct neighbours. NAPs that cannot handoff to one another are indirect neighbours of a certain degree, this being the smallest number of handoffs that is required for a call to be transferred between these two NAPs. These neighbour degrees enable the definition of an *n-layer neighbour map*. An n-layer neighbour map of a NAP is the set of all NAPs that have a neighbour degree equal to or less than n. A prediction of the future behaviour of an MT is represented as the set of NAPs that the MT will visit in the future time period specified. This set is referred to as the *Future Location Set*.

4.2   Data Gathering and Input Generation

As an MT hands-off from one NAP to another in the network, it creates a history of NAPs it has visited at times in the past. The exact form of this history is an ID vector of length *Histlen* as defined in Table 1. This history vector contains in it two types of information about the recent mobility behaviour of that MT. The first piece of information is when this MT connected to which NAPs. Intuitively this information should represent a general direction of the MT's motion. The other piece of information contained in this history vector is how long the MT spent at each NAP it connected to. This intuitively carries information about the speed of the MT. A fast MT will spend less time at NAPs than a slow one.

These two pieces of information about the recent connection behaviour of the MT need to be incorporated into one piece of input that can be presented to the neural network. This *input vector* is created as follows: The size of this input vector is defined by the number of neighbours found in the n-layer neighbourhood of the current NAP (cNAP), where the cNAP is the NAP whose neural network is being trained. The parameter n is tuneable and represents how large a neighbourhood the cNAP should be aware of. An n-layer neighbourhood map is created for the cNAP which is a mapping of some network imposed neighbour NAP ID to an index in the input vector. The values of the input vector are then set to an initial value of 0. The parameter lambda (λ) has a value in the range (0, 1], where a value of 1 places all the weight on the absolute time spent at a NAP and disregards any historical sequence and a value close to 0 puts almost all the weight on the historical sequence of NAPs and little on the absolute time spent there. If the present time is $t= 0$, then $t= -k$ is k time steps in the past. The input vector is created by adding the value λ^{k+1} to the value in the input vector that represents the NAP the MT was connected to at time $t= -k$. If this NAP is not in the neighbourhood of the cNAP, the value for that time step is ignored and its information lost. An example can be seen in Figure 3 where each arrow represents one time step in the movement of an MT on its way to the cNAP. The MT is currently in the cNAP for one time step, has spent the previous two time steps connected to NAP 7 and the two before that to NAP 8. The neighbourhood that cNAP is aware of is depicted by a circle, and if the neighbour mapping is such that the ID of the NAP is the position in the input vector and Histlen is 5, then the resulting input vector of this

Table 1. Parameter Definitions Table.

$FLS_t(a)$	The Future Location Set at time t time units into the future according to the predictor at NAP a.
$neighbours(a)$	The set of NAPs that are direct neighbours of NAP a.
T	The threshold such that an output from a neural net predictor corresponding to a certain NAP will only result in this NAP being included in the FLS if this output is higher than or equal to T.
λ	The lambda parameter affects the weight given to the absolute length of time spent at a NAP as opposed to the relative time since that NAP has been visited.
$nno(a \rightarrow b)$	The output corresponding to NAP b, from the neural network predictor at NAP a.
$Histlen$	The length of the history vector used to classify the MT. This is as far as the system can see in the past on a per user basis.

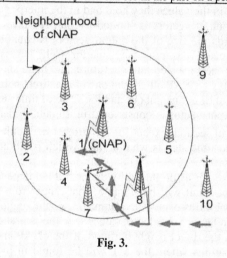

Fig. 3.

movement is: $[\lambda^1,0,0,0,0, \lambda^2+ \lambda^3, \lambda^4+ \lambda^5]$ (shown transposed to save space) Mathematically the input vector can be expressed as:

$$input = \sum_{k=0}^{Histlen} \lambda^{k+1} \times P_k \qquad (1)$$

P_k is a position vector such that it has size equal to the input vector size, and has 0 value for all positions other than the position representing the NAP where the MT was located at time $t= -k$ which is equal to 1. For example, $P_1 = [0,0,0,0,0,0,1,0]$.

4.3 Training Data Generation

In order to train the neural network, it is necessary to have input-output pairs that are examples of what the network is supposed to be able to produce once trained. The input vector of such a training data point is gathered and created as described above. The corresponding output vector of this data point needs to somehow represent the desired prediction output which is in essence some representation of the NAP that the MT will move to in the next time step. This is obviously impossible to obtain at the time the input vector is created since the future behaviour of the MT is not known. This problem is solved by waiting until the next time step to see where the MT actually goes and creating the desired output vector accordingly. This is then coupled together with the already existing input vector and stored as a training data point to be used when training the neural network.

4.4 Output Interpretation

There are essentially two types of output vectors in this prediction system. The first kind are the artificial ones, that is to say the ones created by the system in order to train the neural network. The second kind are the ones that are actually produced by the neural net after it has been trained. These vectors are identical in structure, but there is a difference in the values they hold and in the interpretation of these values.

The size of all output vectors is limited by the 0+1-layer neighbourhood of the cNAP. In other words the size of the output vectors is equal to the number of direct neighbours that the cNAP has, plus one value for itself. This is because the neural net is trained to predict one time step into the future, and there should be no possible way that the MT connects to a NAP other than one of the direct neighbours of the cNAP or itself, by definition of direct neighbour and the scale of time steps.

The artificial output vector is constructed in a manner identical to the P_k vectors described in the input section, except for the stricter size limit. The NAP that the MT moves to in the next time step is what defines which position in the otherwise zero-vector has value 1.

The true output vector as produced by the neural net depends on the characteristic of the neural network, but will have values that range from 0 to 1 in all positions. These are not probabilities even if the numbers would suggest it, although they are similar. These are relative confidence values that the neural net has assigned to the respective NAPs in the direct neighbourhood of the cNAP and to the cNAP itself as potential future locations where the MT will be found in the next time step. From these, the *Future Location Set* (FLS) is constructed. The FLS is the set of locations, or NAPs, that the neural net has a sufficient confidence in as potential connections of MT in the next time step. Sufficient confidence is defined by a tuneable threshold parameter T as defined in Table 1. The higher this threshold, the more critical the predictor is of which NAPs will be part of the FLS. Other than the specifics of the neural network, this is the general one time step prediction mechanism employed in this predictor. In the case of multiple time step prediction, there is an additional step before the comparison of the confidence values and the threshold.

4.5 Neural Network Specifics

At the heart of the predictor lies the neural network. The performance of the prediction system is heavily influenced by the design choices made here. Neural networks are not all alike, and each type of neural net is suited best for a different type of problem. [22]

The type of neural net used in this predictor is a back-propagation network. The main idea behind a back-propagation network is that it starts out with a random pattern encoded in it and as it is trained it modifies this random pattern based on how well the pattern performs on the training data. Depending on how far off the guess is, the network adjusts its internal state and proceeds to the next training point.

There are a few design decisions that need to be made regarding the neural network. First the number of layers in the network needs to be decided. A typical back-propagation network consists of three layers, which is also the number of layers used for this predictor network. There is an input layer, a hidden middle layer and an output layer. Each of these layers server a specific function, refer to [22] for a complete discussion. Then the number of neurons in each layer needs to be decided. The input layer was created such that it could be presented with the input vector, and thus the number of neurons in this layer is the same as the number of entries in the input vector. The number of output layer neurons is similarly dictated by the size of the output vector. The middle layer is then the only layer for which the number of neurons is not dictated by the design of the system.

Second, the transfer functions between the neuron levels need to be decided. There is a number of these, the most common being sigmoid and linear functions. These are mathematical functions that determine how the inputs to an individual neuron determine the output of that neuron. The neural network in this system uses a log-sigmoid function between the input layer and the middle layer and a linear function between the middle layer and the output layer. This configuration is a typical configuration for a back-propagation neural network.

The last major decision that needs to be made is the learning algorithm used to train the network. A typical back-propagation neural network uses a gradient descent algorithm which is what was chosen for the predictor.

The neural network used in this predictor is a typical back-propagation neural net that is quite generic and can likely be improved with studies similar to that in [20]. The focus of this paper is the design of a complete predictor and therefore a generic neural network is sufficient.

4.6 Predicting Multiple Time Steps

So far the system has been described as only able to predict one time step into the future. Since the size of a time step has to be small relative to the call length, the predictor needs to be able to predict farther into the future in order for the prediction to be useful to a dCAC scheme. While it is possible to train a neural network to predict for times farther in the future, such a network is required to capture patterns that are much more complex than those of a one time step prediction and is thus more difficult to create successfully. Due to this, the multiple time prediction system is designed such that only one time step predictions are required. This is achieved using a recurrence relation that defines a prediction of arbitrary time step number as a function of previous predictions. The main idea behind this recurrence relation is that the prediction of some future time step t depends on the prediction of the previous time step $t-1$, such that the one step prediction of all the NAPs from $t-1$ will create the prediction sought after for time step t. The exact recurrence relation is:

$$FLS_t(a) = \{(b, w_b) \mid b \in neighbours(FLS_{t-1}(a)) \wedge w_b > T\} \qquad (2)$$

$$w_b = nno(a \rightarrow b) \qquad (3)$$

The only information missing in equation 3 is how w_b is computed. There are three methods of combining the outputs from multiple NAPs in order to compute w_b. The combination method presented in equation 4 represents a method based on the idea of voting. Each NAP in the FLS at time $t-1$ produces some output confidence value for all its direct neighbours. Then all the output confidence values for a given NAP are added up, and if there is enough combined confidence, the NAP in question is included in the FLS for time t. A potential problem with this method is that an error in prediction at one time step that produces a large FLS will propagate and create a very large FLS from that point on.

$$w_b = \left(\sum [nno(c \rightarrow b)] \forall c \in FLS_{t-1}(a)\right) \tag{4}$$

The combination method presented in equation 5 attempts to prevent the potential problem with the voting method. This is done by taking the maximum individual confidence value as the confidence value compared to the threshold. In essence it means that there is some NAP that expects the MT to travel to the NAP being predicted with a confidence that is enough such that the predicted NAP will be included in the FLS for time t.

$$w_b = \left(Max[nno(c \rightarrow b)] \forall c \in FLS_{t-1}(a)\right) \tag{5}$$

The last combination method presented in equation 6 is similar to the way probability is computed for multiple events. This method is identical to the voting method except it includes a weight on each vote. This means that the confidence values produced by each NAP are modified according to the confidence with which the NAP was predicted in the previous time step.

$$w_b = \left(\sum [nno(c \rightarrow b) * w_c] \forall c \in FLS_{t-1}(a)\right) \quad \text{where } w_c \text{ is from } FLS_{t-1} \tag{6}$$

The threshold value to be used in any of these methods has to be determined experimentally with regard to each situation the predictor would be used in.

5 Simulation

In order to validate the performance of the proposed prediction mechanism, a simulation was performed. The simulation consists of a number of parts. The first and underlying part is the mobility model that dictates how users move throughout the network and the structure of the network itself. For this we chose the activity based model as presented in [4]. We modify the network structure however such that there are only 16 NAPs as opposed to the original 45. The network is also constructed such that there are two separate clusters divided by a linear structure. This attempts to model two cities connected by a highway, and is intended to represent the different types of environments that the predictor may have to be used in. The number of users in the simulation is 1000 and each one of these follows the activity based model. The second part of the simulation is the neural network prediction system. Six neurons were used at the middle layer at each NAP, as this number seemed to be reasonable after some initial experimentation. One minute represented one time unit in this simulation. The lambda parameter used to create the input vector was set at 0.5 in order to create a balance between the absolute and relative time spent at every previous NAP. The length of the history vector used was 30 time units, or 30 minutes. The neighbourhood depth each NAP is aware of is two levels. The predictor has been tested on a 7 minute into the future prediction, and as configured, the mobility model allows users to traverse up to three NAPs in the 7 minute interval, thus the two level neighbour maps. The 1000 users were allowed to move around the network for 24 hours during which training data was gathered. After this the neural network at each NAP was trained with the data collected. The next 100 minutes of the simulation were used to test the predictor. Various threshold values were tested at each NAP to discover which would provide the best performance. The range of threshold values tested was [0.15, 0.2]. This range was selected as a result of a number of previous short experiments.

5.1 Evaluation Methodology

Due to the widely varied methods of evaluating mobility prediction mechanisms present in current literature [9], [11], [12], [14] and none of these evaluating the type of prediction that our system produces, we chose to evaluate our system by comparing it to an ideal predictor of the same type as our predictor. What this means with respect to the proposed prediction mechanism is that one and only one NAP should be predicted for any time step. This would be the NAP where the MT will actually be connected to at that time. A predictor that is capable of such accurate prediction is a perfect predictor. We use two numeric parameters to perform this evaluation. The first parameter is what's called a correctness ratio. This ratio is calculated by comparing the number of times the predicted FLS actually contains the NAP that the MT will be connected to at the time being predicted to the total number of predictions. The second parameter is the predicted set size. The smaller the set size, the more accurate predictor is, as long as the predicted set contains the real future location of the MT. It is obvious that there is a trade-off between the correctness ratio and the set size.

6 Results

Three simulations were performed in total, each one with a different combination method for the inter-time step predictions. As stated each prediction was performed with a number of thresholds. The overall prediction performance per threshold was then calculated using the correctness ratio and set size parameters. The aim was to see how small the average set size could get given a required correctness ratio. Figure 4 shows the smallest average set size per NAP in the network using the different confidence methods for correctness ratio of 0.8. More results are available but not presented due to space constraints. Note that when the correctness ratio could not be reached, it was assumed that the whole network would have to be included in the FLS and therefore the value reflected in the graphs as the FLS size is the size of the network. In order to gauge the complexity of the patterns that are present at the various NAPs, it is important to note that a high number of users were seen in NAPs 5, 7, 8, 9, and 16 while the other NAPs only had a low to moderate number of users pass through them.

6.1 Result Analysis

There is a general trend in all the results that the NAPs encountering a large number of unique users are ones where the predictor performs poorly. This can be seen in

NAPs 5, 7, 9 10, 16. NAPs 5, 7, 10 and 16 are NAPs that are frequently visited by MTs since they are on the main route in the network (the line from one cluster to the other), but are not in an area that would impose strict geographical restrictions such as NAP 8, 9. These represent the highway like scenario that is somewhat one dimensional and thus imposes considerable geographical limits on motion. We say somewhat represents because MTs can still reach an FLS of size 7 from each of there in the 7 time steps. NAPs 8 and 9 would then be expected to have a predictor with better performance than the other main-line NAPs. The outer cluster NAPs would also be expected to have a well performing predictor since not as many users are expected to pass through them. In general we see that these expectations are met; however there is some unexpected behaviour that happens with each combination method.

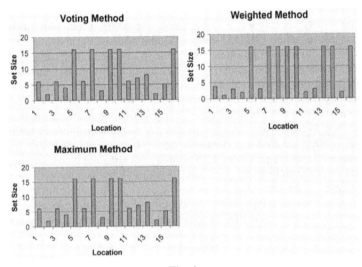

Fig. 4.

With the Voting method, the outer cluster NAPs have predictors that are able to achieve quite high correctness ratios with FLS sizes that are reasonably small. There are a few NAPs that can achieve over 80% correctness with an FLS size of only 2 or 3, and some of these can achieve even higher correctness ratios with such small FLS sizes, such as NAPs 4 and 14. NAP 8 also has a well performing predictor. The NAPs that are expected to have predictors of a lesser performance quality due to their geographic location also fall within expectation, these being NAPs 5, 7, 10 and 16. NAP 9 was expected to have a predictor comparable in performance to NAP 8, however this is not the case. Further investigation into raw data shows that NAP 9's predictor is of quality comparable to that of NAPs 5, 7, 10 and 16. The reason for this in unclear but there are a number of explanations discussed later on.

The maximum method is identical in performance to the voting method; again most expectations are met as before. Further investigation into the result data shows that this method does vary slightly in some scenarios, but the close similarity to the voting method is intriguing.

The results for the weighted method are quite different than those of the previous two methods, since the predictor seems to work either quite well or not at all. This can be seen when the outer cluster NAPs are considered vs. the NAPs on the main line between the two clusters. Most of the outer cluster NAPs show predictor is with very good performance and FLS sizes of less than four. The main line NAPs and two of the outer cluster NAPs (13, 14) however contain predictors that show very poor performance. This suggests that this method is highly sensitive to the pattern complexity present at a location, since the predictions are either very accurate or not accurate at all.

6.2 General Comments

Is clear that the neural net predictor is very successful in certain situations. It is also clear however that there are situations where the performance is unacceptable. There are a number of potential causes of this. First it is possible that the neural net used is simply too small or too simple to be able to capture the complexity of the patterns present at those locations. It's also possible that there simply are no patterns at those locations or the patterns present are very faint. The possibility is there that the neural predictor simply cannot be used in such situations, however the success of the neural predictor in other situations would lead us to believe that such a conclusion is premature and requires more proof. Although the neural net predictor obviously requires more work in order to be successful in the simulated scenario, we feel it is more important to focus on the development of a mobility model that is more reflective of reality than the one currently used. The extent of mobility models in research today is not sufficient such that a model exists which reflects real mobility in wireless networks [8], [11], [13]. Too many mobility models make assumptions that are not realistic and have an extreme influence on the performance of mechanisms like ours.

7 Conclusion

In this paper we present a mobility predictor that is able to learn and predict connection patterns of MTs and abstracts completely from user mobility. The predictor is an aggregating predictor, in that it does not keep any per user information but rather focuses on using a general behaviour exhibited by MTs at a certain location. This ensures user privacy.

The performance of the predictor was measured using a simulation based on the activity based mobility model [4]. Multiple prediction methods were tested and the general result was that the prediction mechanism is quite successful in some scenarios, while not successful in others. While it is possible to tune the predictor for each simulated scenario, there is no simulation scenario available that is close enough to real mobile networks and thus makes this tuning a marginally useful effort. Therefore the current results are sufficient to conclude that the presented prediction mechanism is useful, and further improvements in its performance will need to be made only after it has been tested either in a real wireless network or with a simulator that is sufficiently reflective of a real wireless network.

References

1. F. Erbas, J. Steuer, D. Eggesieker, K. Kyamakya, K. Jobmann, "A Regular Path Recognition Method and Prediction of User Movements in Wireless Networks", Proc., VTC - IEEE VTS 54th, Fall 2001, Volume 4, pp. 2183 -2187
2. Y. Iraqi, R. Boutaba, "A Novel Distributed Call Admission Control For Wireless Mobile Multimedia Networks", Proc., ACM WoWoMoM, 2000, pp. 21-27

3. X. Shen, J. W. Mark, J. Ye, "User Mobility Profile Prediction: An Adaptive Fuzzy Inference Approach", Wireless Networks 6, 2000, pp. 363-374

4. J. Scourias, T. Kunz, "An Activity-based Mobility Model and Location Management Simulation Framework", Proc., Second ACM International Workshop on Modeling, Analysis and Simulation of Wireless and Mobile Systems (MSWiM), 1999, pp. 61-68

5. W.-S. Soh, H.S. Kim, "QoS provisioning in cellular networks based on mobility prediction techniques", IEEE Communications Magazine, Jan 2003, pp. 86- 92

6. J.R. Moorman, J.W. Lockwood, "Wireless call admission control using threshold access sharing", Proc., IEEE GLOBECOM, 2001, Volume: 6, pp. 3698 -3703

7. D. A. Levine, L. F. Akyildz, M. Naghshineh, "A resource estimation and call admission algorithm for wireless multimedia networks using the shadow cluster concept", IEEE/ACM Trans. Net, 1997, Vol. 5, No. 1, pp. 1-12

8. T. Kunz, A. A. Siddiqi, J. Scourias, "The peril of Evaluating Location Management Proposals through Simulations", Wireless Networks 7, 2001, pp. 635-643

9. I. R. Chen, N. Verma, "Simulation Study of a Class of Autonomous Host-Centric Mobility Prediction Algorithms for Wireless Cellular and Ad-Hoc Networks", Proc., 36th Annual Simulation Symposium, March 2003, pp. 65 -72

10. K. Curran, G. Parr, "A Framework for the Transmission of Streaming Media to Mobile Devices", Int. J. Network Mgmt, 2002, Vol 12, pp. 41-59

11. J. Chan, A. Seneviratne, "A Practical User Mobility Algorithm for Supporting Adaptive QoS in Wireless Networks", Proc., IEEE International Conference on Networks, Fall 1999, pp. 104 -111

12. A. Jayasuriya, J. Asenstorfer, "Mobility Prediction for Cellular Networks Based on the Observed Traffic Patterns", Proc., 2nd IASTED International Conference Wireless and Optical Communications, 2002, 356-235,

13. J.Chan, B. Landfeldt, A. Seneviratne, P. Sookavatana, "Integrating Mobility Prediction Pre-allocation into a Home-Proxy Based Wireless Internet Framework", Proc., IEEE International Conference on Networks, Sept 2000, pp. 18- 23

14. W. Su, S. J. Lee, M. Gerla, "Mobility Prediction in Wireless Networks", Proc., MILCOM, Oct 2000, Volume 1, pp. 491 -495

15. J. Ye, J. Hou, S.Papavassiliou, "A Comprehensive Resource Management Framework for Next Generation Wireless Networks", IEEE Transactions on Mobile Computing, Fall 2002, Vol 1, No 4, pp. 249 - 264

16. H. Kim, J. Jung, "A Moblity Prediction Handver Algorithm for Effective Channel Assignment in Wireless ATM", Proc., IEEE GLOBECOM, Nov 2001, Volume 6, pp. 3673-3680

17. A. Aljadhai, T. F. Znati, "Predictive Mobility Support for QoS Provisioning in Mobile Wireless Environments", IEEE Journal on Selected Areas in Communications, Oct 2001, Vol 19, No 10, pp. 1915-1930

18. A. Bhattacharya, S. K. Das, "LeZi-Update: An Information-Theoretic Framework for Personal Mobility Tracking in PCS Networks", Wireless Networks 8, 2002, pp. 121-135

19. W.T. Poon, E. Chan, "Traffic Management in Wireless ATM Network Using a Hierarchical Neural-Network Based Predication Algorithm", Proc., 15th International Conference on Computers and their Applications, March 2000,

20. J. Biesterfeld, E. Ennigrou, K Jobmann, "Neural Networks for Location Prediction in Mobile Networks", Proc., International Workshop on Applications of Neural Networks to Telecommunications, 1997

21. B. P. V. Kumar, P.Venkataram, "Prediction-based Location Management using Multilayer Neural Networks", J. Indian Inst. Sci., 2002, 82, pp. 7-21

22. M. T. Hagan, "Neural network design", Boston: PWS Pub., c1996, 1996, ISBN: 534943322

Author Index